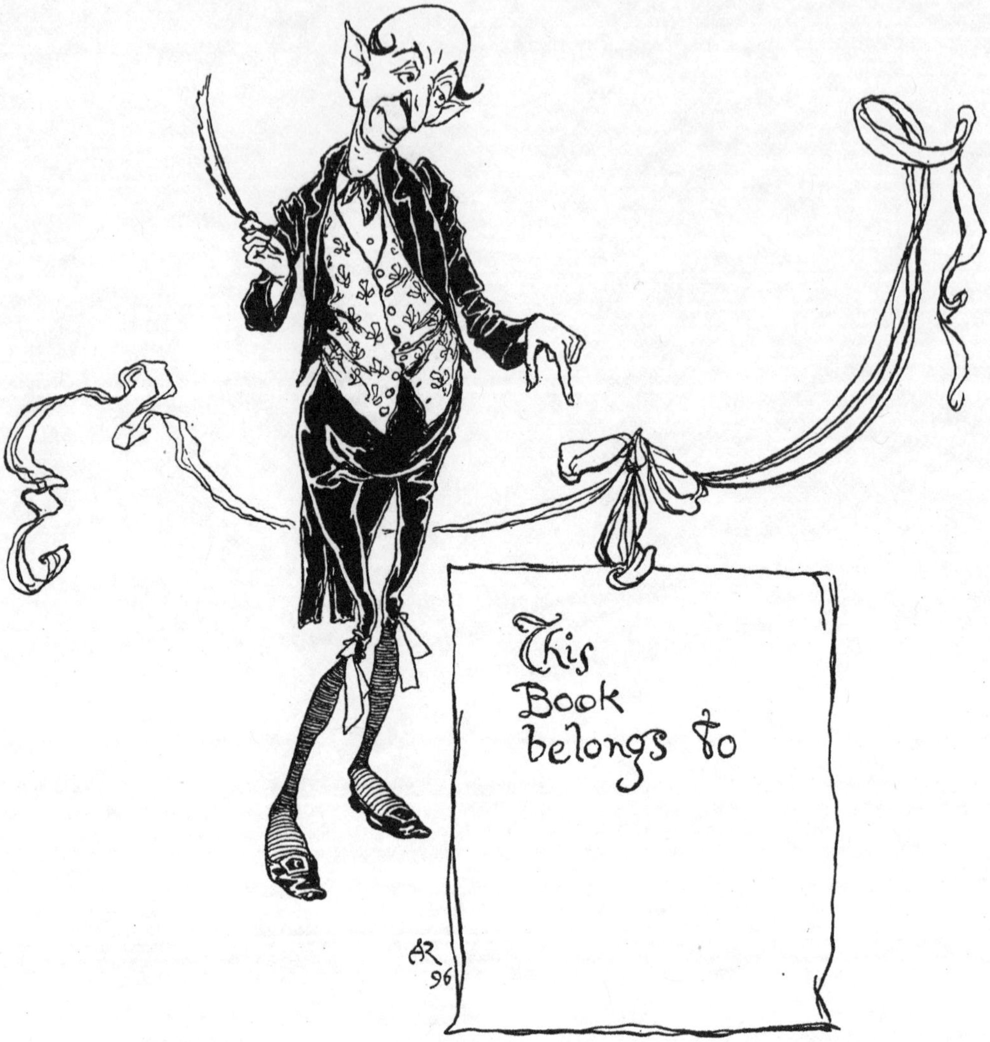
This
Book
belongs to
AR
96

The Fantastic Line Art of
Arthur Rackham

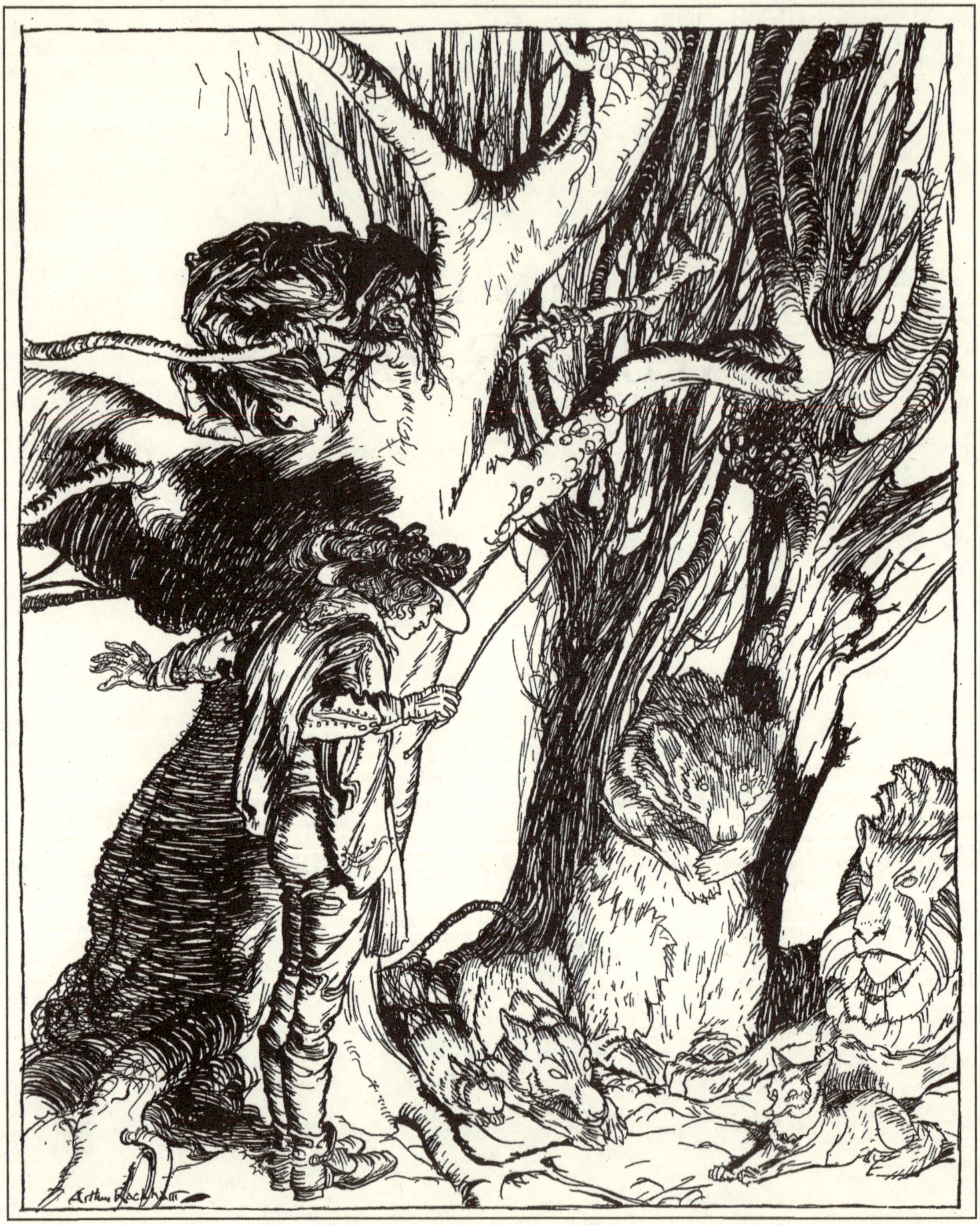

Instantly they lay still, all turned into stone.

Little Brother and Little Sister, 1917

The Fantastic Line Art of Arthur Rackham

Selected and Edited by Jeff A. Menges

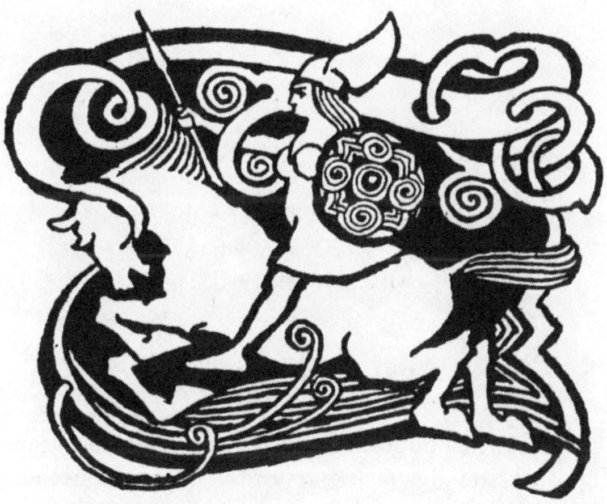

Dover Publications, Garden City, New York

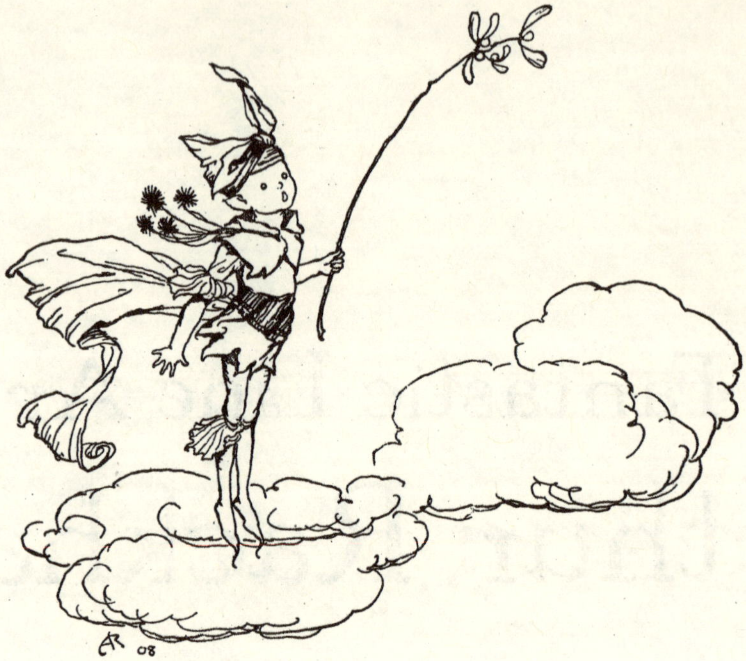

Copyright

Bibliographical Note

This Dover edition, first published in 2017, is an original compilation of Arthur Rackham illustrations reprinted from various sources.

Library of Congress Cataloging-in-Publication Data

Names: Rackham, Arthur, 1867–1939, artist. | Menges, Jeff A., editor.
Title: The fantastic line art of Arthur Rackham / Arthur Rackham ; selected and edited by Jeff A. Menges.
Description: Garden City, New York : Dover Publications, 2017.
Identifiers: LCCN 2017038331 | ISBN 9780486814223 (paperback) | ISBN 048681422X
Subjects: LCSH: Rackham, Arthur, 1867–1939—Themes, motives.
Classification: LCC NC978.5.R32 A4 2017 | DDC 741.942—dc23
LC record available at https://lccn.loc.gov/2017038331

Printed in Canada
81422X06 2026
www.doverpublications.com

Contents

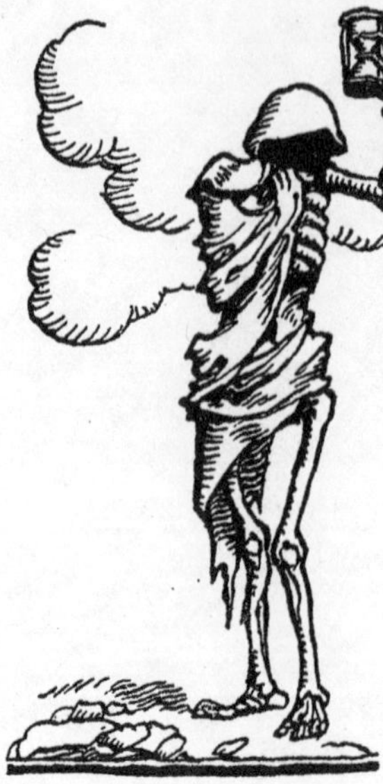

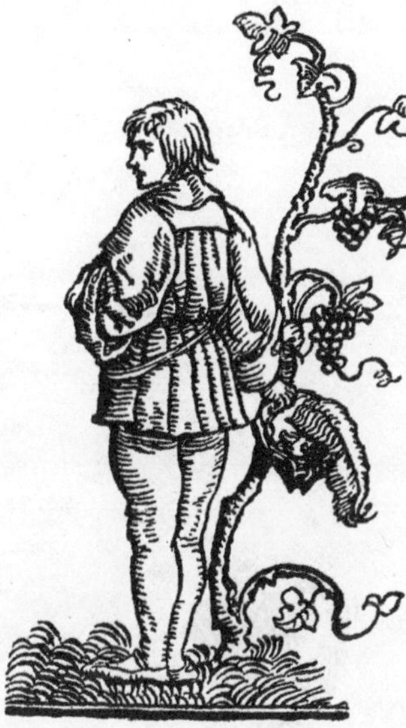

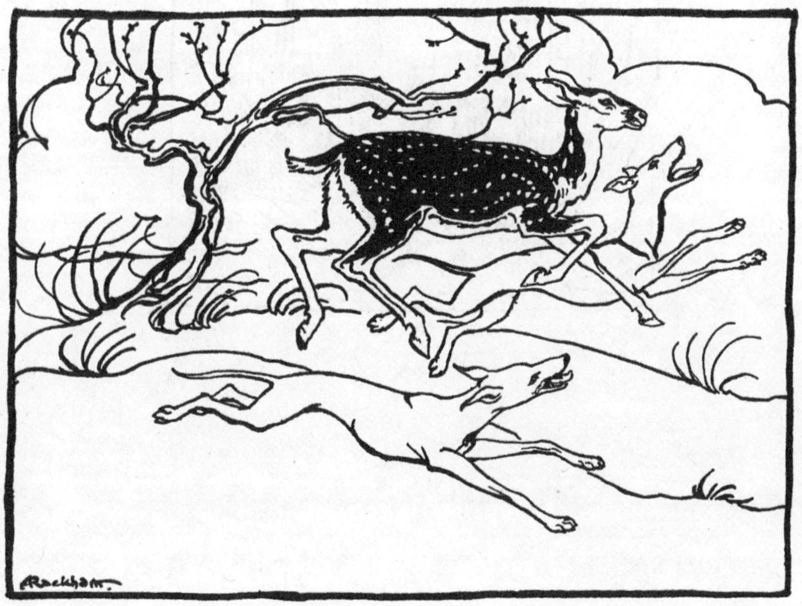

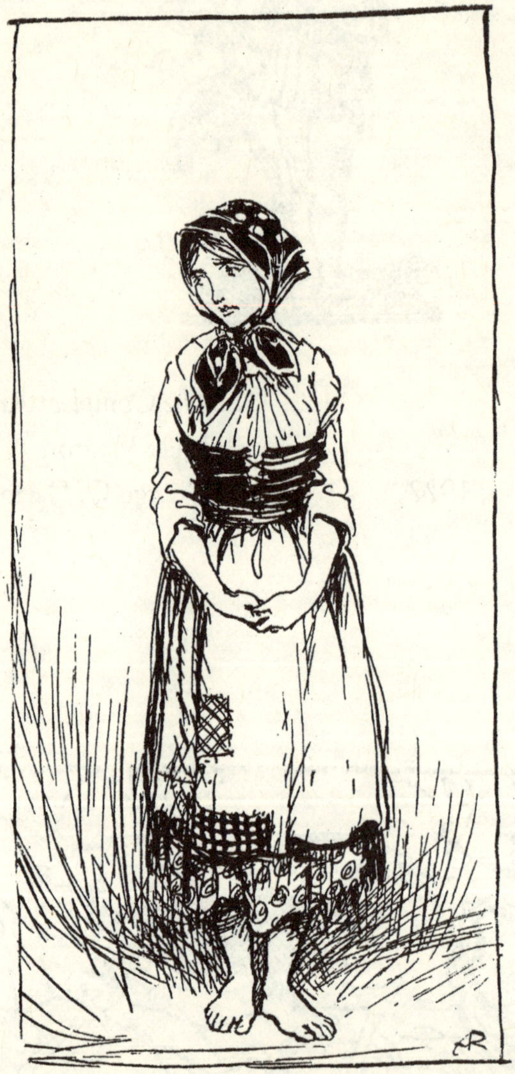

Introduction

Jeff A. Menges

The year of this publication—2017—marks 150 years since Arthur Rackham's birth; truly a worthy celebration. Few creative minds have shaped the generations that followed them as much as Arthur Rackham's did in the early twentieth century. Rackham's career as an artist and illustrator had longevity, depth, and was successful enough to reach all over the world. The diversity of his output ranged from Mother Goose to the writings of Milton. What was more amazing was the fact that he handled this wide variety of work equally well from one assignment to the next.

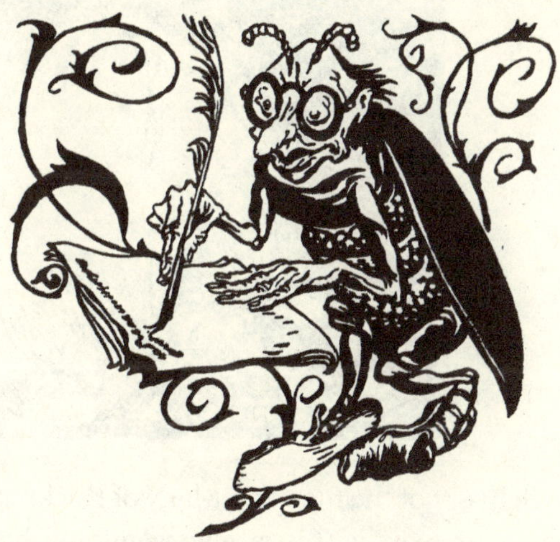

At the foundation of it all were both his imagination and his ink line. Arthur Rackham entered publishing at a time when the hard, solid edge of the ink line was king; it had a firm grip above all other forms of graphic marks for being the best method of making a reproducible drawing. Every area striving to be a soft tone was made from a net of fine, solid lines. As every journeyman illustrator did, *mastering* ink—in both brush and pen—gave Rackham versatility, and expandedhis pool of work. It wasn't long before he had his pick of the jobs that most suited him.

The interest that Rackham had for storytelling seemed to strengthen his own communication in his image making. When he finally had the chance to contribute to classics, he was free to do the work as he saw fit, rather than tailoring his art to satisfy a client.

There were a number of qualities that made Rackham an exceptional inker. He could make great communicative statements very simply. Rackham was able to capture a playful mood in a smile or a stance; sinister intent with the crooked sweep of a hand; or convey the darkness in a bank of gnarled roots. He was not unlike a skilled translator, who is aware of the most nuanced phrases, reviews a work of writing, and then makes it his own by successfully aiding in

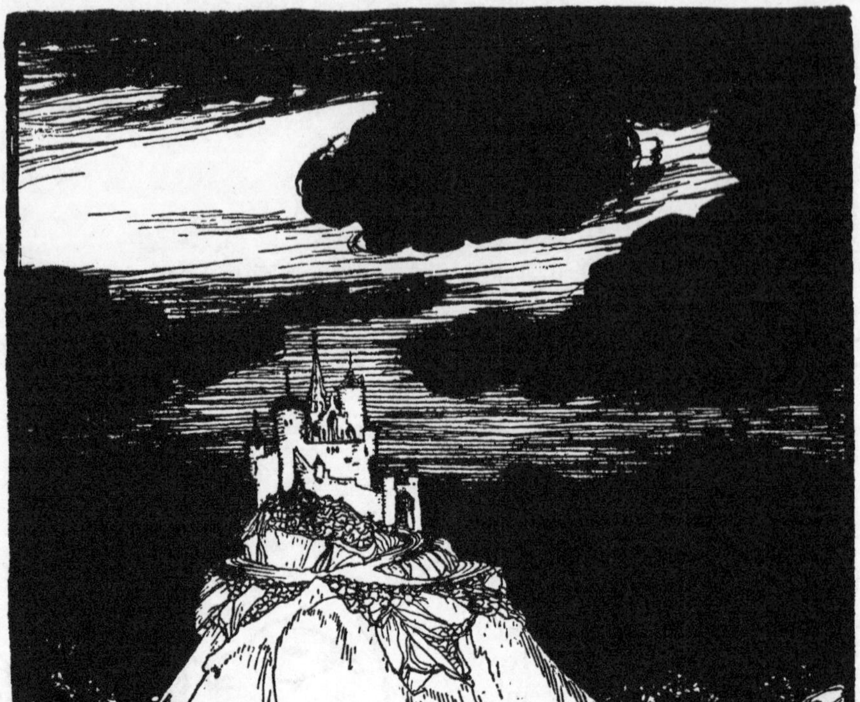

the delivery of the message. Many of Rackham's characters exist within a few seemingly hasty lines, alongside a full-page image that has been labored over to the finest detail. His ink work carried him to great heights, and he never let go of that.

Even as technology advanced into the age of machinery, he held on to his quill, connecting him to an earlier time. Rackham's line is known for its organic quality—rarely straight, it travels through an image in a variety of widths, and his most iconic works often add the sweep of brush line, not simply to fill in blacks, but to seamlessly be an arbiter of the placement of light and dark.

Lastly, and perhaps most important in this artist's career, was his consistency. Being a leader in his field allowed for freedoms that would not be afforded to an illustrator of a lesser reputation. Work for him continued steadily, from the turn of the century until his death in 1939. When many of his contemporaries in the fading gift-book market began to look elsewhere for work, Rackham continued with the practices he knew. Despite changes in current trends—the looks of Art Nouveau, the Arts and Crafts movement, and Art Deco all surrounding his active period—Rackham used ink work *and his own style* as his primary means of picture making. Other artists whose work was produced in the same period often absorbed the look of the moment, to keep up with the current demand. If not, they often went out of favor. Rackham's look was timeless, and he continued to be

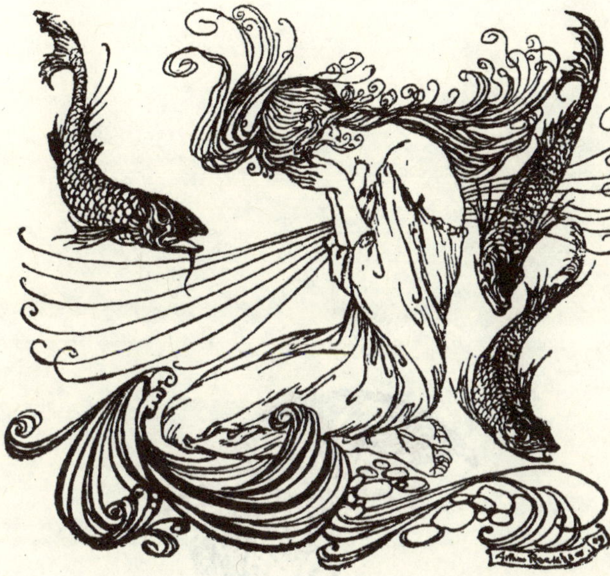

a strong and sought-after contributor to the field of book illustration throughout his career.

Rackham's direct approach to his work has spoken to generations of readers. For many, his work defined what Grimm's stories looked and felt like, or what sort of moods were set through the writings of Wagner when Siegfried slays Fafnir. Although Rackham worked in a tradition and format that was already outdated when he was using it, the strength of his creativity speaks from his ink line, and that still resonates with those who read the works he illustrated today.

May 2017

A NOTE ABOUT THE FOLLOWING TWO ARTICLES:

The following two articles are reprinted from publications that championed Rackham's work in his day. The first is from *The International Studio* (1905), the premiere arts magazine of Britain at that time. Illustration was serious business at the start of the twentieth century, and no doubt a commercial endeavor, but *The Studio* embraced the application of art into all forms of materials, from publishing to pottery. Illustration, and all aspects of drawing, were the backbone of artistic expression that the magazine was built around.

The second article is from 1914, first published in *St. Nicholas*, a magazine directed toward children. The text here speaks of a visit to Rackham's home and discussion with the illustrator directly. This candid, close look at the artist in his environment offers a fascinating insight into his work.

While neither article looks exclusively at his ink work, both pieces of writing contribute to the knowledge of what Rackham has brought to public consciousness, and provide a glimpse into what kind of celebrity an illustrator of his stature experienced in the first decades of the twentieth century.

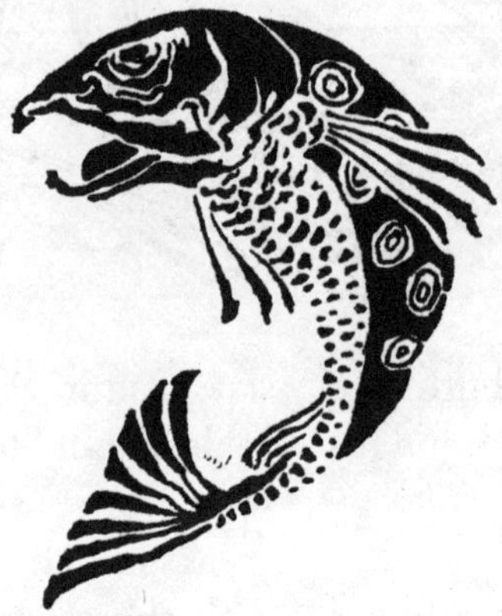

ARTHUR RACKHAM: A PAINTER OF FANTASIES

A. L. BALDRY, *THE INTERNATIONAL STUDIO*, APRIL 1905

One of the best and most interesting characteristics of the British Water-Colour School has always been its wonderful variety. During the century and a half which is approximately the period that has elapsed since water-colour painting began to be seriously studied in this country, there has been an astonishing development in this form of art practice. The first attempts of the early water-colourists were, it can be admitted, purely tentative technical essays, and aimed at nothing more than the representation of commonplace facts in a timid and conventional manner. But in a very short time, as the school increased the number of its adherents and acquired fuller authority, a broader conception of the functions of the art was substituted for the earlier formalities and a much more vigorous type of effort was encouraged. All kinds of subjects quickly came to be regarded as permissible in water colour, and the widest varieties of treatment were allowed to the men who had the strength and originality necessary for marked departures from the beaten track. Conventions gave way to freedom of action and to the legitimate experiments which led to substantial and valuable progress.

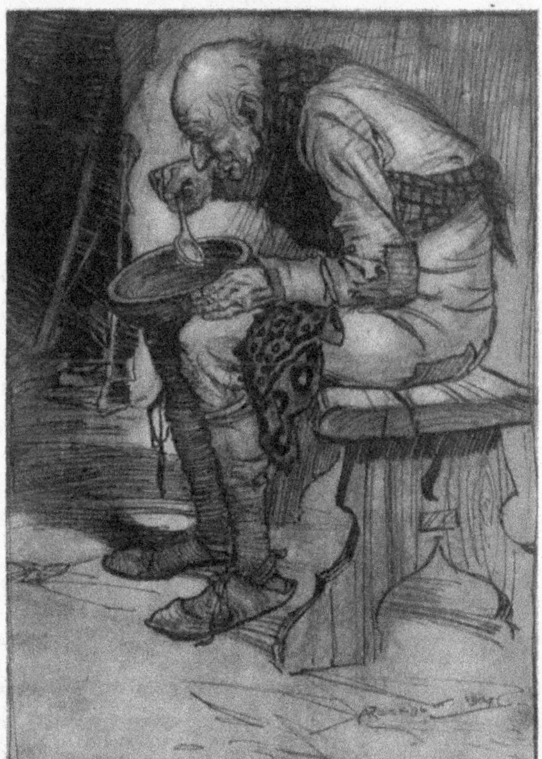

"The Old Man," illustration for *Grimm's Fairy Tales*, 1904.

Fortunately, this love of experiment has not diminished with the lapse of years. The present day water-colour painters are as ready as their predecessors to seek new ways of expressing themselves, and consequently there has been no slackening in the progress of the school, and no decrease in the vitality of the art itself. New men who have something fresh to say are constantly making their appearance and are adding steadily of value to the sum total of England's artistic achievement. There is evidence of continuous movement, of that vigourous expansion which better than anything else proves the sincerity of the workers to whose efforts it is due, and, as well, the thoroughness of their recognition of their professional responsibilities. Among these workers, neither enthusiasm nor capacity is wanting; they are amply fulfilling their mission in the art world, and are doing complete credit to the school to which they belong.

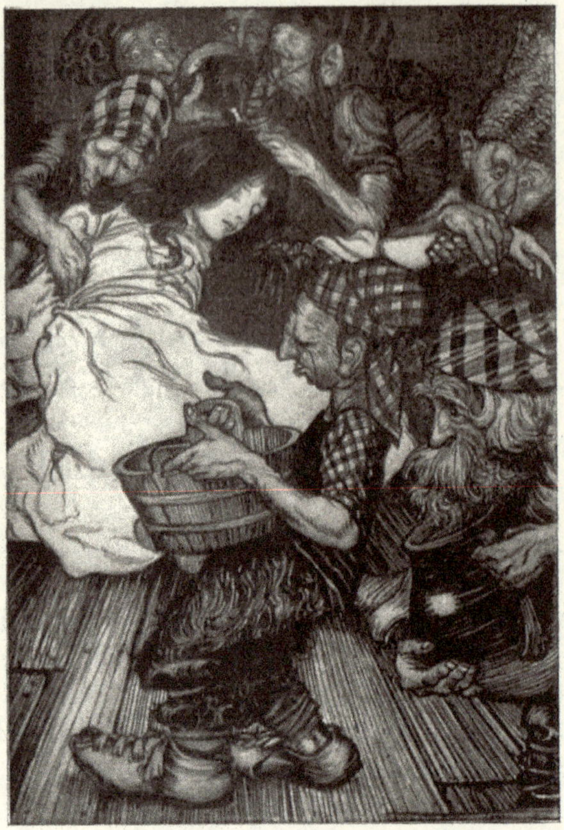

"Snowdrop," illustration for *Grimm's Fairy Tales*, 1904.

There is most certainly no apology necessary for assigning to Mr. Arthur Rackham a prominent place among the most distinguished of these modern water-colourists. We have no one who can quite be compared with him, no one who uses his particular executive method with a tithe of his ability or approaches him in fanciful originality. Nor is there any of his predecessors who can be said to have shown him the way to work the unusual pictorial vein that is providing him with such ample material. Mr. Rackham has found for himself the field in which he is now labouring with conspicuous success, and has developed with delightful ingenuity an absolutely personal style. He owes his position to his special endowment of quaint imagination, and to a rare understanding of the executive devices by which his fancies can be made properly credible.

He had, indeed, no peculiar advantages in his youth which were calculated to develop in him an extraordinary inventiveness, and his art training was neither exceptionally complete nor marked by unaccustomed features. It is true that from his earliest childhood he loved to amuse himself with a pencil and paintbox; and that, like many other boys, who have in later life excelled as artists, he was constantly sketching and scribbling, and trying to give form to the ideas with which even then his mind was filled; but he had no systematic art education during his boyhood. His childish essays were mostly fantastic creations, or drawings of animals; but as a lad in his teens he began to take himself seriously and to have convictions about the need for careful study of nature. So at this period he started landscape painting assiduously, seeking in all sincerity to master the problems which nature presented for solution, and searching out unaided the facts which he felt would provide him with a useful foundation on which to build much later achievement.

As he grew towards manhood the opportunity came to him to acquire a more disciplined type of training, something in which he could be guided by the experience of men who had a skilled knowledge of the matters with which he was experimenting. Even then the best he could do was to attend the evening classes at the Lambeth School of Art—where, however, he had the advantage of being taught by a very able master, Mr. W. Llewellyn—and to devote

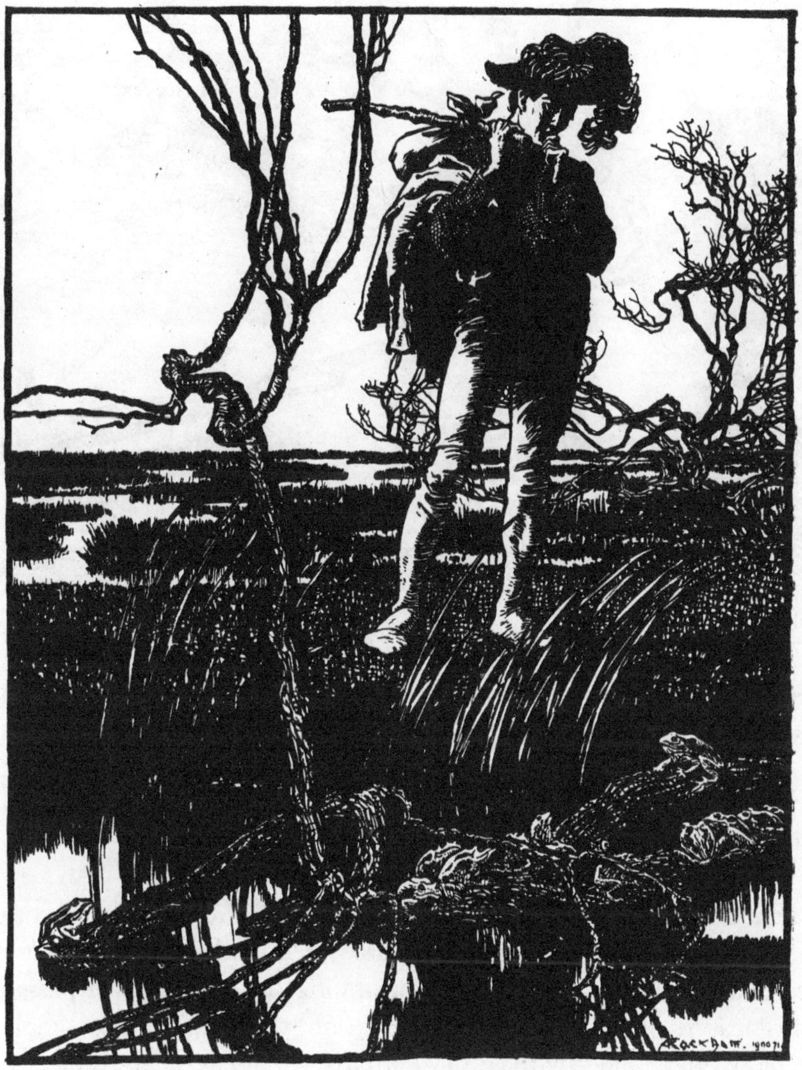

"The Young Count and the Frogs," illustration for *Grimm's Fairy Tales*, 1904.

mature mind what were his chances of success. His confidence in his powers was certainly not misplaced, for he found immediately that there was a demand for his work, and that there was a place in the art world for him to fill. At first he was chiefly occupied with drawings for reproduction, with journalistic illustrations for the "Pall Mall" and "Westminster Budget," the "Graphic," the "Sketch," "Black and White," and other weeklies of the same order, and with more imaginative work for books and magazines. He illustrated the "Ingoldsby Legends," "Grimm's Fairy Tales," and a number of his drawings were published in the children's magazine, "Little Folks." All kinds of subjects engaged him, fairy tales and fantasies, realistic modern life, dramatic motives drawn from fiction, and others which offered him scope for invention and imaginative expression; and the variety, it may well be assumed, was helpful in the development of his art and in the widening of his professional outlook.

Meanwhile he was steadily advancing in his command over the practical details of his art. He was becoming a draughtsman of remarkable power and an eminently accomplished water-colourist, a painter, indeed, with much more than ordinary skill. So satisfactory was his development that in 1902 he was able to secure admission to the Royal Society of Painters in

a portion of his time to the work in which he desired to excel. That this mixture of self-education and school training was of value to him, and that it really helped him to progress in the right direction, may be judged from the fact that he was able at this period to figure as an exhibitor at the Academy, the Royal Institute of Painters in Water Colours, and other galleries, and to rank himself among the abler craftsmen at a comparatively early stage of his career.

It was not until 1892 that he finally gave himself up to art work and made painting his sole profession. He was born in 1867, so that by this time he had reached the age of five-and-twenty, and was in a position to judge with a

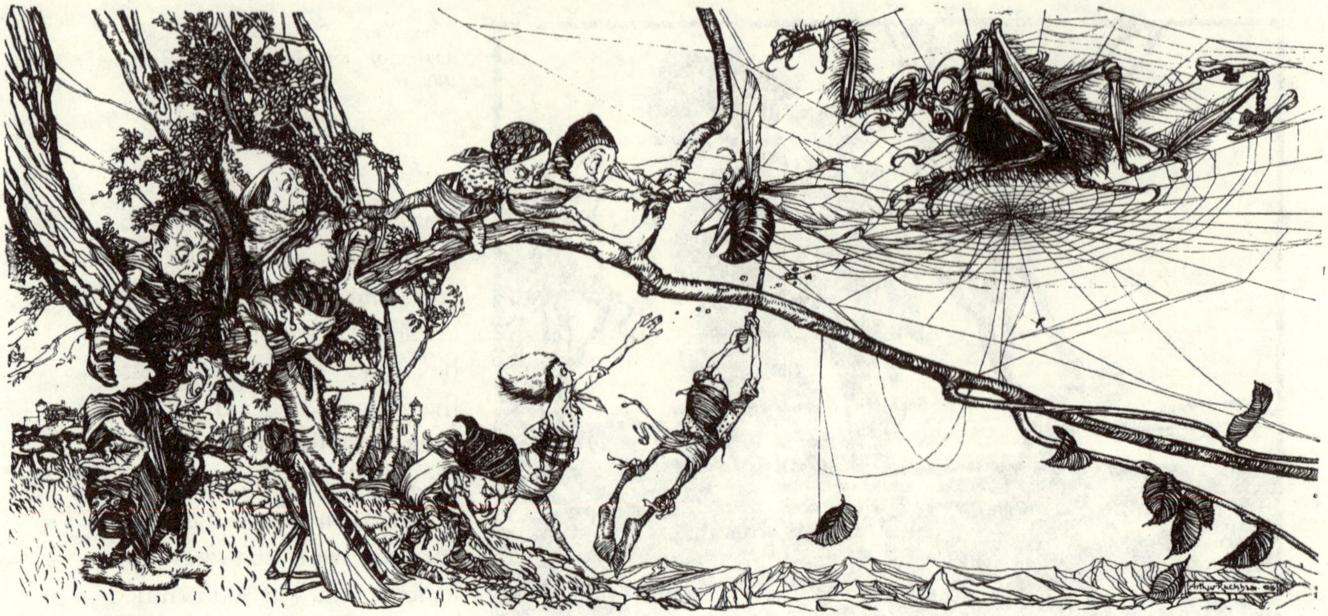

"The Rescue," from a pen-drawing by Arthur Rackham.

Water-Colours on the first occasion that he offered himself. This prompt recognition of his claims deserves to be recorded, because it is no uncommon thing for artists of distinction to have to make a succession of attempts to satisfy the Society of their fitness for election. That the doors should have been opened to him at once is evidence enough that he was regarded then as a specially desirable Associate, and that the members thought his contributions likely to increase appreciably the attractiveness and interest of the Society's exhibitions. No one who has seen the drawings by which he has since been represented in the gallery in Pall Mall would feel disposed to question the correctness of this opinion. He has given to the shows some very novel features, and he has taken in the Society an absolutely unique position; there is certainly no one else among the supporters of this catholic and energetic association who approaches him in that form of pictorial expression which he has made so emphatically his own, and there are few who can be said to rival him in thoroughness and completeness of craftsmanship.

Indeed, there is no harm in repeating what has already been stated, that neither among present day artists nor among those who have passed away is there anyone who is quite comparable with him. Perhaps the nearest to him was Richard Doyle, but Mr. Rackham surpasses even

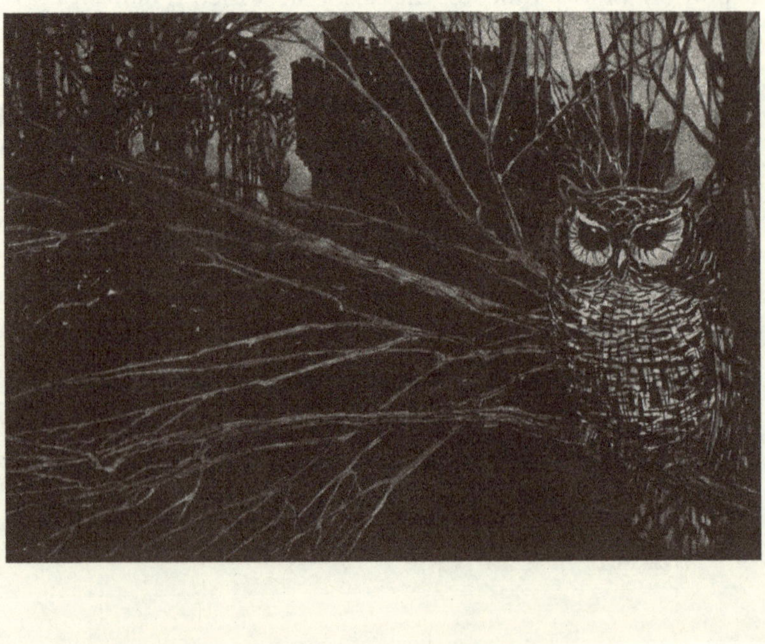

"The Little Owl," illustration for *Grimm's Fairy Tales*, 1904.

that master by fanciful contrivance in the richness and strength of his work. He has undeniably an extraordinary imagination, extraordinary in its intricacy, in its unfailing resource, and its endless variety. Mere grotesque extravagance does not by any means satisfy him; there is much more in his art than simple twisting of facts into absurdities, or than the travestying of serious things in a broadly humorous manner. Such an example of it as *The Rescue*, is really an intensely dramatic story cast in a definitely comic mould, a drama in which all the actors are playing their parts in deadly earnest, and with the most serious conviction. The humour of it is grim—not so grim, perhaps, as that which distinguishes that other amazing creation, the Langham sketch *Alone*—but in the grimness there is a charming hint of tenderness and of sympathy with the weaker things that suffer under nature's inflexible code of laws. In this drawing Mr. Rackham appears as a moralist, and as a commentator on the tragedies of existence; in *Cupid's Alley*, with its wonderful insight into character, he is quite as convincingly a satirist, and in *Alone* he tells a complete and tragic story in which there is a plain and intelligible symbolical intention. In all these fantasies of his, with their quaint and grotesque presentation, there is an underlying meaning that is well worth seeking out; to treat them simply as clever fooling would be a serious mistake.

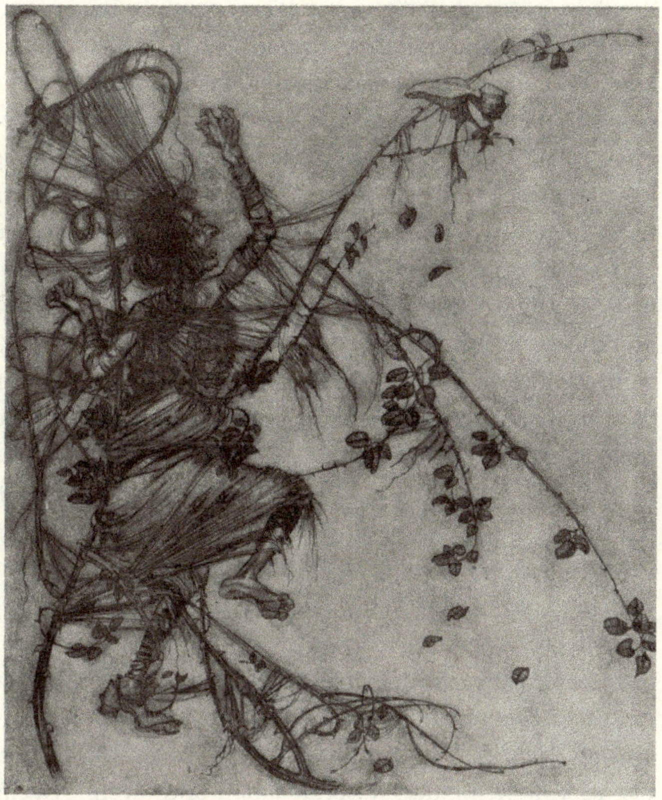

"The Witch who Danced to Death in the Briar Hedge," illustration for *Grimm's Fairy Tales*, 1904.

But when he ceases to deal with these problems and turns to ideas which are essentially dainty and delicate in sentiment he loses none of his attractiveness as an artist. His illustrations to *Grimm's Fairy Tales* (London: Constable & Co.), *The Old Man*, *Snowdrop*, *The Cat*, and *The Young Count*; his exquisite water colours, *Playmates* and *Queen Mab*, even his water colour landscape *The Lakeside*, show a sensitive understanding of artistic refinements which is heartily to be commended. There is in them all an amount of thought, and a degree of ingenuity in design, far beyond what is to be found in the work of the average illustrator, and there is a sympathetic touch which is a clear reflection of his own kindly temperament. Obviously he feels the beauty of nature quite as keenly as her strength, and is as responsive to her charms as to her sternness and inflexibility.

To the executive side of his work, nothing but praise can be given. Whether he is expressing himself in colour, in black-and-white line, in broad masses as in the silhouette, *The Wren and the Bear*, or in that combination of pen-line and tinting in colour-washes which he particularly affects, he is always a complete master of technical method. His practice, indeed, is as intricate and searching as his imagination and as complex as his invention. Everything he does is finished like a miniature and yet is broad, decisive, and confident. The struggle to make himself intelligible, and to keep his mind and hand in proper relation, is never apparent in his drawings; though this struggle is one from which no artist can escape. He has learned with rare completeness how to control the processes of the form of art which he has chosen, and he has acquired that air of spontaneity which more than anything else implies exhaustiveness of preliminary study and long continued effort to acquire a sufficiency of mechanical experience, and in this he has been especially wise; nothing would have hampered more seriously a man of his peculiarly prolific imagination than technical imperfection.

Really, it would be possible to use the whole series of his drawings to illustrate a long and elaborate argument about the importance of careful preparation to the artist who wishes to devote himself to imaginative painting. The realist who is satisfied to present things as they are, to "hold the mirror up to nature"—a cant phrase which is much misunderstood and often misapplied—does not require anything like the same amount of preliminary study, for he proposes to do nothing more throughout his life than he has been accustomed to do at school. He can always sit down before his subject and reproduce it with all the exactness of which he is capable, and with the strictest attention to its trivialities. There is no necessity for him to think, no need even for him to stock his memory with facts to draw upon in later years. As soon as he has acquired the manual dexterity which is expected of every passable student who has gone through the ordinary art school course, he can blossom out as a producing artist, and can secure admission to the exhibitions for his records of the things which are always about him.

All that such a man has to concern himself with is the development of a capacity to see microscopically. If he ever had any power of viewing his material largely or of conceiving his subject as a whole, he is certain to grow more narrow in vision as he goes on. He loses his larger perceptions and he gains in exchange a faculty which is easier to exercise and less

"Lakeside: Evening," from the water-colour by Arthur Rackham.

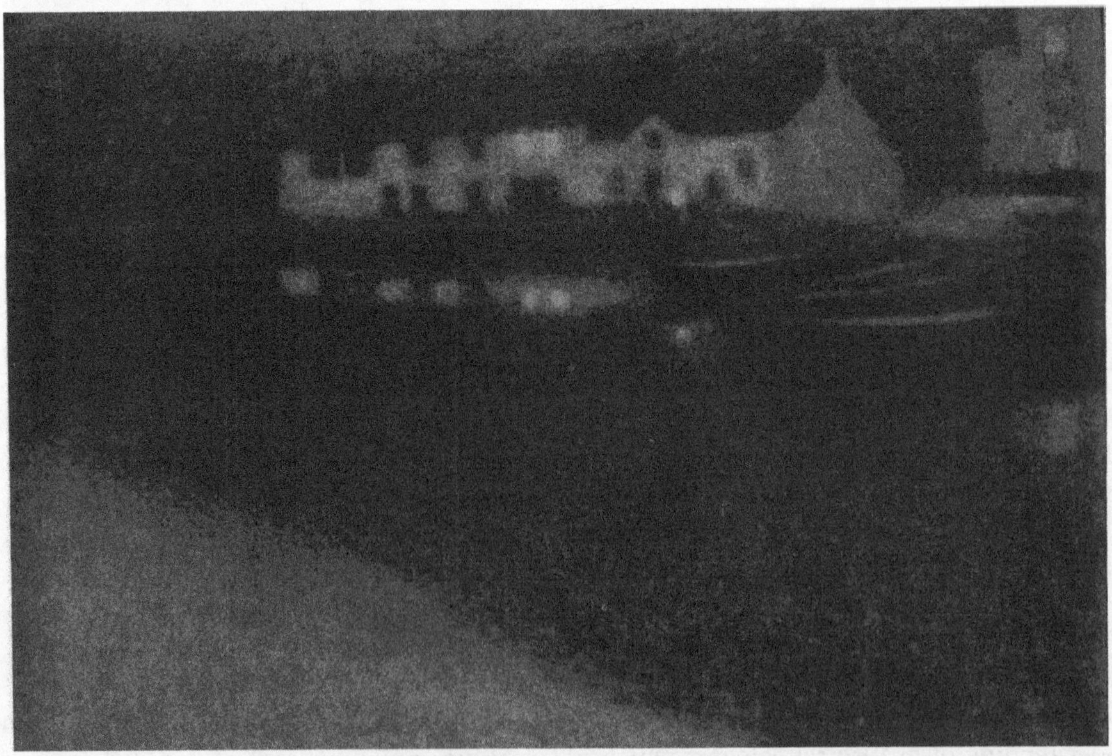

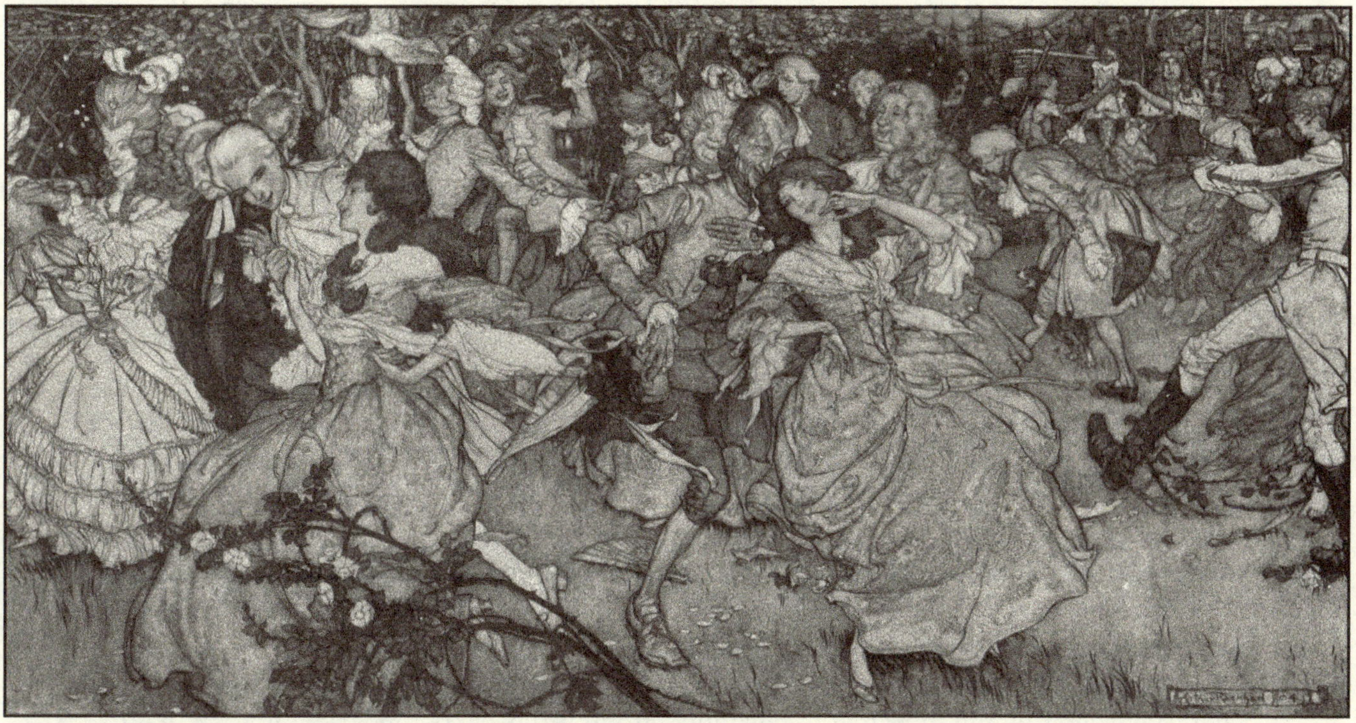

"Cupid's Alley" by Arthur Rackham.

likely to impose any strain upon what intellectual powers he may chance to possess. His one and only ambition is to produce works of art which will be actual enough to be deceptive and which will excite the gaping wonder of the uneducated by their imitative exactness. When he has painted a fly which some deluded observer tries to brush off with a handkerchief, or represented a bunch of grapes which is so like the real thing that it will induce the street-arab to flatten his nose in admiration against the shop-window in which the picture is exhibited, he feels that he has not lived in vain. His triumph seems to him to be assured, his ambition to be completely satisfied.

The unfortunate thing, however, is that triumphs of this sort can be secured so early in the career of any artist who is blessed with sufficiently keen sight. His development begins and ends with his school training, and all he can acquire in later life is merely a little more manual dexterity. Before he has reached middle age he has ceased to be an artist and has become only a manufacturer of stock patterns, who can turn out in any number required things which are quite according to the samples he provided many years before. He stops short on the threshold of art and goes no further because his blunted susceptibilities cannot perceive that there are any more worlds for him to conquer. Possibly he is not unhappy, because, having no ideals he can have no disappointments and can never fall seriously short of what he intended: but his happiness comes simply because he is too fossilised to experience any sensations.

With a worker of Mr. Rackham's type the case is very different. He could not remain a realist, for realism would destroy all the spirit and meaning of his art. He cannot confine himself to the facts that are before him because plain actuality would never satisfy him and would never allow him the scope for expression that he so intensely desires. But he has, all the same, to go through the drilling of the realist or else he would be incapable of expanding in the directions where he can justify his artistic temperament most convincingly. If he had not the basis of sure knowledge he could never construct those delightful perversions of nature which evidently give him such joy and show the rare richness of his imagination. For it must be remembered that his grotesques have to be made credible, and with all their extravagance have to be so dramatically suggestive that they can attract and hold the attention of the people whose first inclination is to laugh at their absurdity.

Directly he began to fumble, or to hint at any uncertainty in his own mind, his power to persuade would be gone; he would seem to be attempting something beyond his reach, or to be deliberately poking fun at his admirers. Such a breach of faith would be inexcusable; for if he is not serious in his art, no matter how amusing or fantastic it may be, he stamps himself as a charlatan who is only attitudinising to draw notice which his merits do not entitle him to claim. Only a consummate command over his craft would allow him to show that his amazing departures from strict veracity are deliberate expressions of a very original aesthetic belief and perfectly sincere in their exaggeration.

When he turns from grotesques to purely poetic drawings, the value of his nature study is not less apparent. The course of landscape painting which he began in his boyhood, and has kept up to the present day, has had a most valuable influence upon his art. It has guided him into exquisite suggestion of nature's subtleties, into a true appreciation of her sentiment and tender beauty. The landscape settings of his grotesques are as decoratively appropriate as they are naturally charming, and have the fullest measure of the true poetic spirit. His landscapes with incidental figures, and his pure landscapes of the *Lakeside* type, are sensitive, dainty, and well observed, distinguished by the happiest observation of atmospheric qualities, and by that perfect refinement which comes solely from intimacy of understanding. If he had not been so close a student, he could never have grasped so firmly the elusive mysteries with which nature veils herself from the unsympathetic soul, and he could never have ranked himself so high as her faithful and earnest interpreter.

Arthur Rackham: The Wizard at Home

Eleanor Farjeon, *St. Nicholas Magazine*, March 1914

There have been three creators of *Rip Van Winkle*. The first, who was Washington Irving, created him with his pen; the second, who was Joseph Jefferson, created him with his personality; and the third, who is Arthur Rackham, created him with his brush. And all three owed much to another, far earlier, and unknown creator—the nameless imagination which, in many lands, through many ages, built up the haunted storehouse of lore and legend to which only the true imaginations of later ages possessed the key. Irving, Jefferson, and Rackham, all true imaginers in their different veins, have all held that key in their possession; and though it is of the third holder, only, that I am writing, it is for a particular reason impossible for me to think of him without thinking of the other two as well. For Joseph Jefferson was my grandfather, and *Rip*, in my family, is regarded as a household god by inheritance.

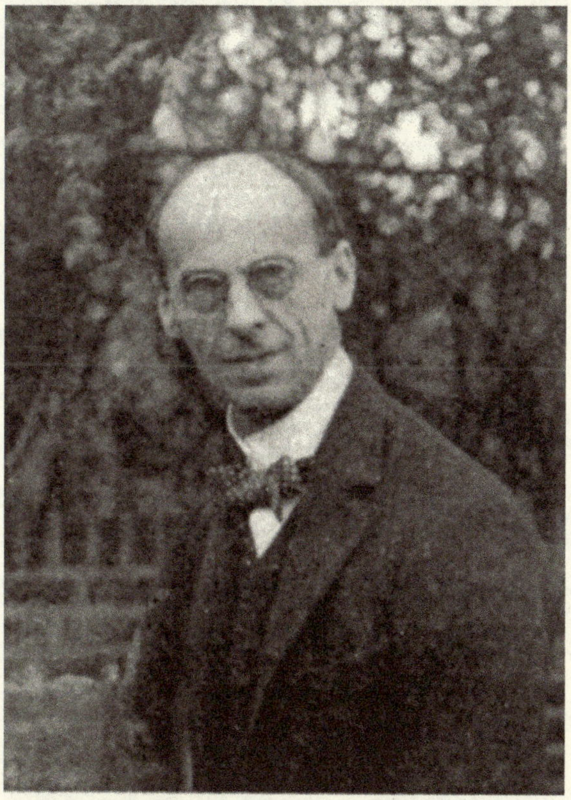

Mr. Rackham in his garden.

Rip was the first book to bring Arthur Rackham fame, and I doubt whether it had to pass through so severe a test at the hands of the qualified critics as at our hands, who judged it from a special personal standpoint. But we were captured instantly. There was never doubt that this dear vagabond figure of *Rip* in his tatterdemalion youth—this wild, pathetic figure of Rip in his lorn age—was *our* "Rip"; or that the red-roofed village under the haunted mountains was his village, or that the haunted mountains were the "Kaatskills" of Hendrik Hudson.

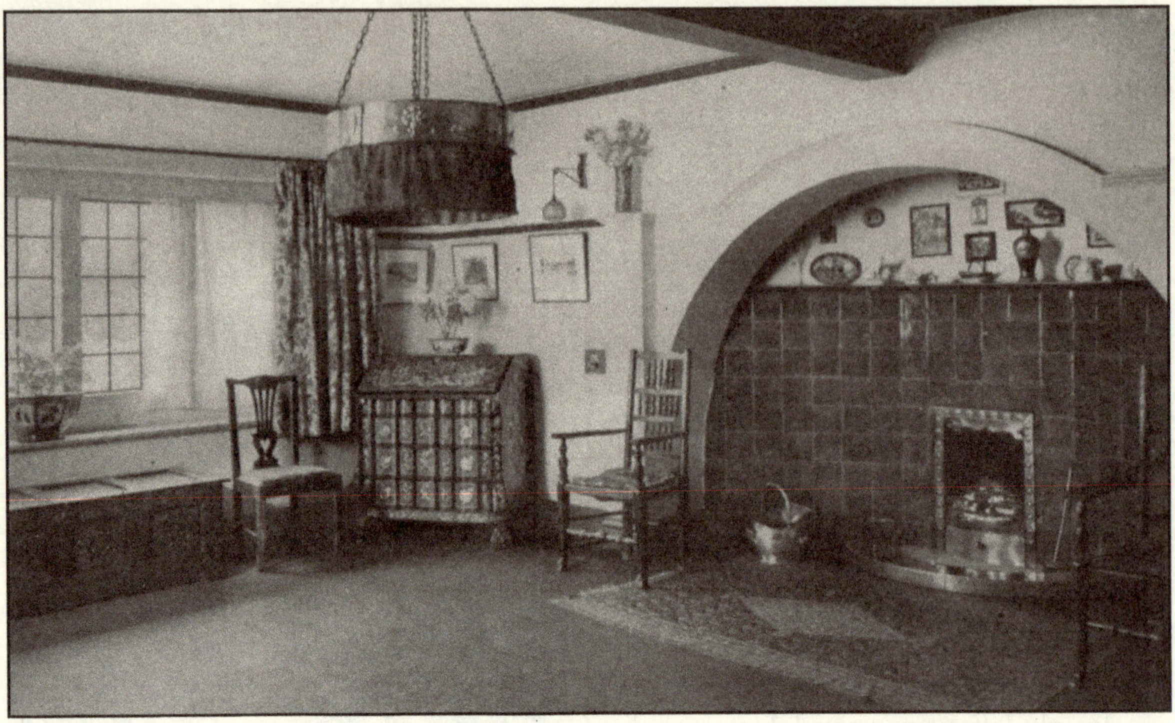

The dining-room.

We knew Arthur Rackham's *Rip* before we knew Arthur Rackham, but it was inevitable that, after knowing the book, we should know the man. A quarter of an hour's walk separates our houses, and it was not long before that ground was covered.

I had always had the impression, from the intimate inside knowledge of Fairy-land which his work betrayed, that Arthur Rackham was a kind of wizard; that he only pretended to call himself Arthur Rackham, and hobgoblins really hailed him by some more mystic name on stormy nights on Hampstead Heath, which is an easy broomstick ride from a certain little house in Chalcot Gardens. Acquaintance has not entirely allayed the suspicion. Arthur Rackham looks rather like a wizard—a wizard of the unmalicious order, who dabbles in sly, freakish, and delightful arts. He watches you from behind the Spectacles of Cunning, and there's a whimsical line in his face that can translate itself into the kindliest of smiles. He is light and spare and alert, so that I imagine his favorite form of transformation to be some kind of a bird. But these are matters I do not inquire into, in case he should turn me into a speckled toad.

If you know Arthur Rackham's fairy-land of books—if you know ancient Aesop and modern *Peter*, and their immortal equals, *Rip*, *Undine* and *Alice*, *Puck* and *Mother Goose;* if you know Grimm, who is better than painted gingerbread and striped sugar-sticks, and if you know the gods and giants and dwarfs and nymphs of the legendary Rhine—not only through the wonder-makers who first shaped them for our hearts, but also through the wonder-maker who has reshaped them for our eyes—then you really know as much of Arthur Rackham as can be told. But nowadays we cannot leave our wonder-makers alone; we must know how they live and where they live, and what they do when they are not weaving the spells that have enchained us.

You must not be disappointed to learn that this particular magician does not weave his particular spells underneath a hollow tree, in one of those tiny caverns with pillars and rafters of twisted roots which time and again in his books he has peopled for us with delicate elves. There is nothing disappointing about the little house in Chalcot Gardens. Outwardly it is not unsuited to the pages of fairy tale. It has a mellow red-and-brown charm, and is the kind of house that could very well have been built of gingerbread and candy. Behind the house is the kind of garden that makes me feel six years old again; a place where the grass and trees seem to preserve, in an atmosphere of quiet sunshine, a share of memories that are almost like expectations—it might be memories of a child they expect to come again. Some gardens have this air for me—I never quite know why, unless they resemble a garden I played in when I was six—and I am filled with momentary hope that I am the child they remember and expect. But this garden has its child, blue-eyed and golden-haired, green-frocked and deep in fancy. Her name is Barbara. If you want to find her, do not walk straight down the road, for that is the way to miss the house. It is a house that says "Come and find me" as it steps back a little in the corner of a curbed inclosure, secure from the common traffic of automobiles and motor-bicycles, things which Arthur Rackham has been heard to declare are at the root of most modern evils. With them he classes telephones and type-writers ("I would rather," he told me, "have a page of hand-writing I couldn't read than a type-written manuscript"); and he ought to include the Automatic Piano-Player that lives in his very beautiful un-automatic dining-room. But he must have music at any price, and he has confessed that he is incapable of playing common time with one hand and triple time with the other, so, for once, he has had to fall victim to a machine. I suppose he *has* been seen in a taxi in his day, but I am sure he would prefer to amble across London on a camel; and I know from experience that a magic carpet is kept in the house for personal use.

There's magic, too, in the green carpets on the stairs. They are the color of grass-rings after

Mr. Rackham's house in Chalcot Gardens, South Hampstead, London.

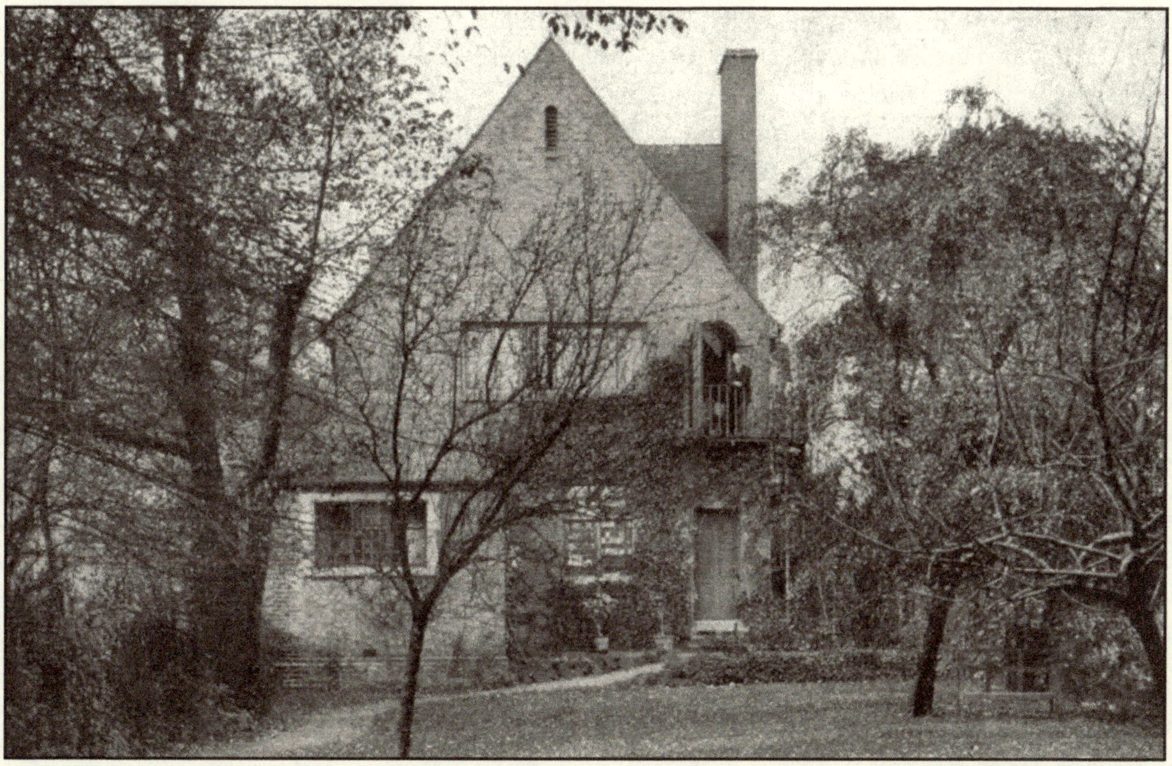

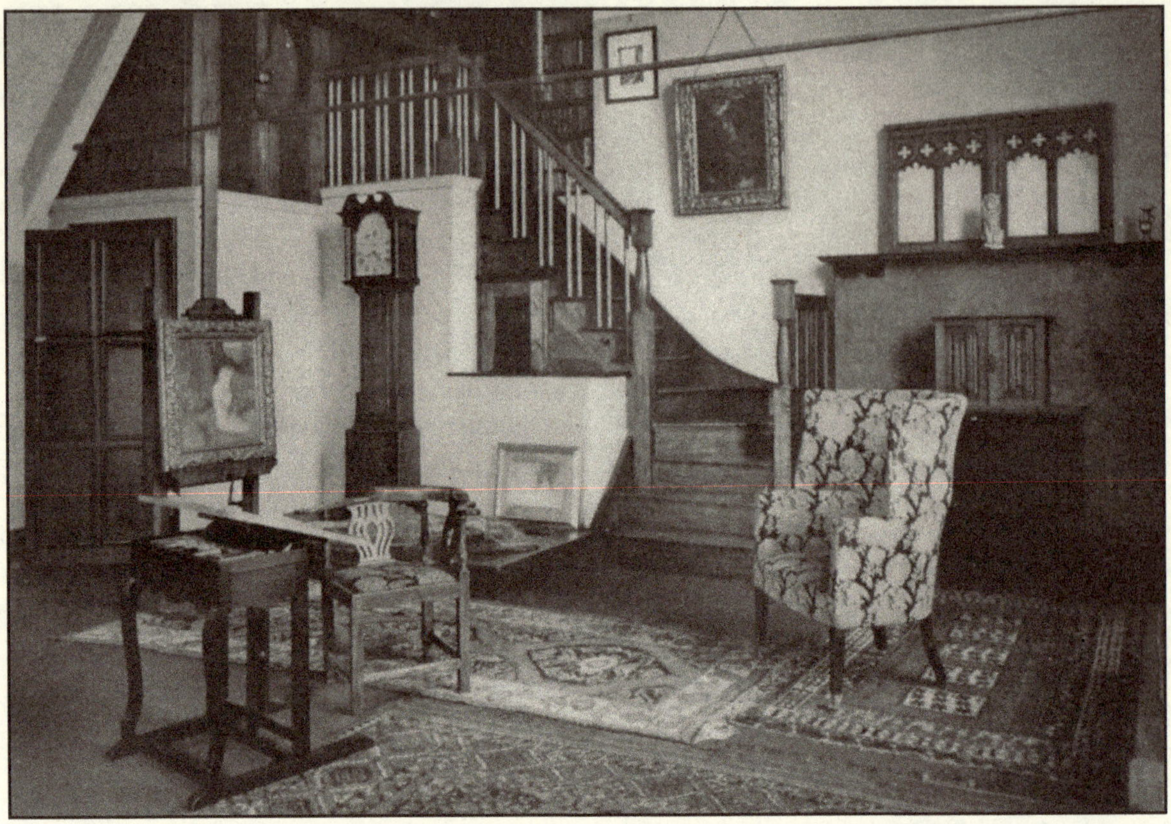
The studio.

fairies have danced in a meadow, so it is not hard to guess what takes place up and down the Rackham staircase after the lights are out. The very stairs are tricksy things, branching different ways like forked twigs on a tree; I am never certain that it is always the same fork which leads me to the Wizard's studio. It is a big room, innocent enough at first sight, but it has its surprises. Look at that easel—half-visible gnomes lurk there, and are on every table, and in every bookcase. In one corner there's a wooden door sunk under an arch, and if you open it unexpectedly, you may find yourself looking over the world in sudden light, on a giddy little platform with a spiral stair running down as fast as it can into the garden. In another corner of the room, almost as far away as possible from the daylight door, the Wizard keeps a second door, up a dark stair. I haven't had the courage to mount that stair and discover the mystery behind that door. I can only guess that, as behind the first door the Wizard keeps his brightest spells, so behind the second he keeps his blackest.

Luckily for me, he was in a harmless mood enough the last time I saw him. I had almost said that, for a wizard, he was in a helpless mood. He was looking for a letter, in much the same way as my mother looks for her housekeeping bag seven times a day. We were chatting about odds and ends as he hovered vaguely among the furniture.

"You see," he was saying, "so-and-so, and so-and-so, and so-and-so... but I must read you that letter... and then such-and-such, and such-and-such—where *is* that letter? did I leave it in Barbara's room?" (Here he vanished without so much as hey presto! and reappeared as rapidly.) "No, I can't find it—and so etc., etc., etc.,—you really should hear the letter, but it isn't here, or here—let me look once more." (Again he

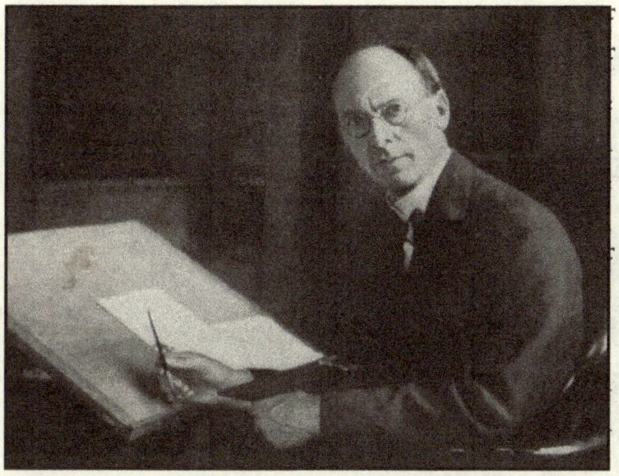

Mr. Arthur Rackham: The wizard at work.

the corner off the highway the moment you try to course," he reflected, picking up some kind of a portfolio in a discouraged way, "this is where it *ought* to be." He opened the portfolio, and that was where it was. Then, looking at me warningly through the Spectacles of Cunning, he observed: "Ah! *now* you see the mistake of putting things in their proper places!"

It is one of his peculiarities that, like his own house, Arthur Rackham steps back a little in the corner off the highway the moment you try to come and find him. I don't mean by this that he literally shuts his mouth and runs away. On the contrary, his instincts are social. He likes company, and he likes fun. And he is far from locking himself up in his studio. He is to be found almost as often in the garden, where, in his own words, he is "continually moving paths and flower beds"—a process that entails long expostulations with a robin, who insists on coming and getting in the way of the spade and the rake whenever there is the chance of a grub turning up. But if the unexplained charm of the garden is due to the Wizard's influence, it is the Wizard's wife who is responsible for the unexplained charm of the house. She really ought to have an article all to herself, but she is as shy and elusive as the little green people of her native Irish hills, so I've small hopes of catching her. In the little house in Chalcot Gardens, the sweet fellowship of daily life is made perfect by the fellowship of work. Under that roof Mrs. Rackham has her own studio; things pass from it now and again to the walls of the Royal Academy, and one of her paintings has lately found a permanent resting-place in the Luxembourg.

Perhaps the most important inhabitant of the house—certainly in his own eyes—is Jimmie, who goes on four feet, and purrs. To formal acquaintances he is Sir James; he was named after J. M. Barrie, and of course he too must have his baronetcy. He does not consider kitchens the place for the toilets of titled cats, and makes a point of being combed, as often as he can, in the studio. Nevertheless, a few of us believe that he is of less account than one other member of the family—the child for whom the garden keeps its memories and expectations.

It is pleasant, after you have been chatting with Arthur Rackham upon every subject from Shakespeare to skeeing, to hear him say, "Now come and see Barbara. We shall have her to ourselves. Mademoiselle is out."

It is pleasanter still to see him, in what is supposed to be Barbara's "Rest Hour," solving puzzles for her that *St. Nicholas* brought on December the sixth; or playing *Cinderella* while she plays the *Prince;* or teaching her to dance with a hop and a skip across the floor; and presently (since it is her Rest Hour) whispering, "Slip out quietly so that she doesn't notice."

Between Barbara and Barbara's mother and Jimmie, and skeeing in Switzerland, and fishing, tennis, and golf in England (he is the only golfer, good or bad, that I ever heard say, "Yes, I play golf," and then talk about something else), and the automatic piano-player in the dining-room, it is rather to be wondered at that the studio sees anything of him. And it is in that part of himself, the part which produces the work we

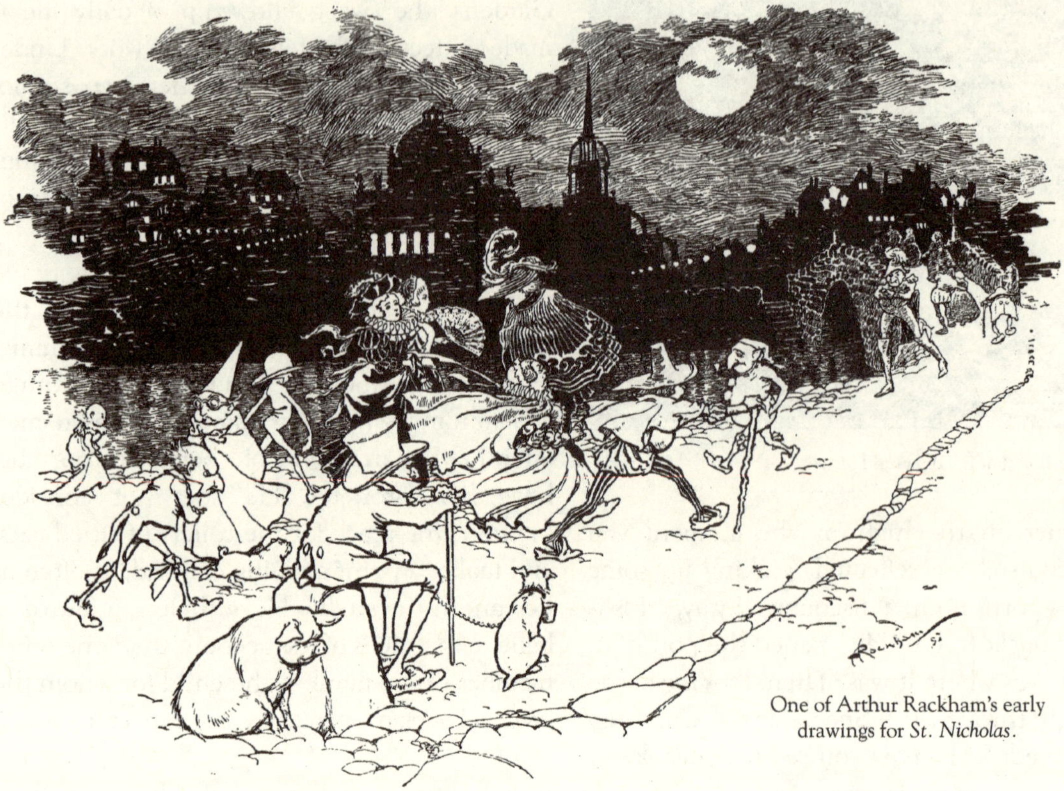

One of Arthur Rackham's early drawings for *St. Nicholas*.

know and love, that Arthur Rackham reminds me of his own house retiring round the corner. He is willing to talk, and does talk, well and definitely, about a multitude of subjects, with equal keenness and interest; but if you mention *Rip*, he will talk of Irving and Jefferson, rather than of Rackham. And it is interesting to hear *Rip's* last creator on his predecessors. Of my grand-father he has said:

"One feels it was he who made the character for all time the great living entity that it is. At least I, for one, very much doubt whether Irving's playful fiction or morality would have become immovably established—to the degree of a creed, a genuine local legend—if Jefferson hadn't given *Rip* the living personality that we now recognize him by. I think *Rip* one of the most remarkable of created characters. Created as the sheerest piece of pleasant moralizing, acknowledging, even, that it was cribbed from old-world sources, here is *Rip* as firmly fixed in the hearts of all good Americans as any genuine myth. I can think of hardly another modern instance."

Personally, I think that among recent inventions *Peter Pan* might have lived as the same kind of local myth, if his author had not created two entirely different *Peters*. The *Peter* of the play is not the *Peter* of the book, and the play has so outdistanced the book in its power of appeal, that the name of *Peter Pan* now instantly calls to mind, not Kensington Gardens, but the Never-Never Land.

Yet it is impossible to say that the chance of a permanently haunted Kensington Gardens has quite been let slip. Arthur Rackham has many times put a fine imagination to the service of the finest imaginations that have set the earth aglow—he has created kingdoms of humorous goblins and fairies with rainbow-colored wings; of two-headed ogres with knotted clubs; of gnomes, and dragons, and witch-wives, and other shapes minute and mighty, fearsome and fair—but his magic never held so firm as when he took the Kensington *Peter* for his theme.

He had done marvels in the Catskills, and was yet to do marvels in the wood near Athens (which is really a wood in Warwickshire). He was to draw *Robin Goodfellow* (and I do not know who could draw *Robin Goodfellow* that had not really seen him). But when our wizard did marvels with fairy-land in London, he perhaps made *Peter* more inseparably his than any other of his creations.

Under the roots that the trees and plants send down into the earth he has fashioned for us an elfin realm so fantastic, so incomparable, so complete, that we can no longer doubt what we should find if, like the icing off a cake, we should slice the top layer off Kensington Gardens. And the seen has as much enchantment as the unseen, the tree-tops as much fairyhood as the tree-trunks, the colors of the Serpentine as much mystery as the glimmering fairy lights which it reflects.

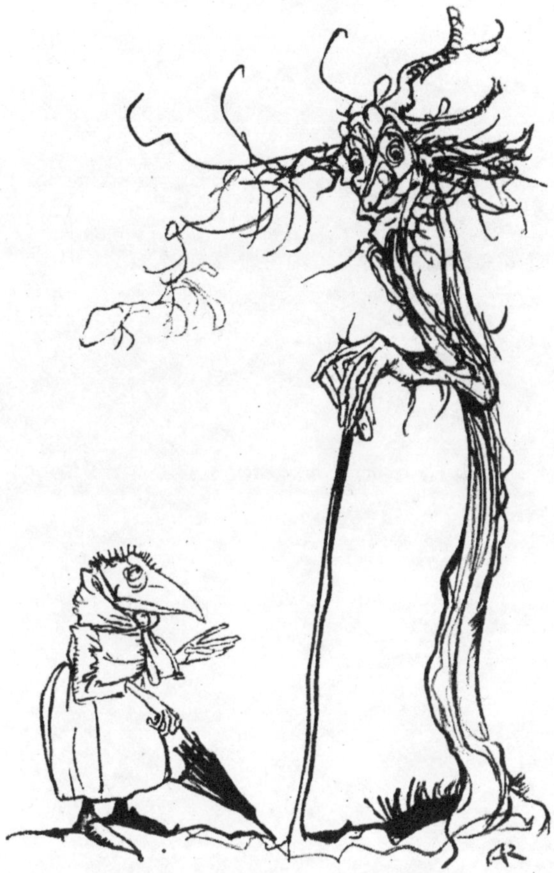

Two of Mr. Rackham's characters.

When the wizard shows us the delicate webs of leafless branches traced against a wintry sky, when he paints evening light for us, or pale marbled clouds, or patterns upon water, or children and flowers as well as fairies in the Gardens—then he reveals a magic which Londoners may encounter day by day. And if, through years of apathy, we have grown numb to it, it is from Arthur Rackham that we may catch the angle of true vision again.

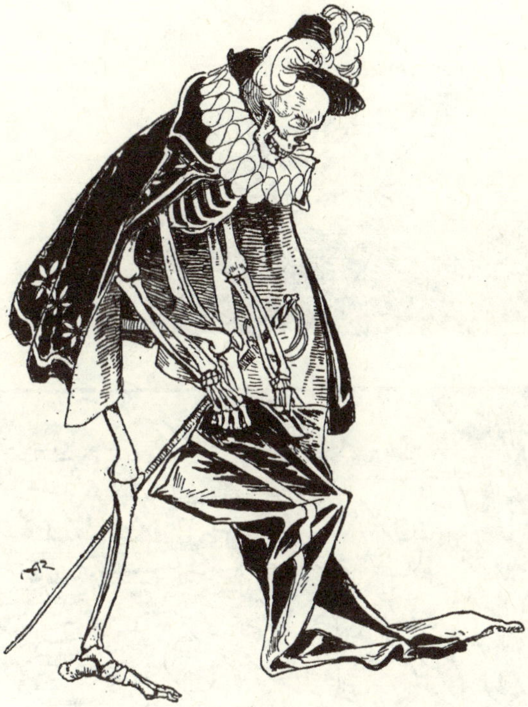

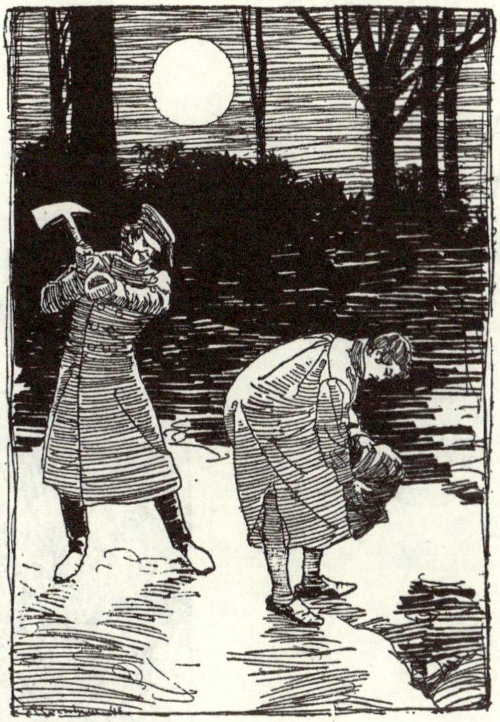

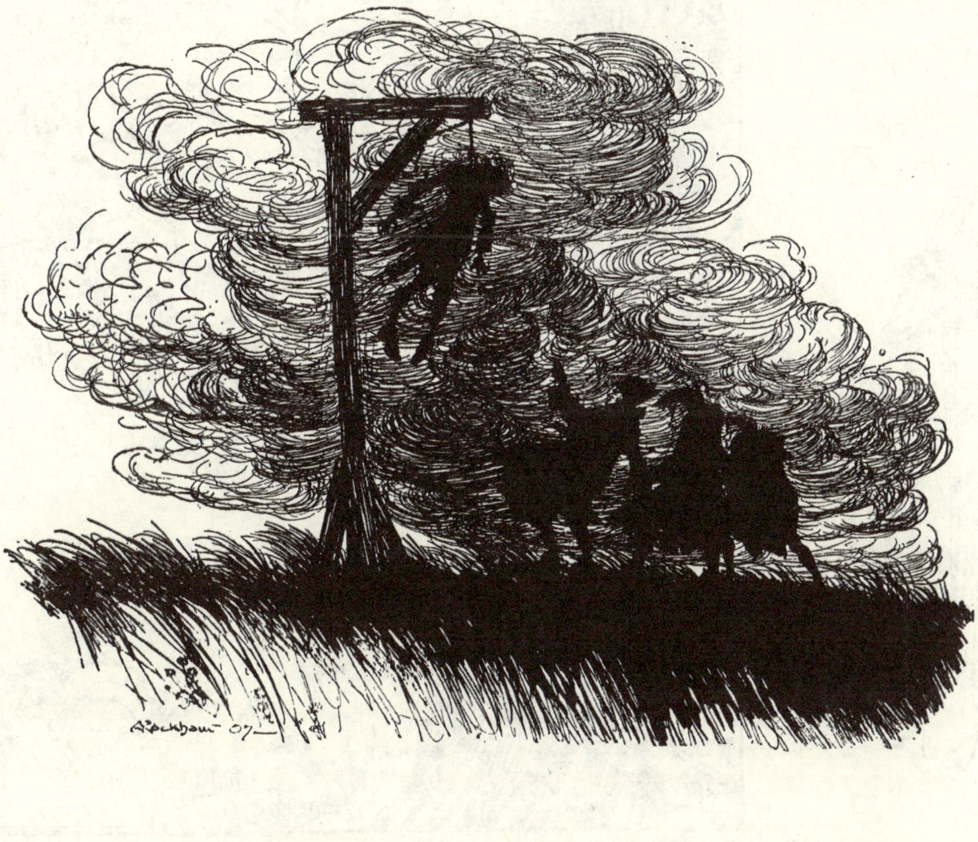

THE INGOLDSBY LEGENDS, 1898

This collection of tales has been reprinted numerous times between 1898–1907, with some editing to the art, colors added, and changes in printing.

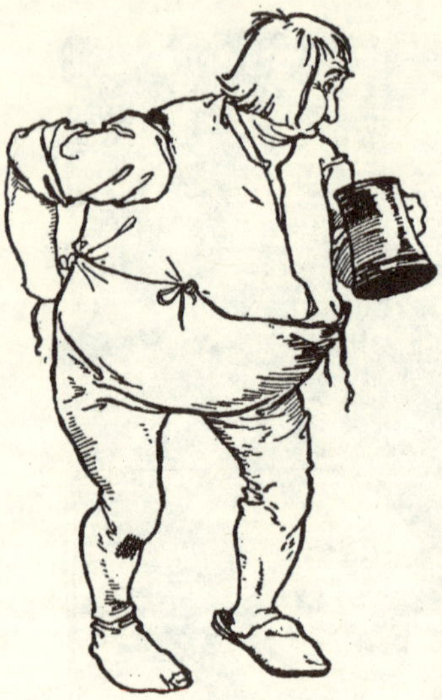

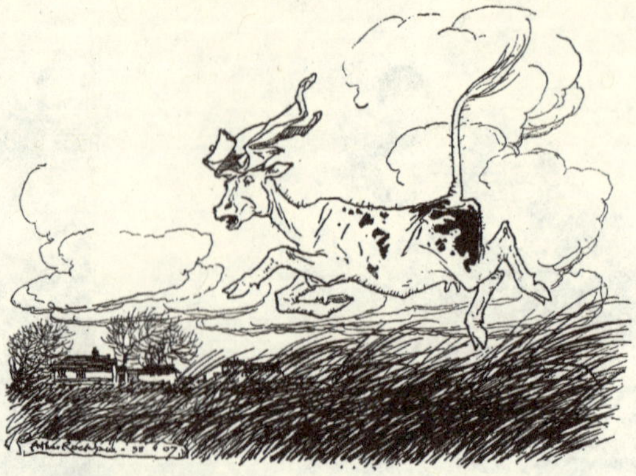

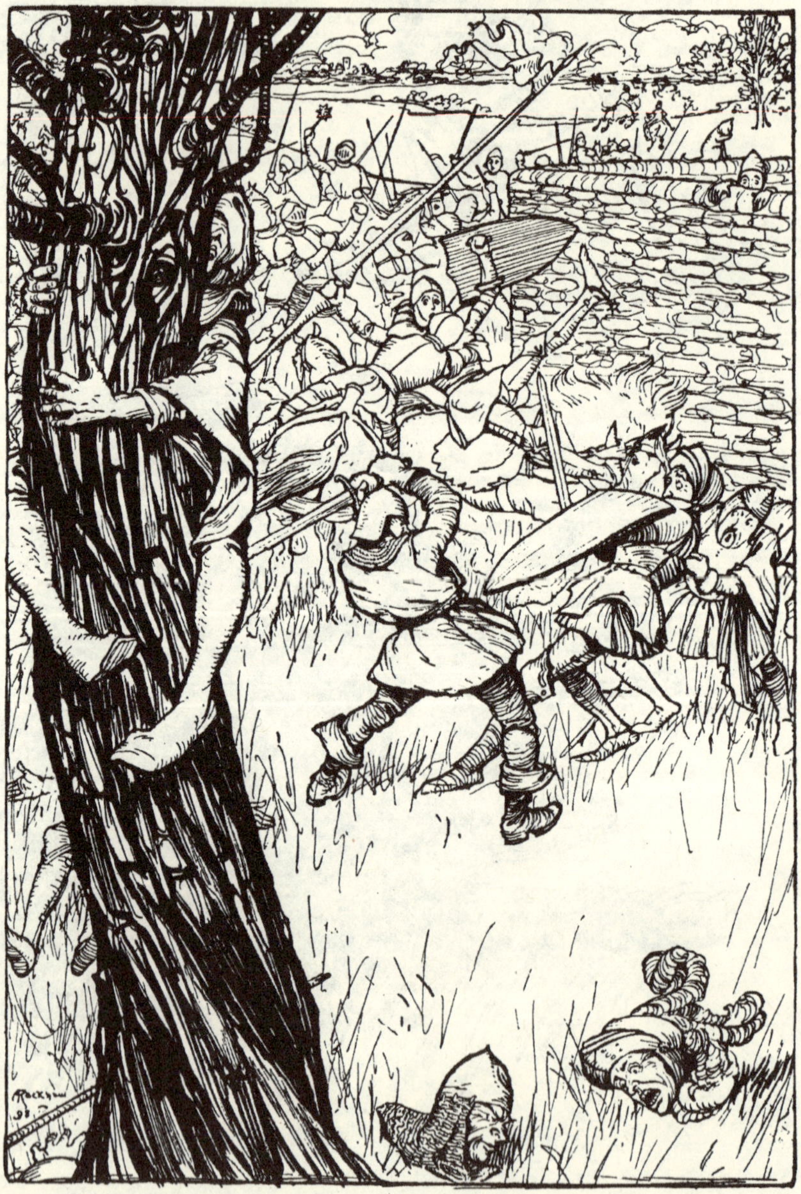

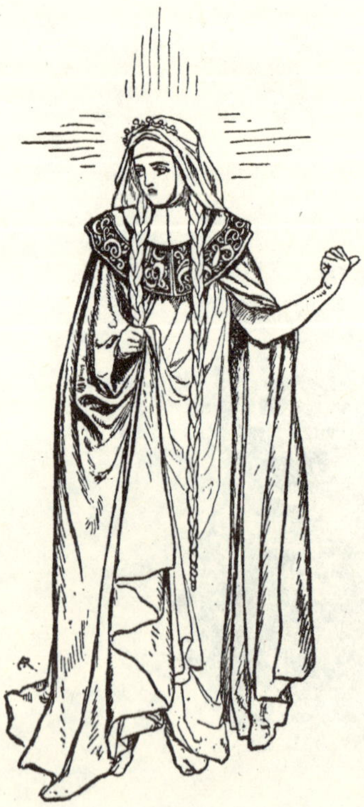

THE INGOLDSBY LEGENDS, 1898

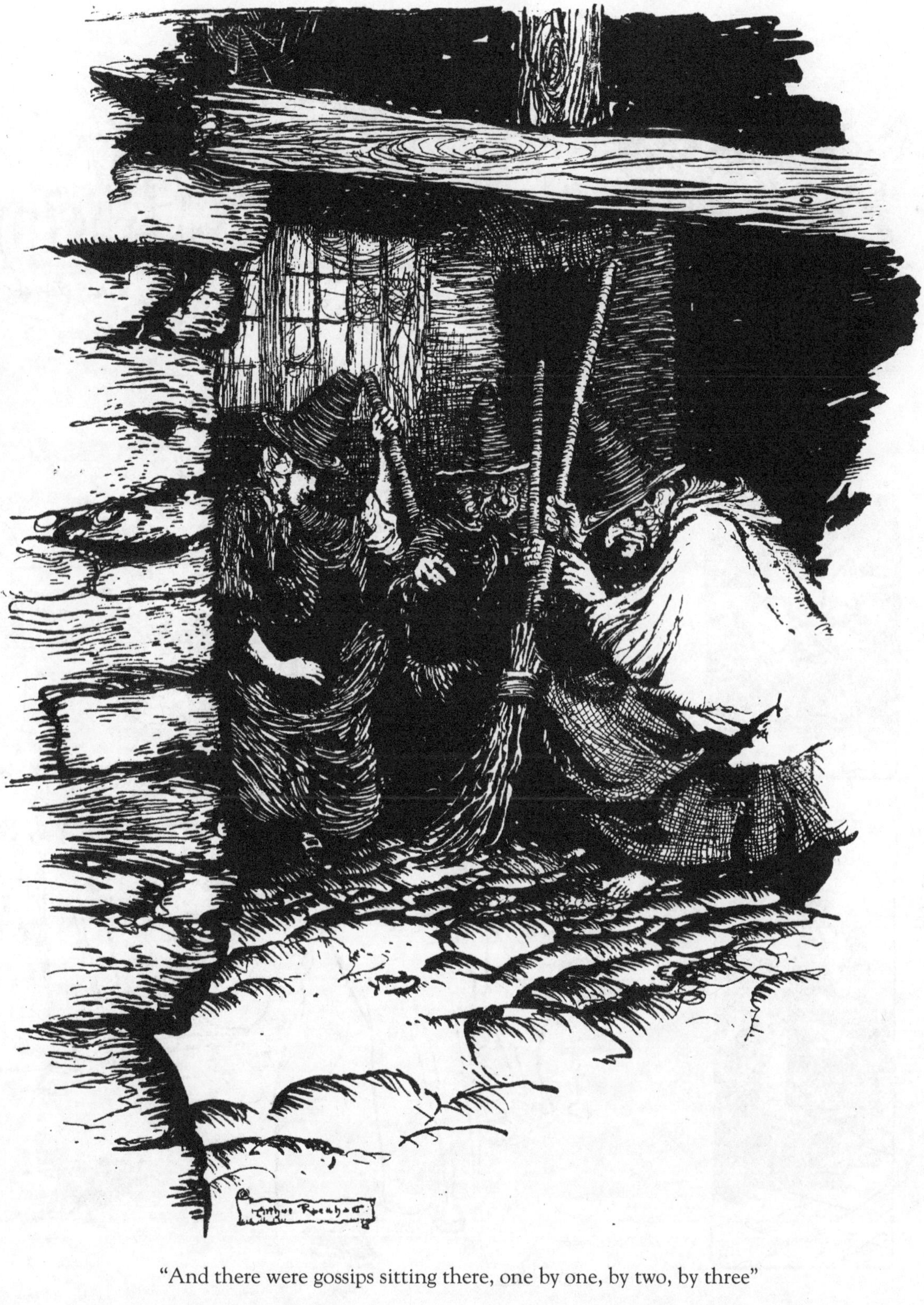

"And there were gossips sitting there, one by one, by two, by three"

The Ingoldsby Legends, 1898

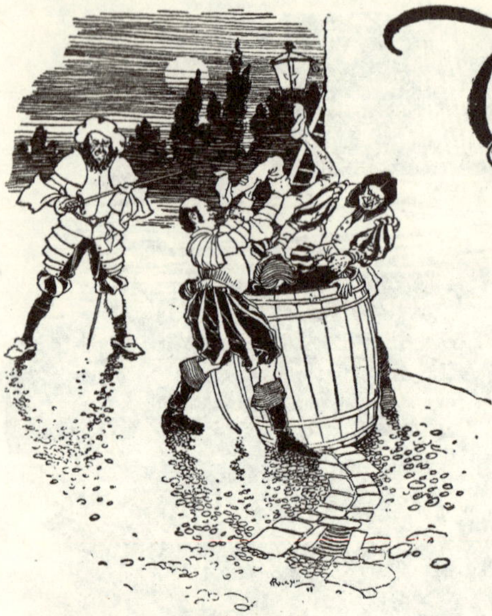

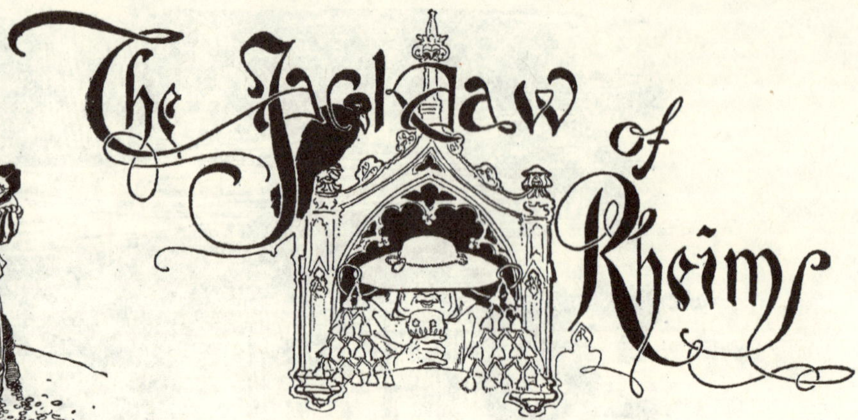

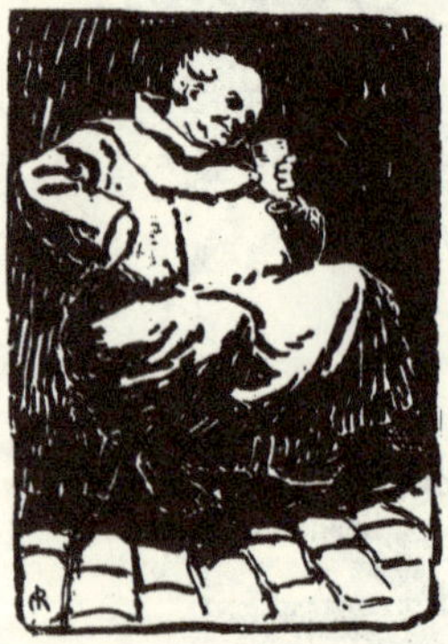

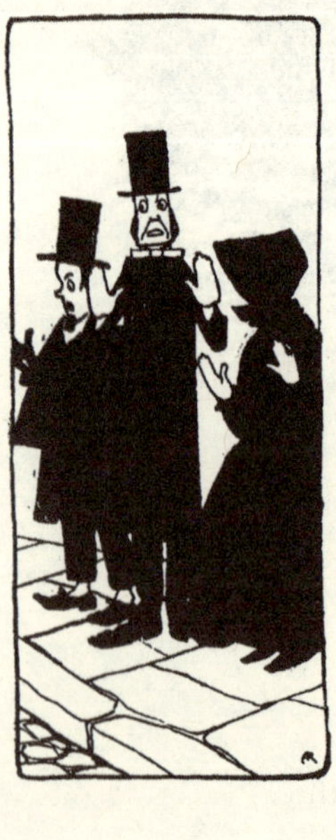

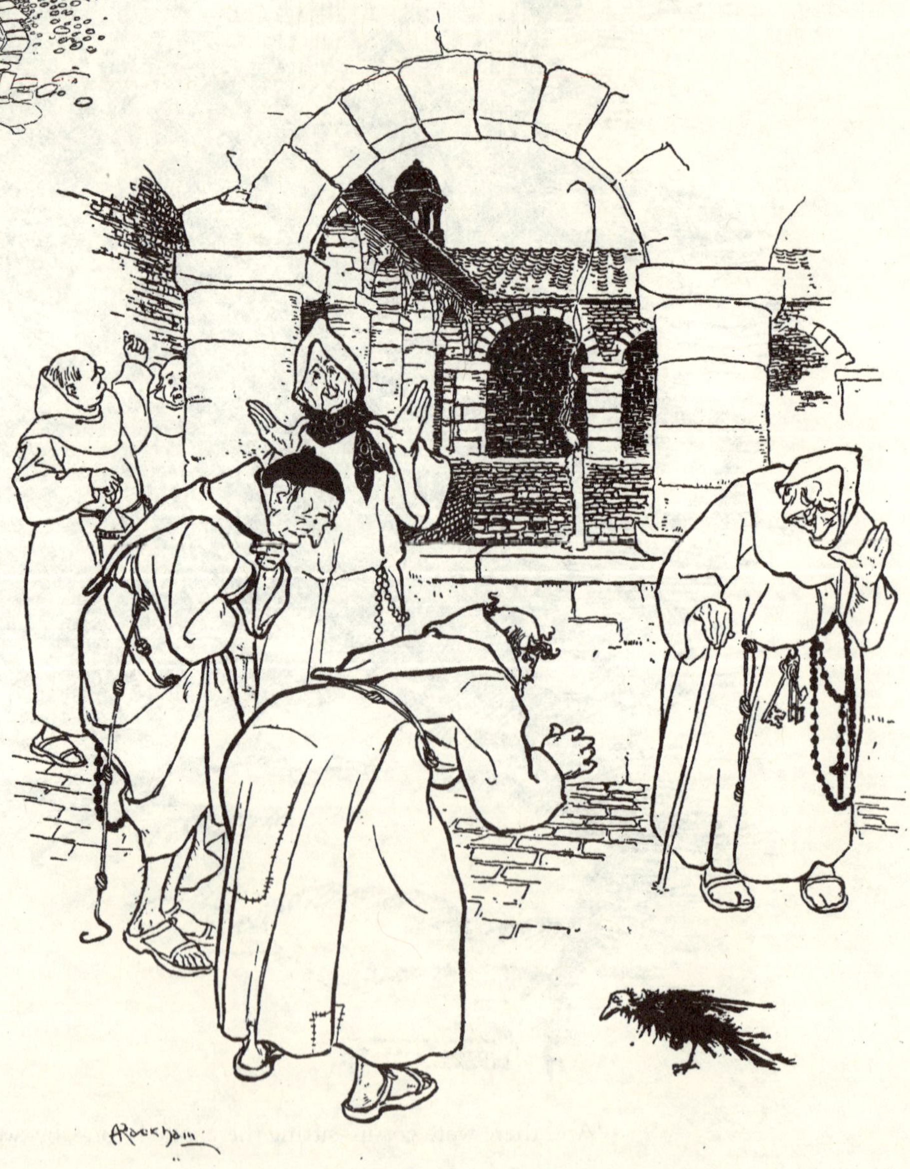

The Ingoldsby Legends, 1898

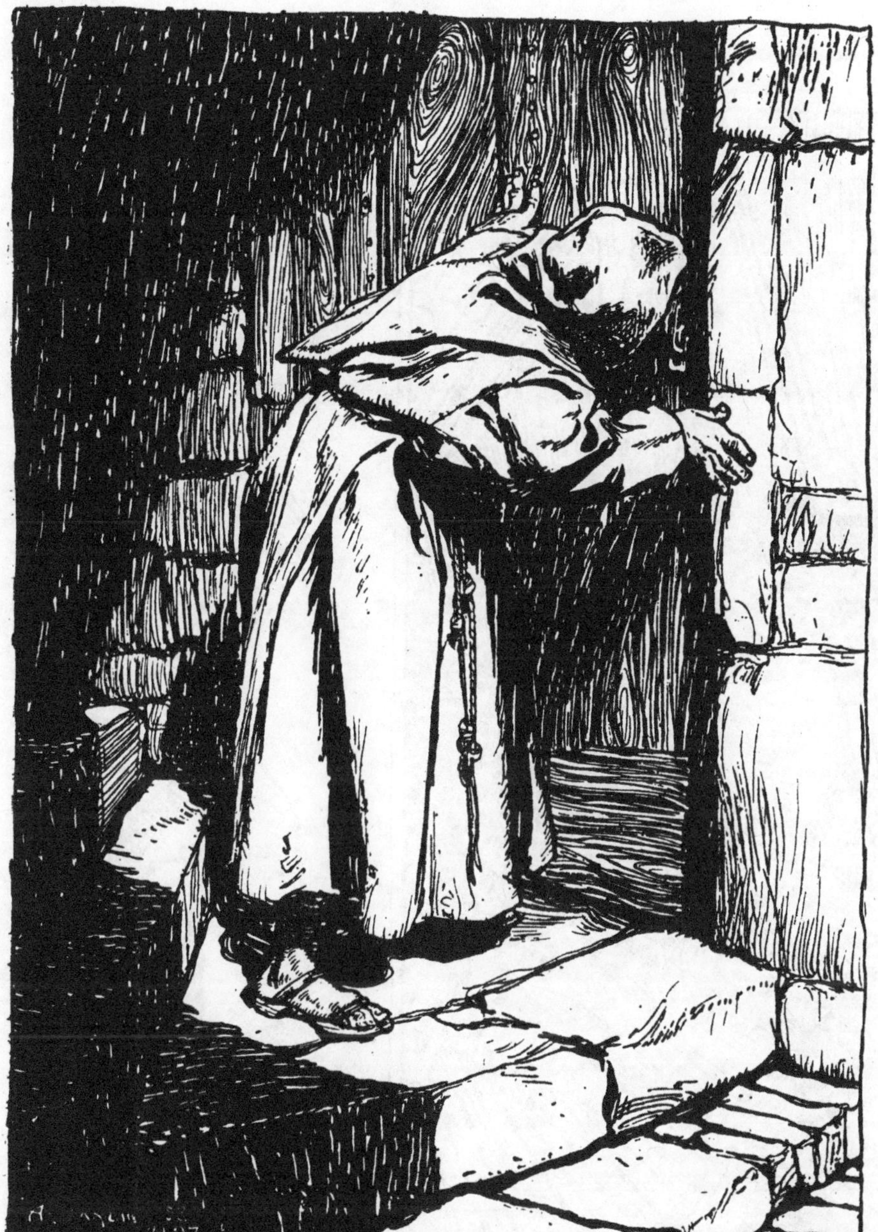

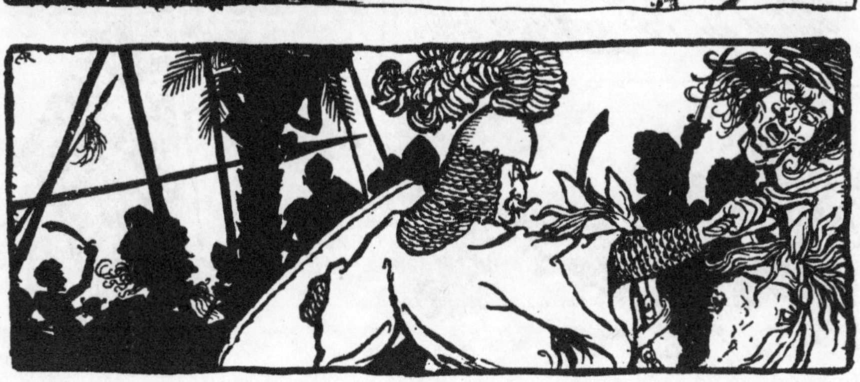

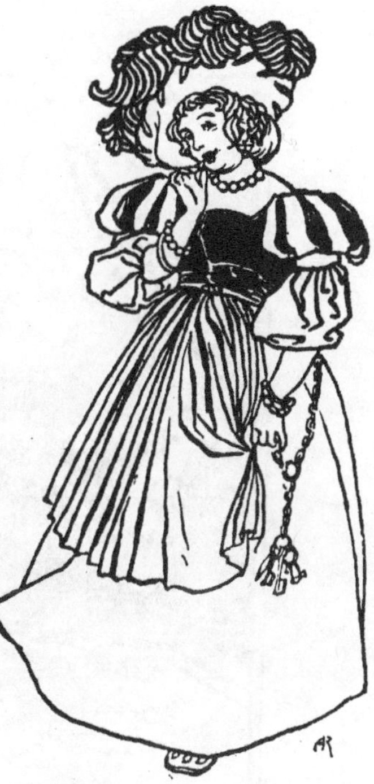

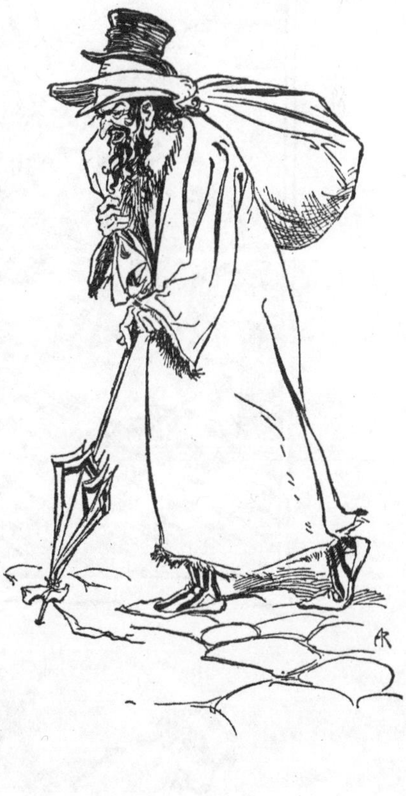

The Ingoldsby Legends, 1898

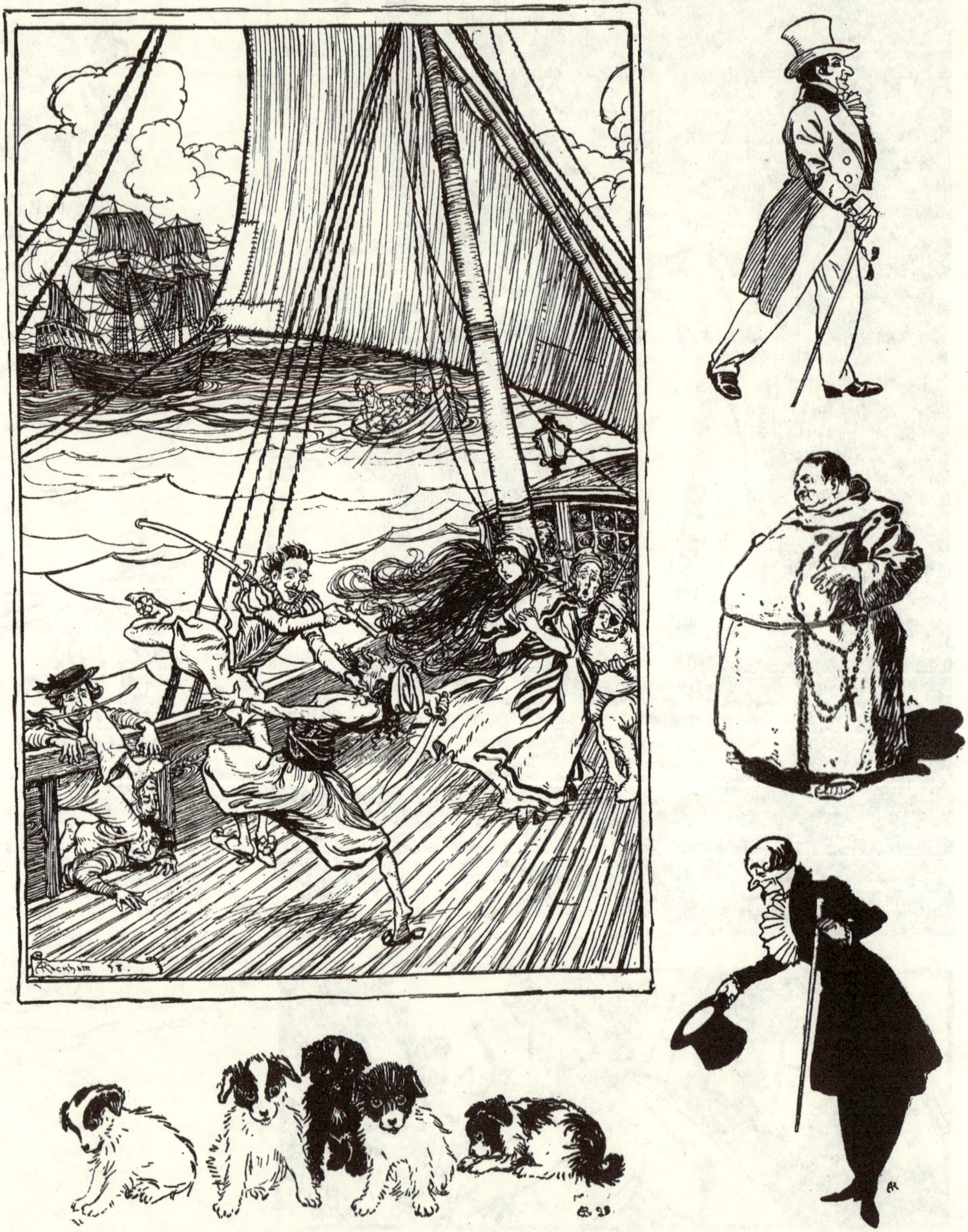

The Ingoldsby Legends, 1898

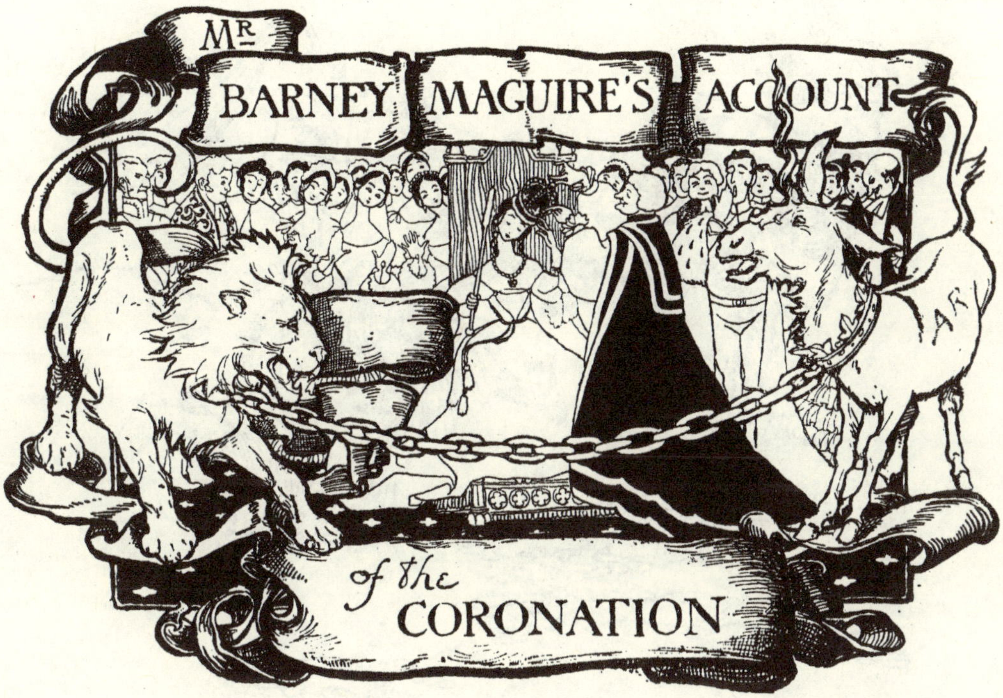

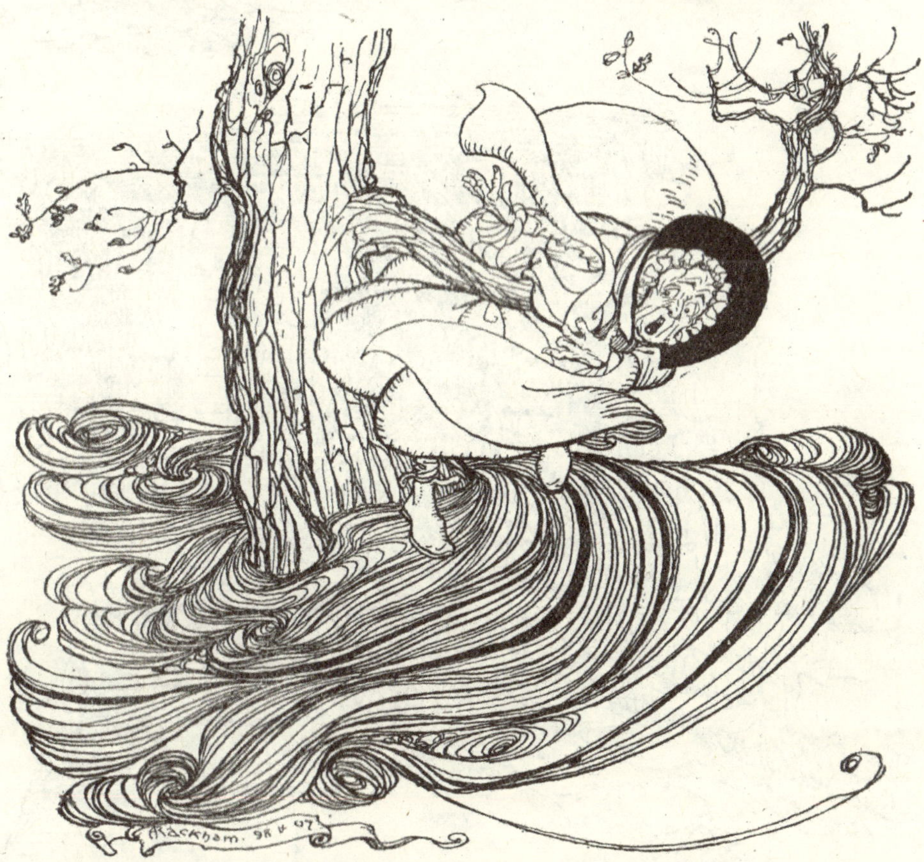

The Ingoldsby Legends, 1898

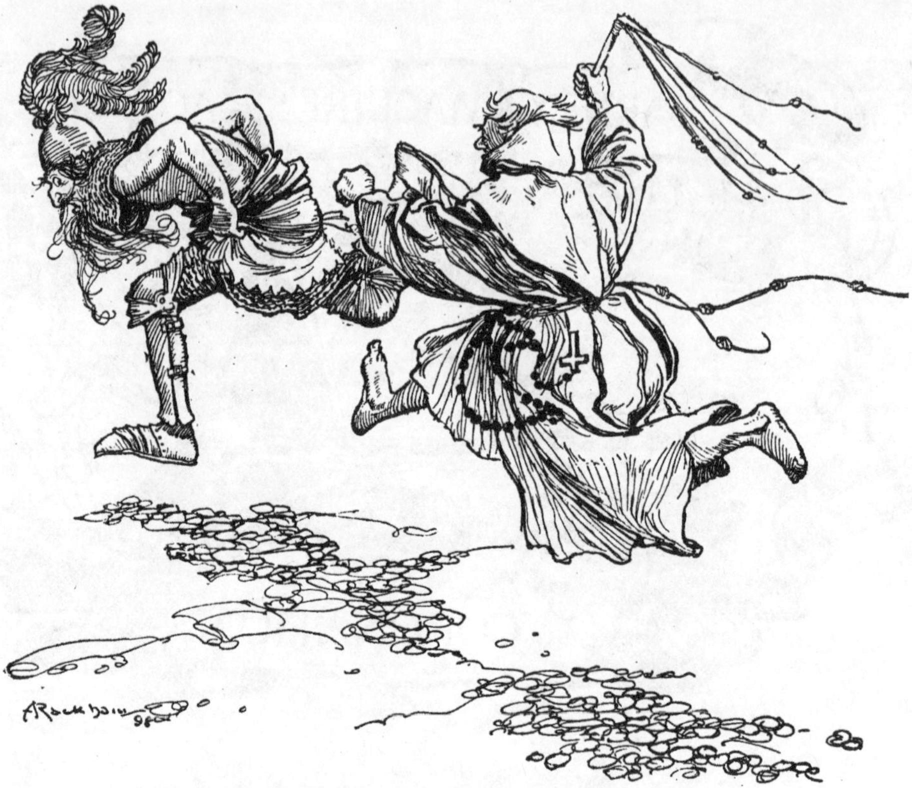

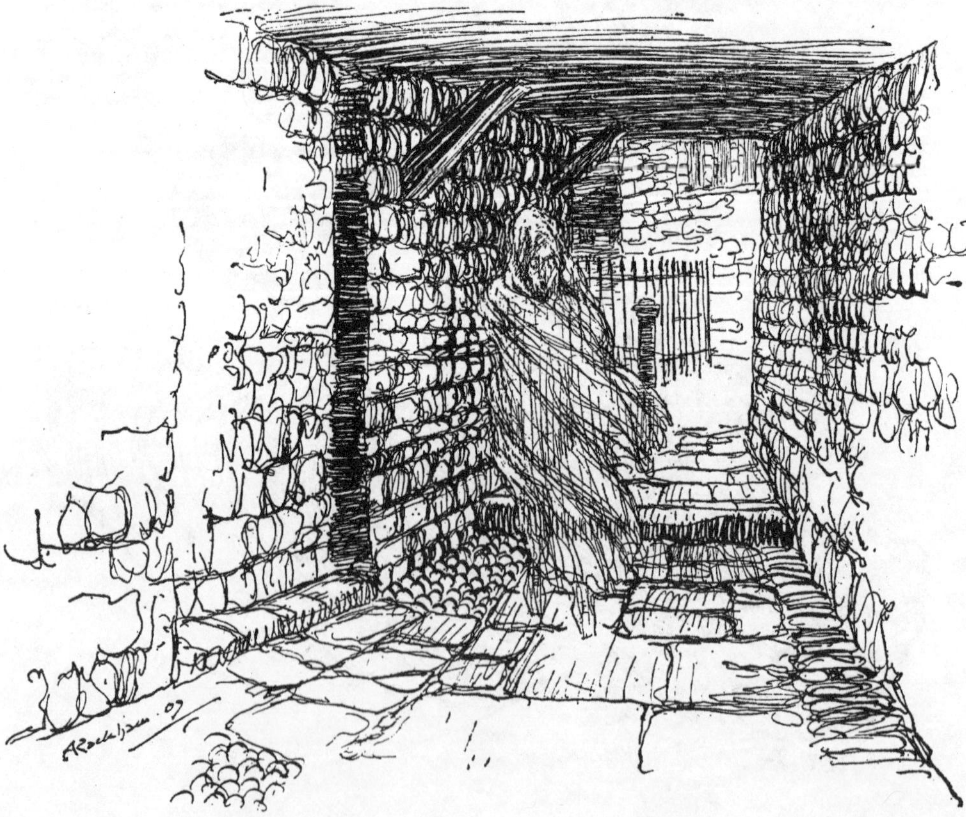

The Ingoldsby Legends, 1898

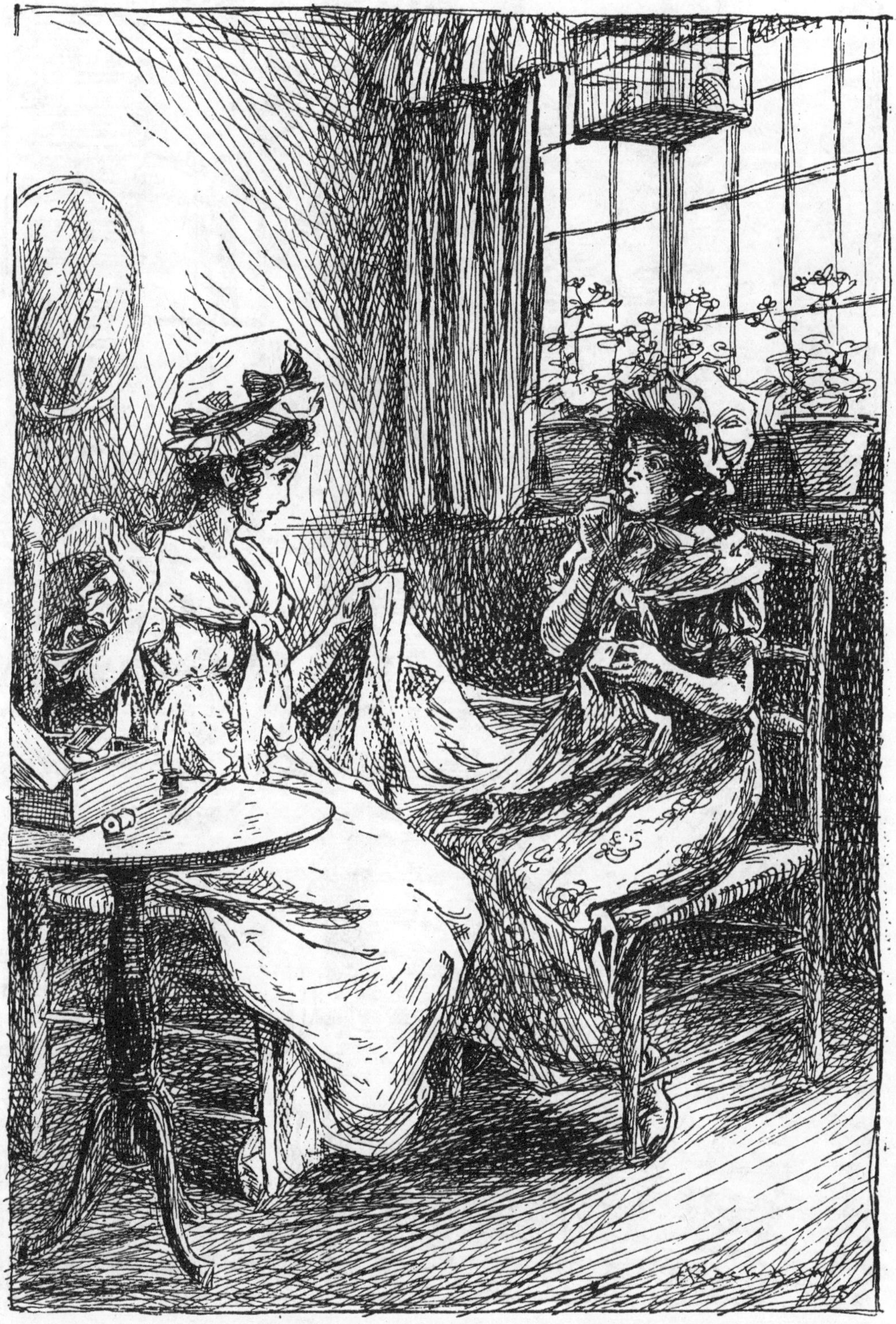

"Ads cuss it! I've spoiled myself now by that 'ere nasty Gusset!"

The Ingoldsby Legends, 1898

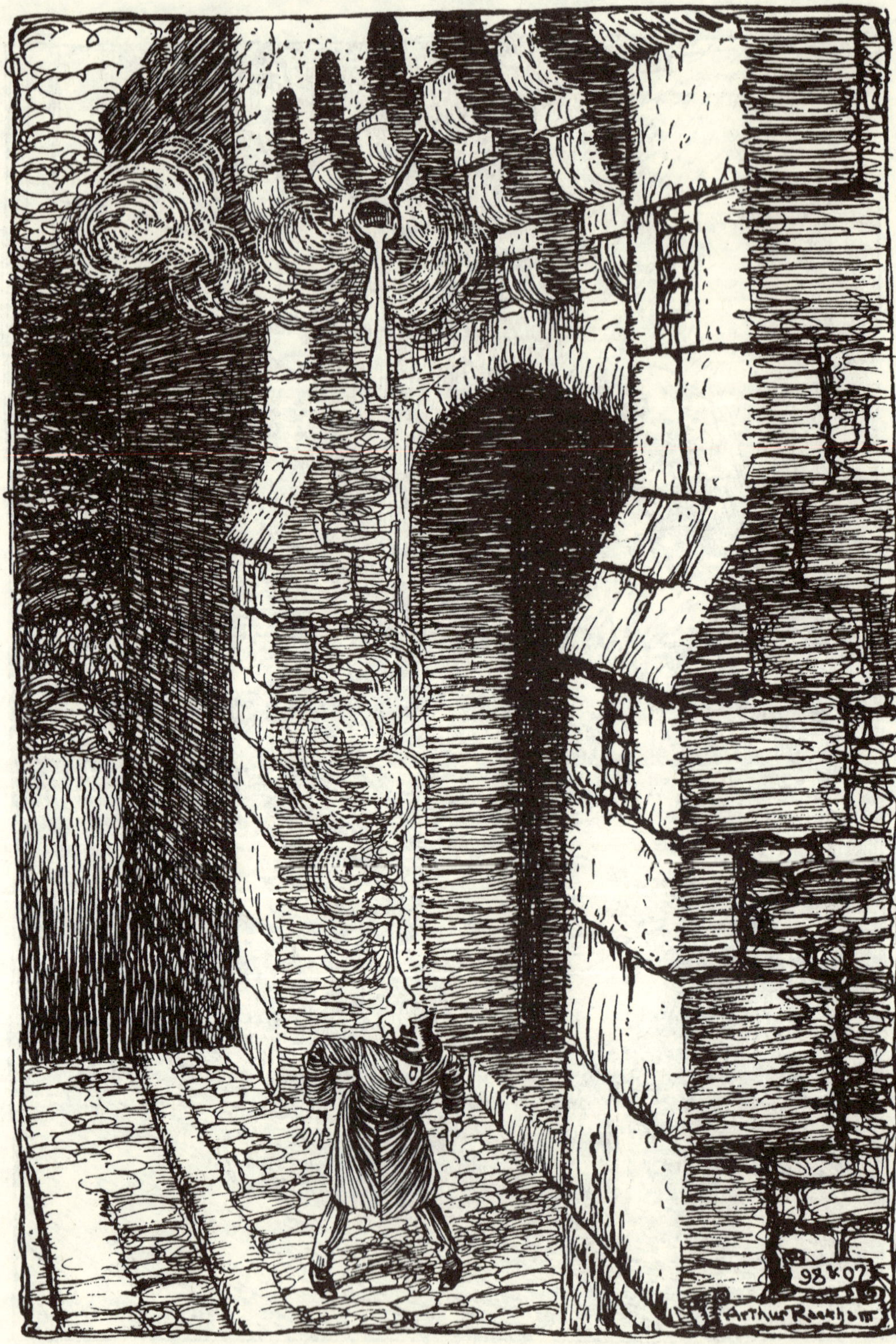

"With iron it's plated, and machecollated, to pour boiling oil and lead down"

THE INGOLDSBY LEGENDS, 1898

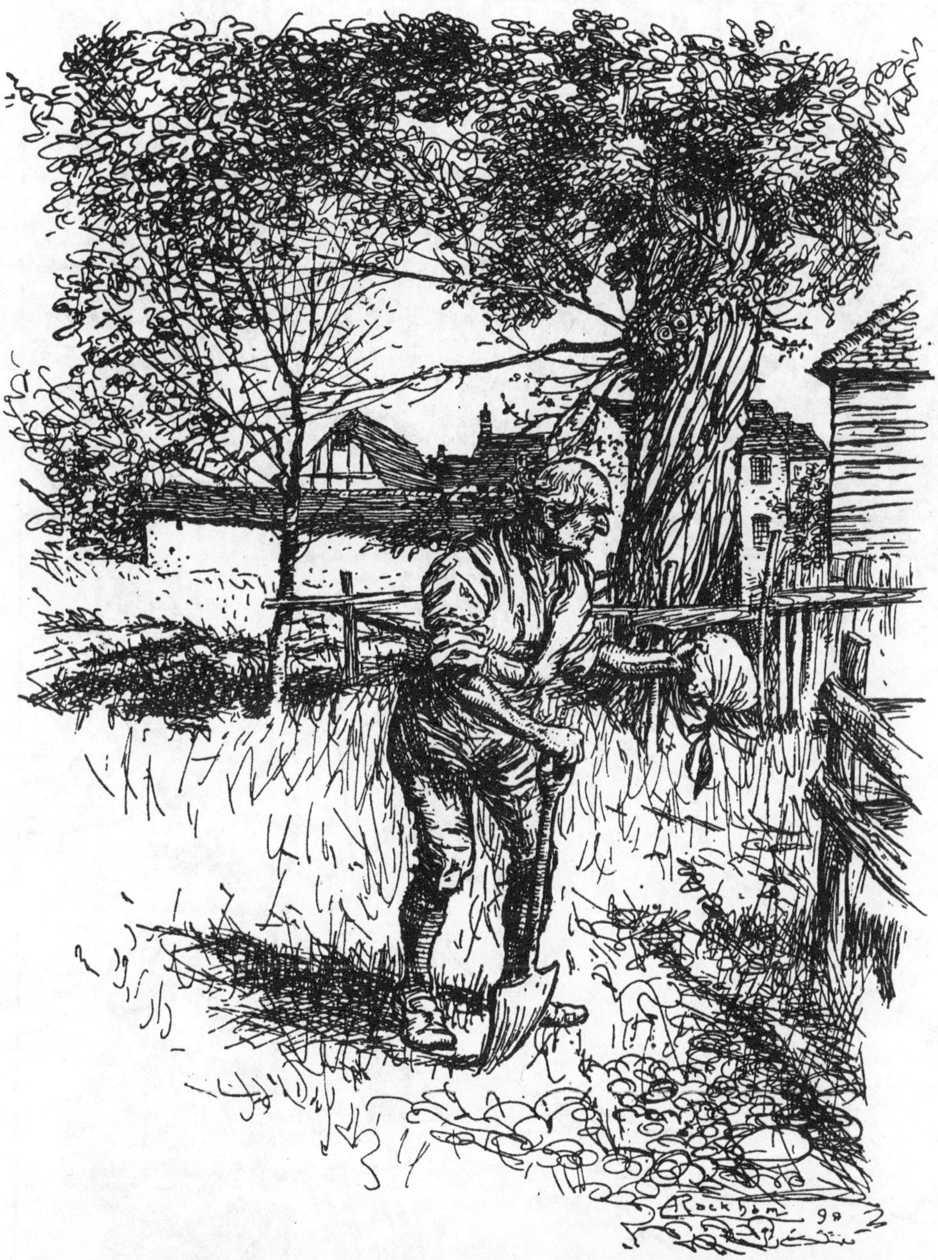

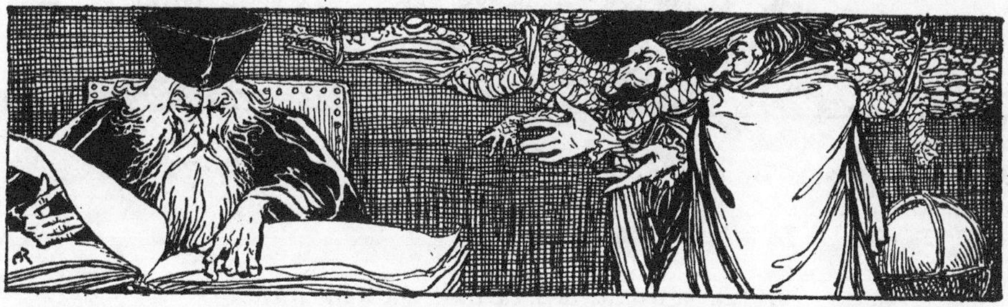

THE INGOLDSBY LEGENDS, 1898

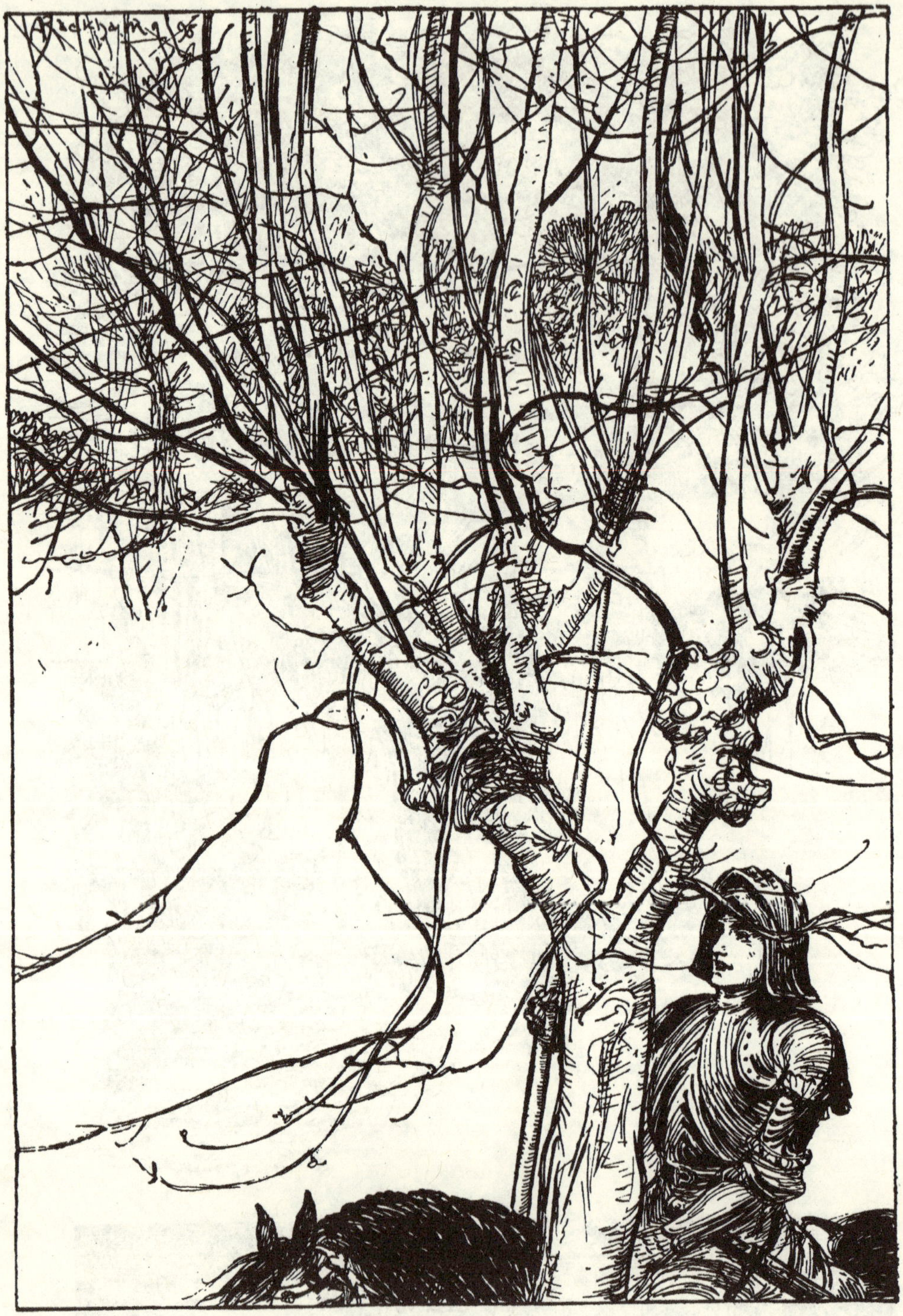

"As I lay a-thynkynge, he rode upon his waye."

The Ingoldsby Legends, 1898

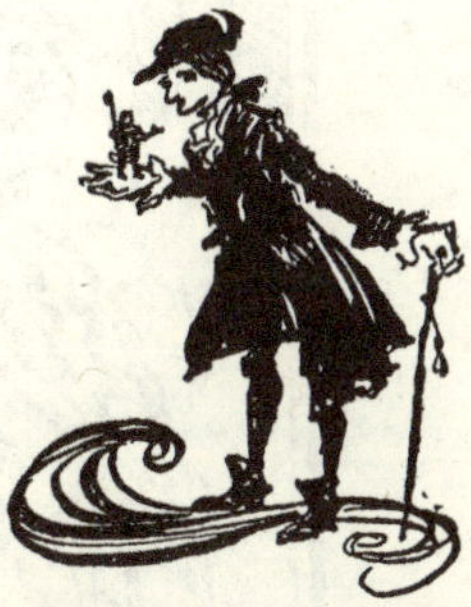

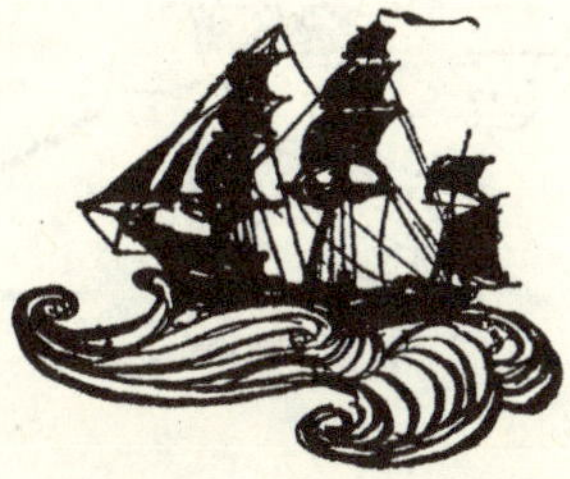

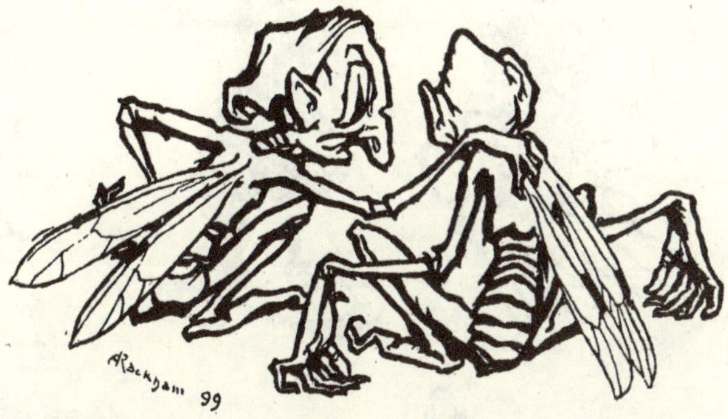

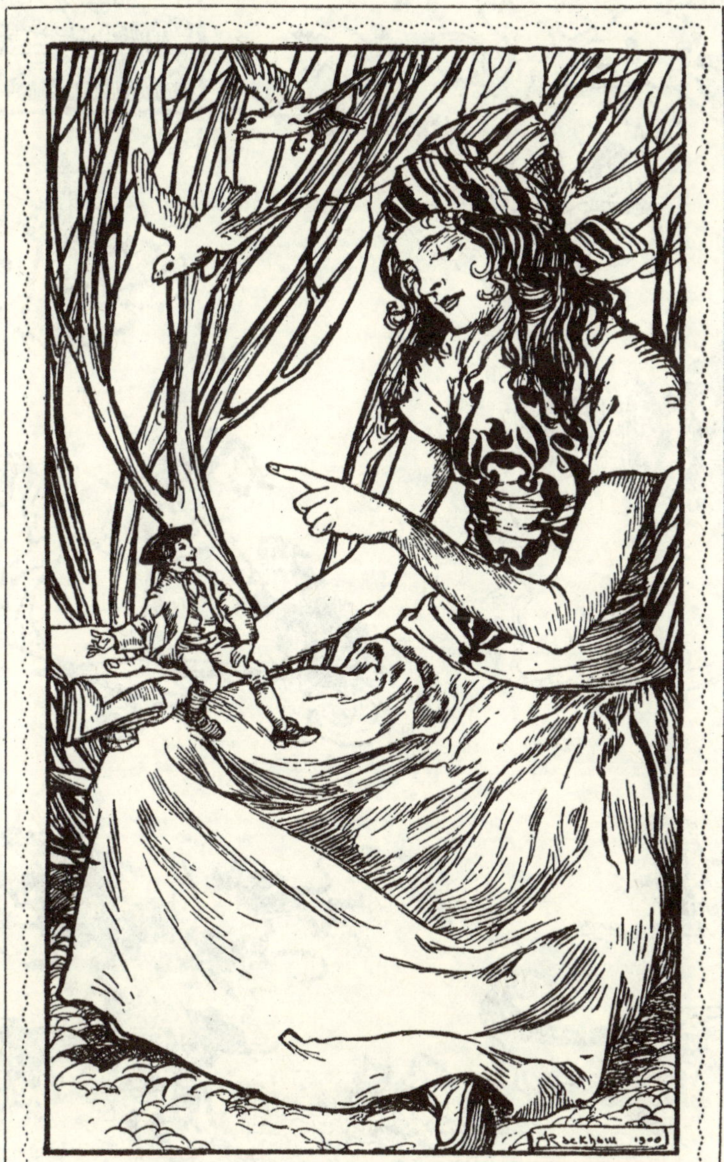

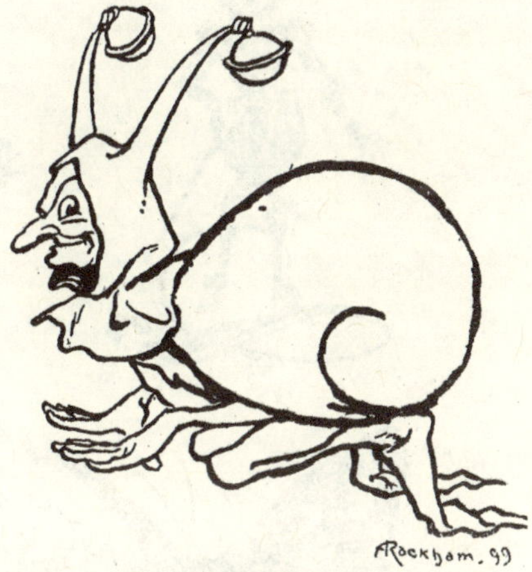

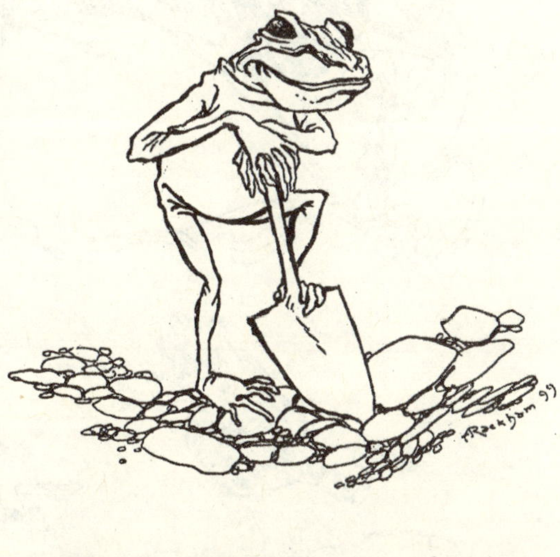

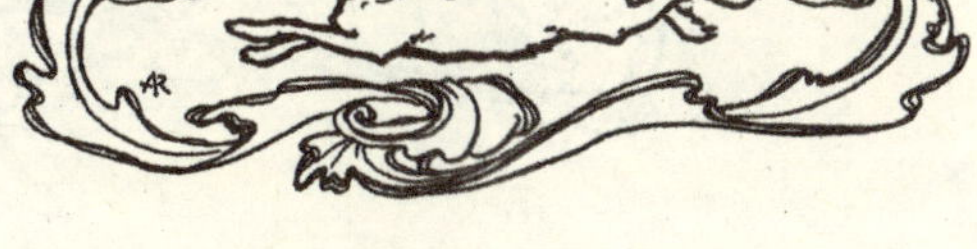

Gulliver's Travels into Several Remote Nations of the World, 1900

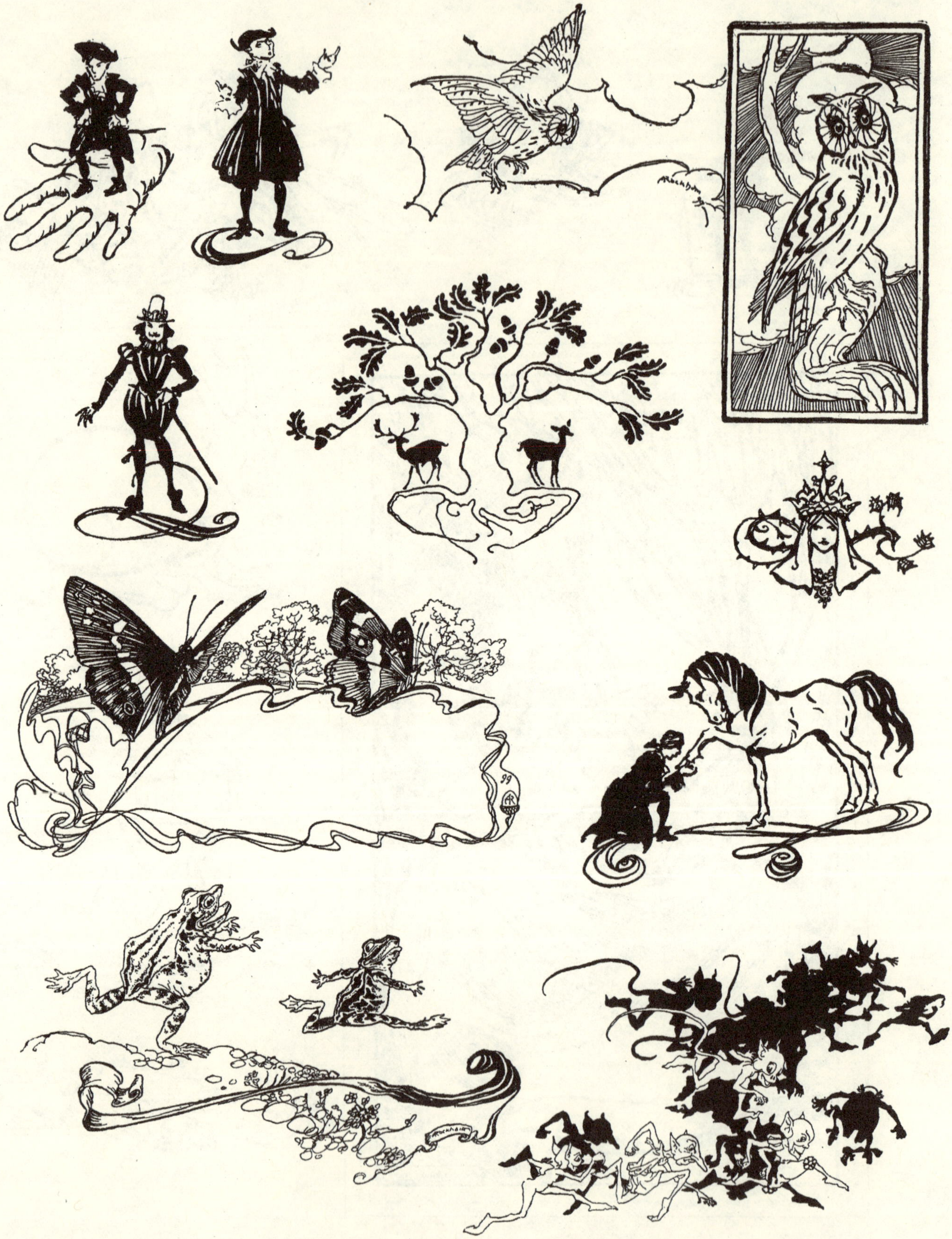

Gulliver's Travels into Several Remote Nations of the World, 1900

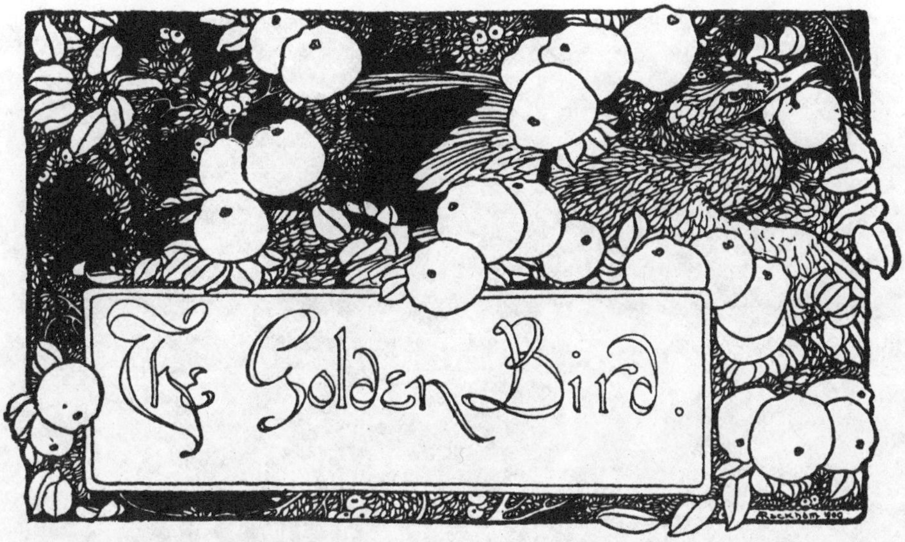

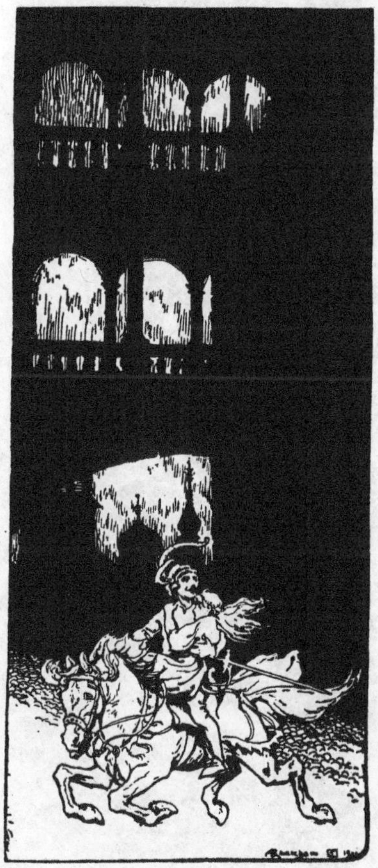

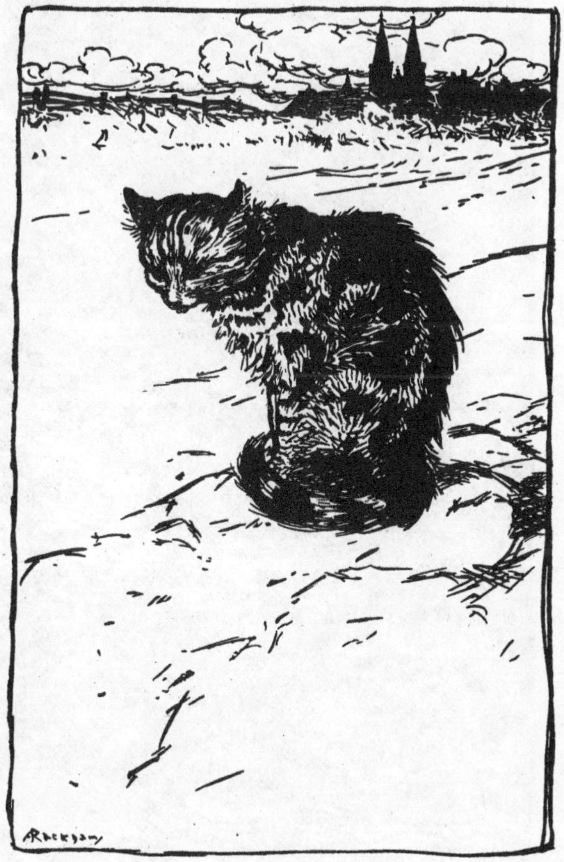

FAIRY TALES OF THE BROTHERS GRIMM, 1900

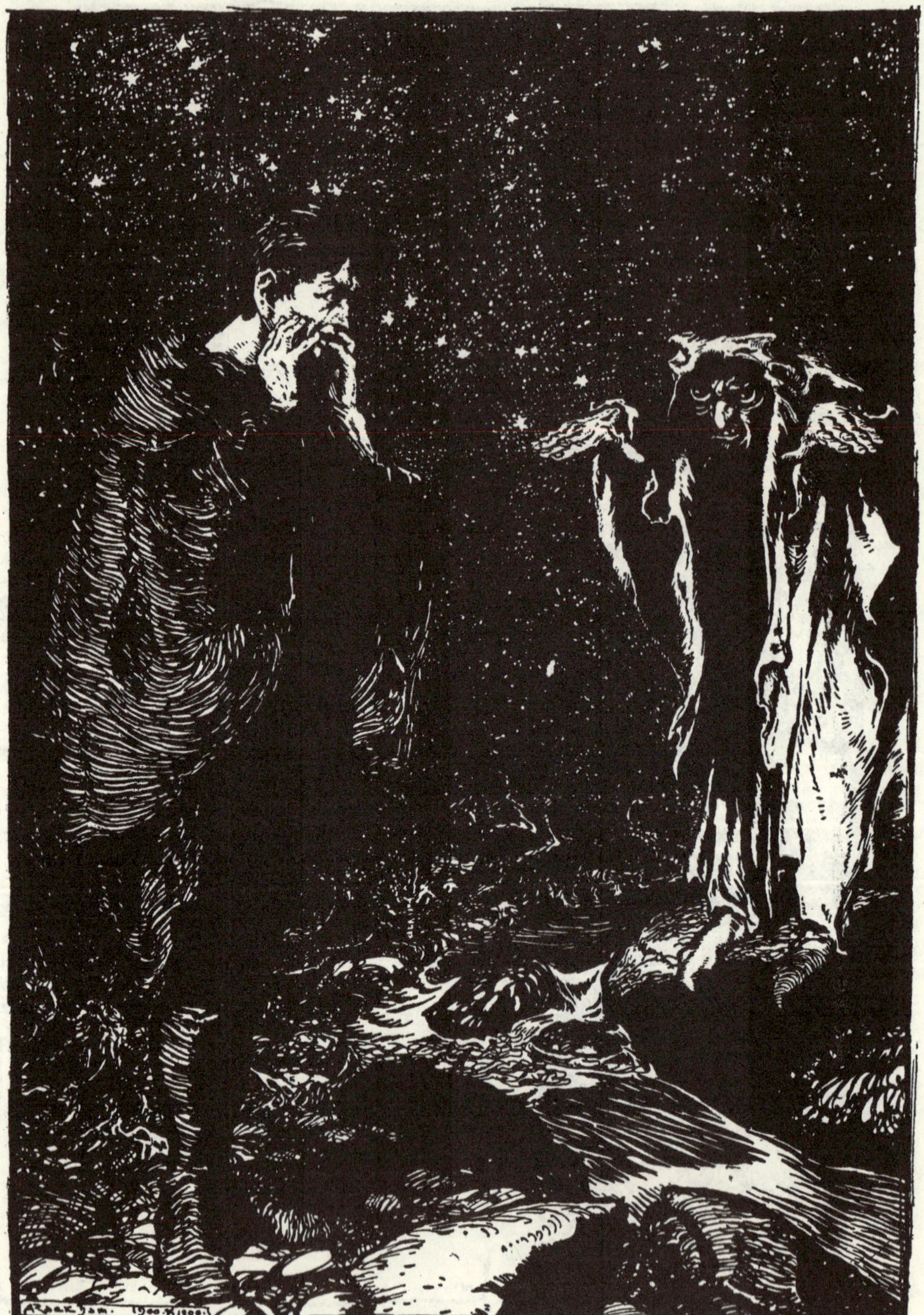

"At last the old woman came back, and said in a droning voice: 'Greeting to thee, Zachiel!'"

Fairy Tales of the Brothers Grimm, 1900

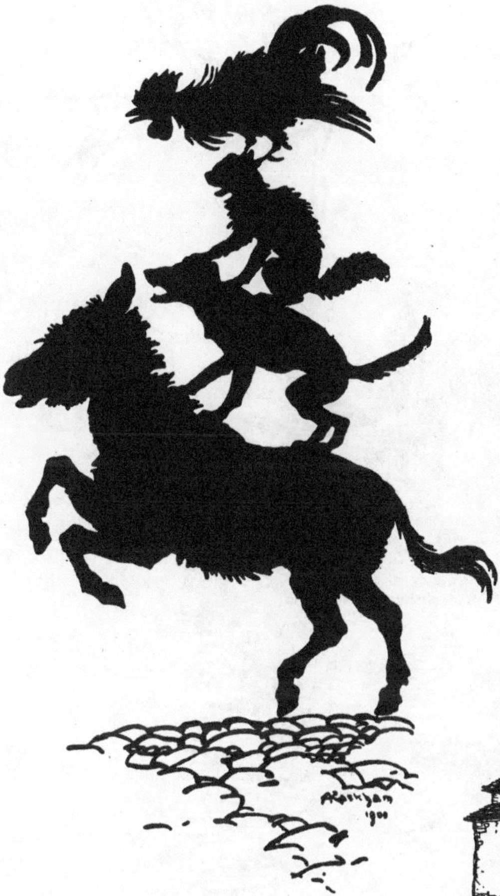

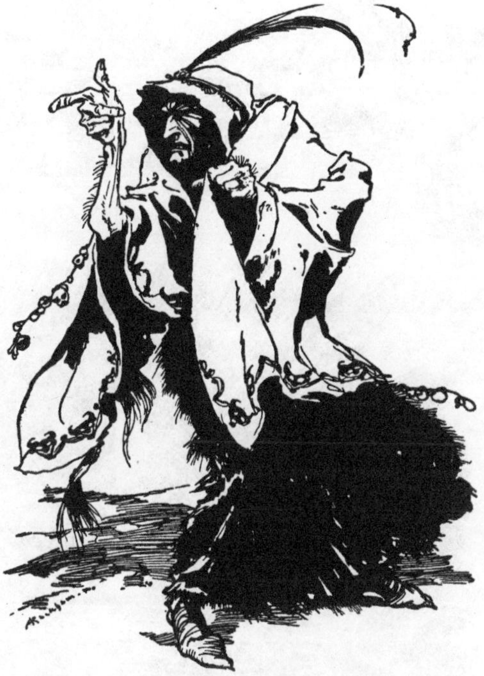

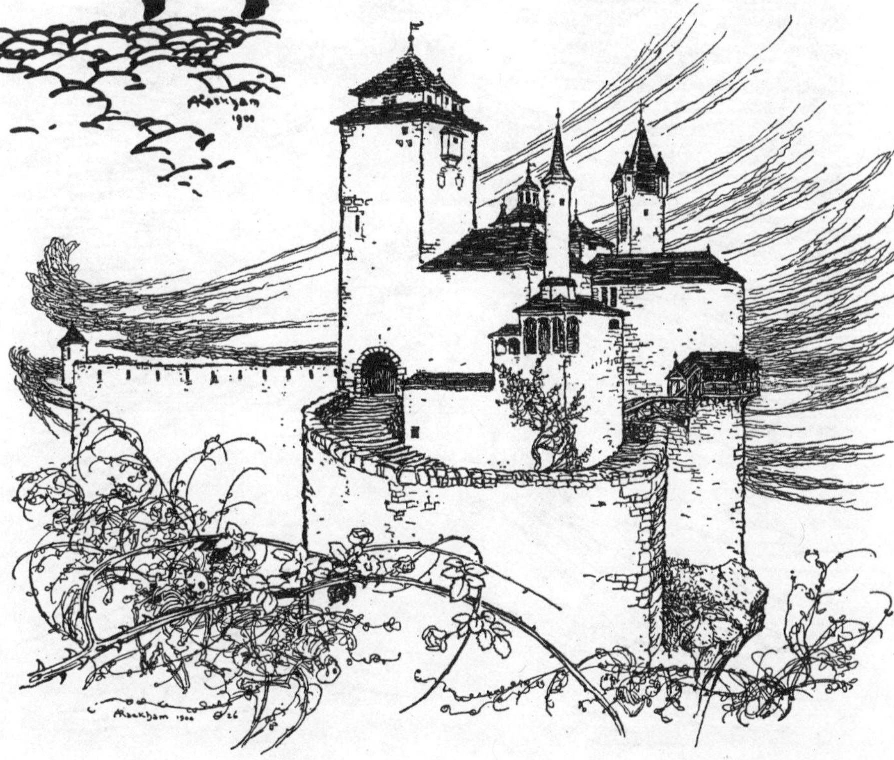

FAIRY TALES OF THE BROTHERS GRIMM, 1900

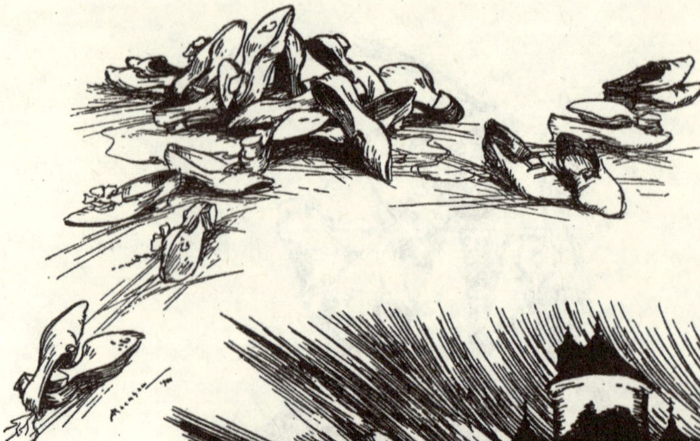

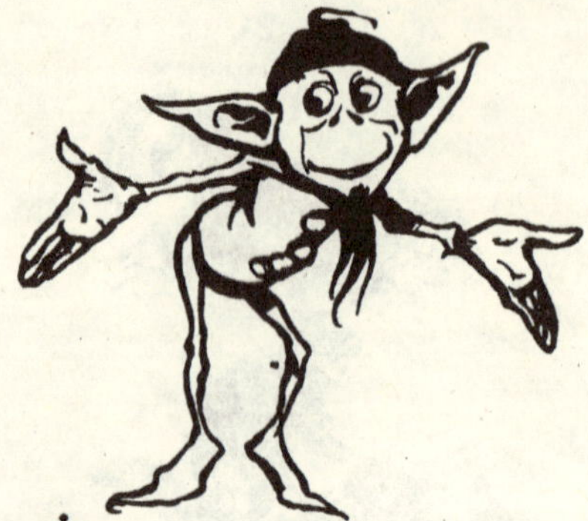

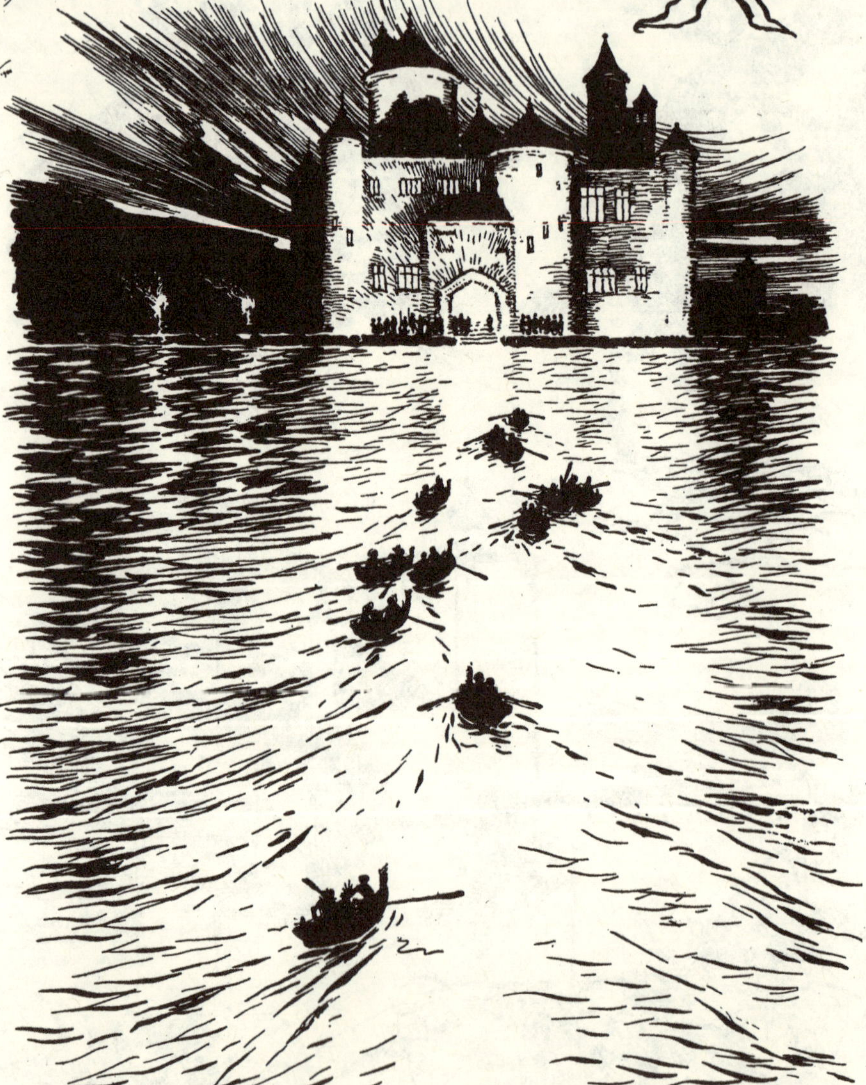

Fairy Tales of the Brothers Grimm, 1900

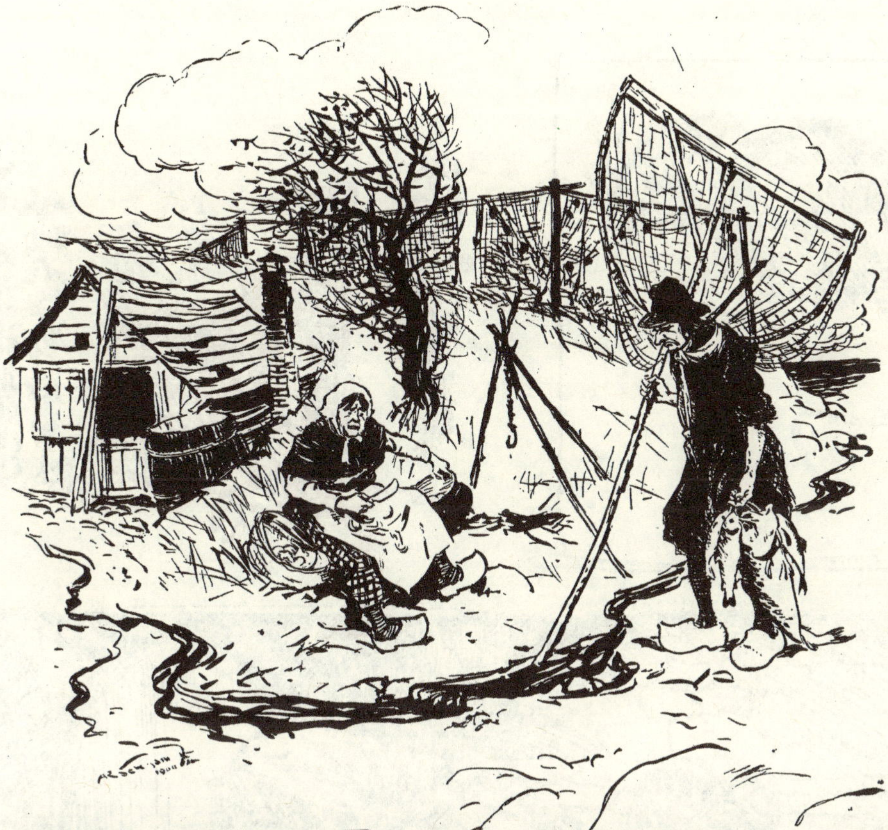

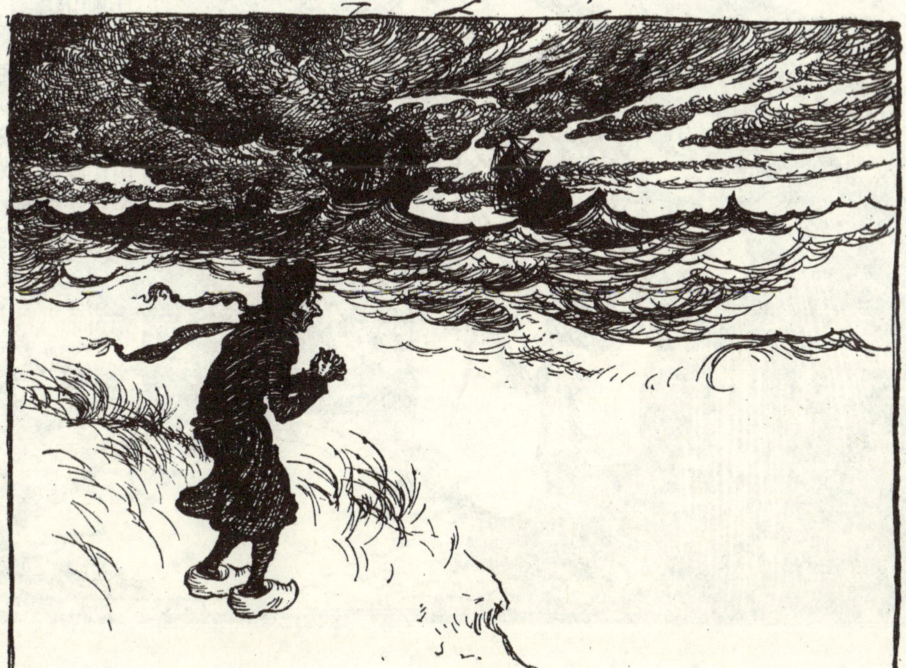

Fairy Tales of the Brothers Grimm, 1900

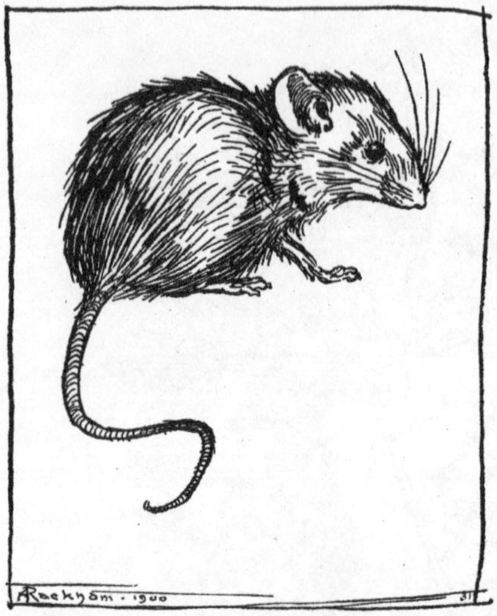

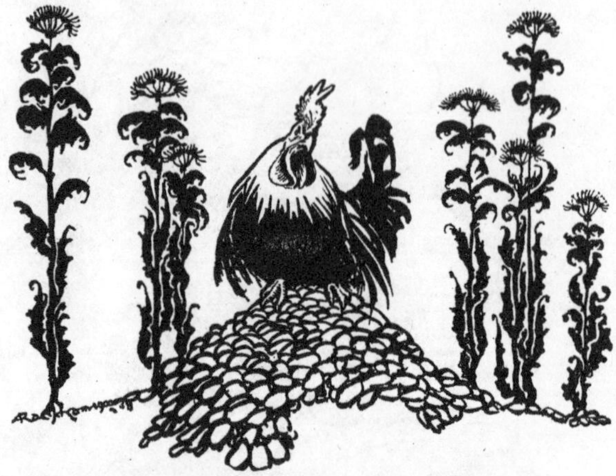

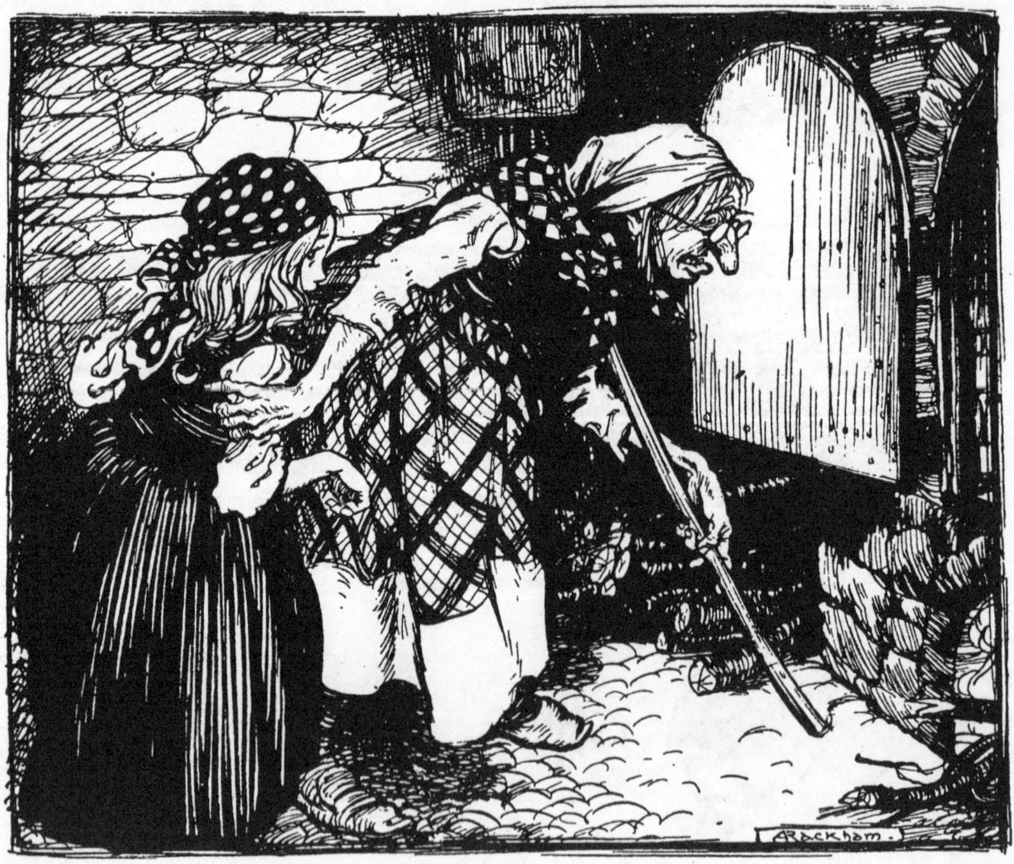

Fairy Tales of the Brothers Grimm, 1900

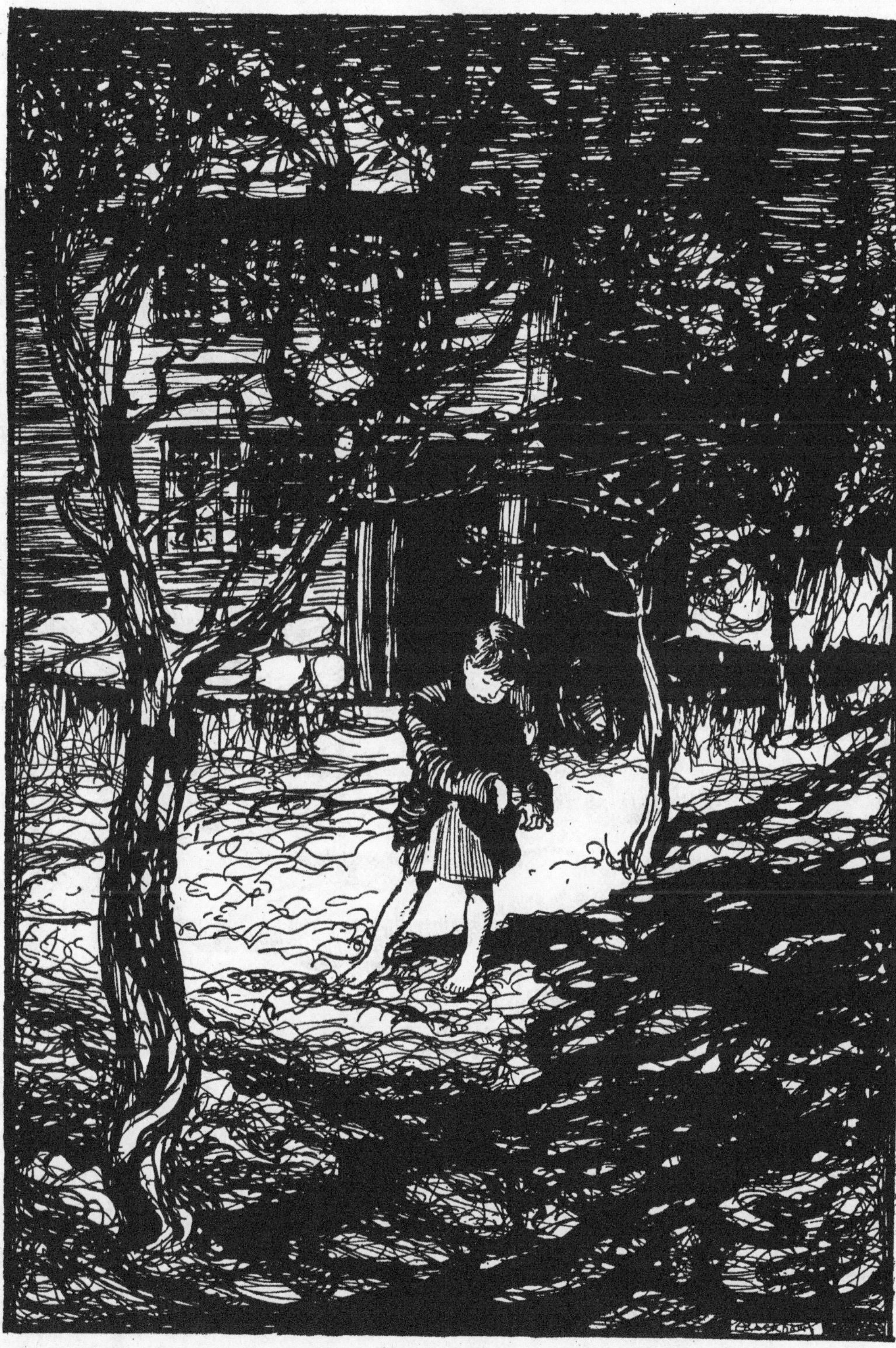

"Hansel picked up the glittering white pebbles and filled his pockets with them"

FAIRY TALES OF THE BROTHERS GRIMM, 1900

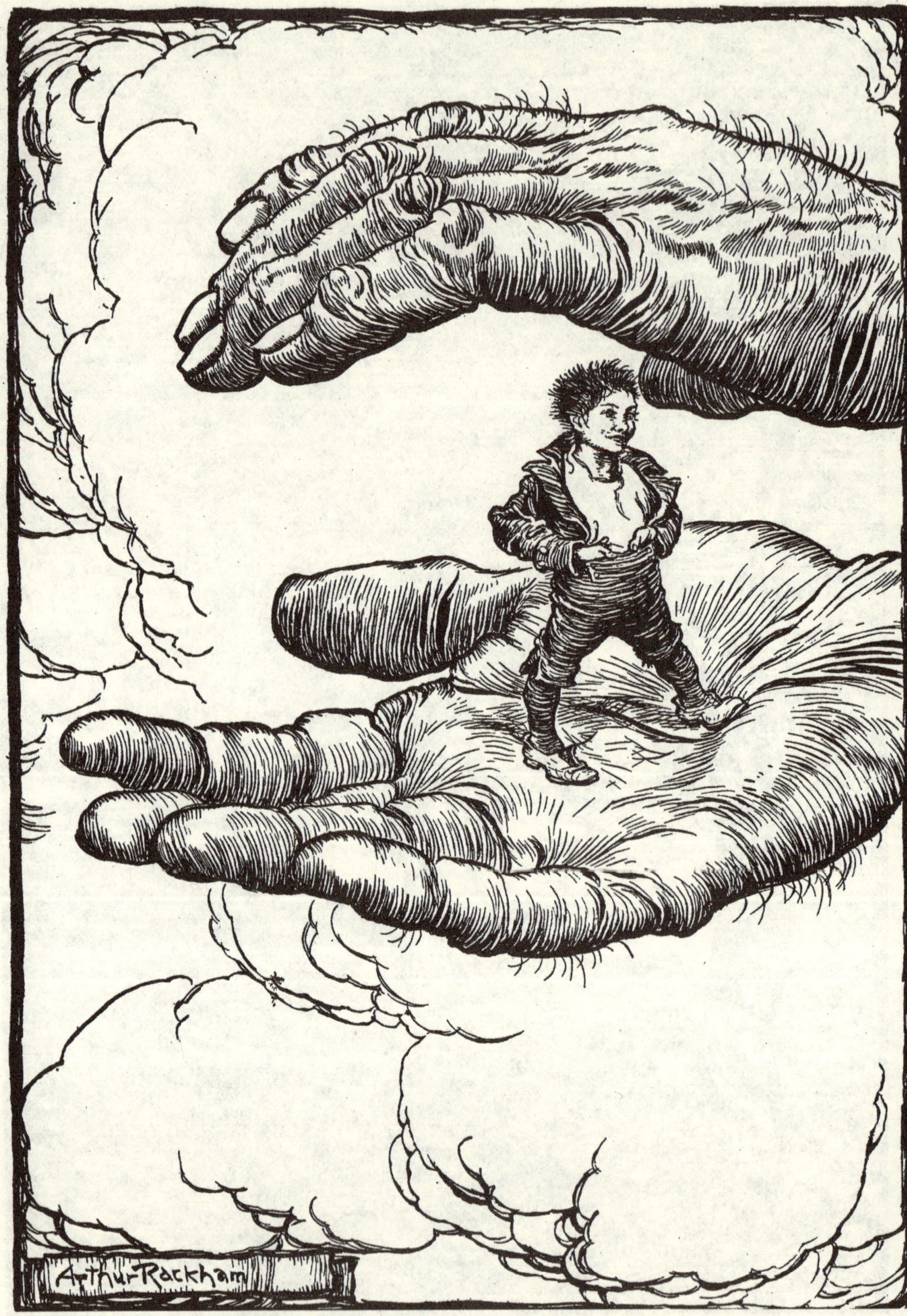

"Tom Thumb"

Fairy Tales of the Brothers Grimm, 1900

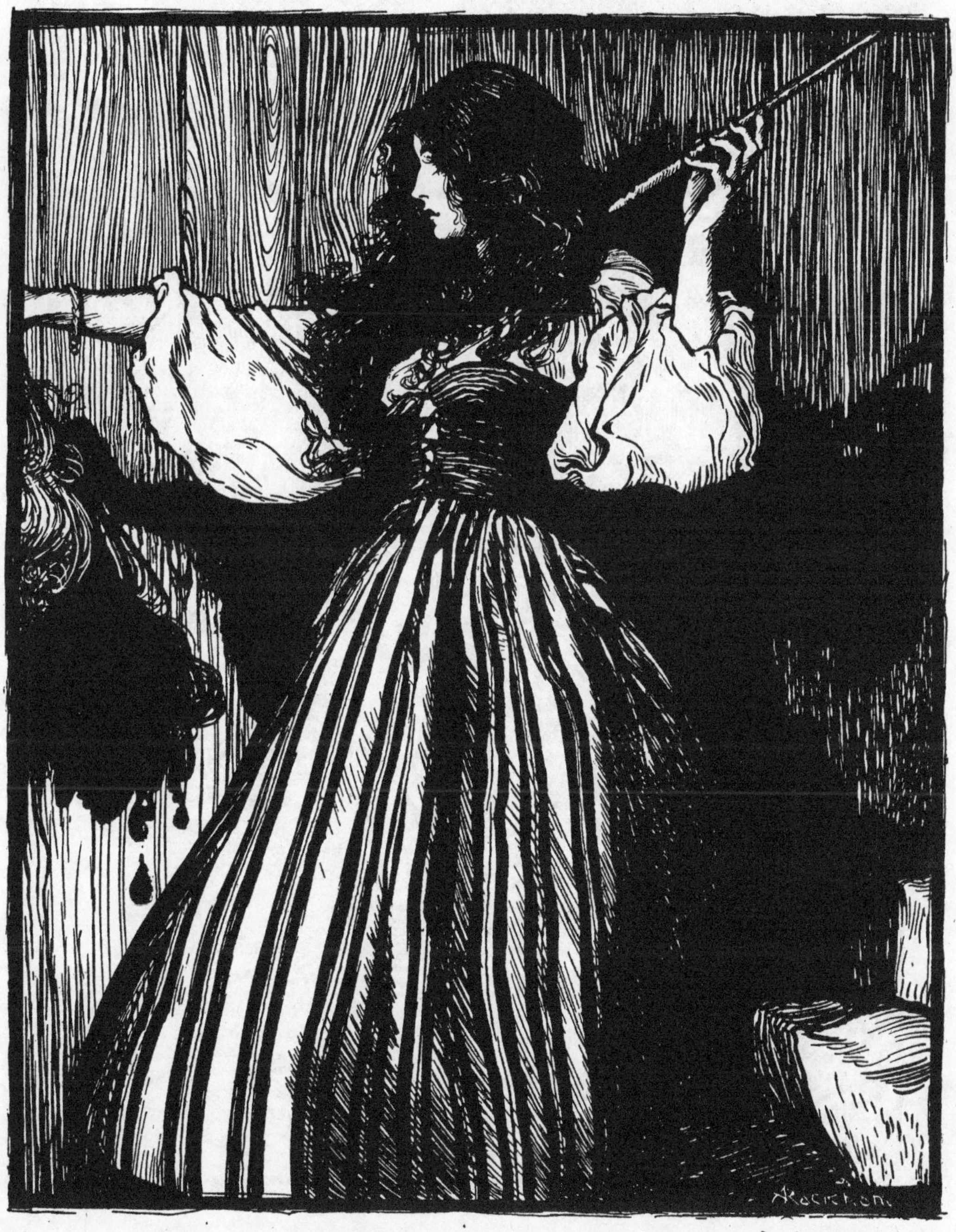

“The Maiden fetched the magic wand, and then she took her step-sister’s head, and dropped three drops of blood from it”

FAIRY TALES OF THE BROTHERS GRIMM, 1900

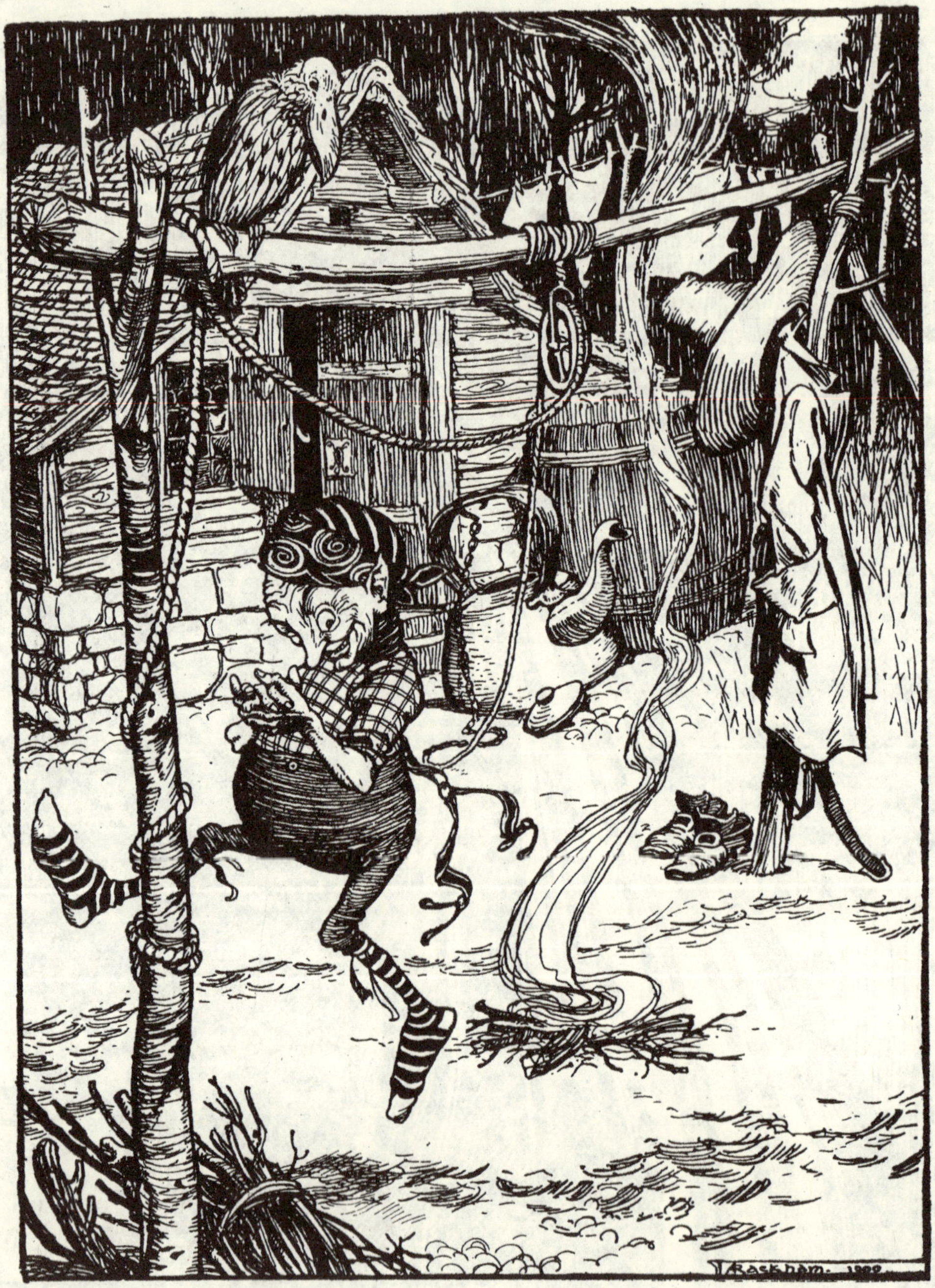

"Round the fire an indescribably ridiculous little man was leaping, hopping on one leg, and singing"

FAIRY TALES OF THE BROTHERS GRIMM, 1900

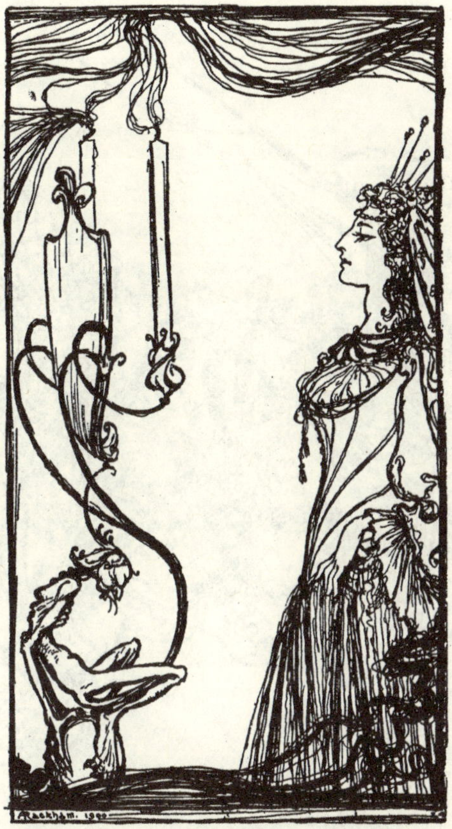

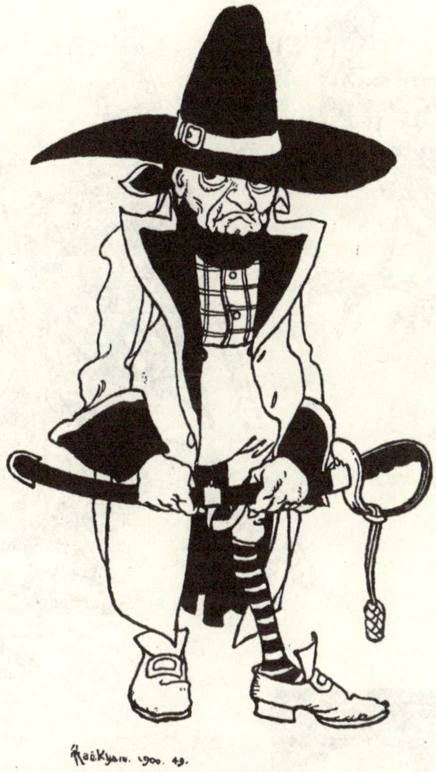

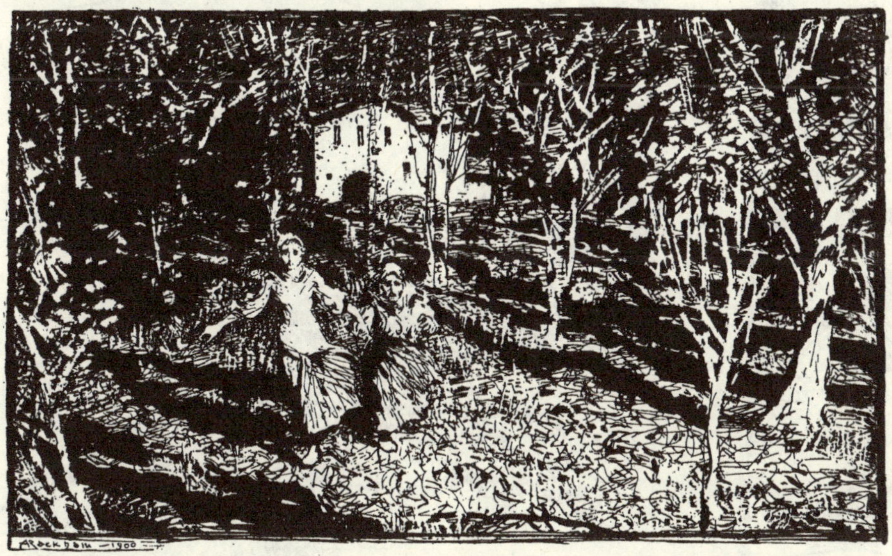

FAIRY TALES OF THE BROTHERS GRIMM, 1900

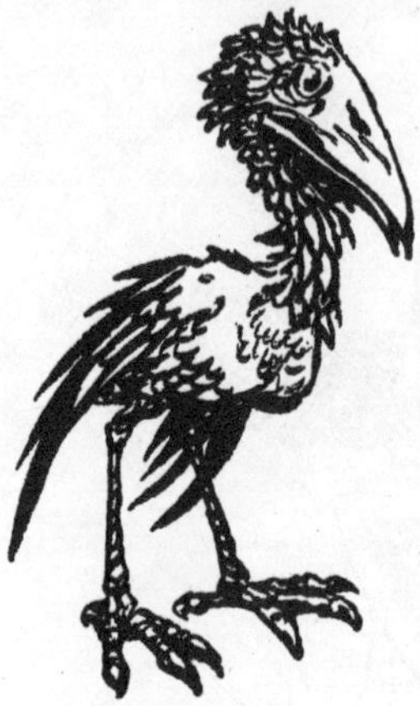

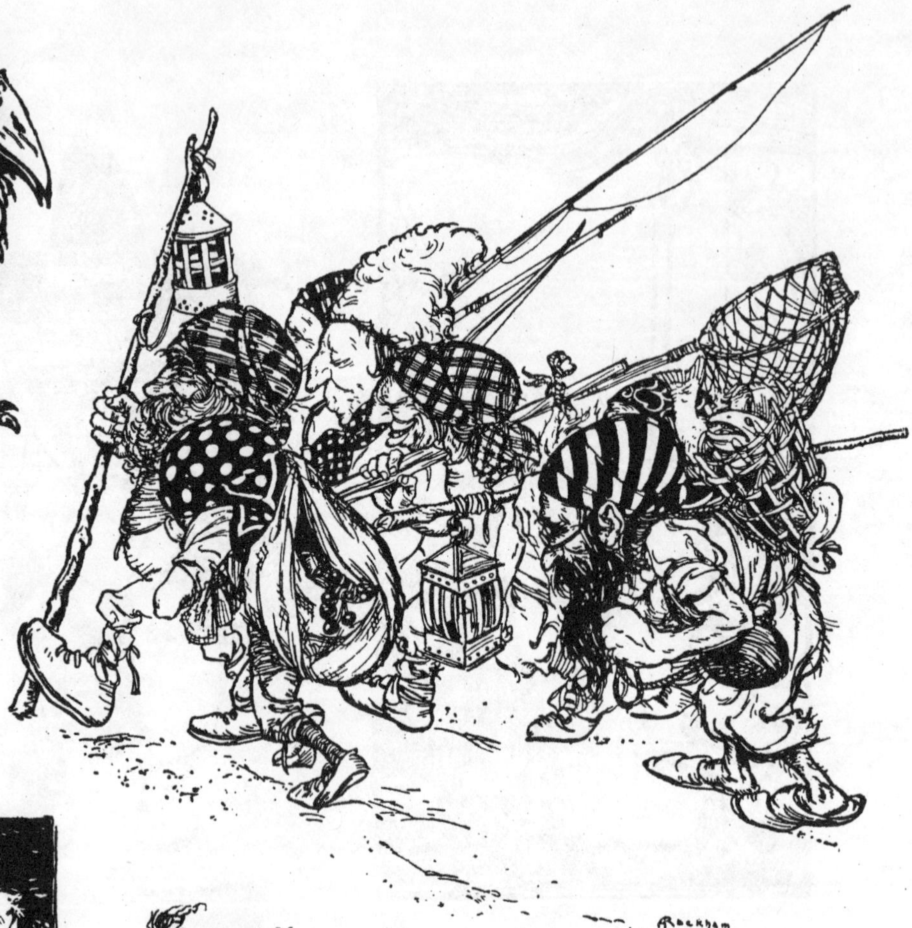

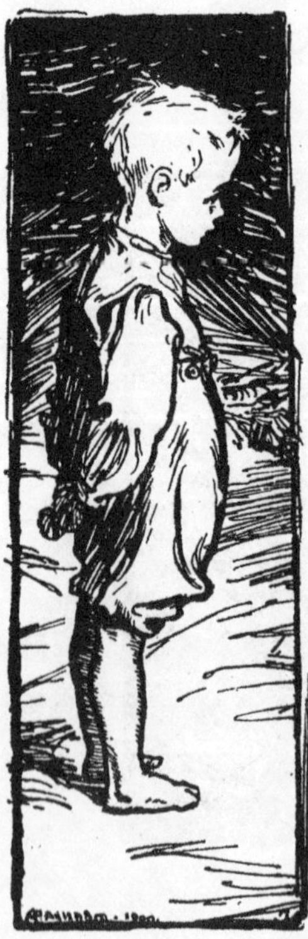

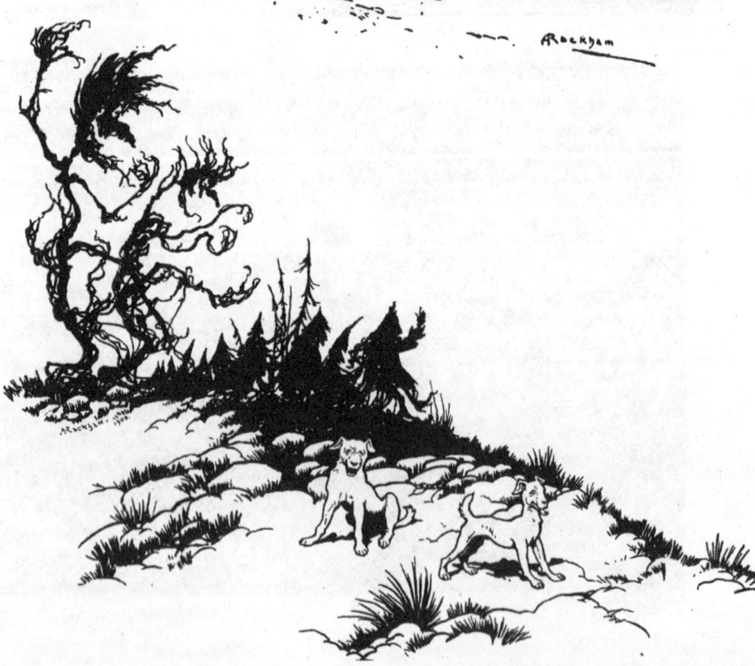

Fairy Tales of the Brothers Grimm, 1900

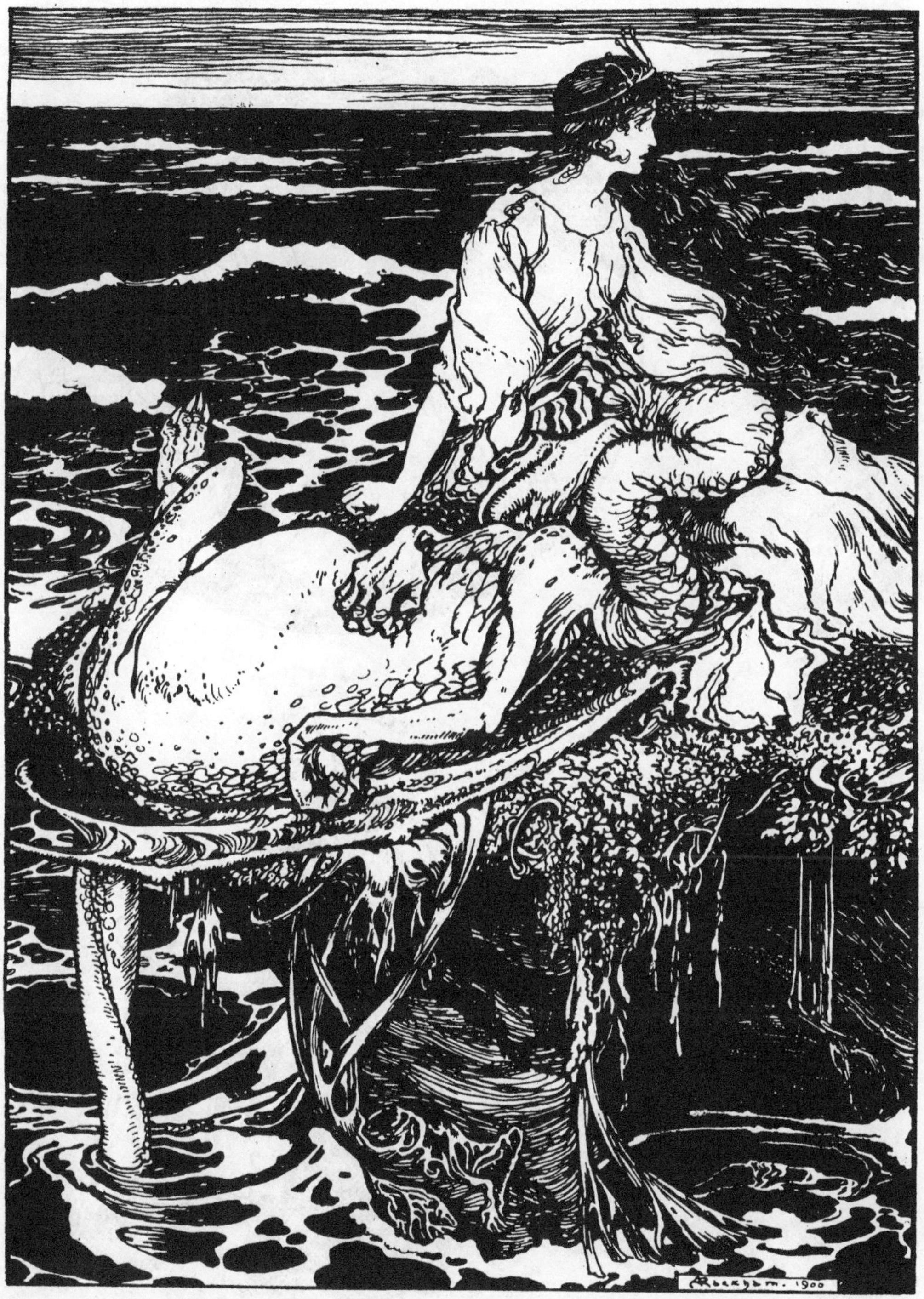

"They found the princess still on the rock, but the dragon was asleep with his head on her lap"

Fairy Tales of the Brothers Grimm, 1900

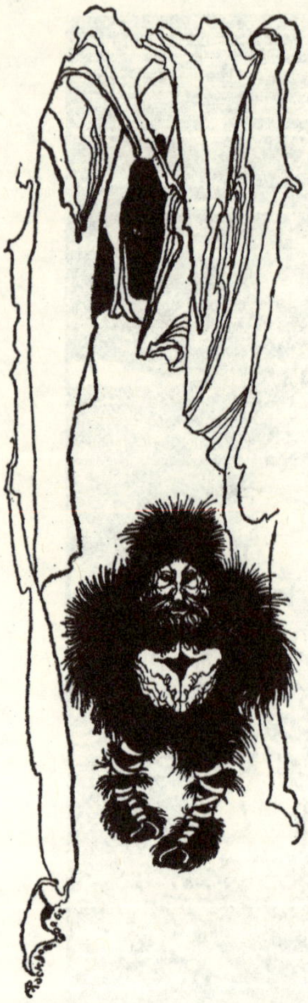

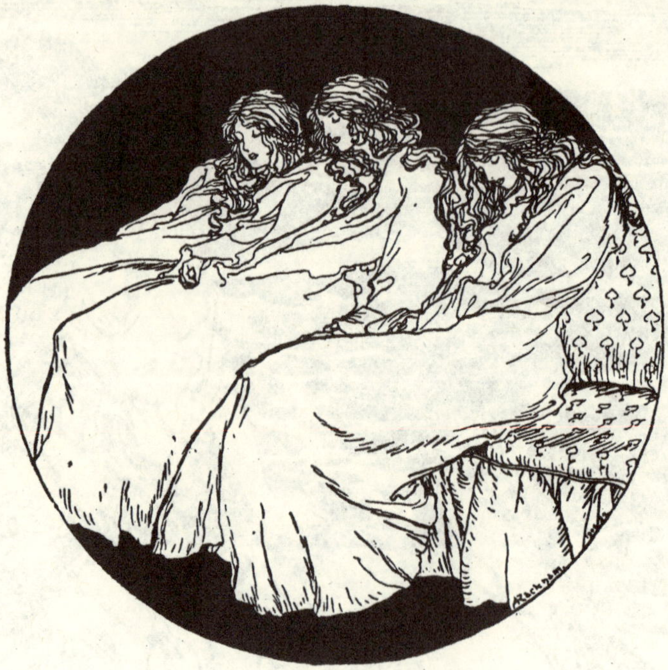

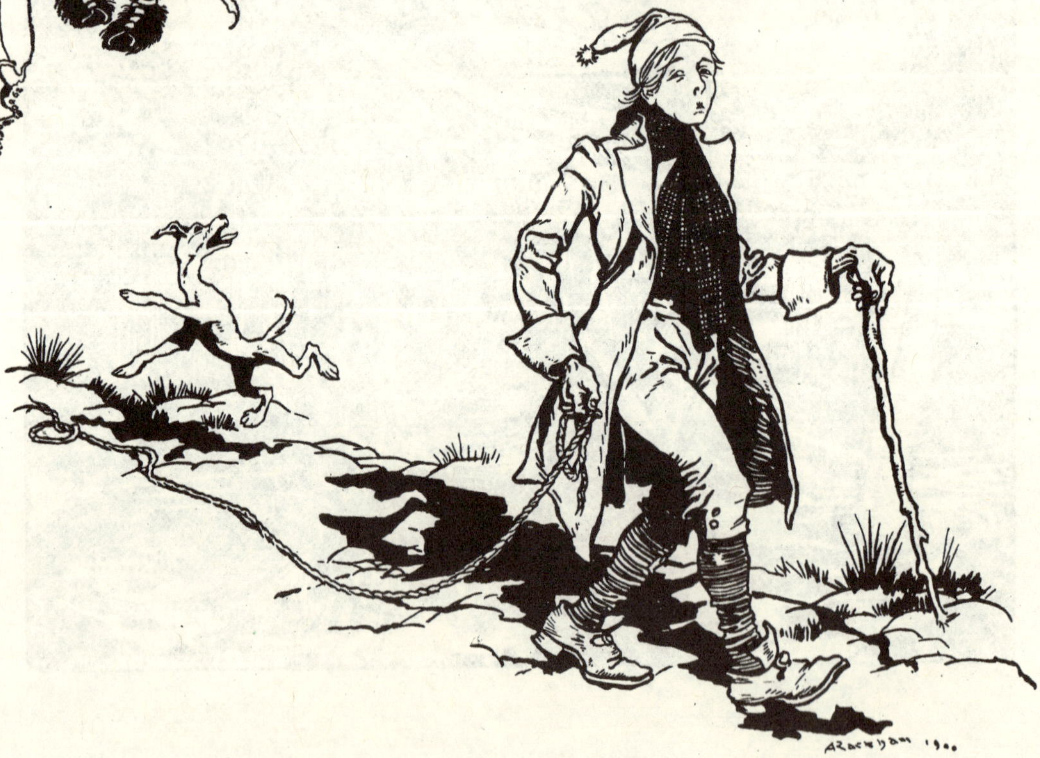

Fairy Tales of the Brothers Grimm, 1900

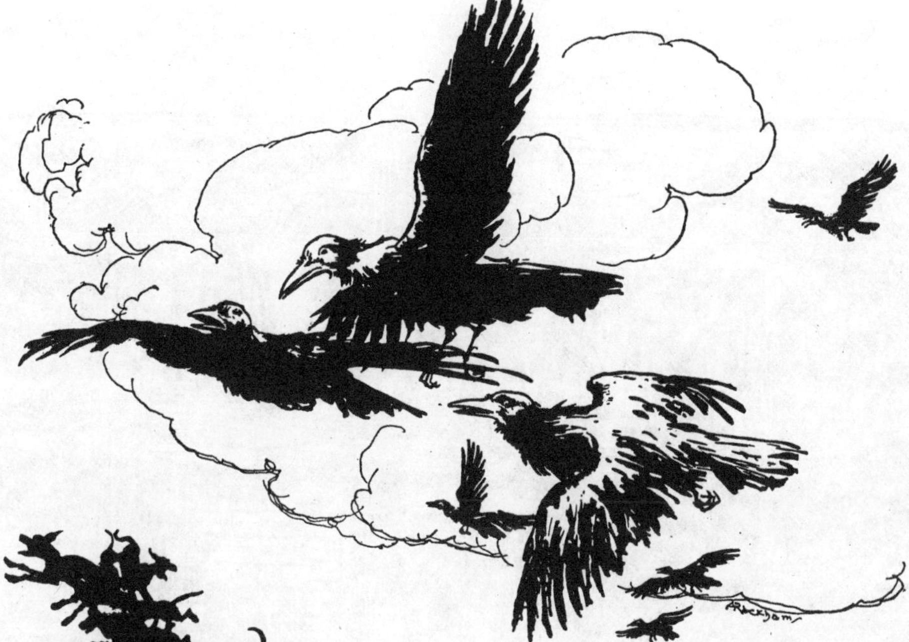

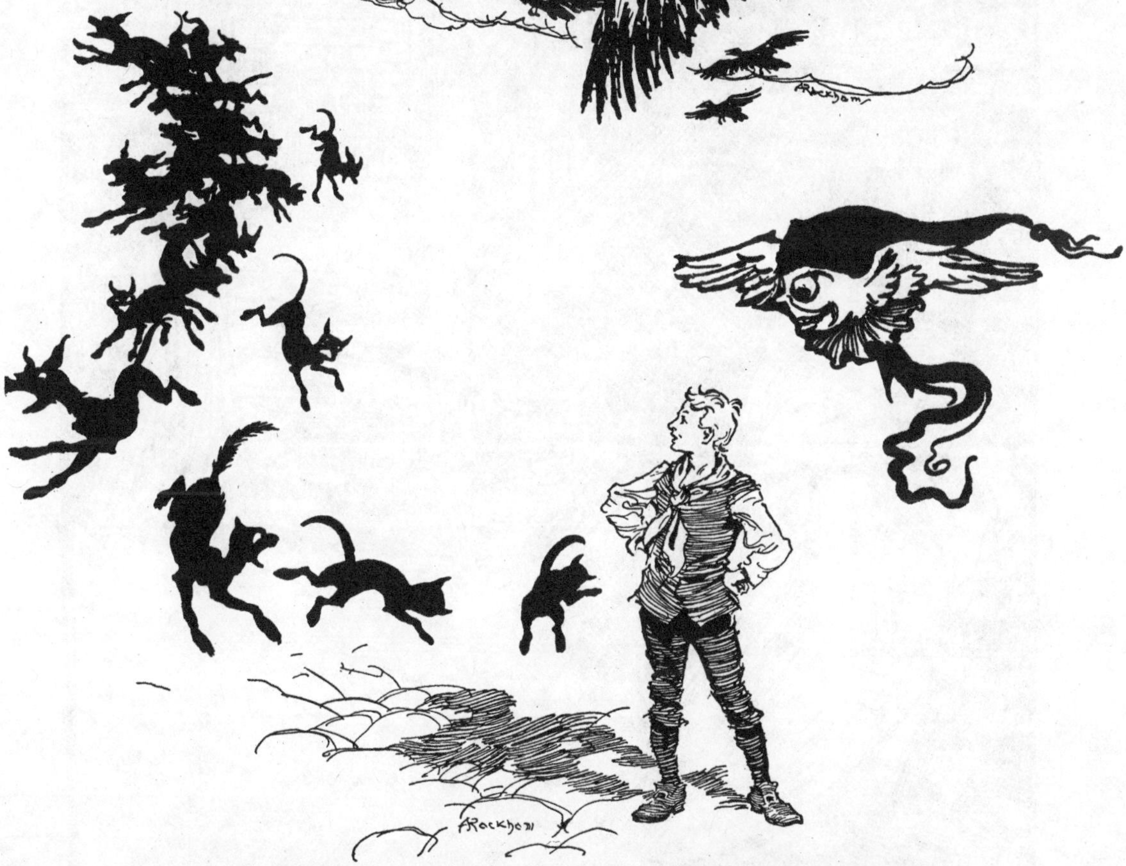

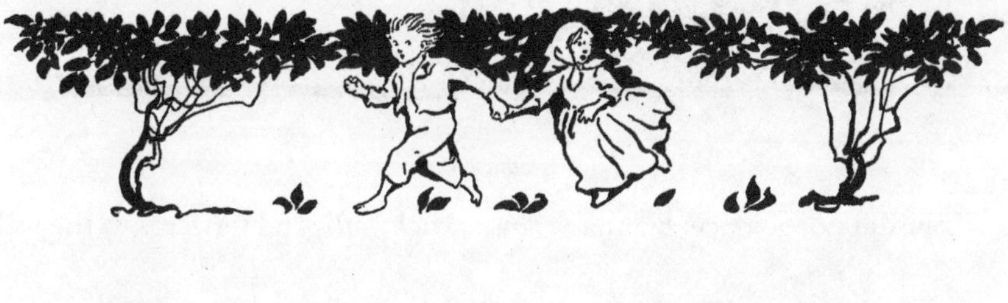

Fairy Tales of the Brothers Grimm, 1900

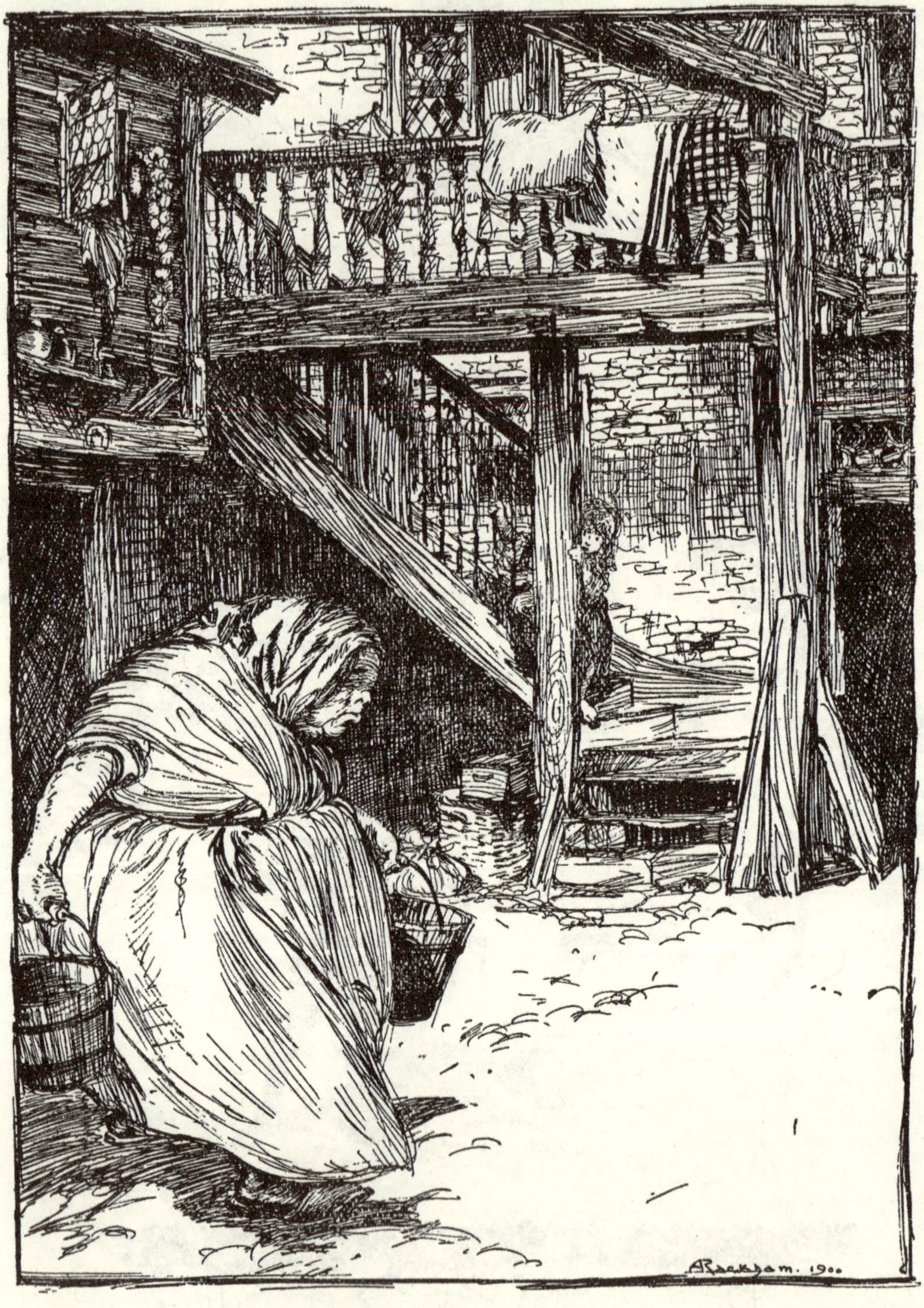

"She did not go once, but many times, backwards and forwards to the well."

Fairy Tales of the Brothers Grimm, 1900

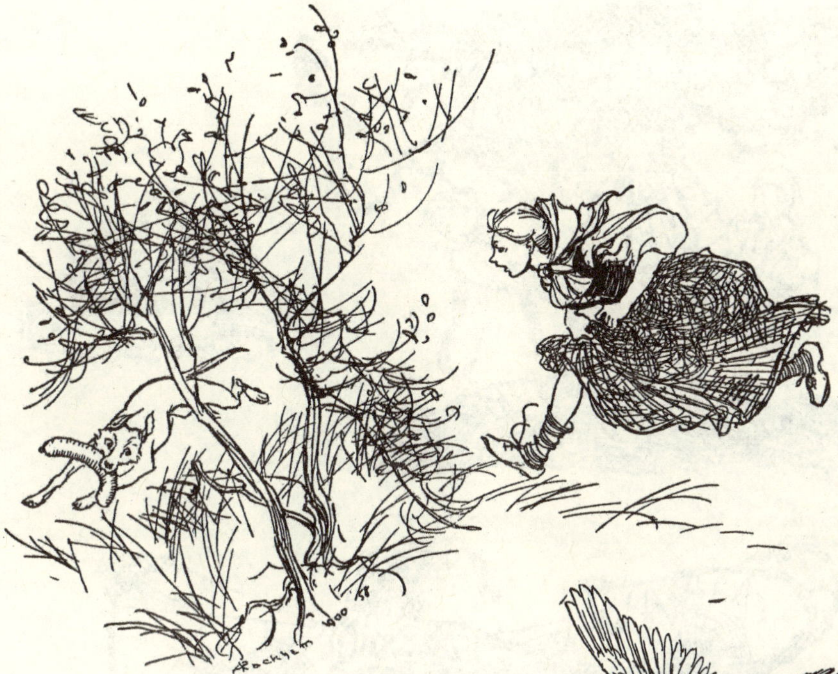

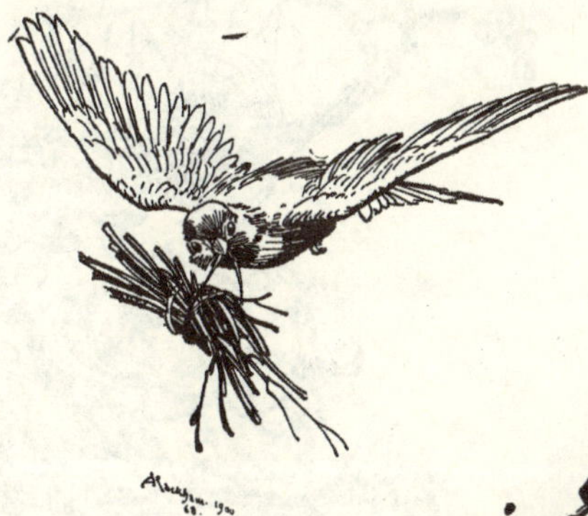

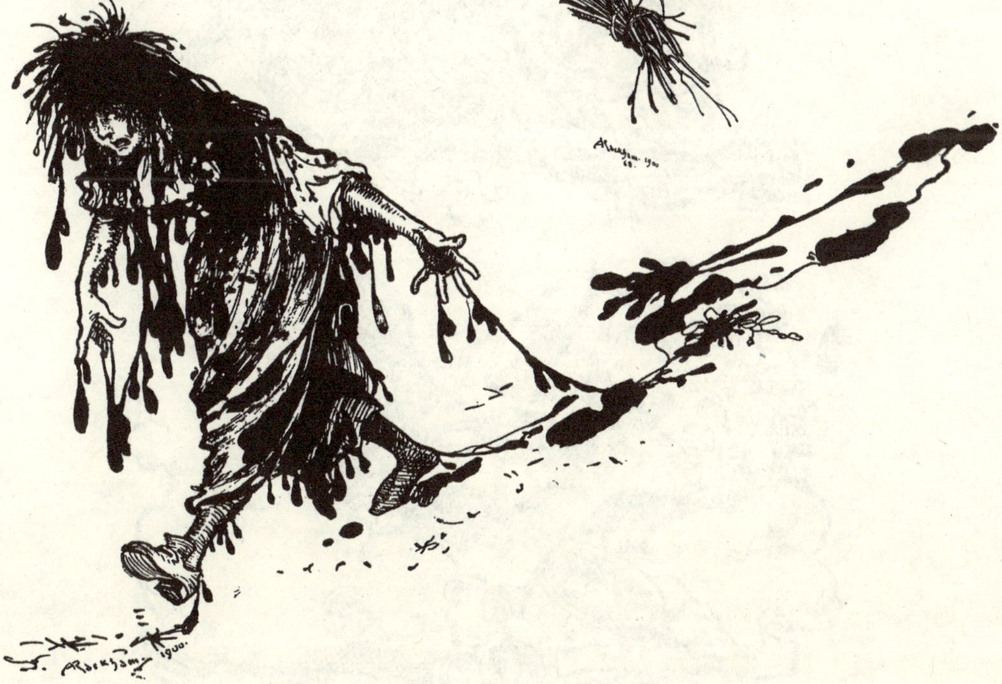

Fairy Tales of the Brothers Grimm, 1900

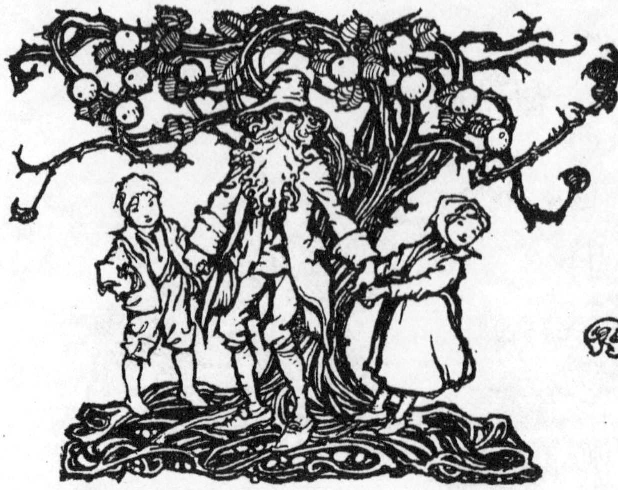

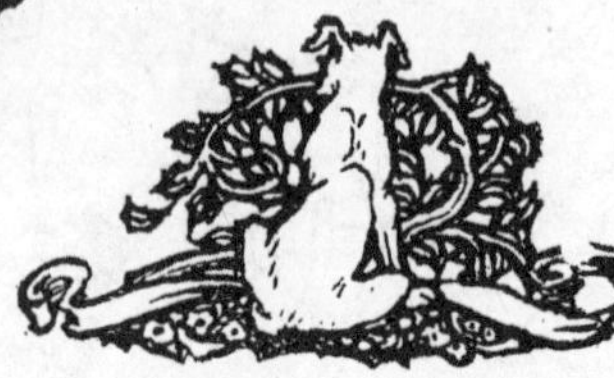

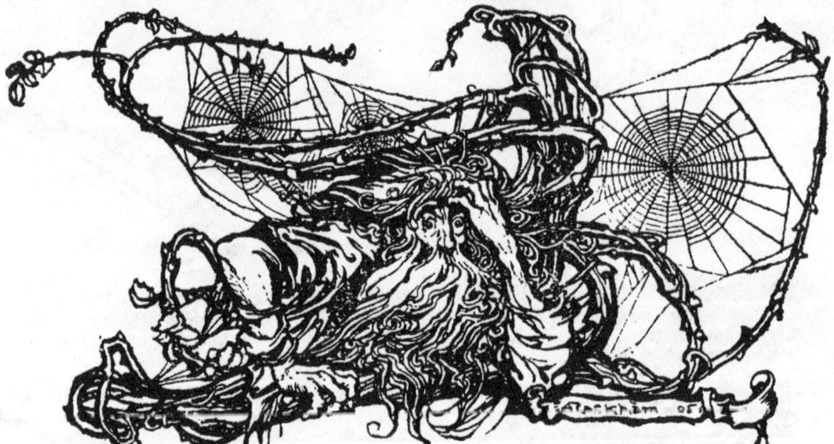

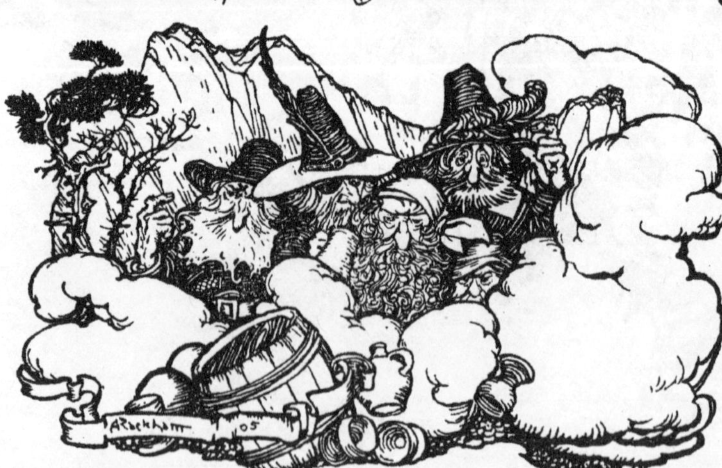

Rip Van Winkle, 1905

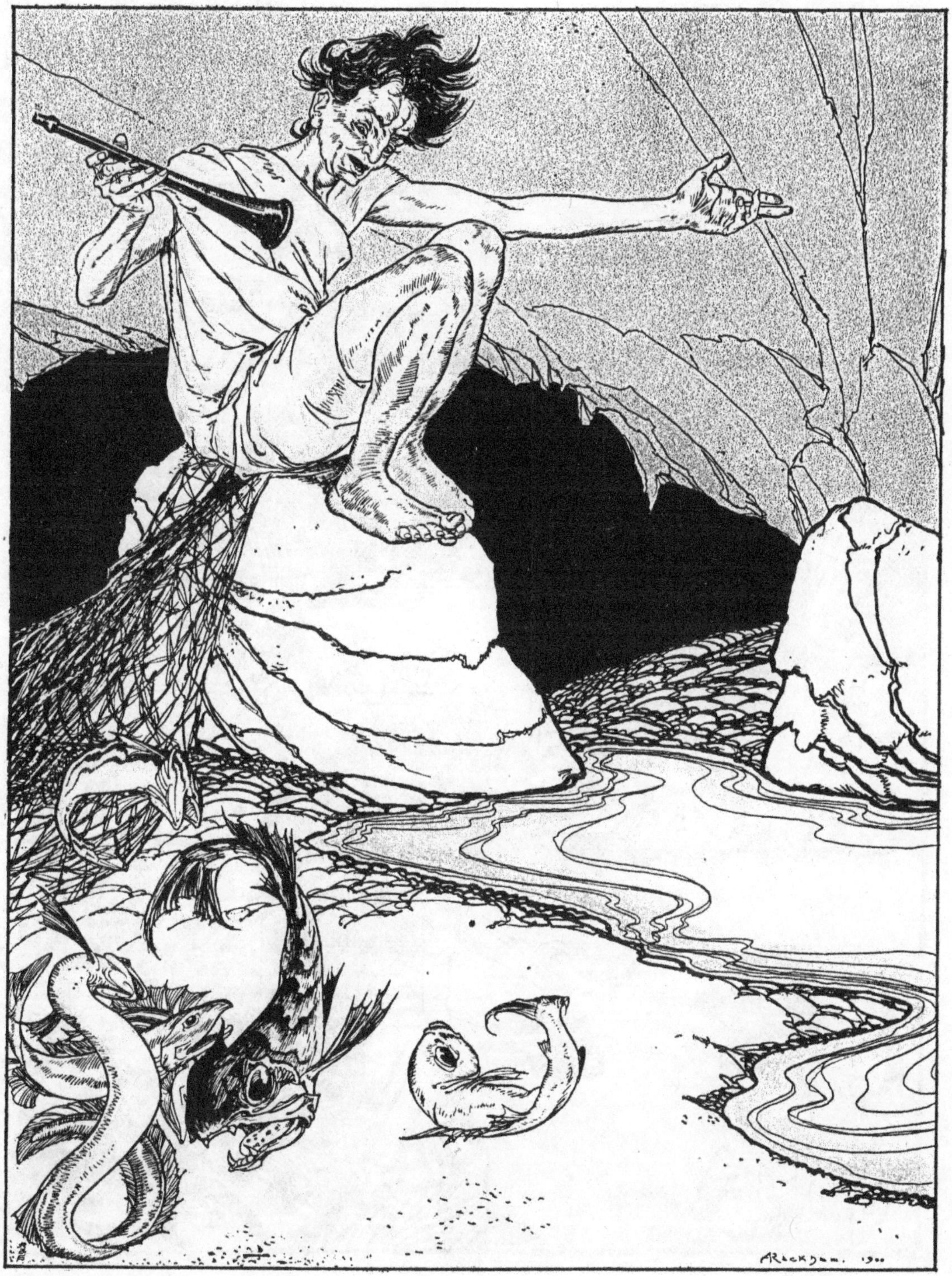

"I want none of your leaping and dancing now"

The Land of Enchantment, 1907

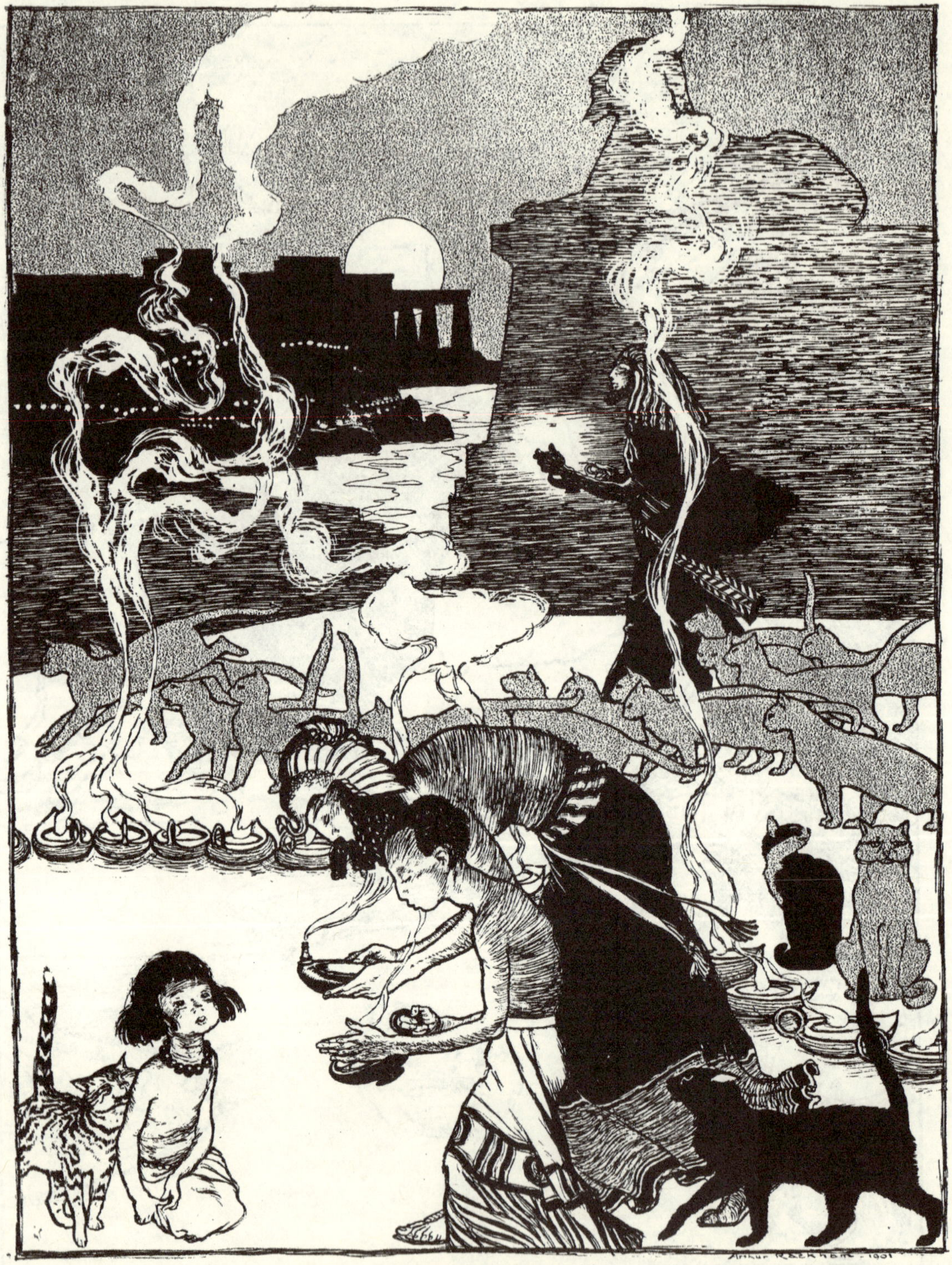

"All through Egypt every man burns a lamp"

THE LAND OF ENCHANTMENT, 1907

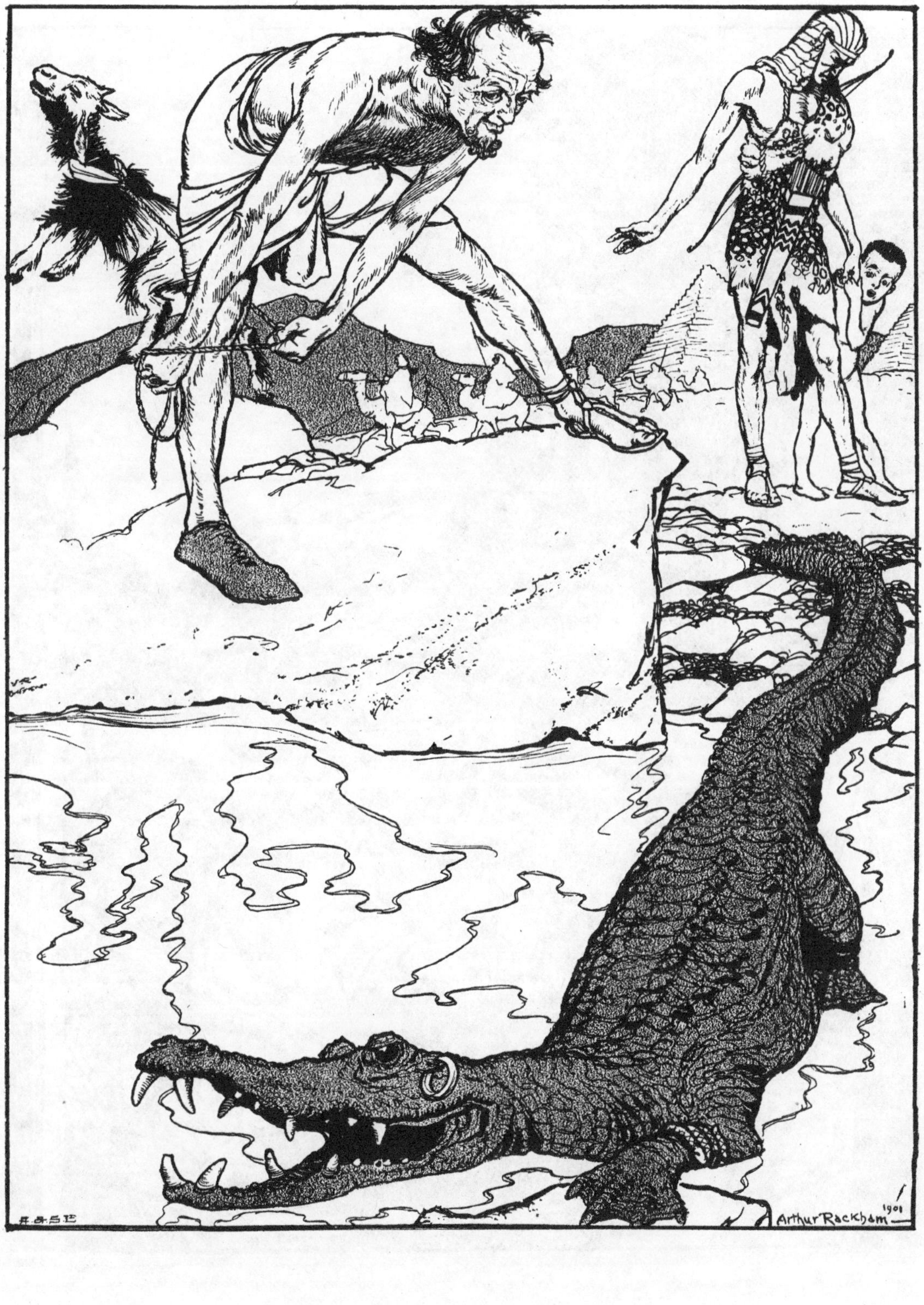

"Special food was prepared for him"

The Land of Enchantment, 1907

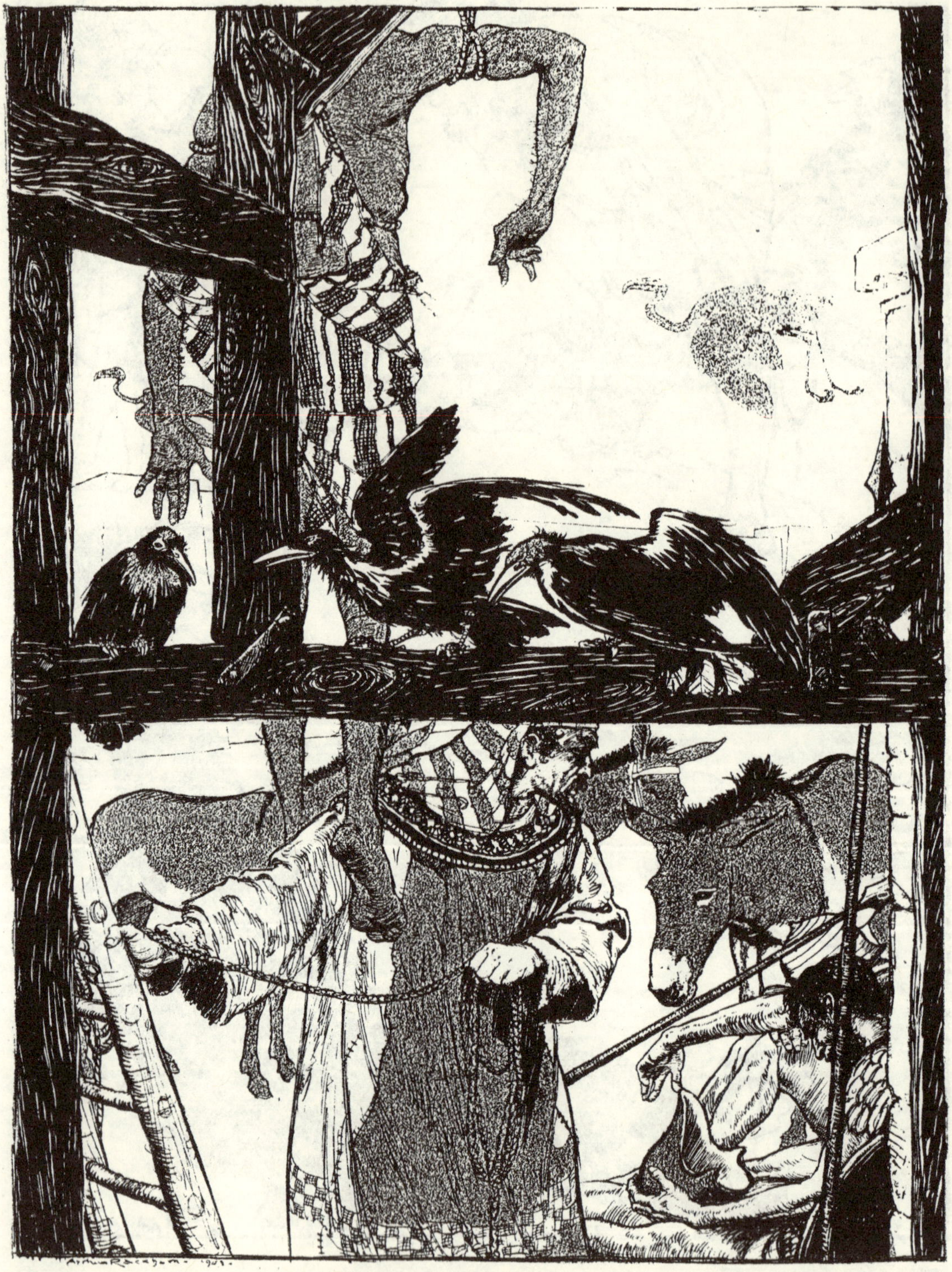

"Then was the thief's opportunity"

The Land of Enchantment, 1907

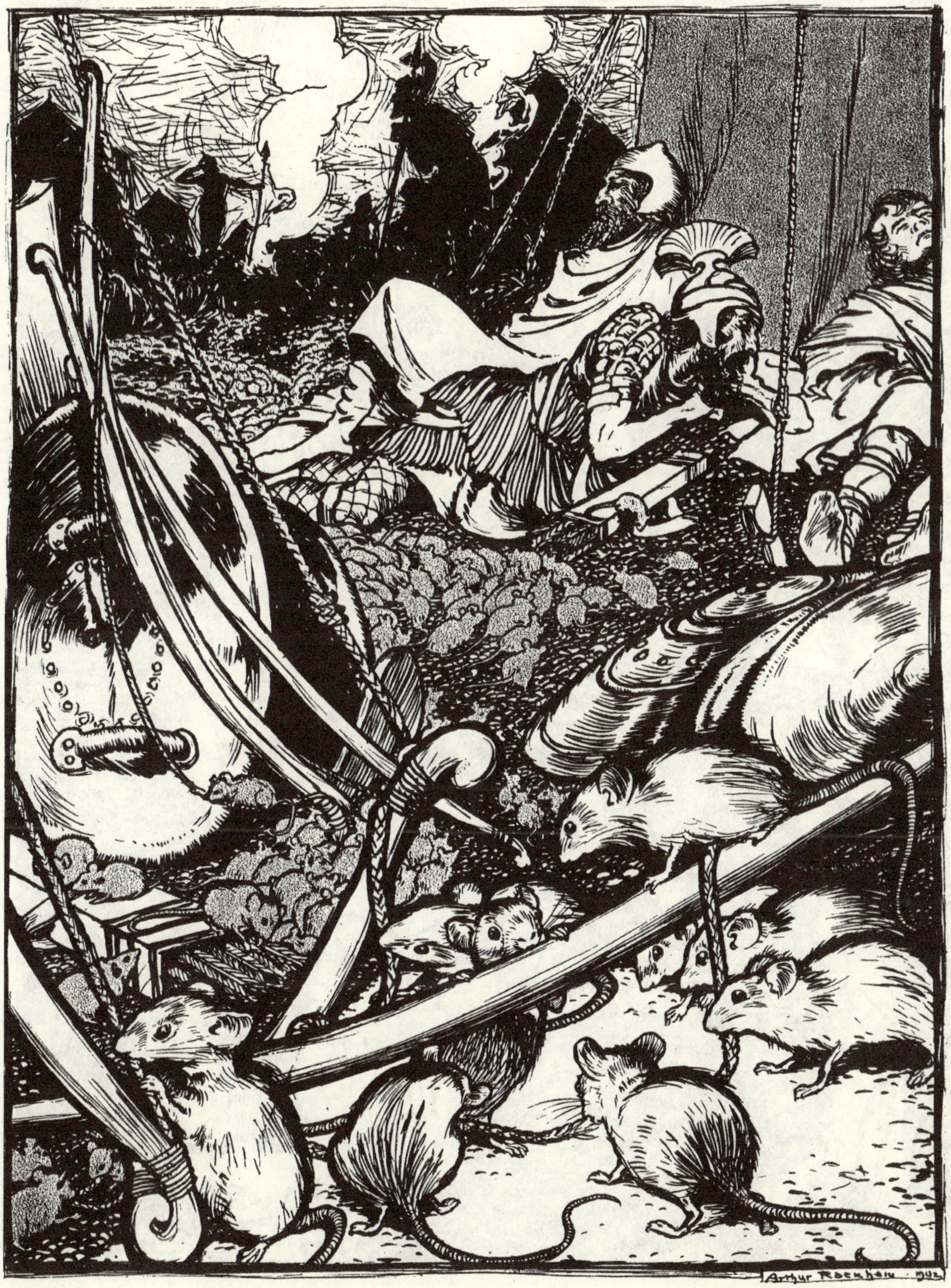

"A swarm of field-mice gnawed the quivers and bow-strings"

THE LAND OF ENCHANTMENT, 1907

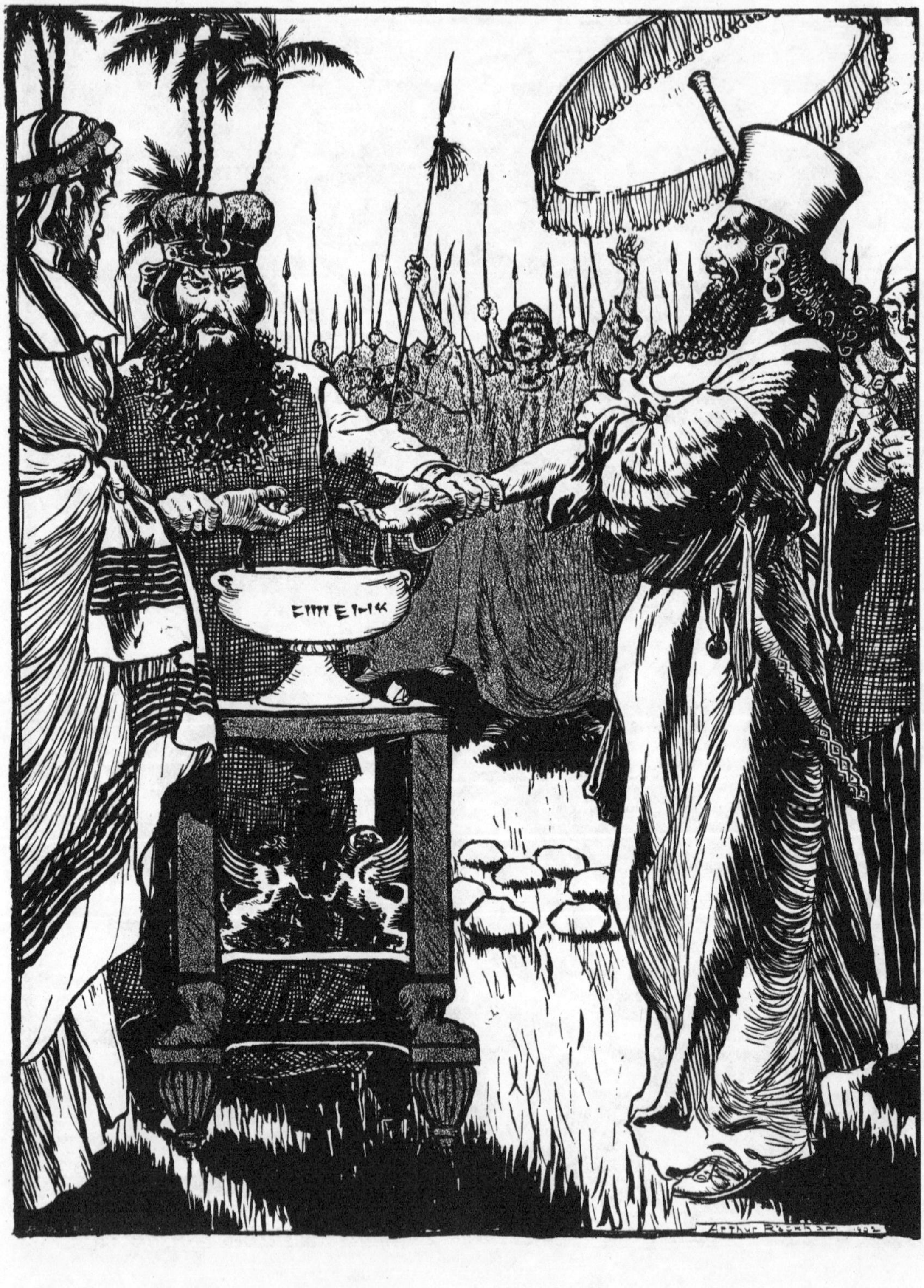

"Cambyses and the Arabian king pledged faith with each other"

THE LAND OF ENCHANTMENT, 1907

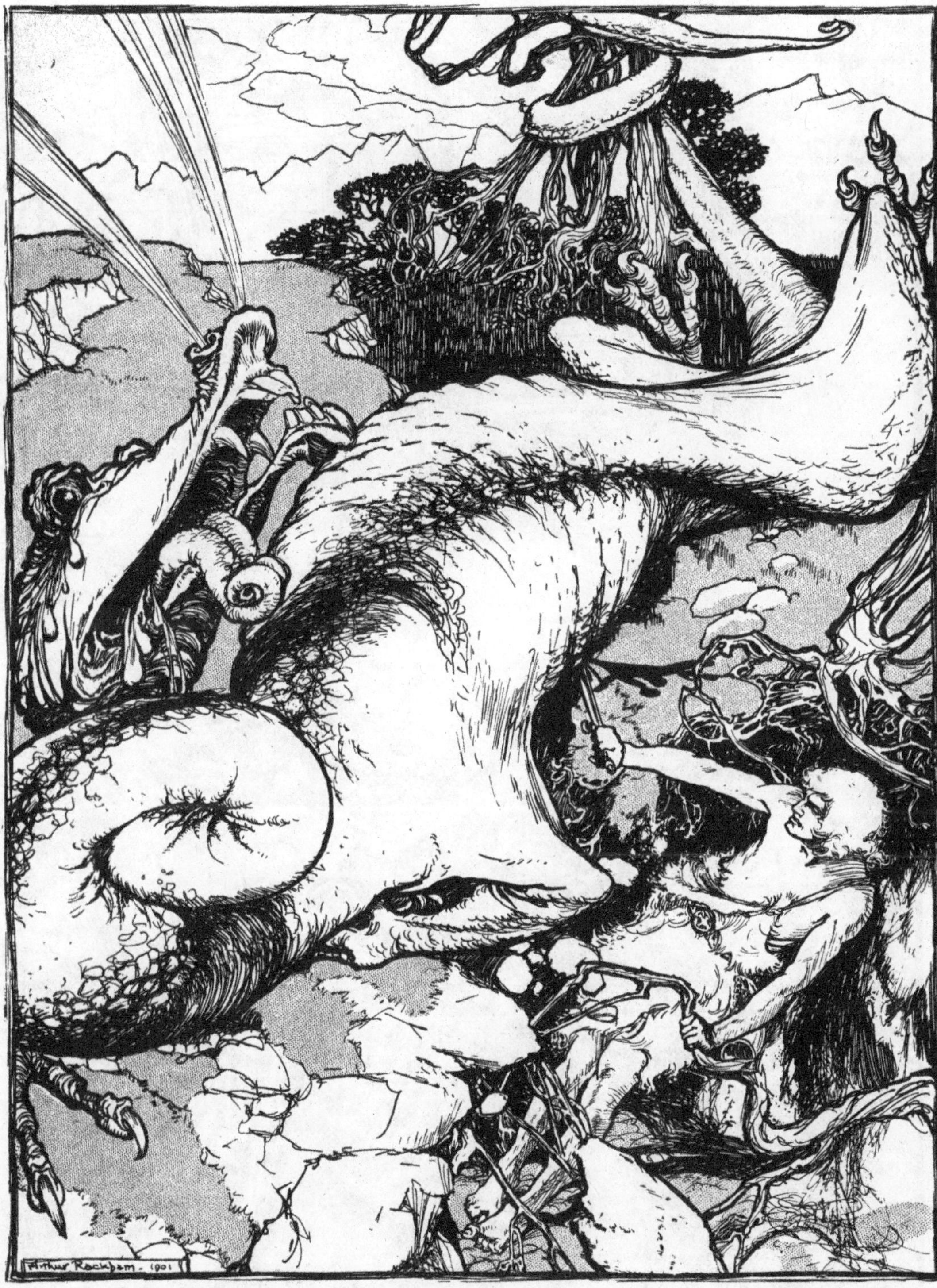

"Sigurd pierced him with his sword, and he died"

THE LAND OF ENCHANTMENT, 1907

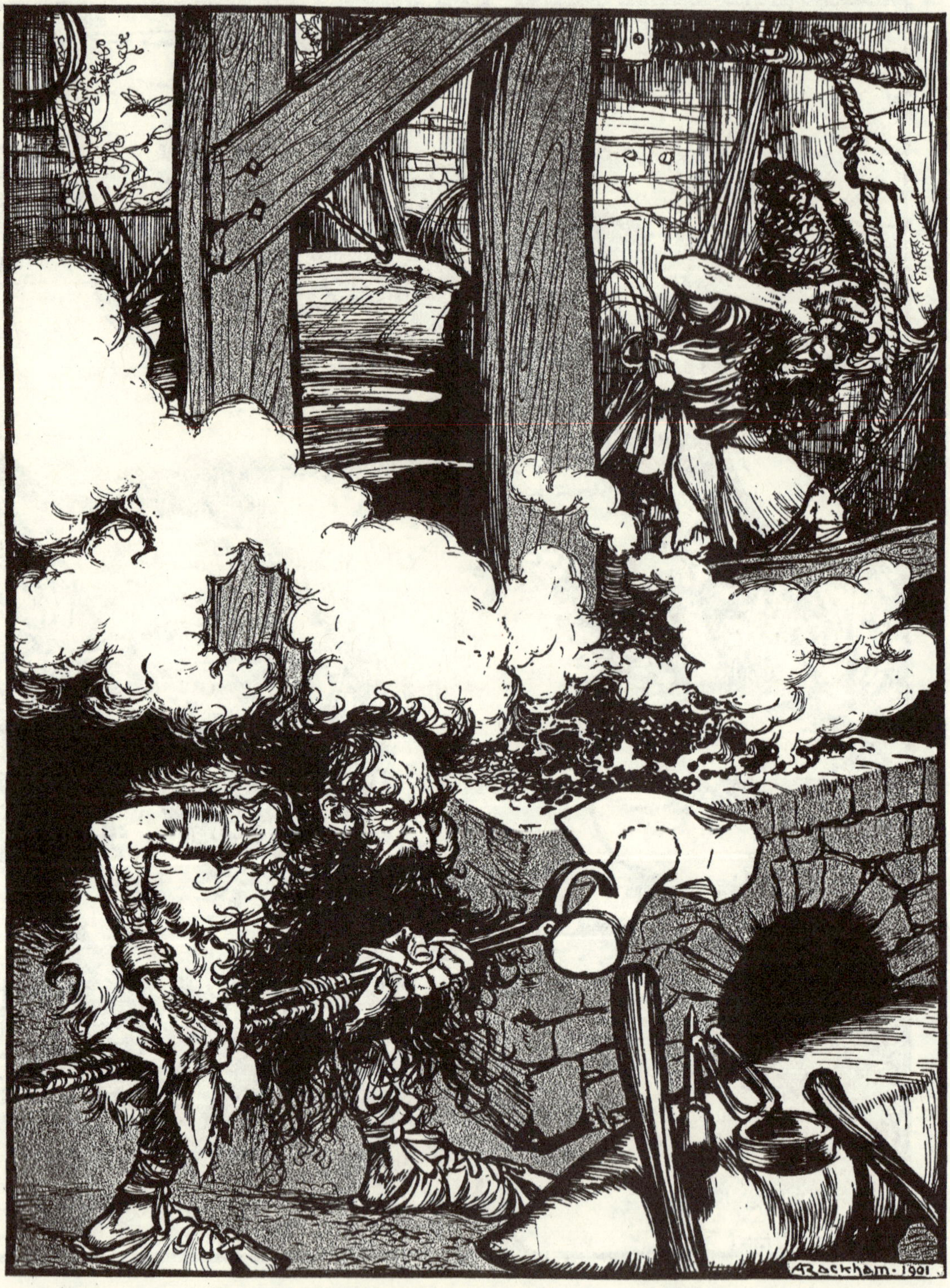

"Once again the buzzing fly came in at the window"

THE LAND OF ENCHANTMENT, 1907

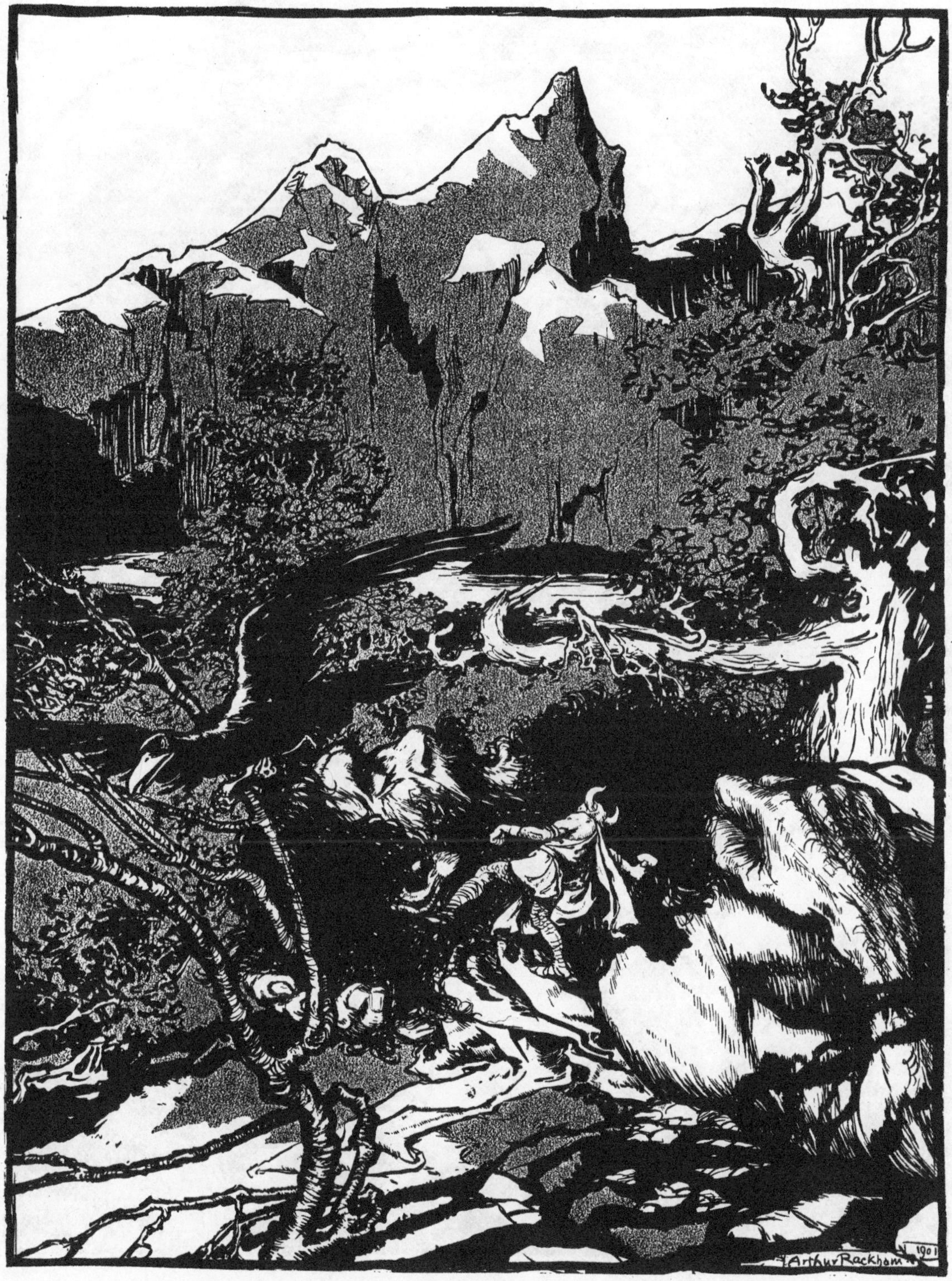

"He raised his hammer with a mighty swing"

THE LAND OF ENCHANTMENT, 1907

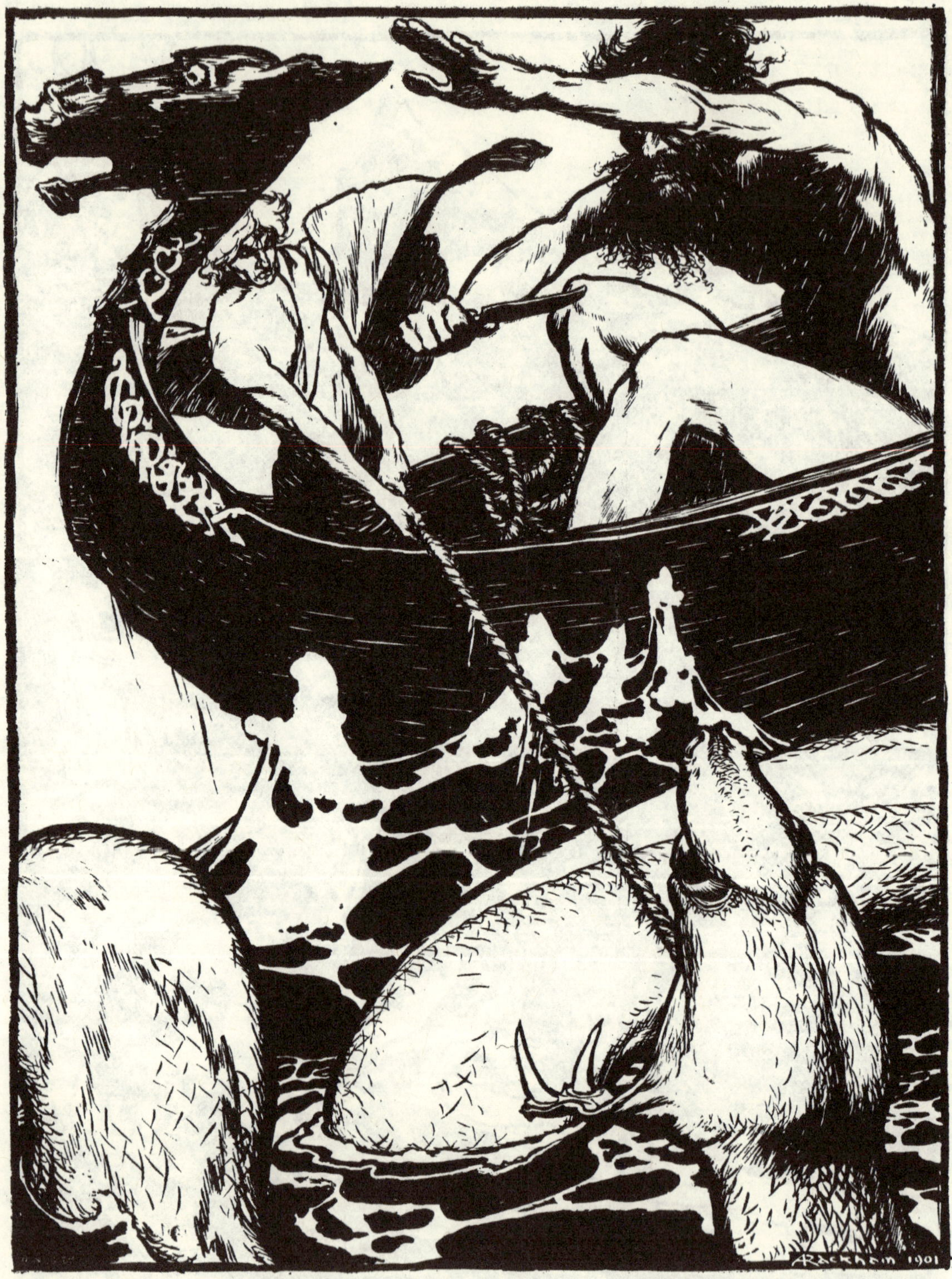

"Hymir rushed forward and cut through the line"

The Land of Enchantment, 1907

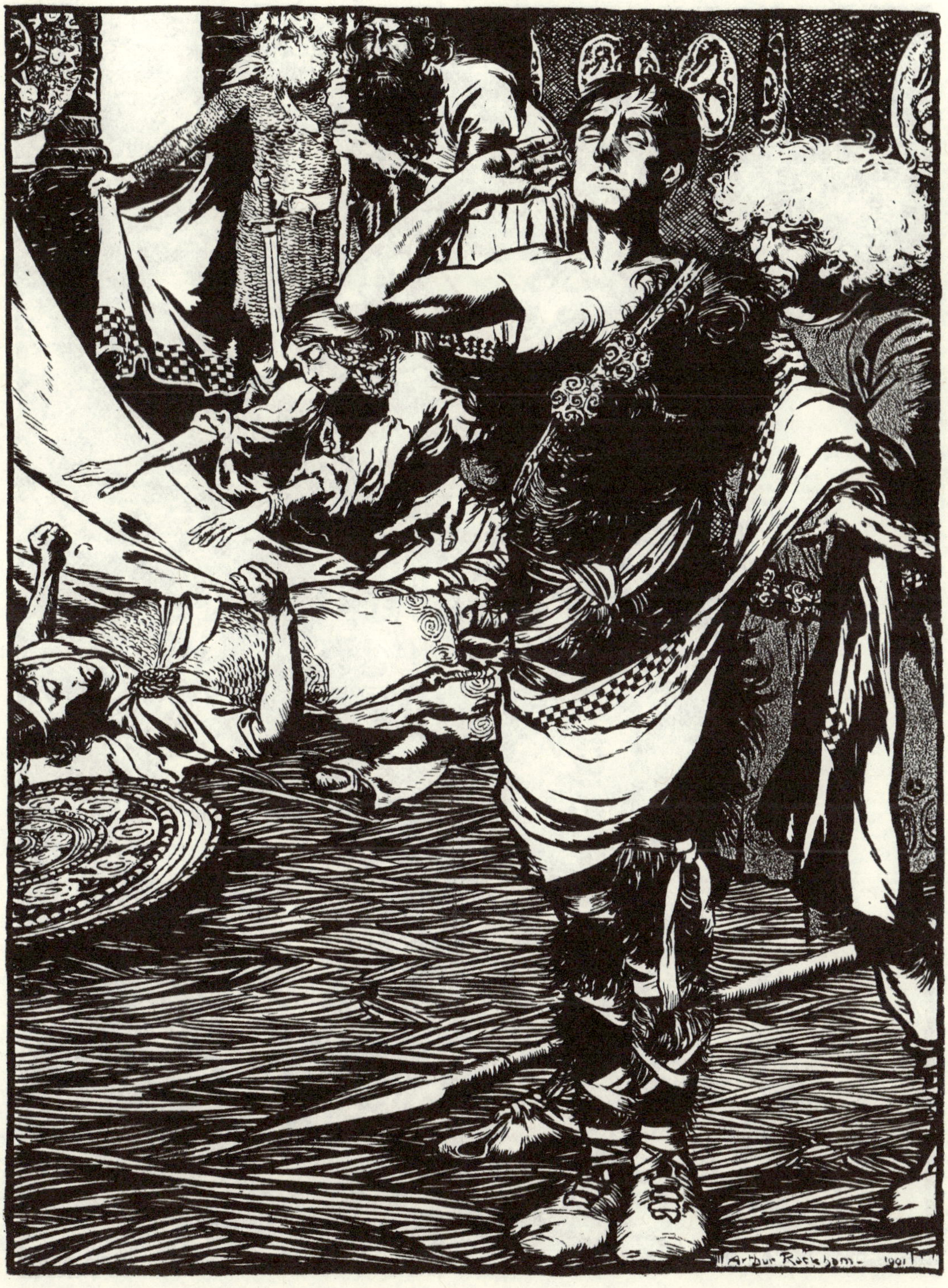

"There broke forth a wailing and a lamentation"

THE LAND OF ENCHANTMENT, 1907

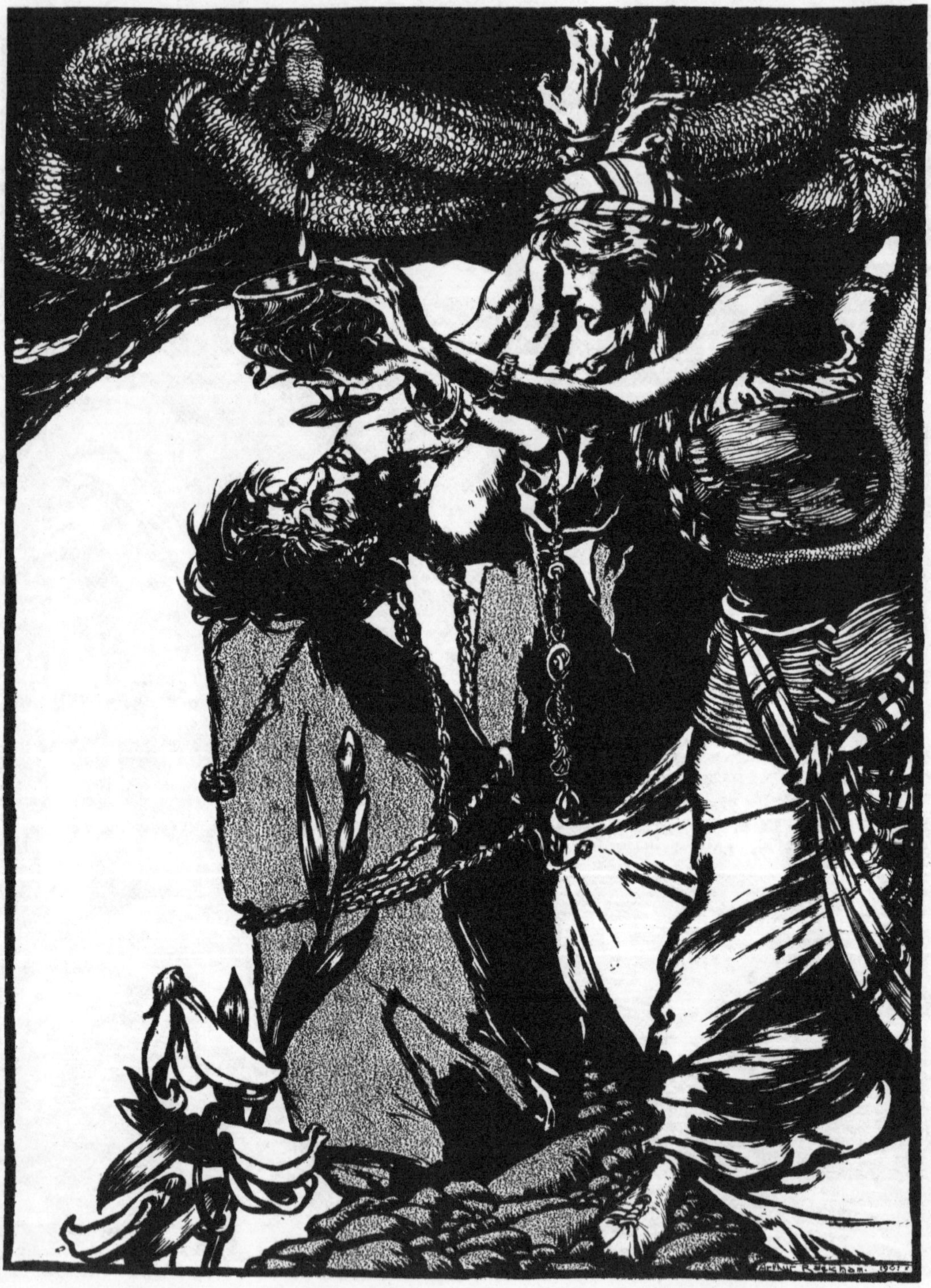

"Held a cup to catch the venomous drops"

THE LAND OF ENCHANTMENT, 1907

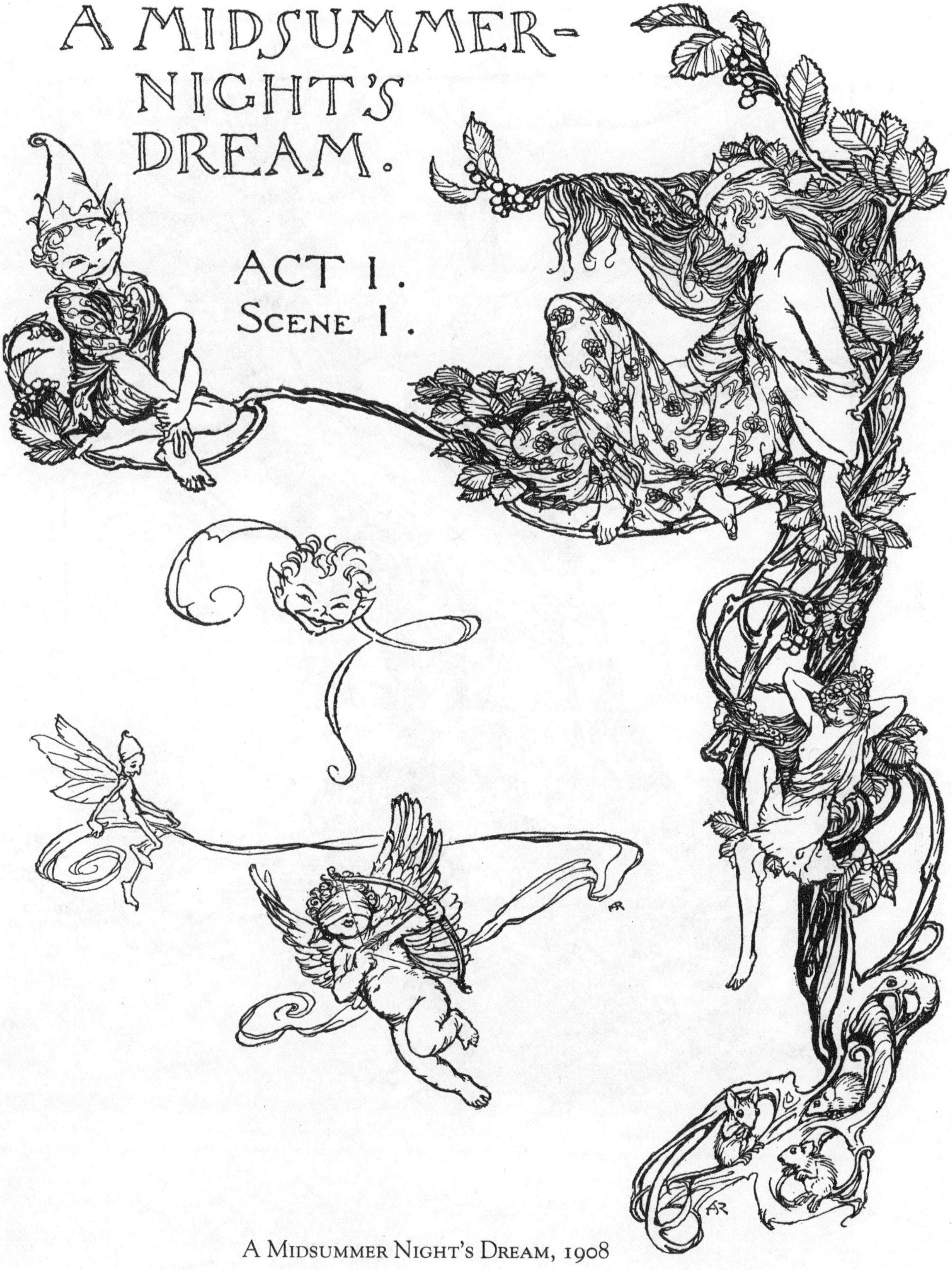

A Midsummer Night's Dream, 1908

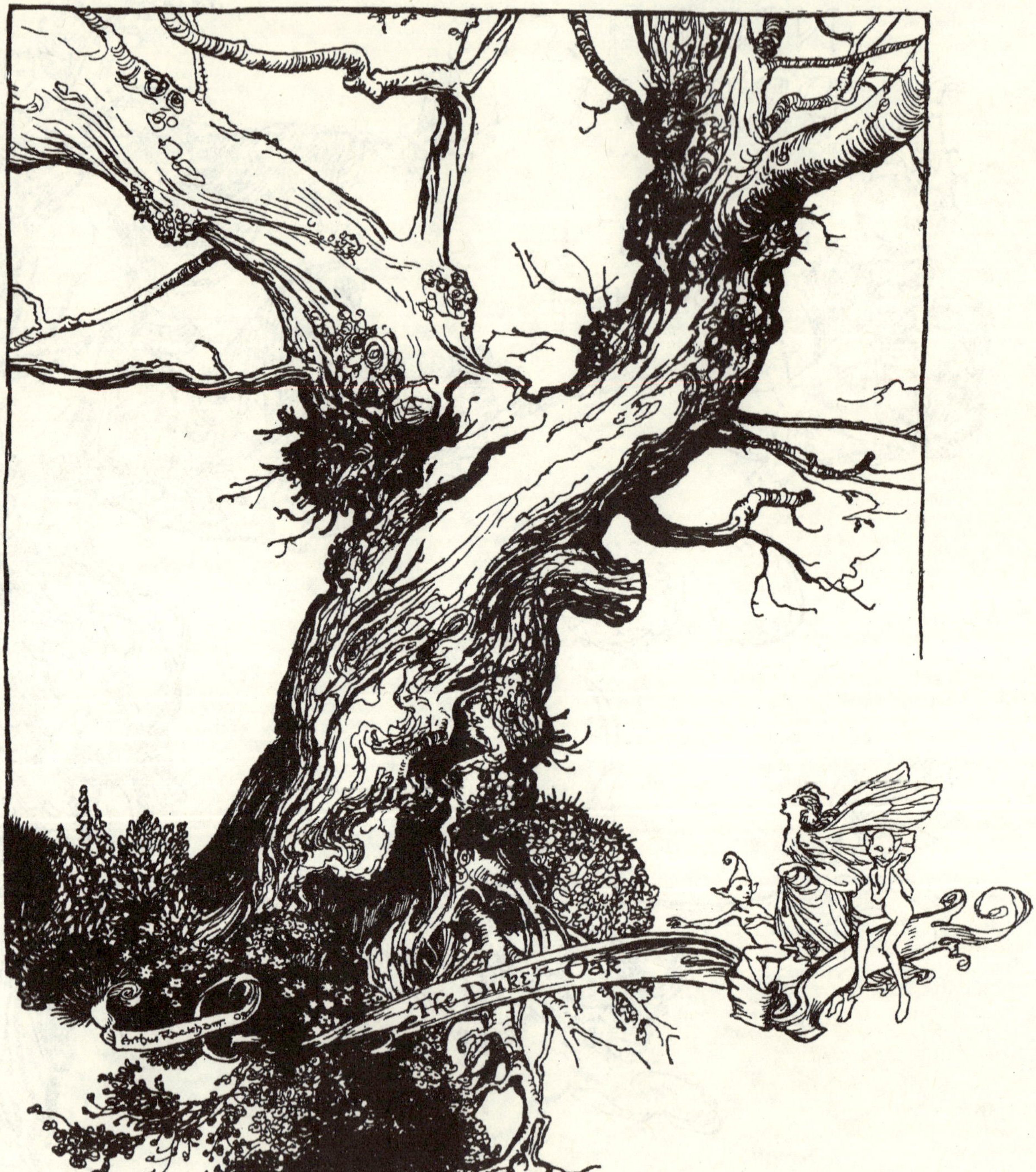

"The Duke's Oak"

A MIDSUMMER NIGHT'S DREAM, 1908

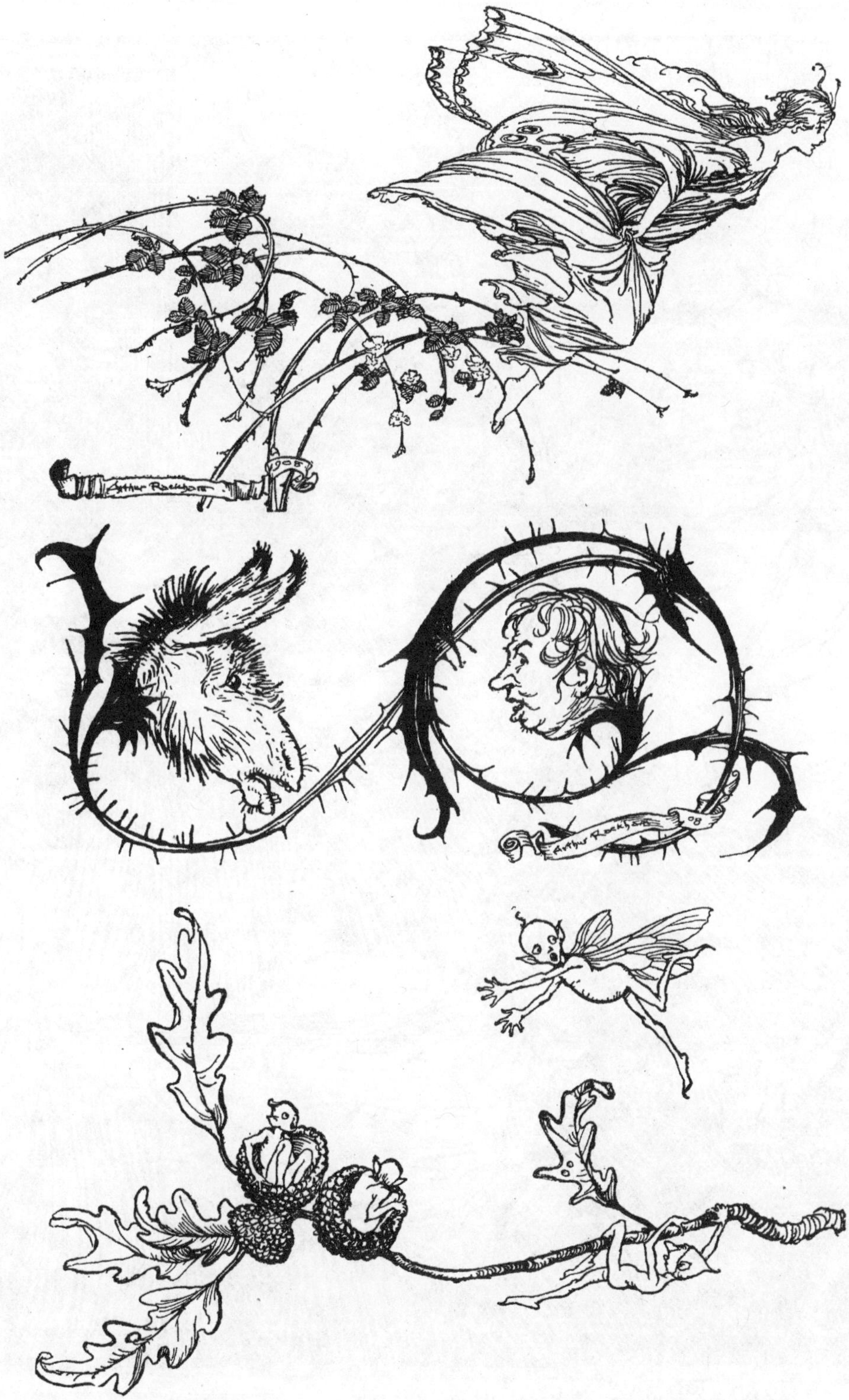

A Midsummer Night's Dream, 1908

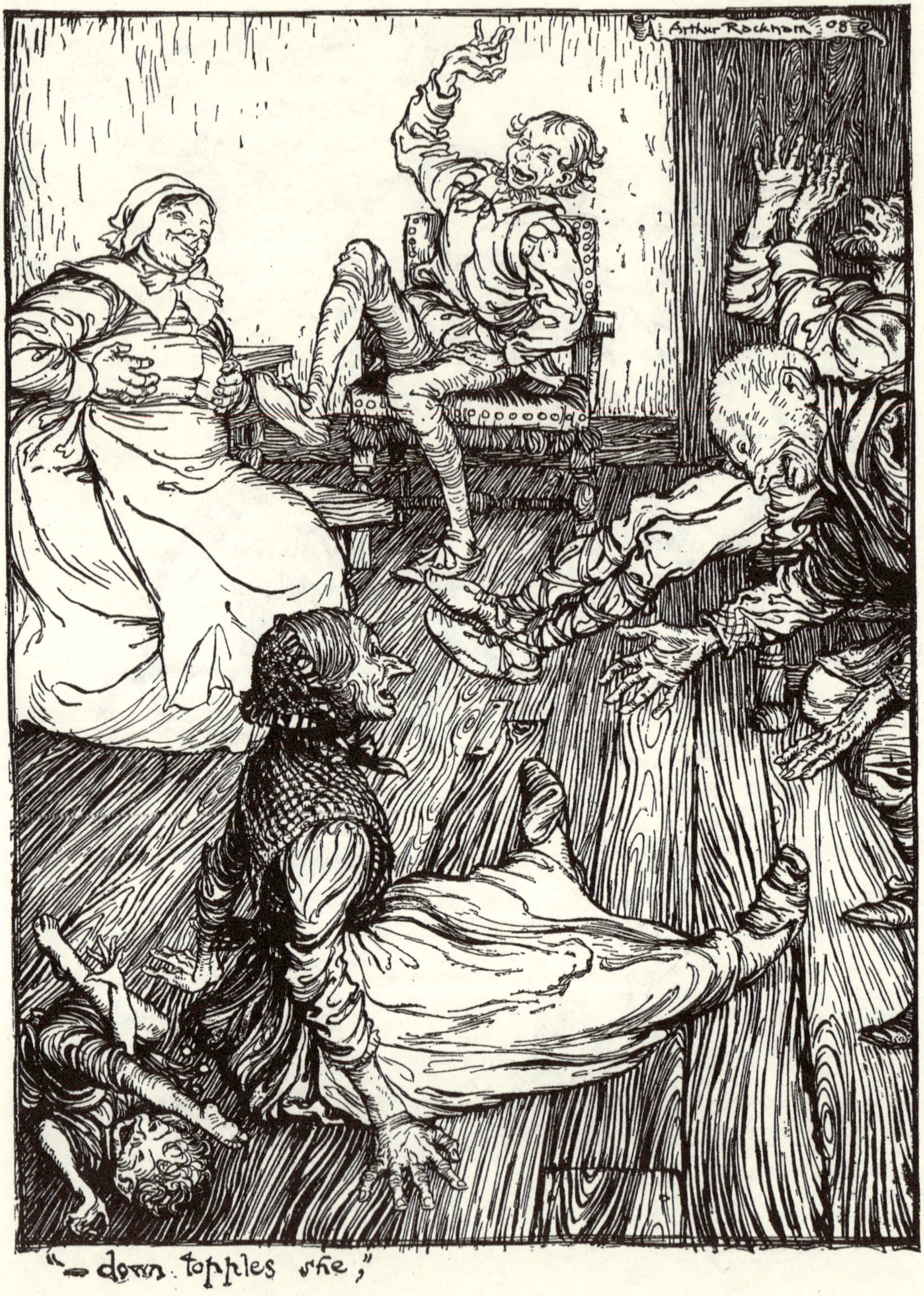

A MIDSUMMER NIGHT'S DREAM, 1908

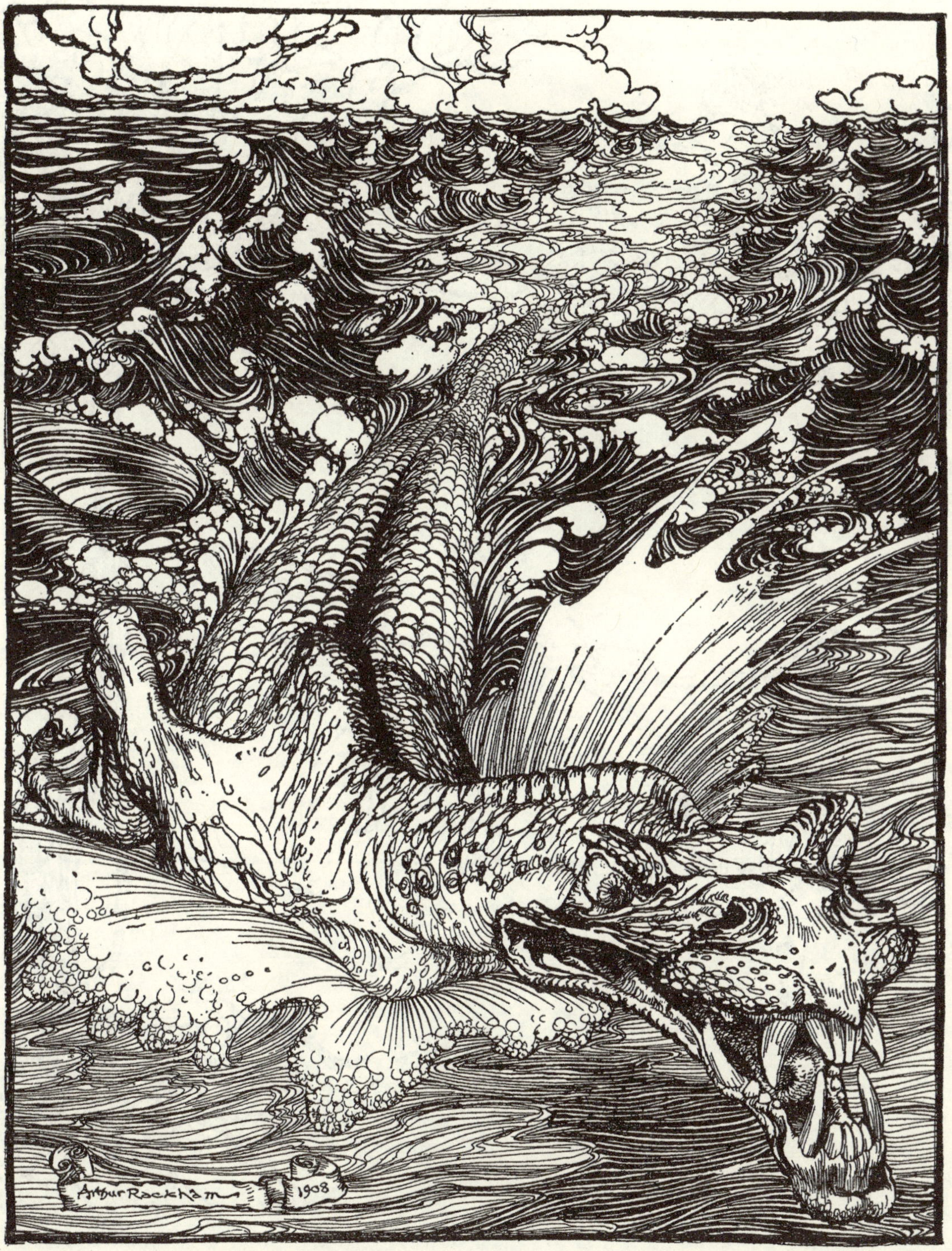

"Ere the Leviathan can swim a league"

A MIDSUMMER NIGHT'S DREAM, 1908

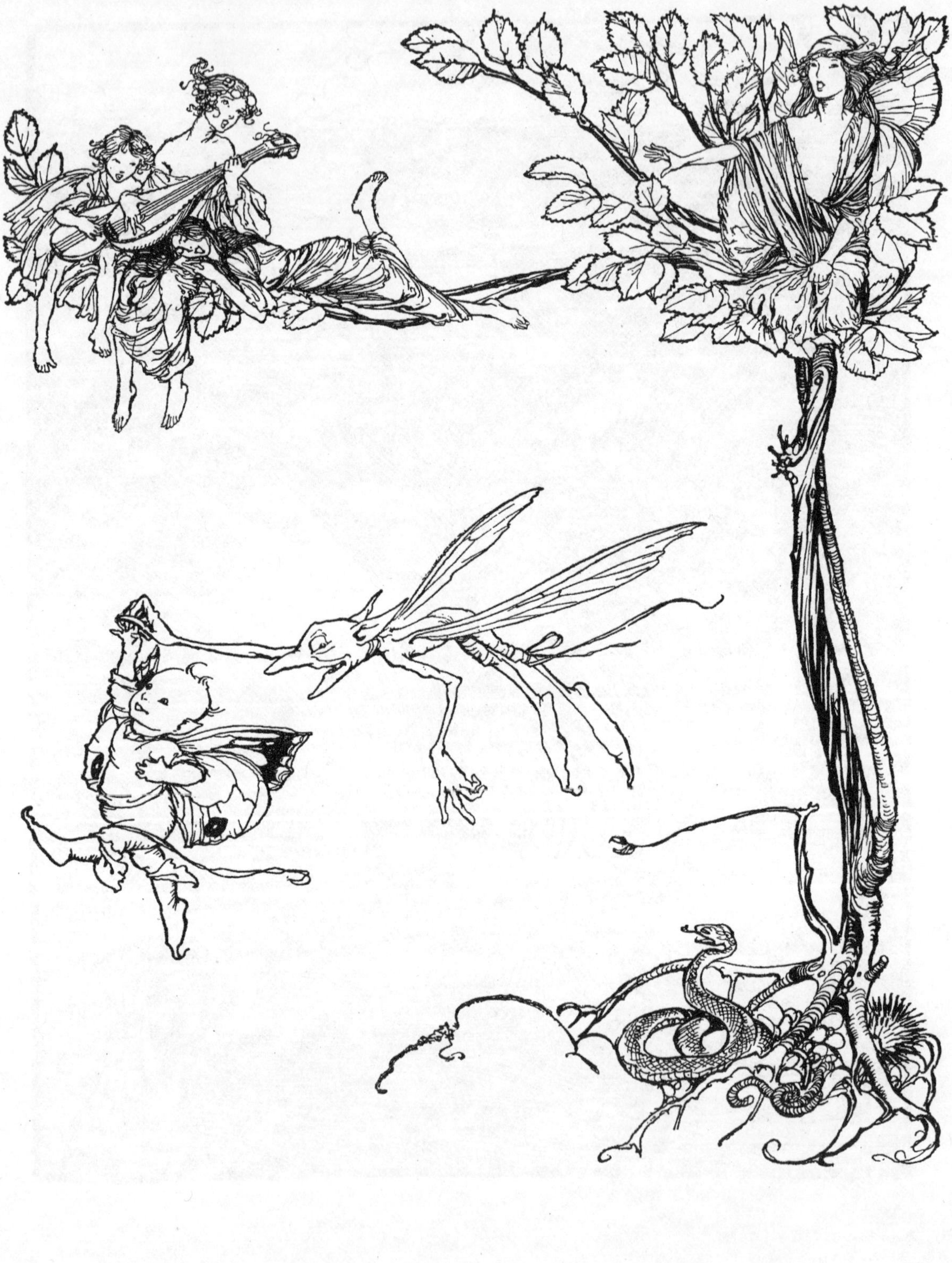

A Midsummer Night's Dream, 1908

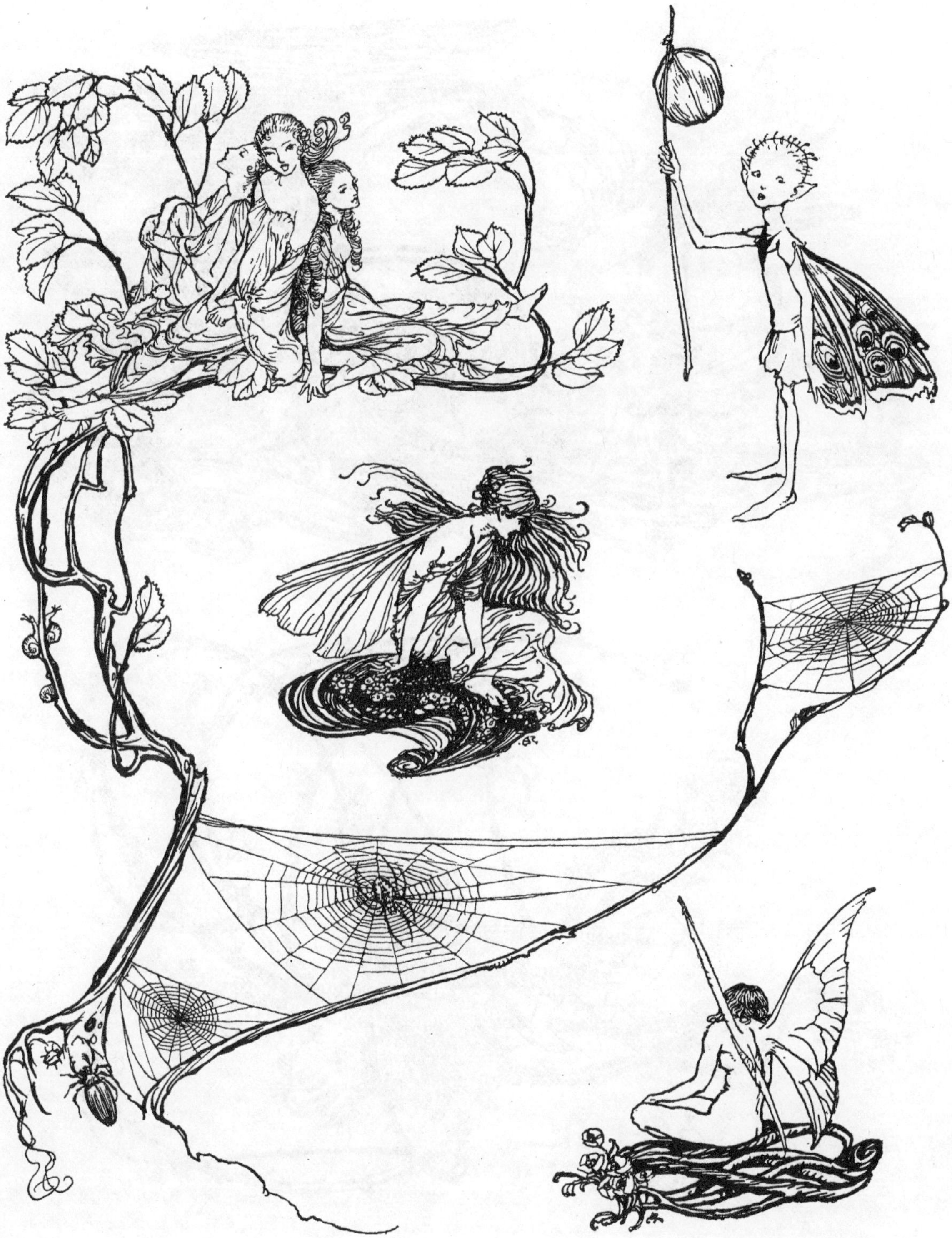

A Midsummer Night's Dream, 1908

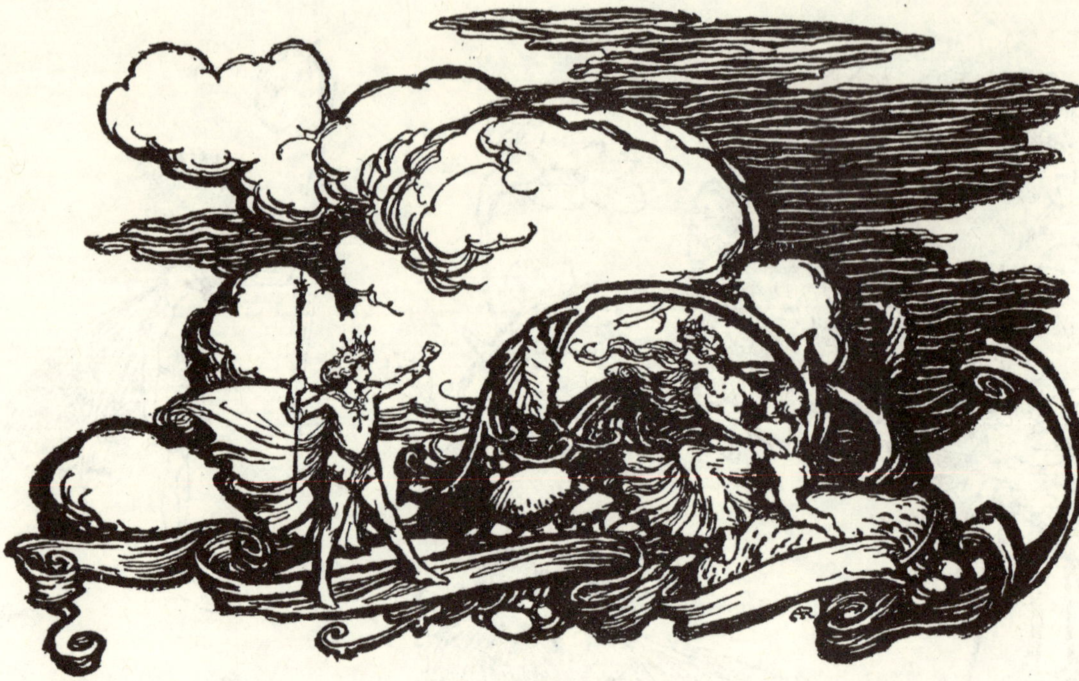

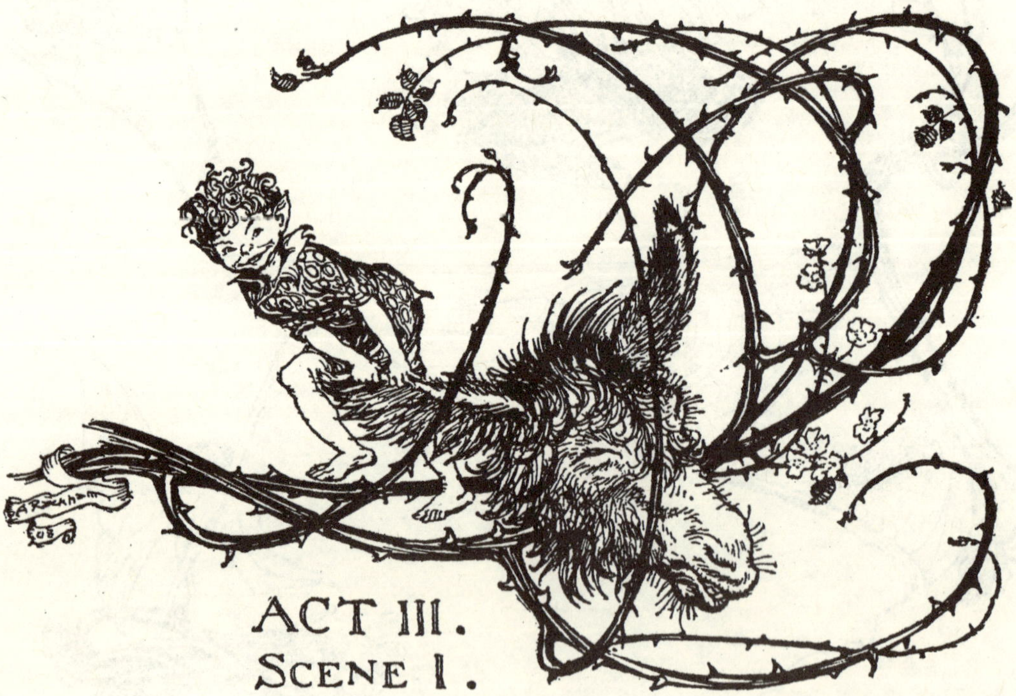

A Midsummer Night's Dream, 1908

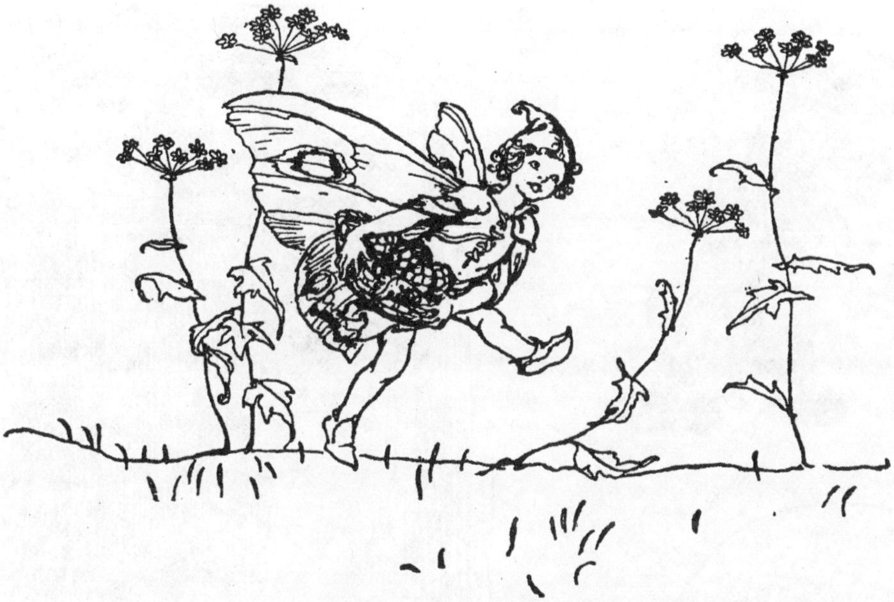

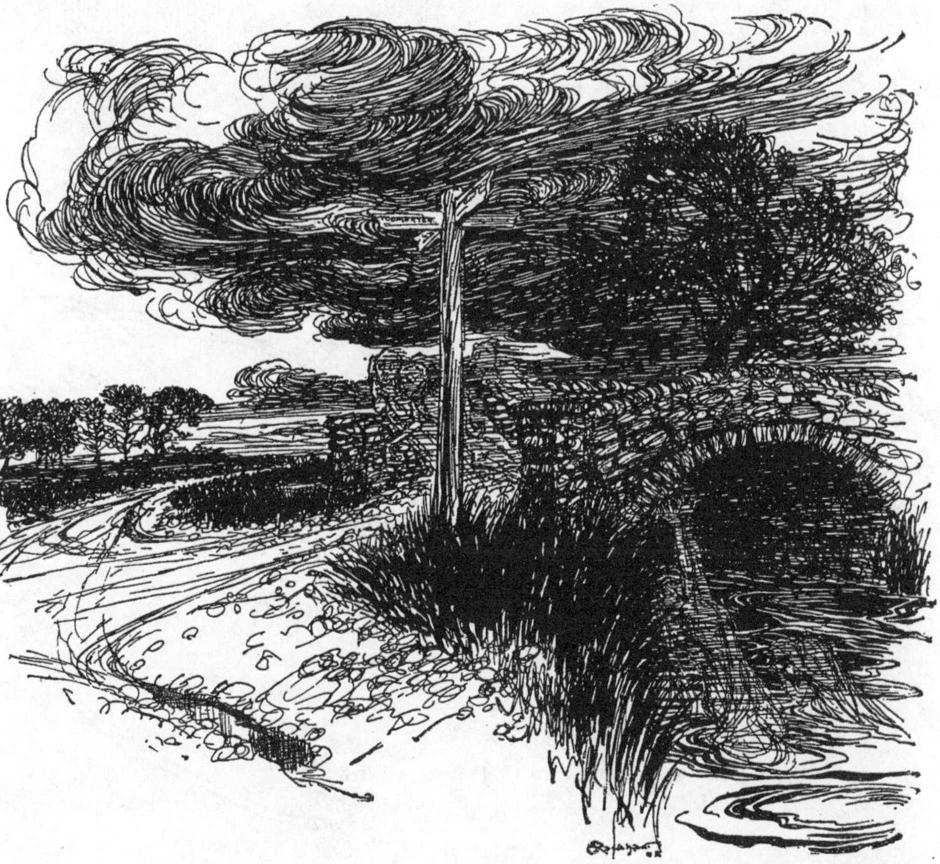

A Midsummer Night's Dream, 1908

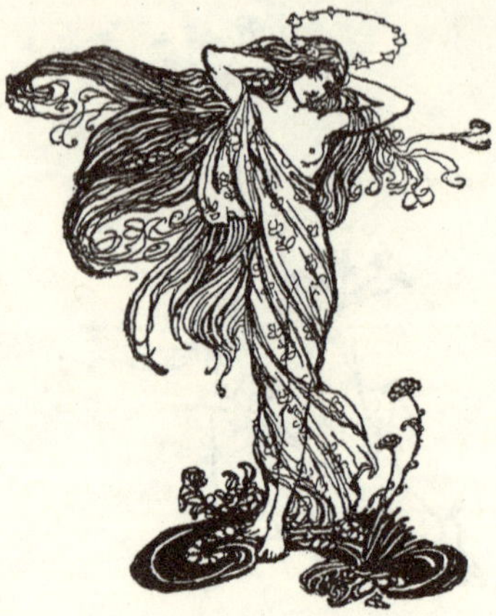

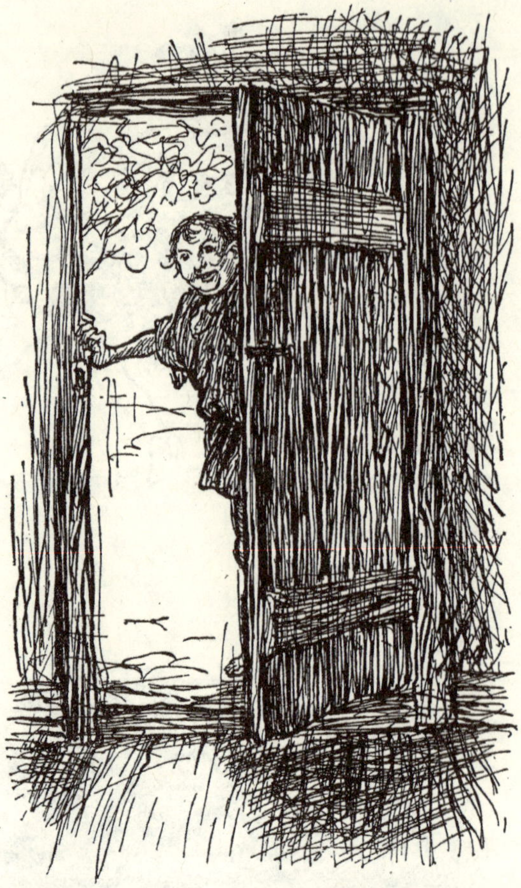

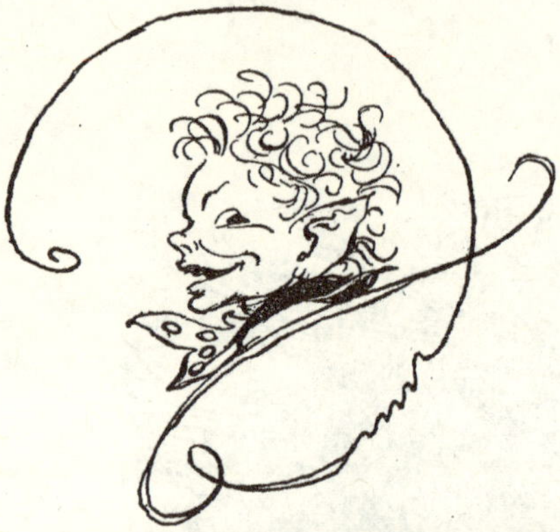

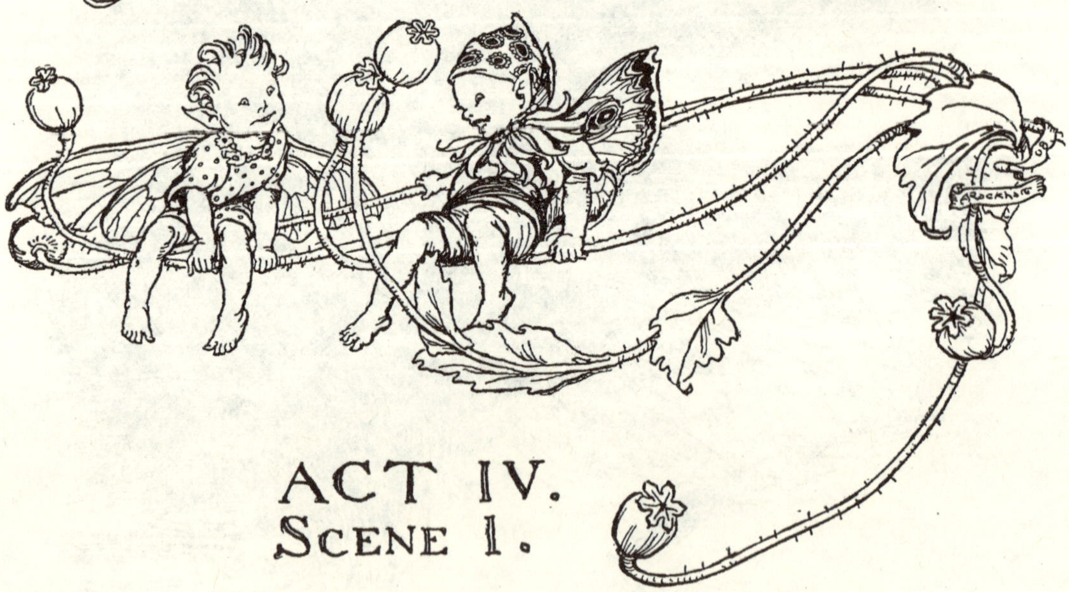

A Midsummer Night's Dream, 1908

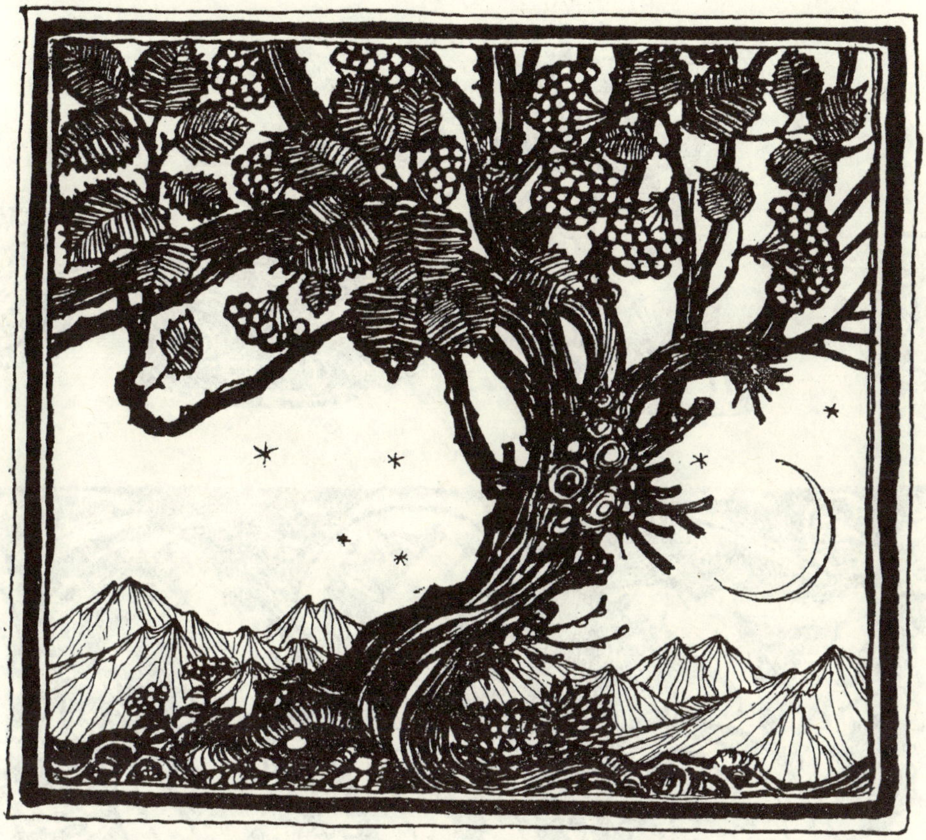

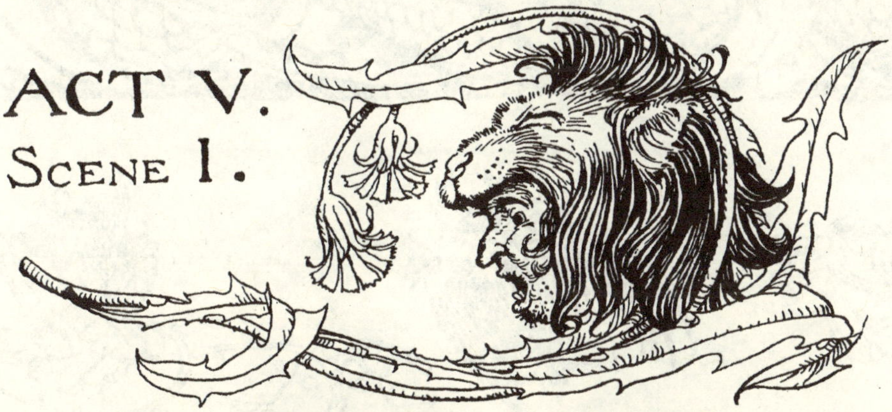

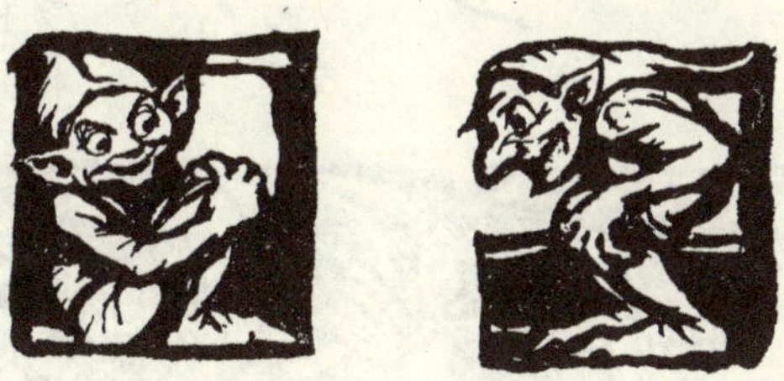

A Midsummer Night's Dream, 1908

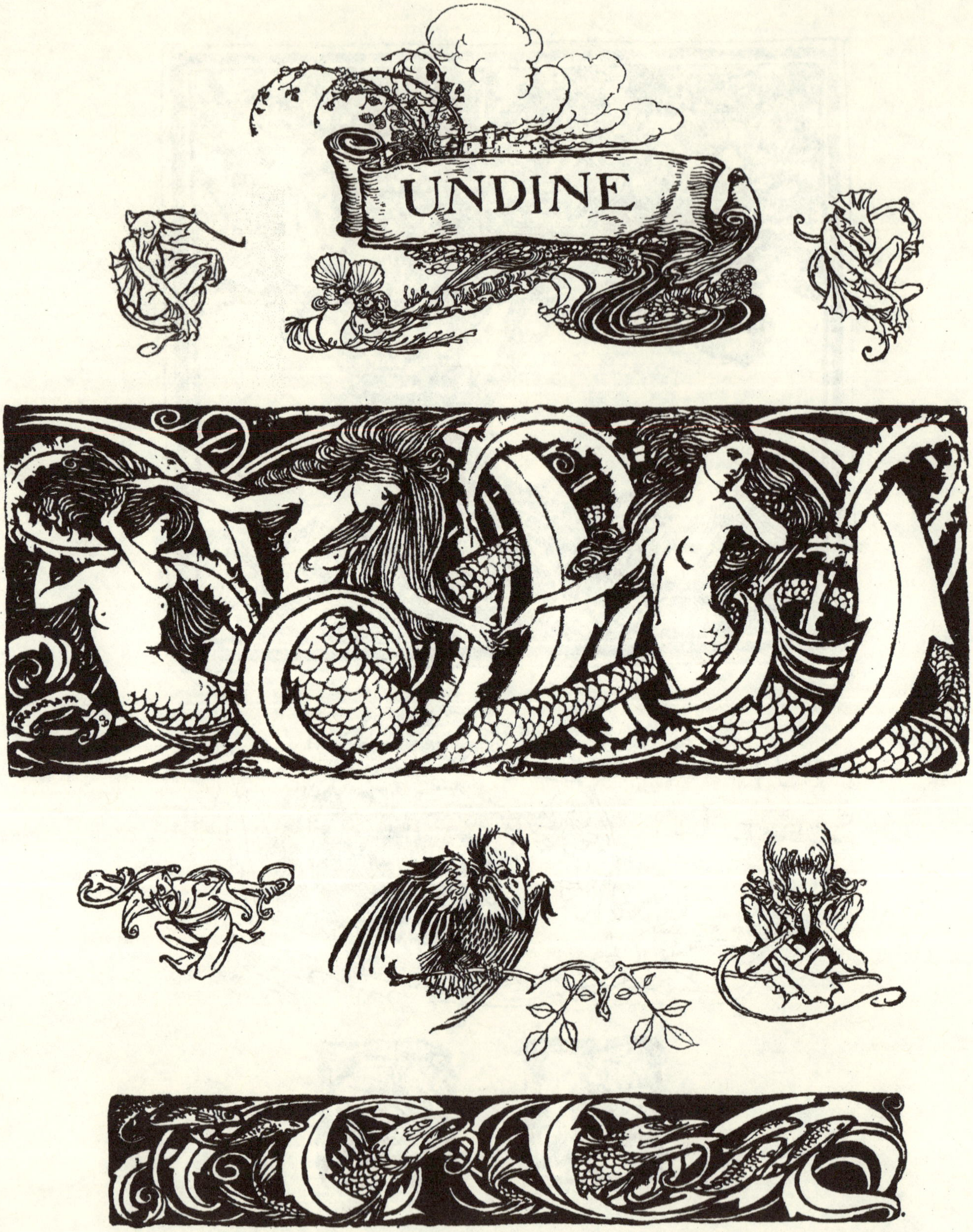

UNDINE, 1909

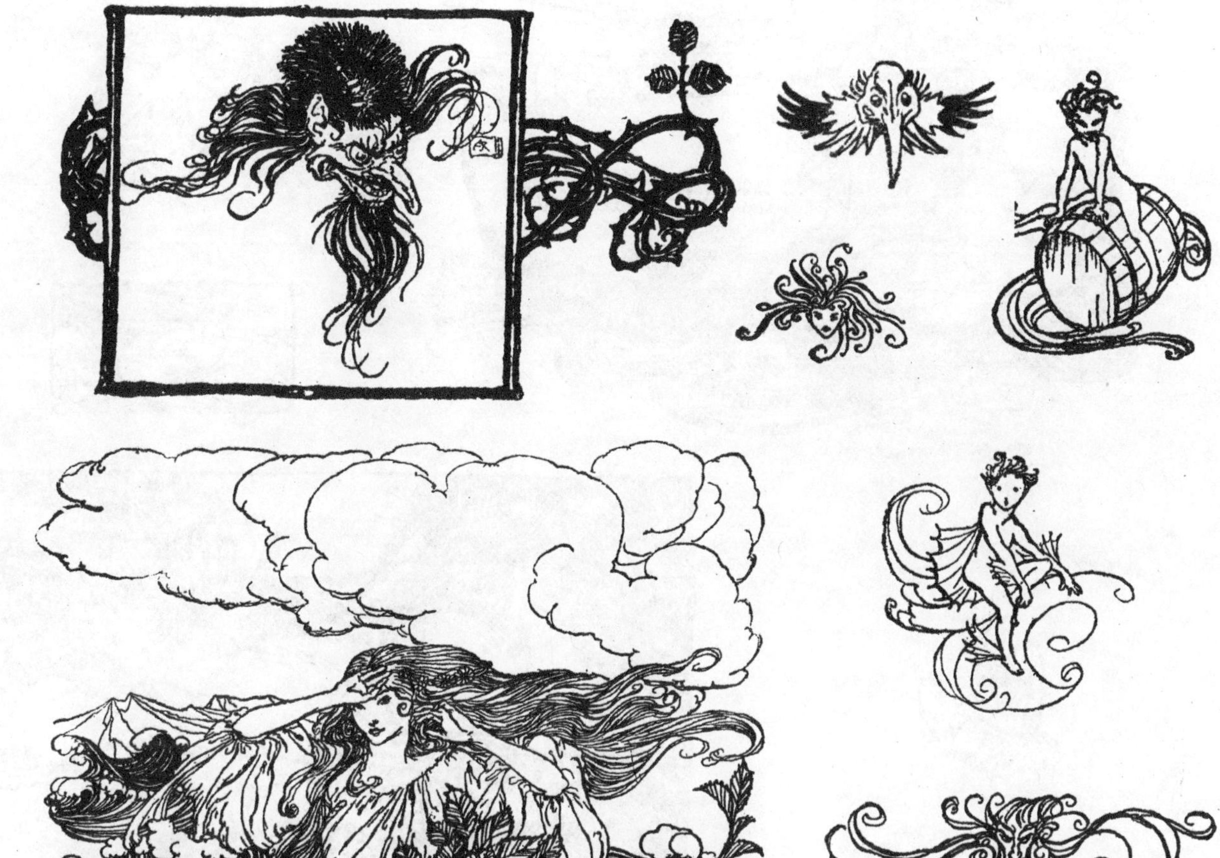

UNDINE, 1909

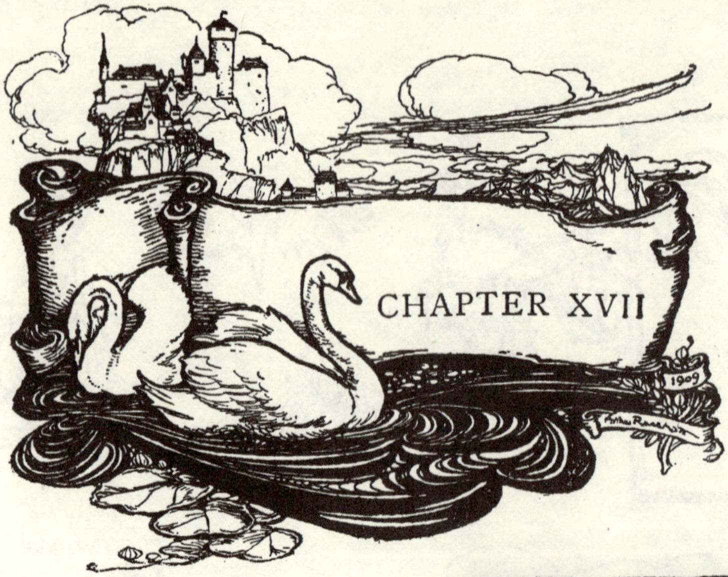

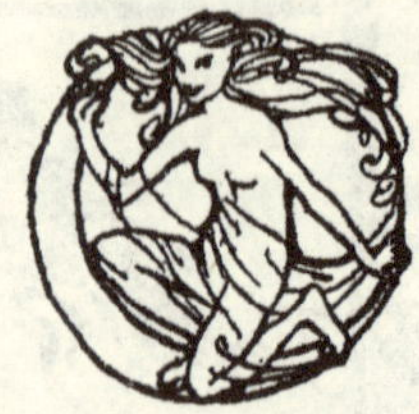

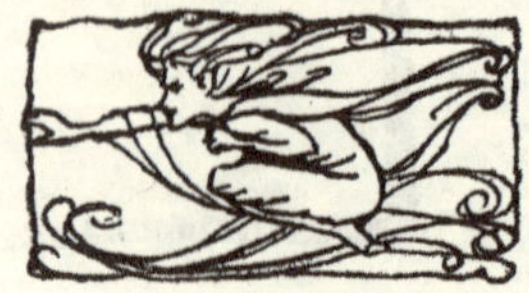

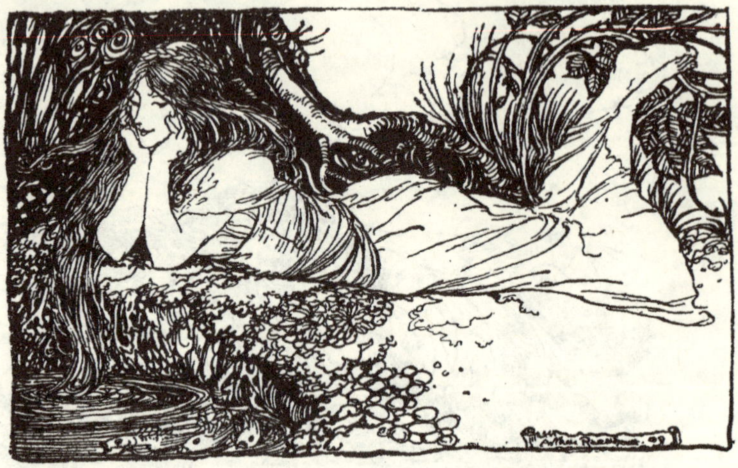

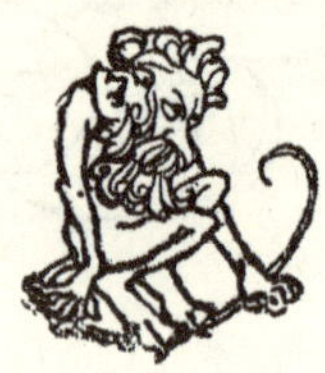

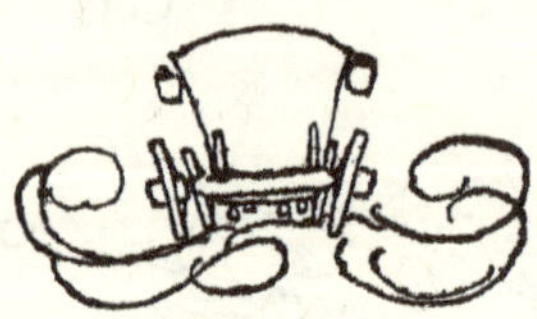

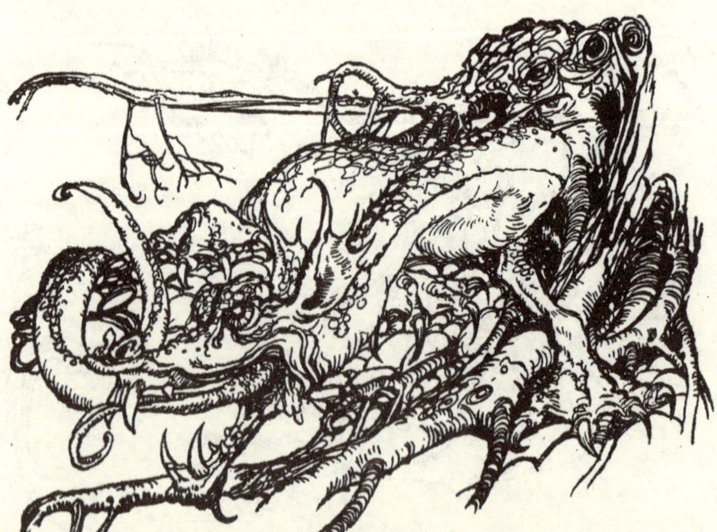

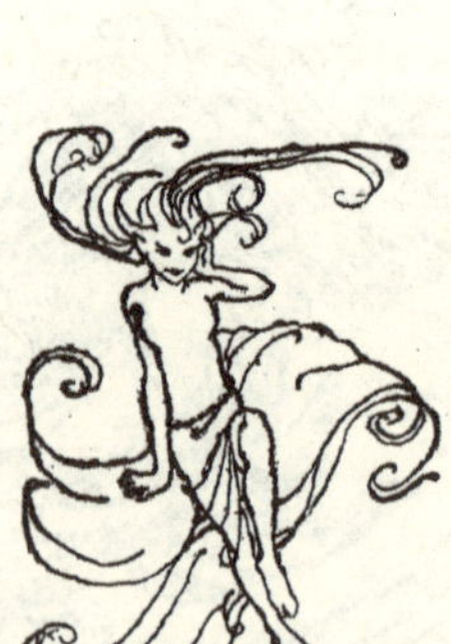

UNDINE, 1909

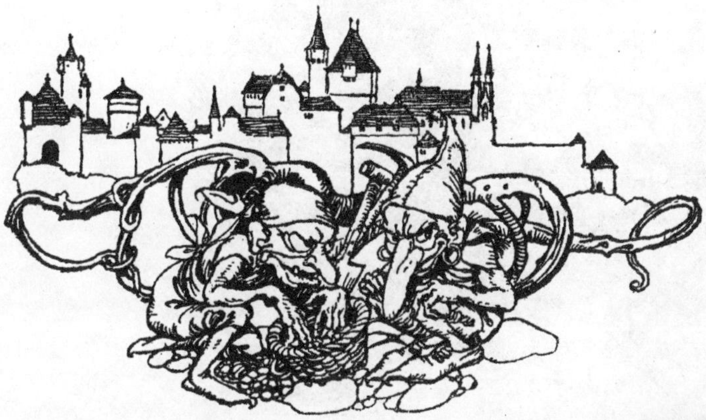

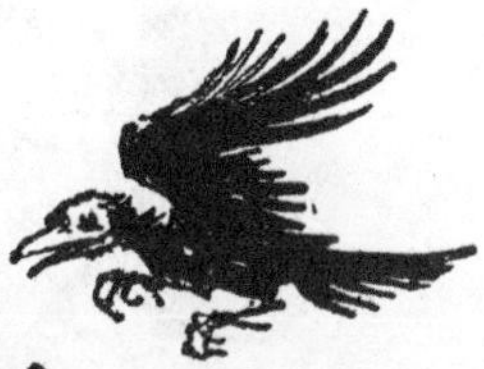

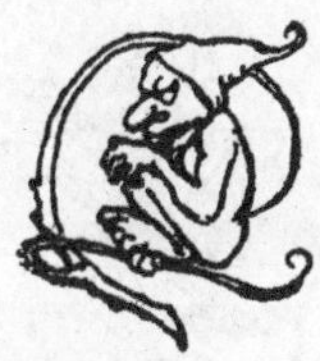

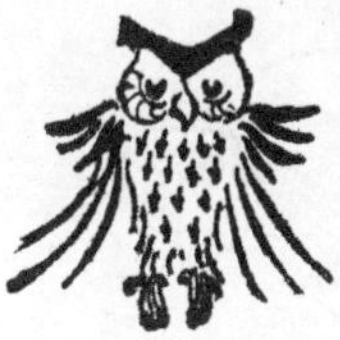

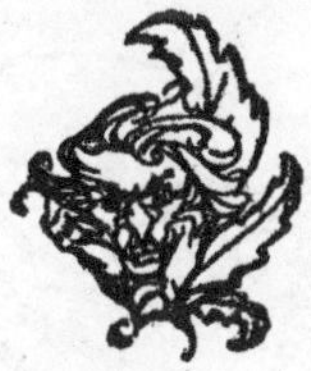

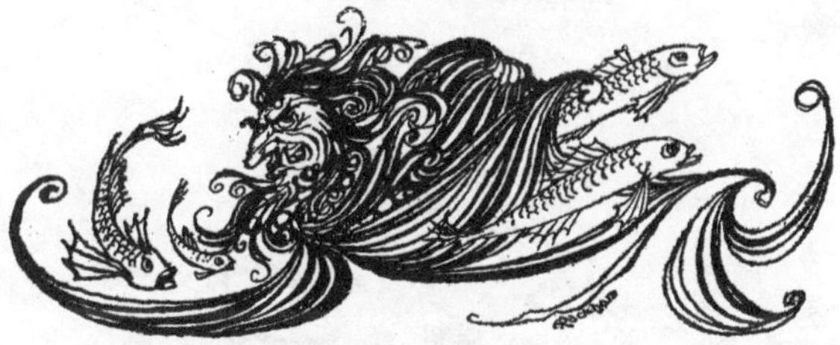

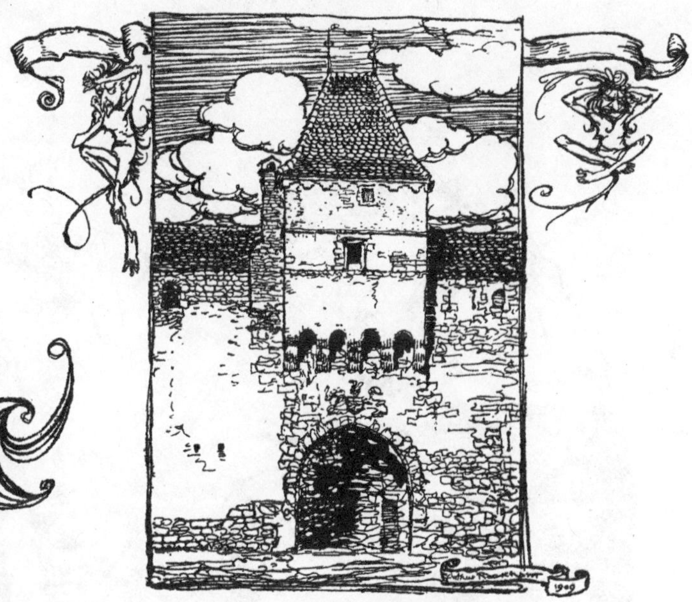

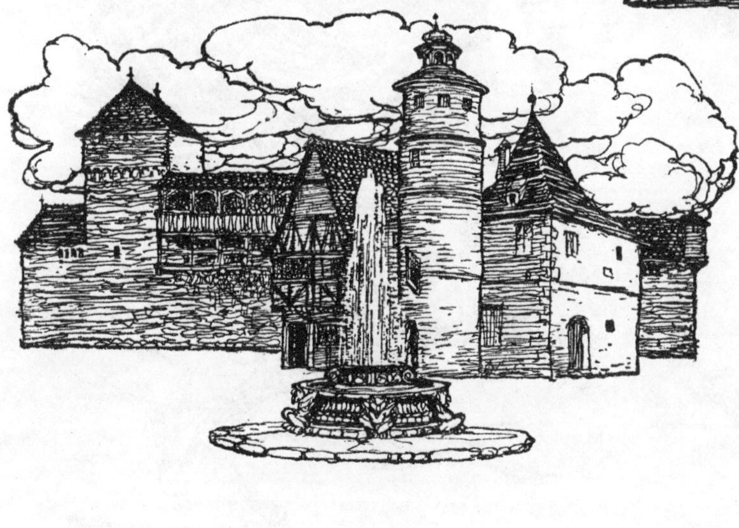

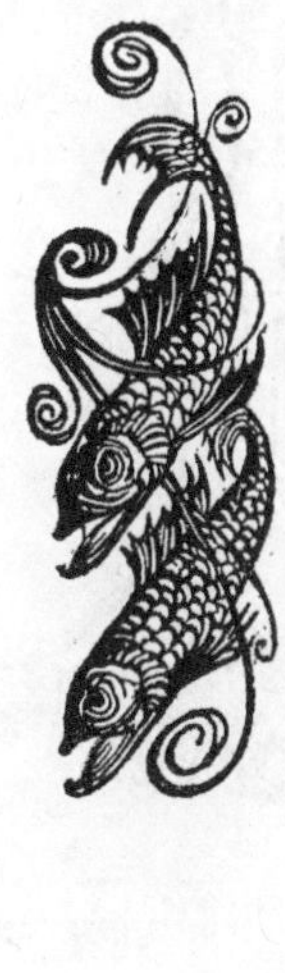

Undine, 1909

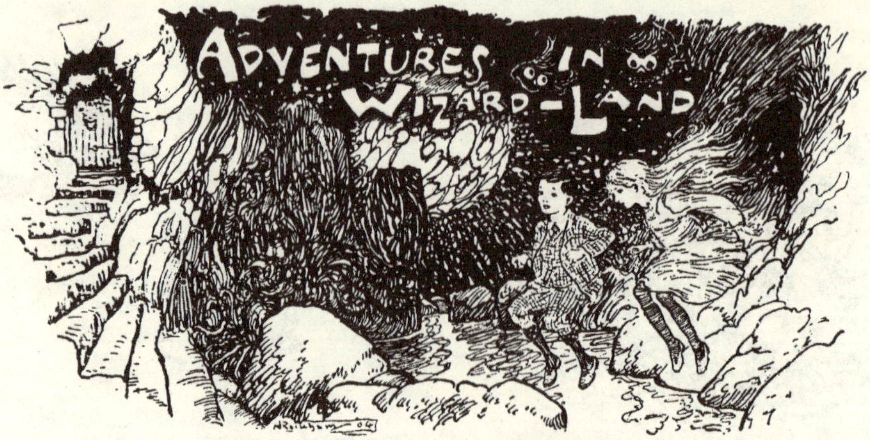

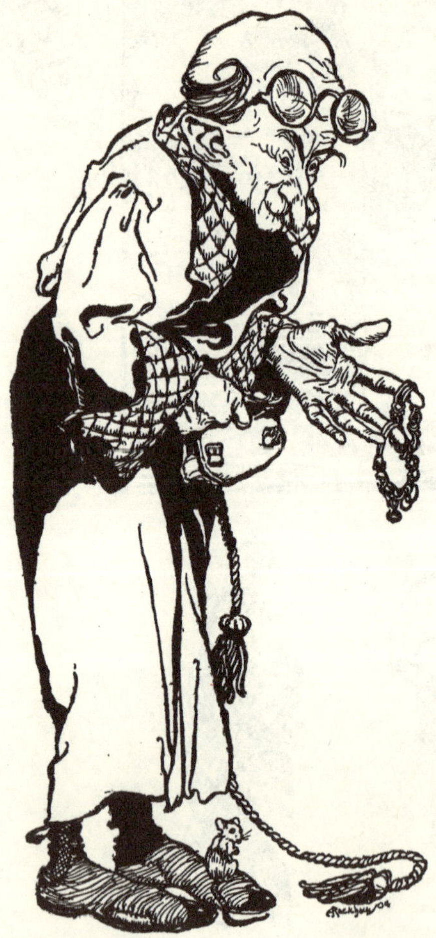

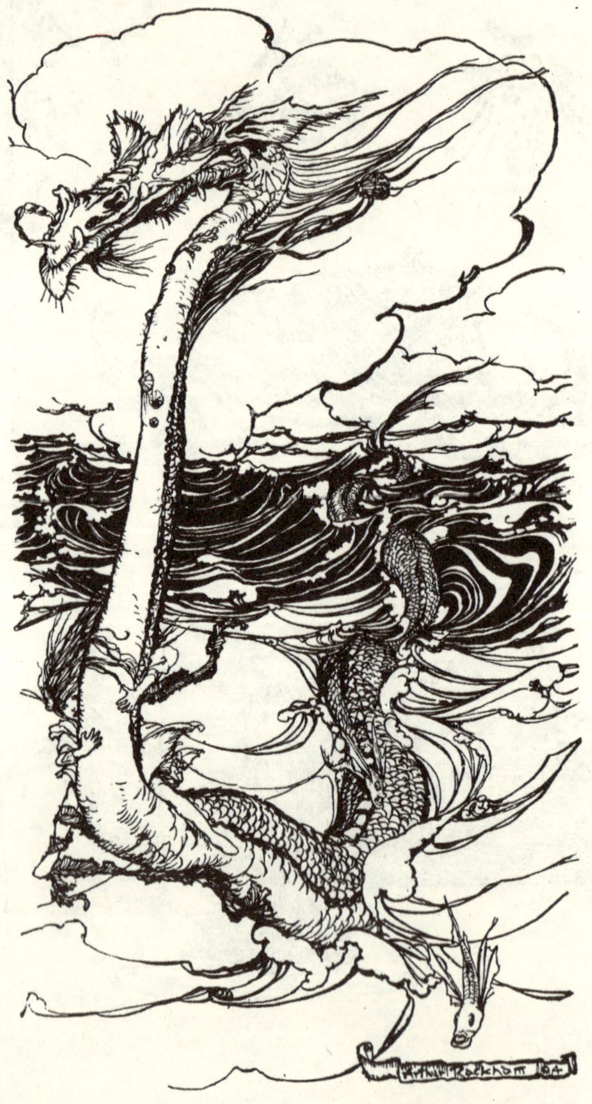

THE RAINBOW BOOK, 1909

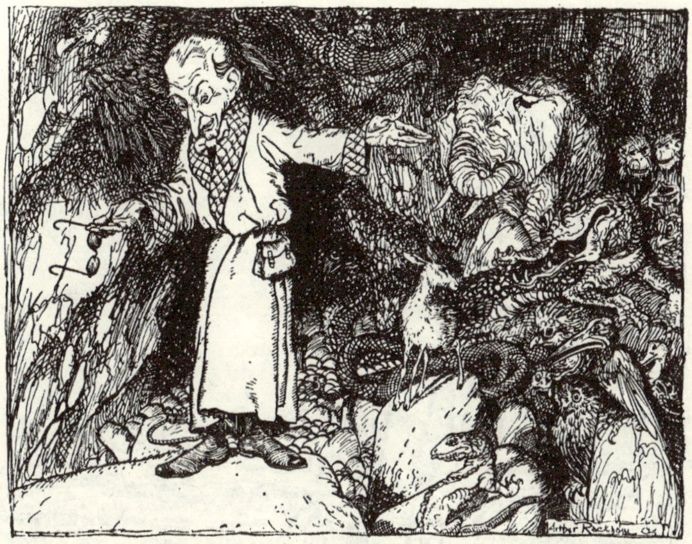

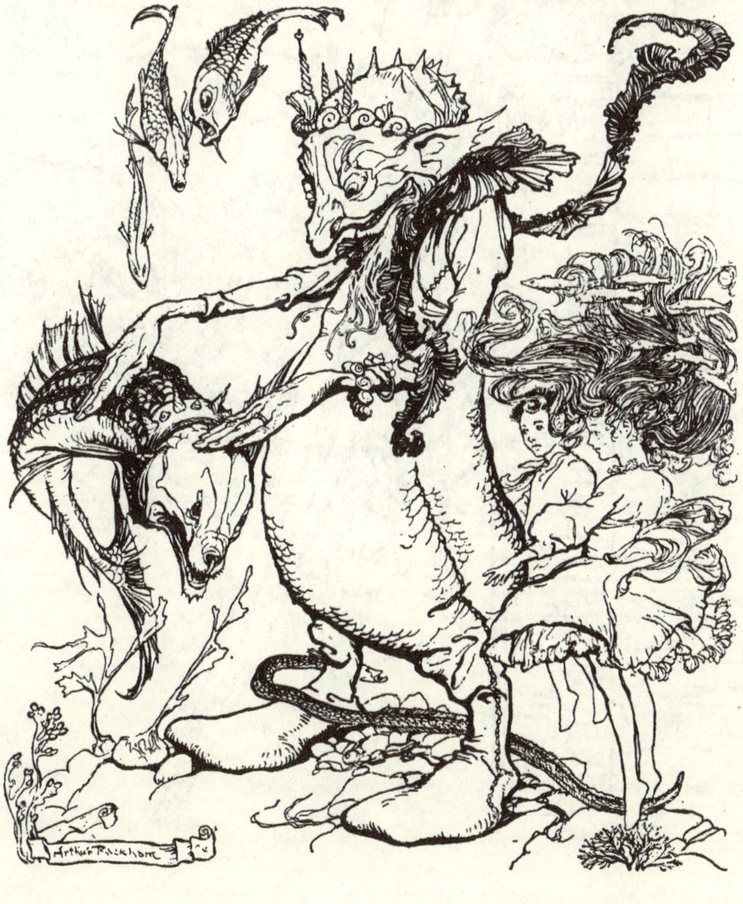

The Rainbow Book, 1909

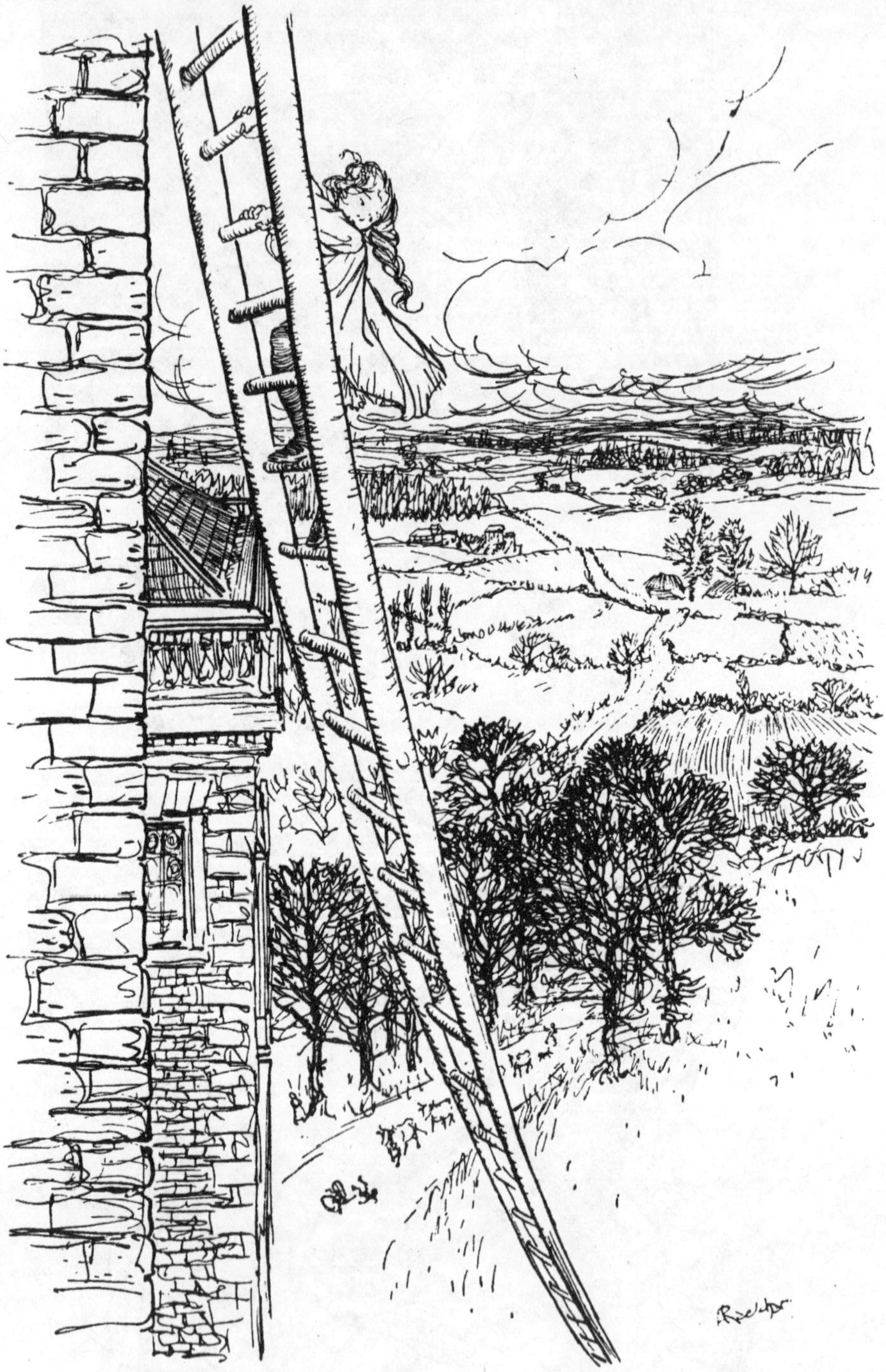

"It was a very, very long ladder"

THE RAINBOW BOOK, 1909

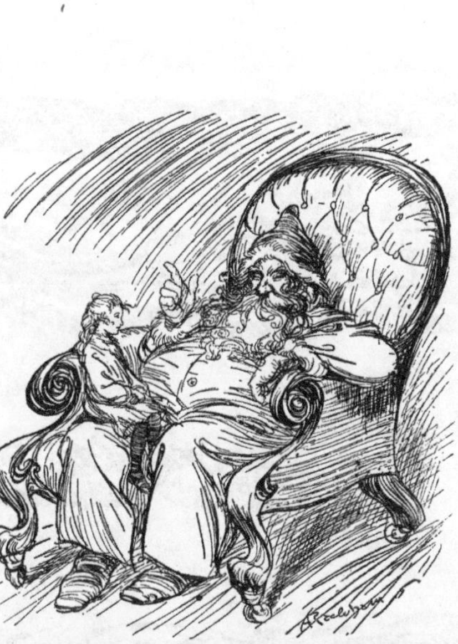

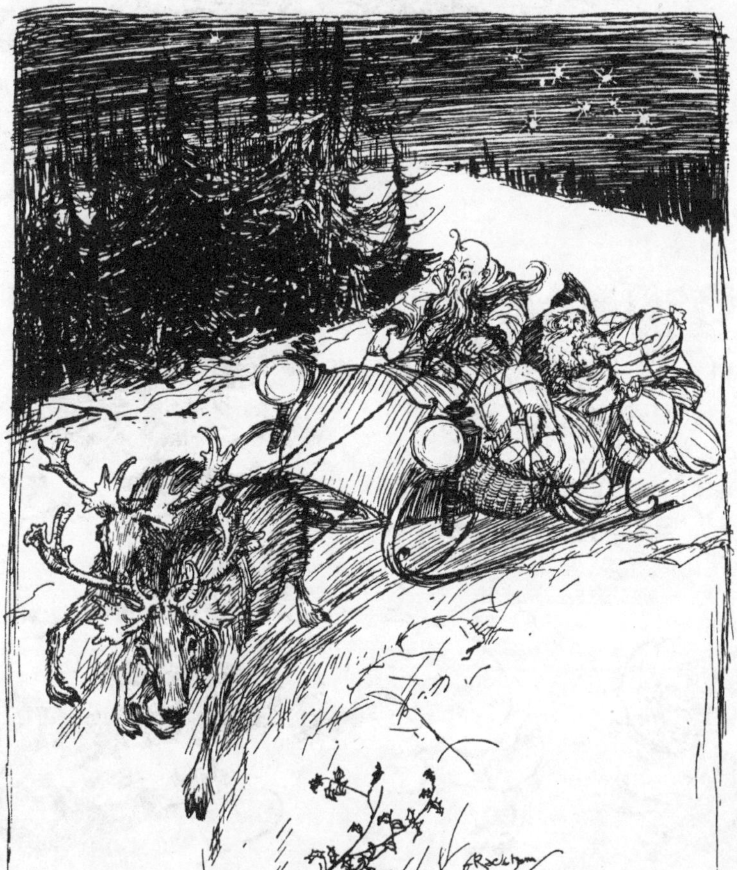

The Rainbow Book, 1909

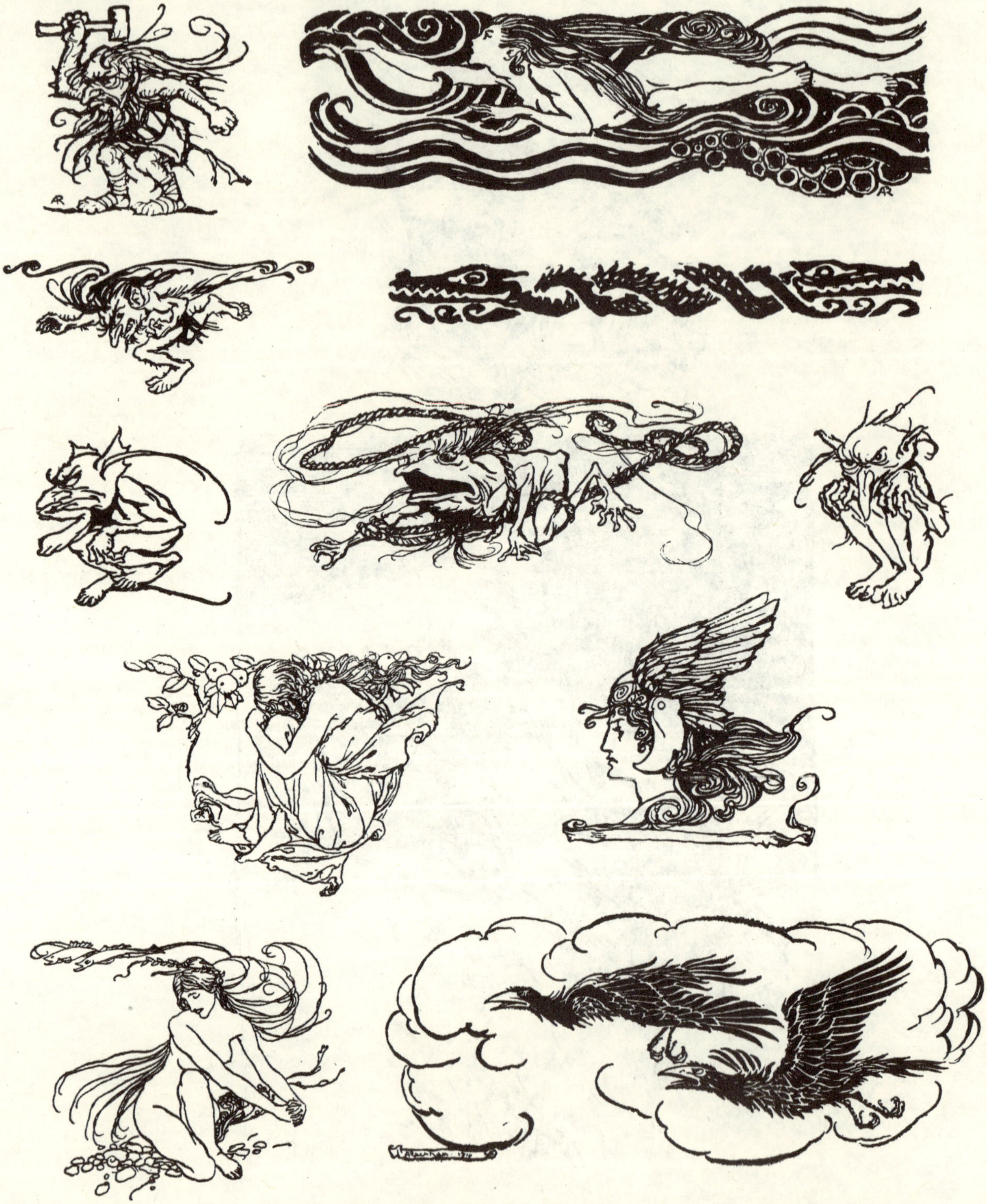

The Rhinegold and the Valkyrie, 1910

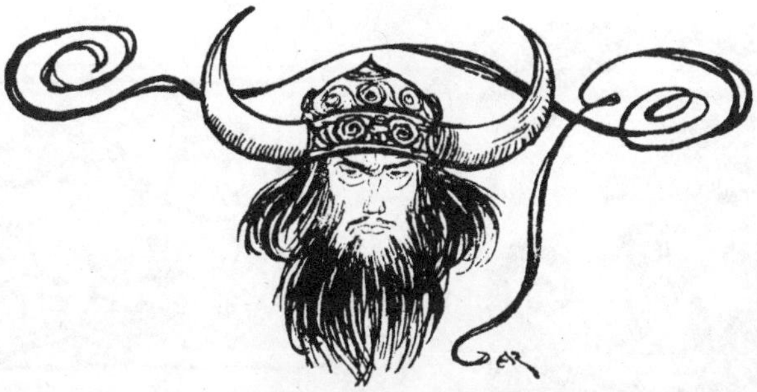

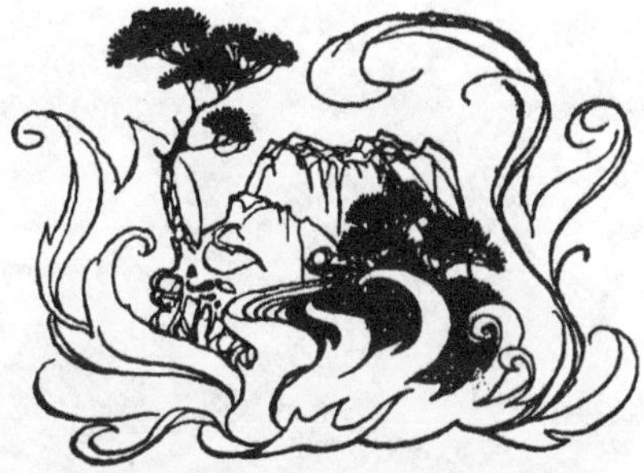

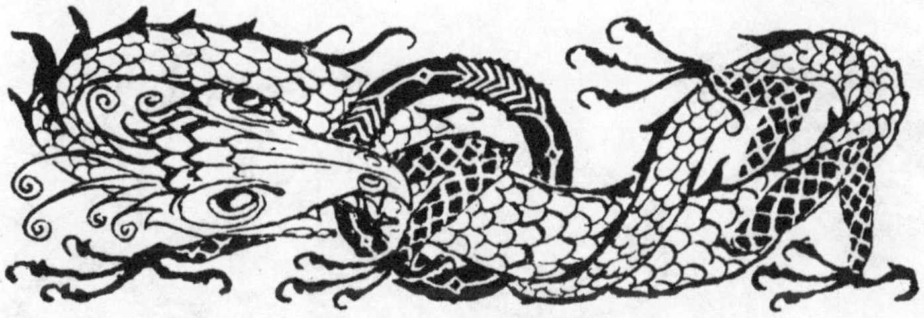

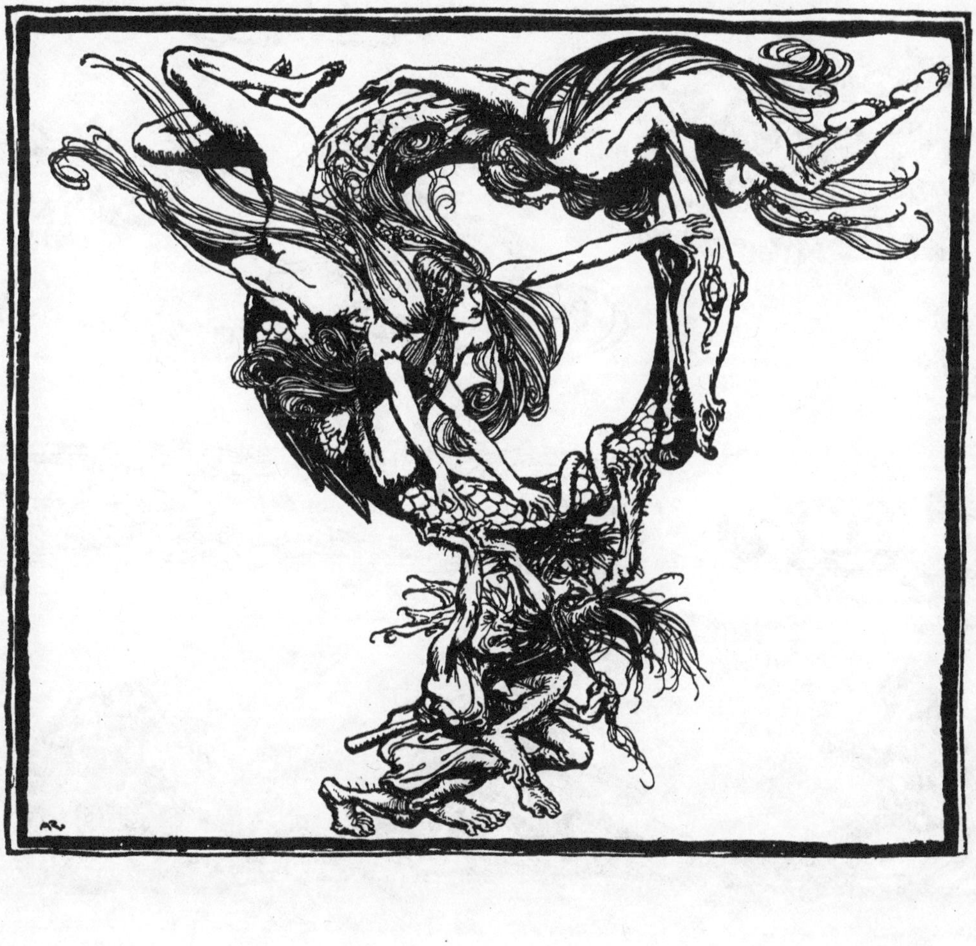

THE RHINEGOLD AND THE VALKYRIE, 1910

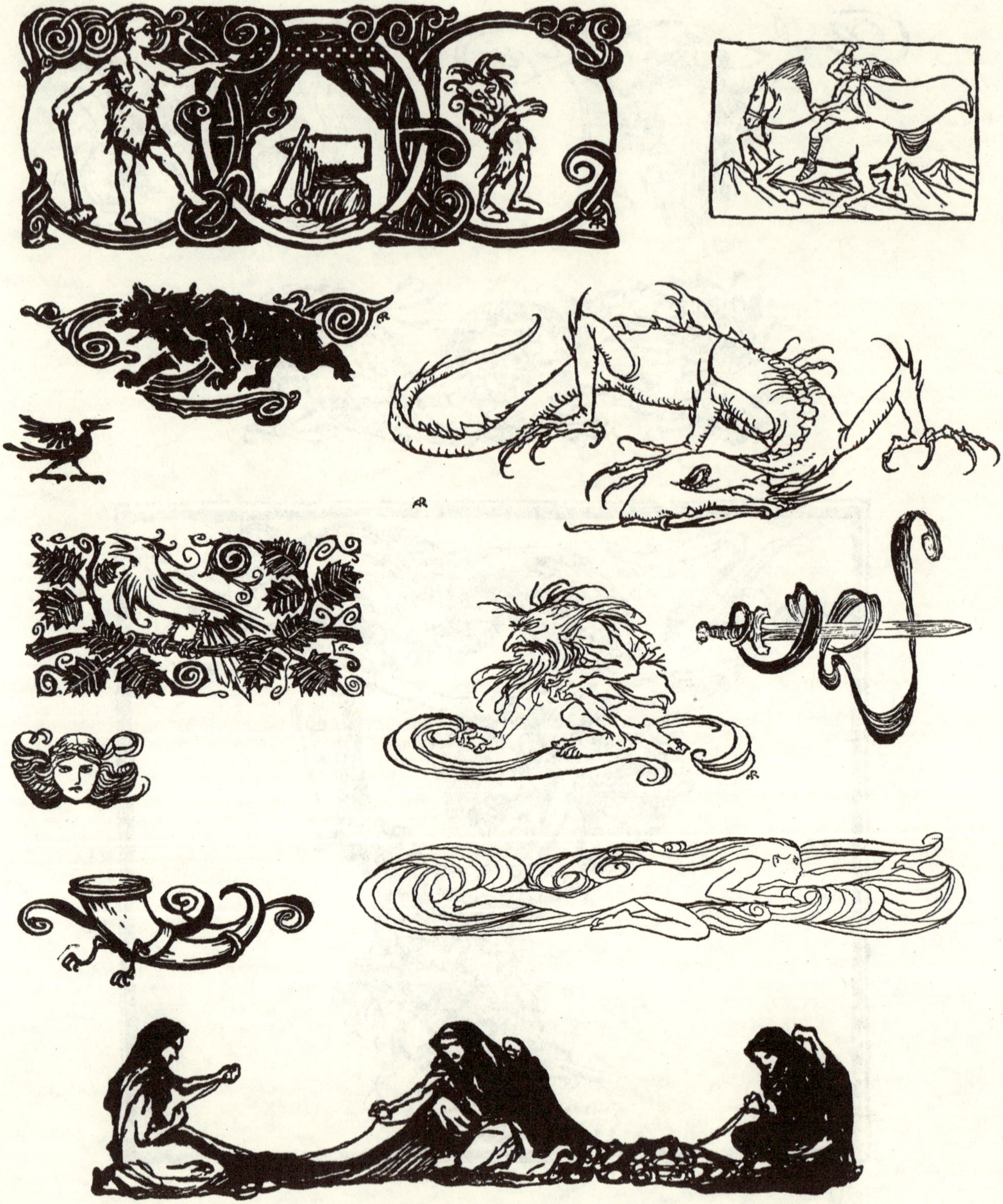

Siegfried and the Twilight of the Gods, 1911

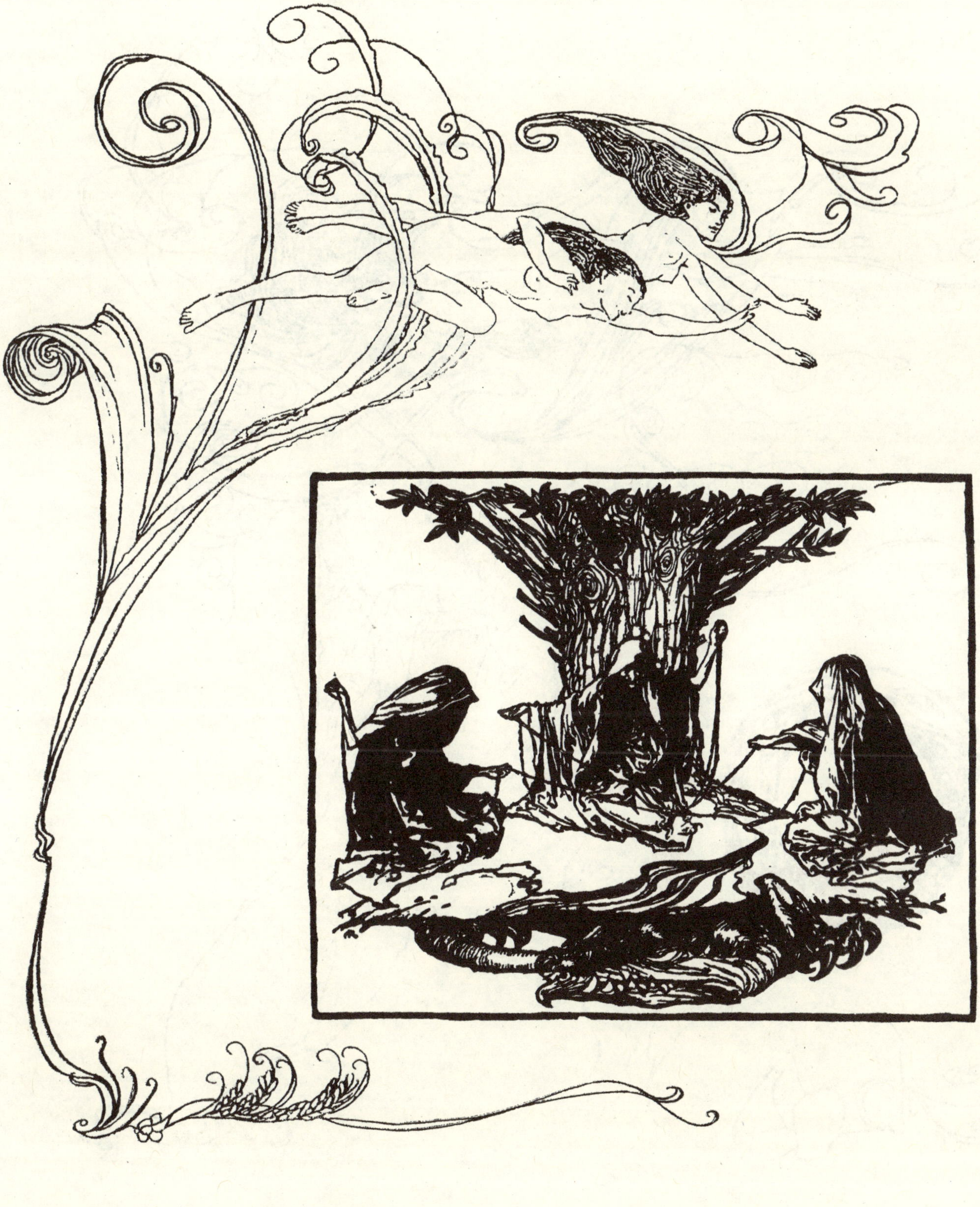

SIEGFRIED AND THE TWILIGHT OF THE GODS, 1911

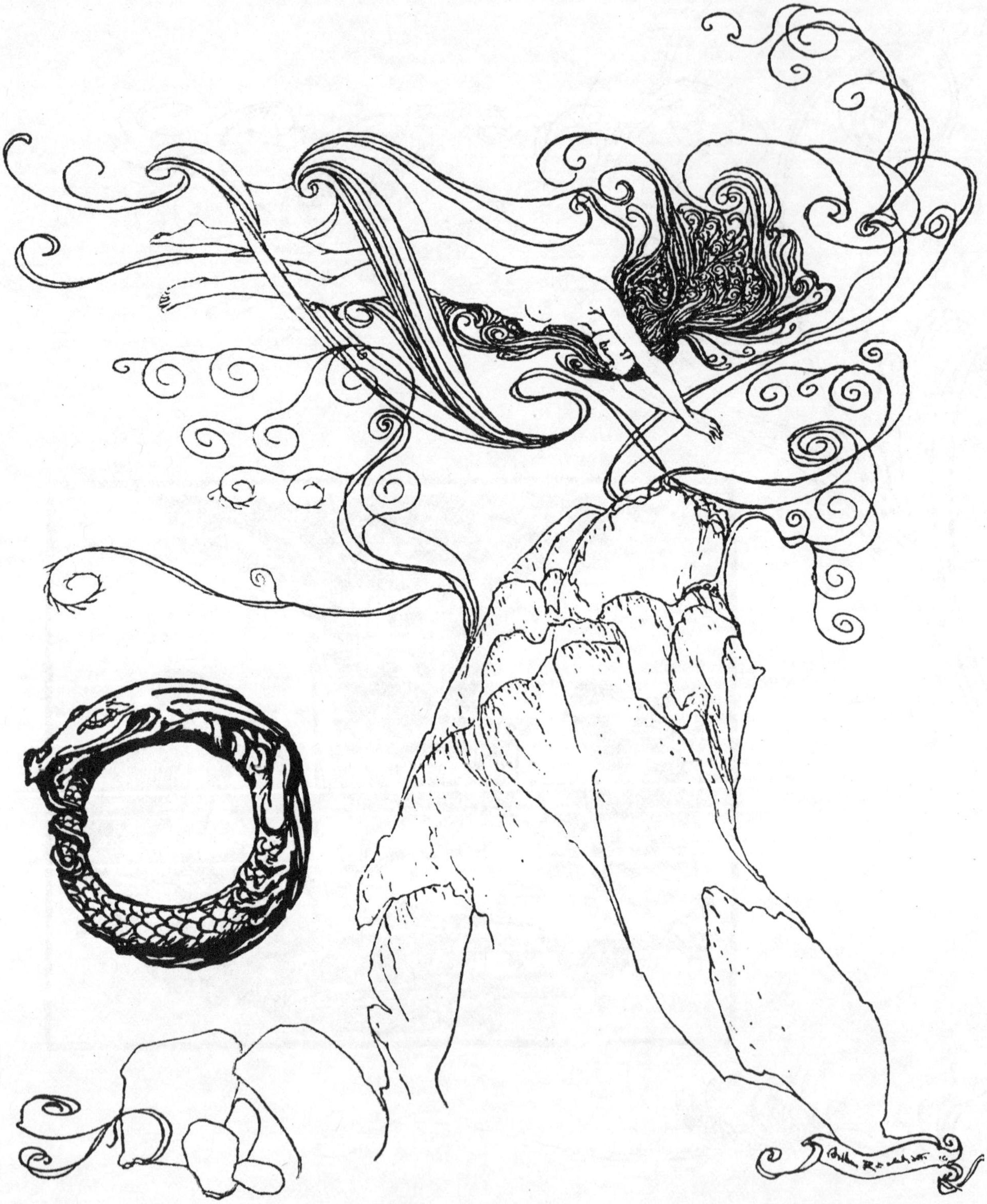

Siegfried and the Twilight of the Gods, 1911

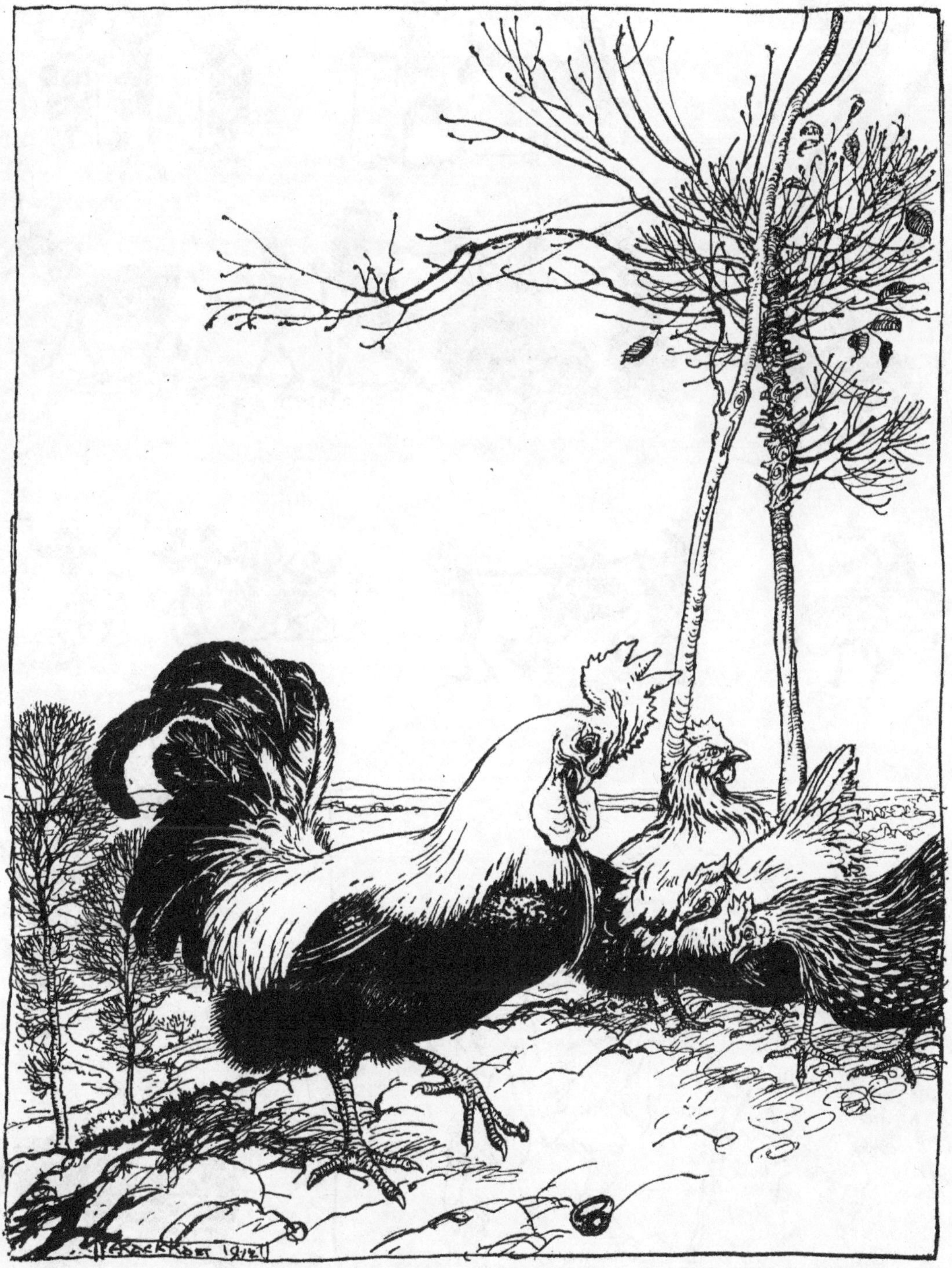

The Cock and the Jewel

Aesop's Fables, 1912

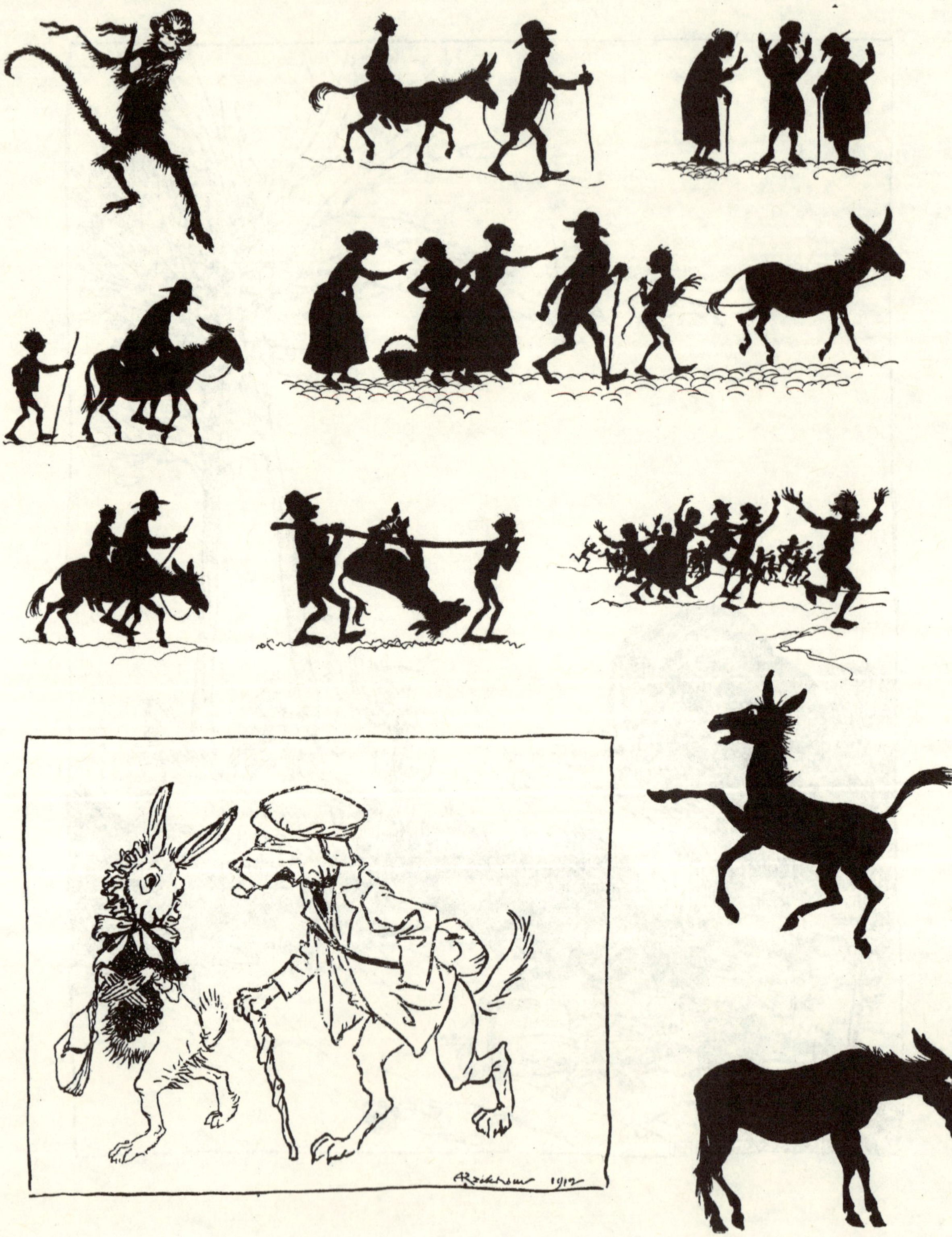

Aesop's Fables, 1912

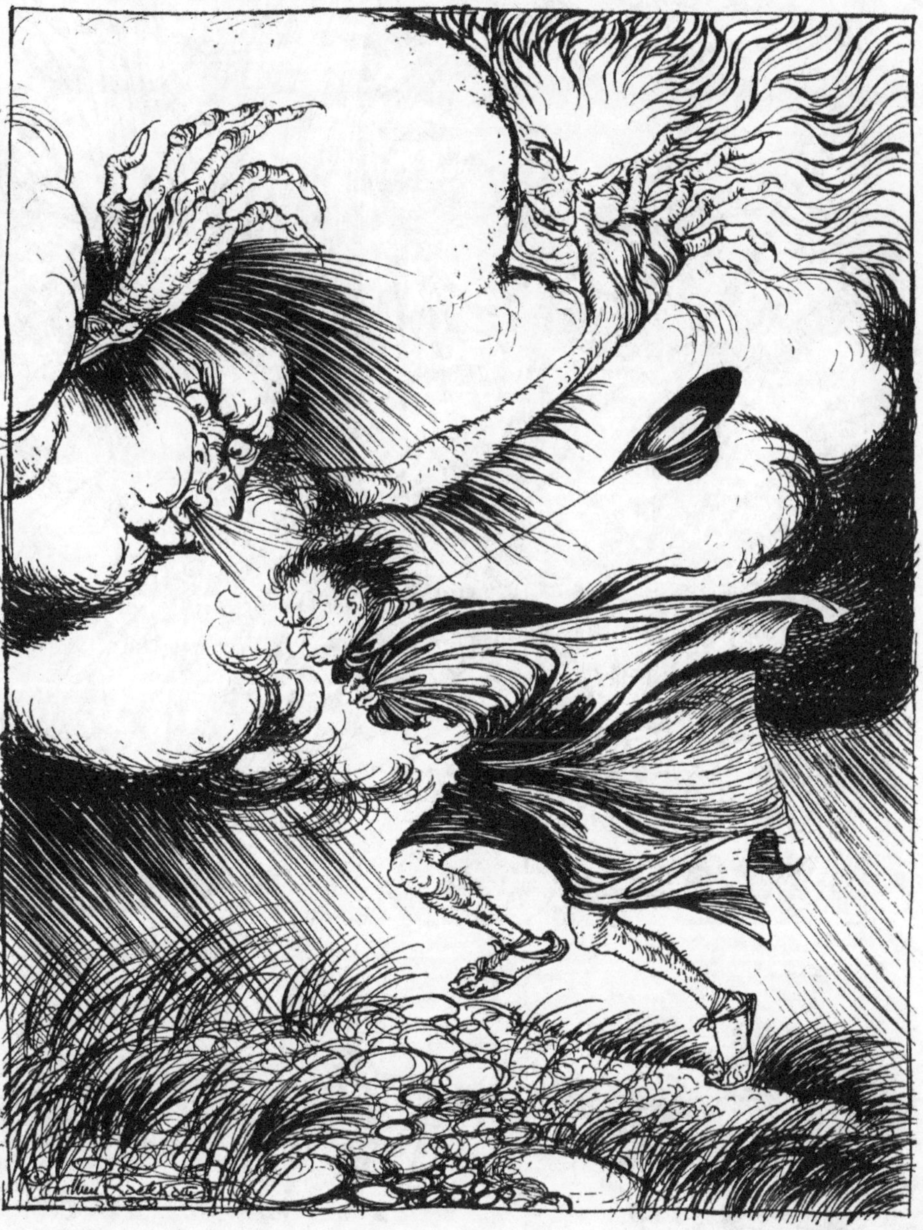

Aesop's Fables, 1912

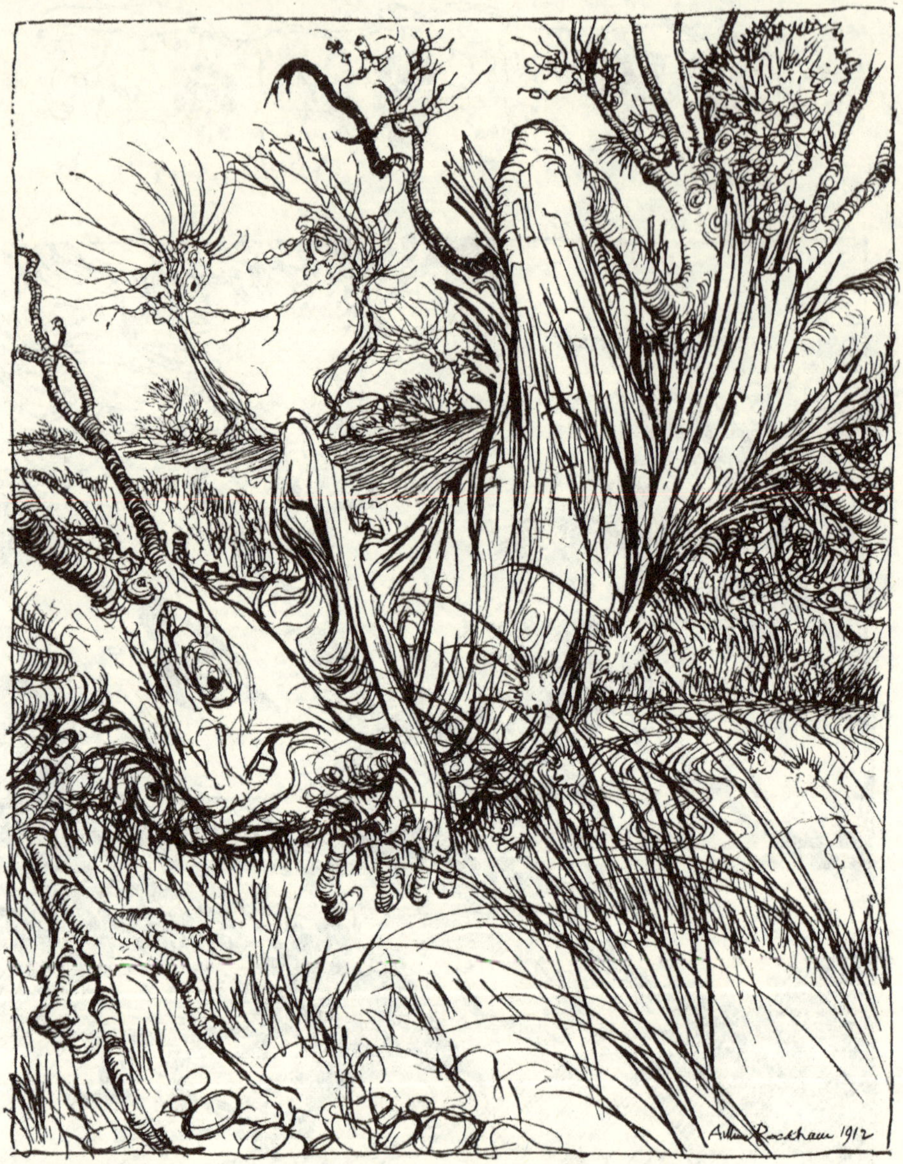

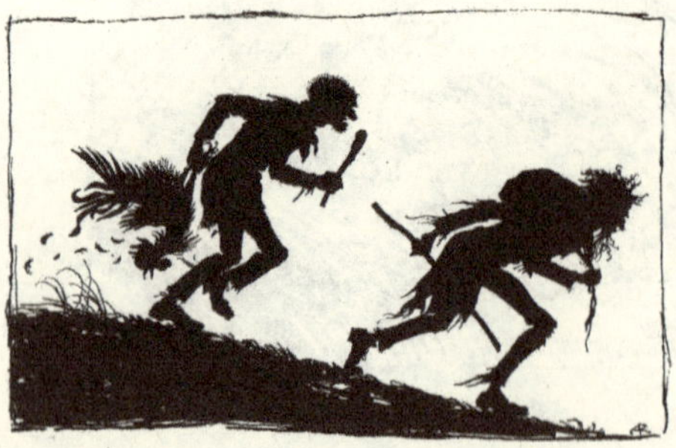

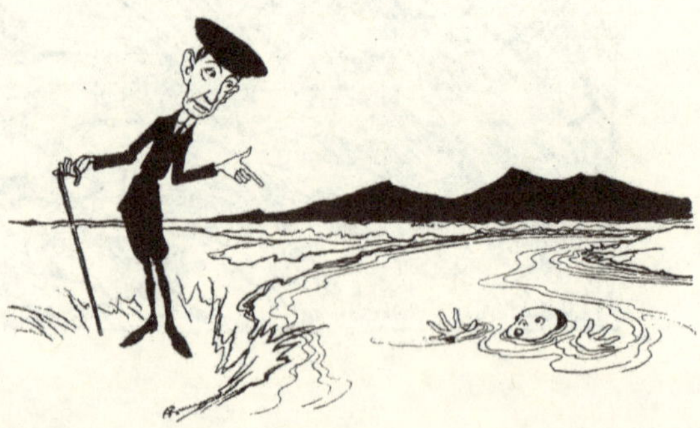

Aesop's Fables, 1912

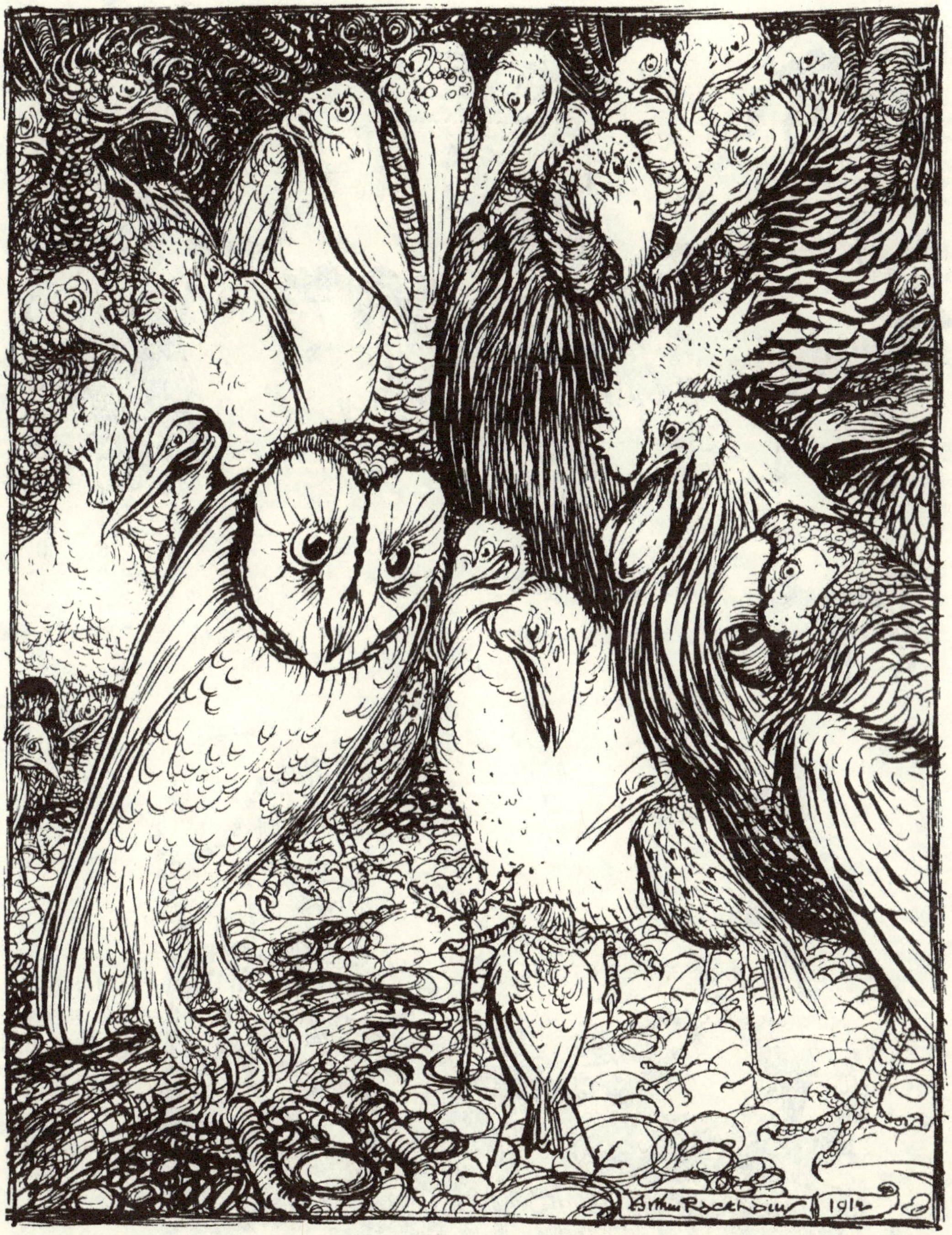

The Owl and the Birds

Aesop's Fables, 1912

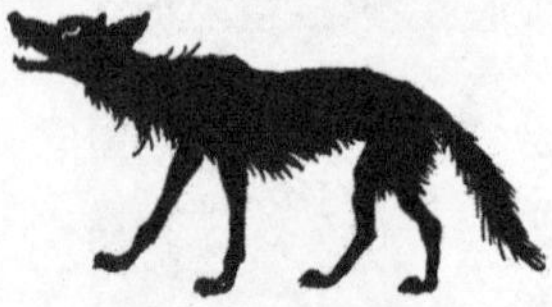

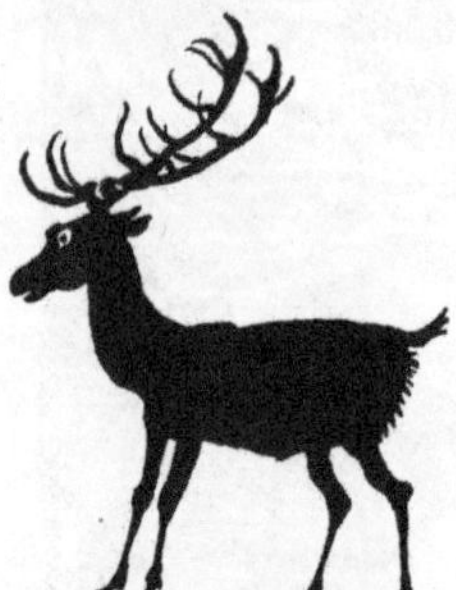

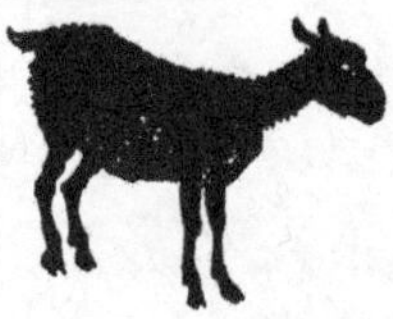

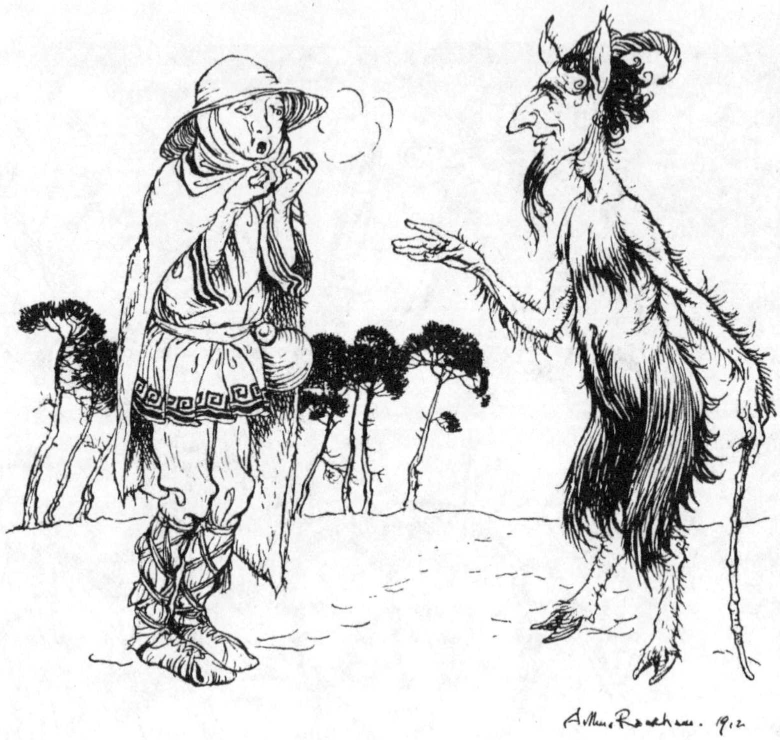

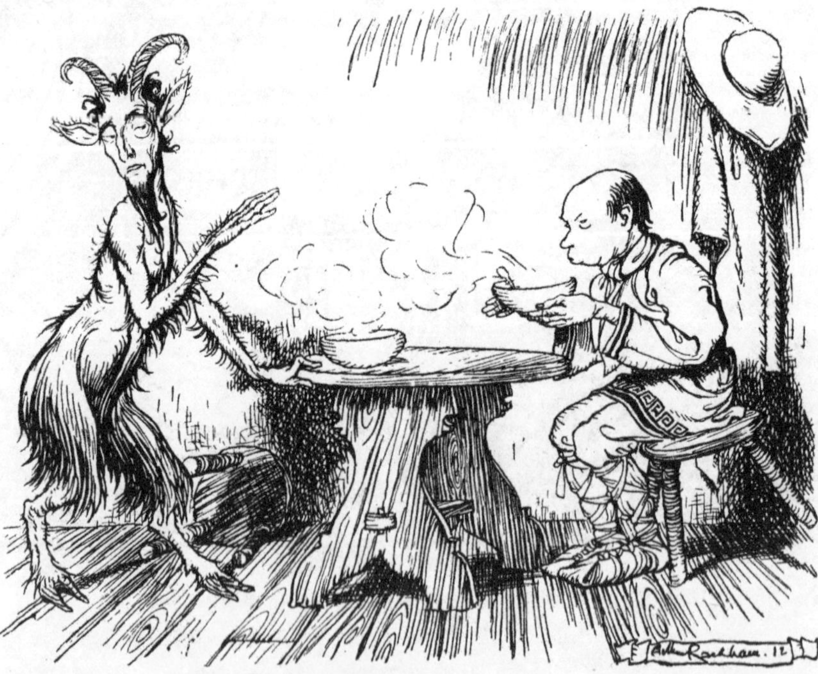

Aesop's Fables, 1912

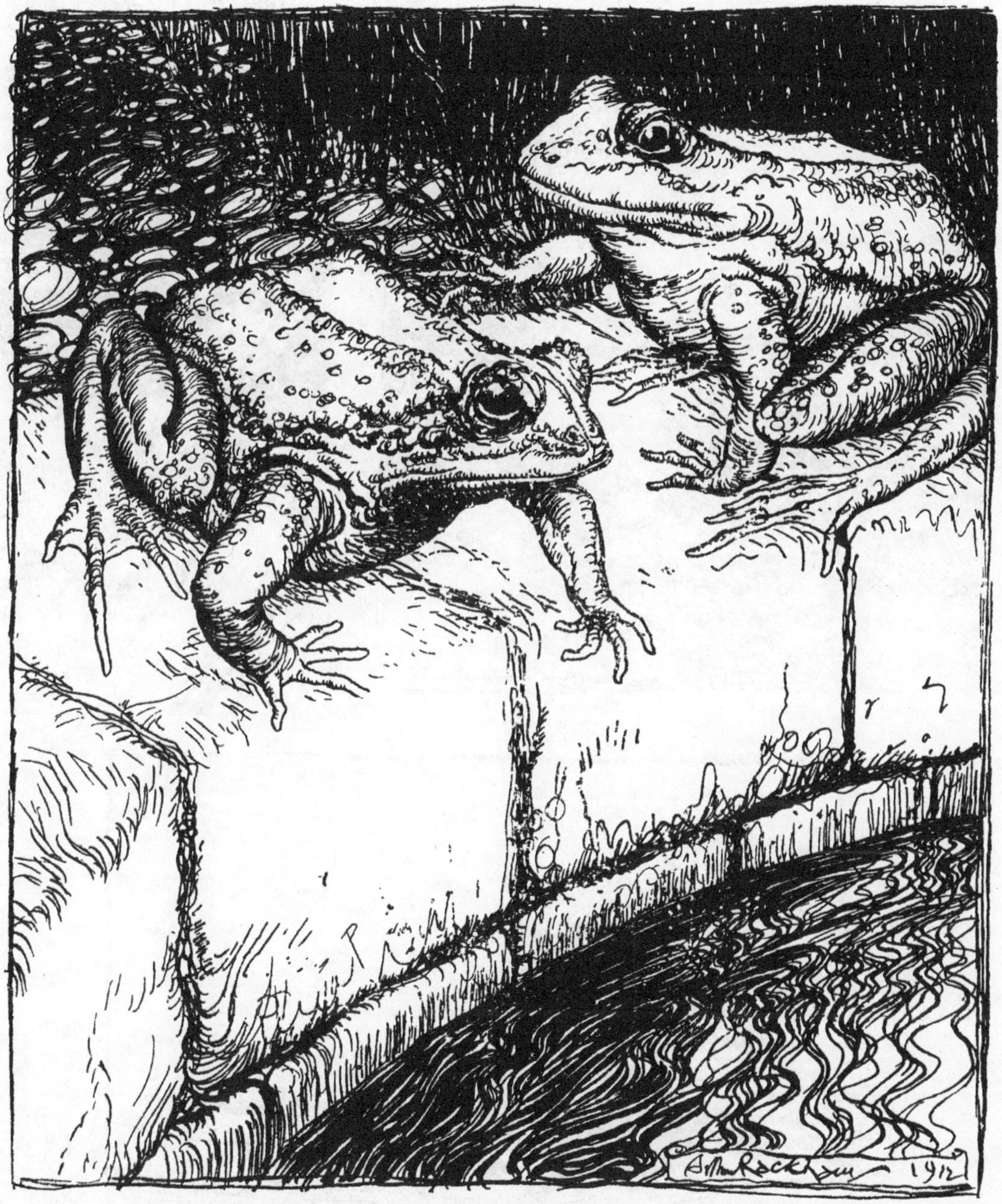

The Frogs and the Well

AESOP'S FABLES, 1912

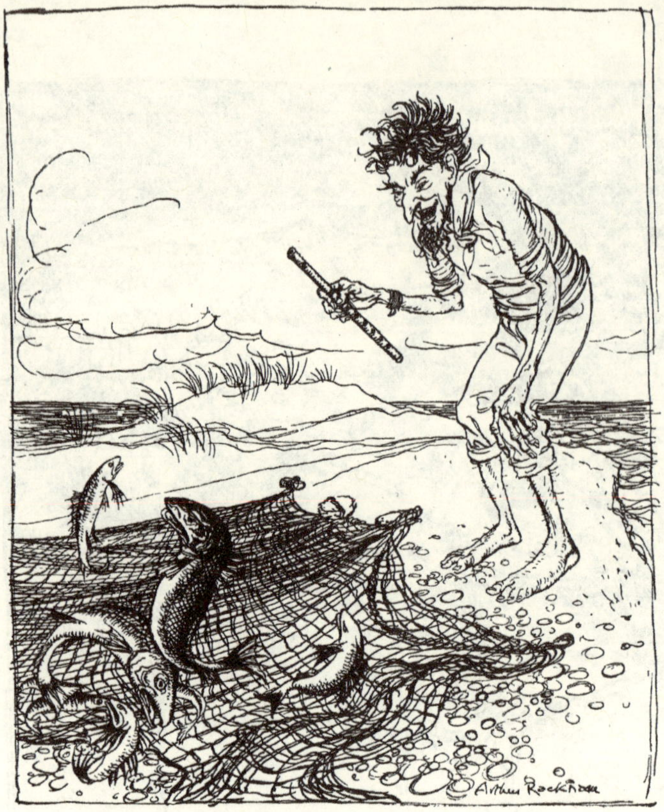

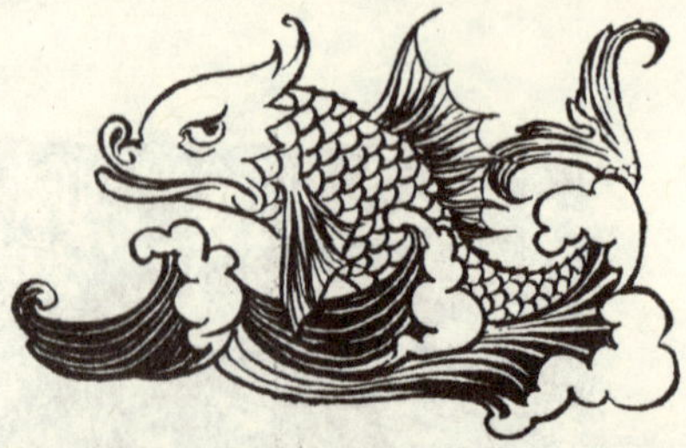

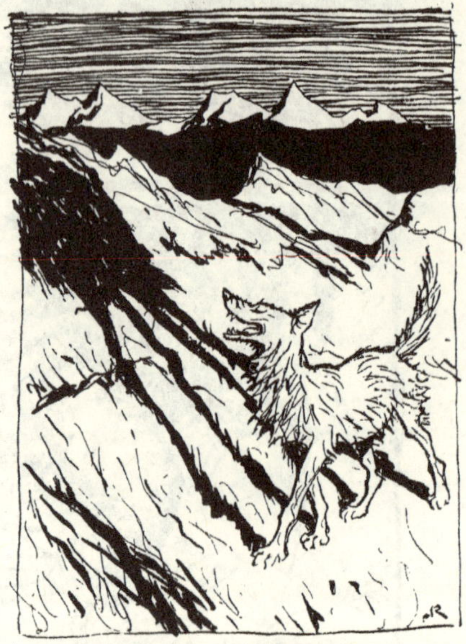

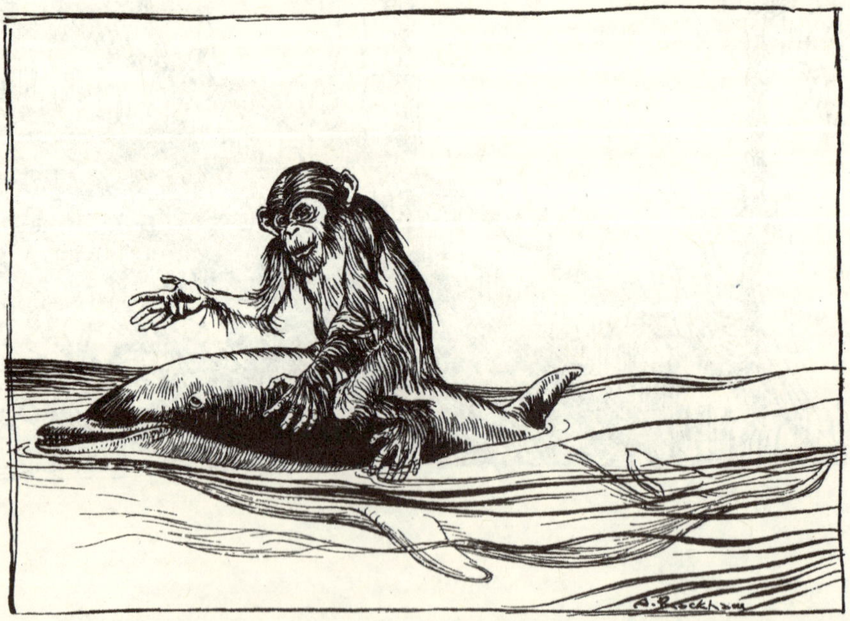

Aesop's Fables, 1912

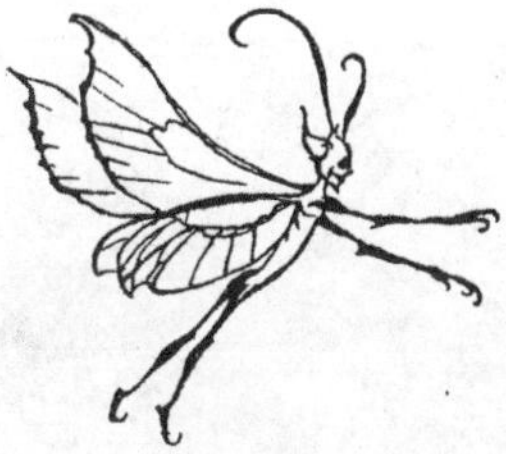

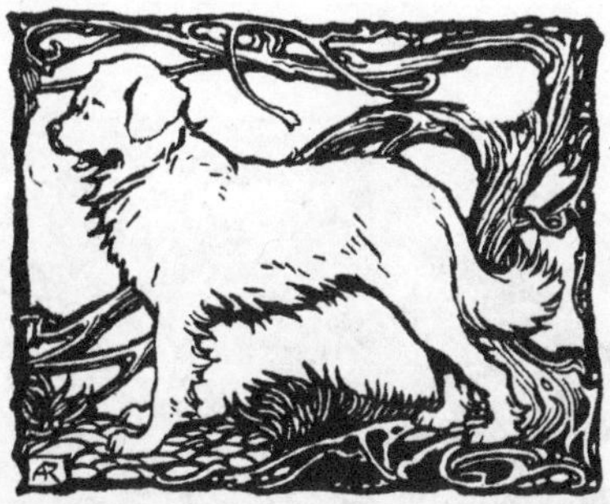

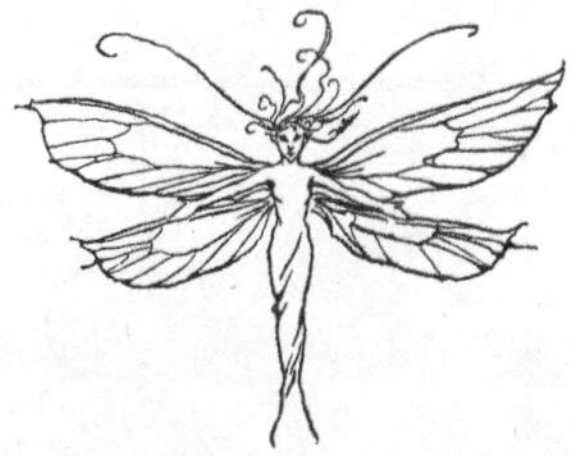

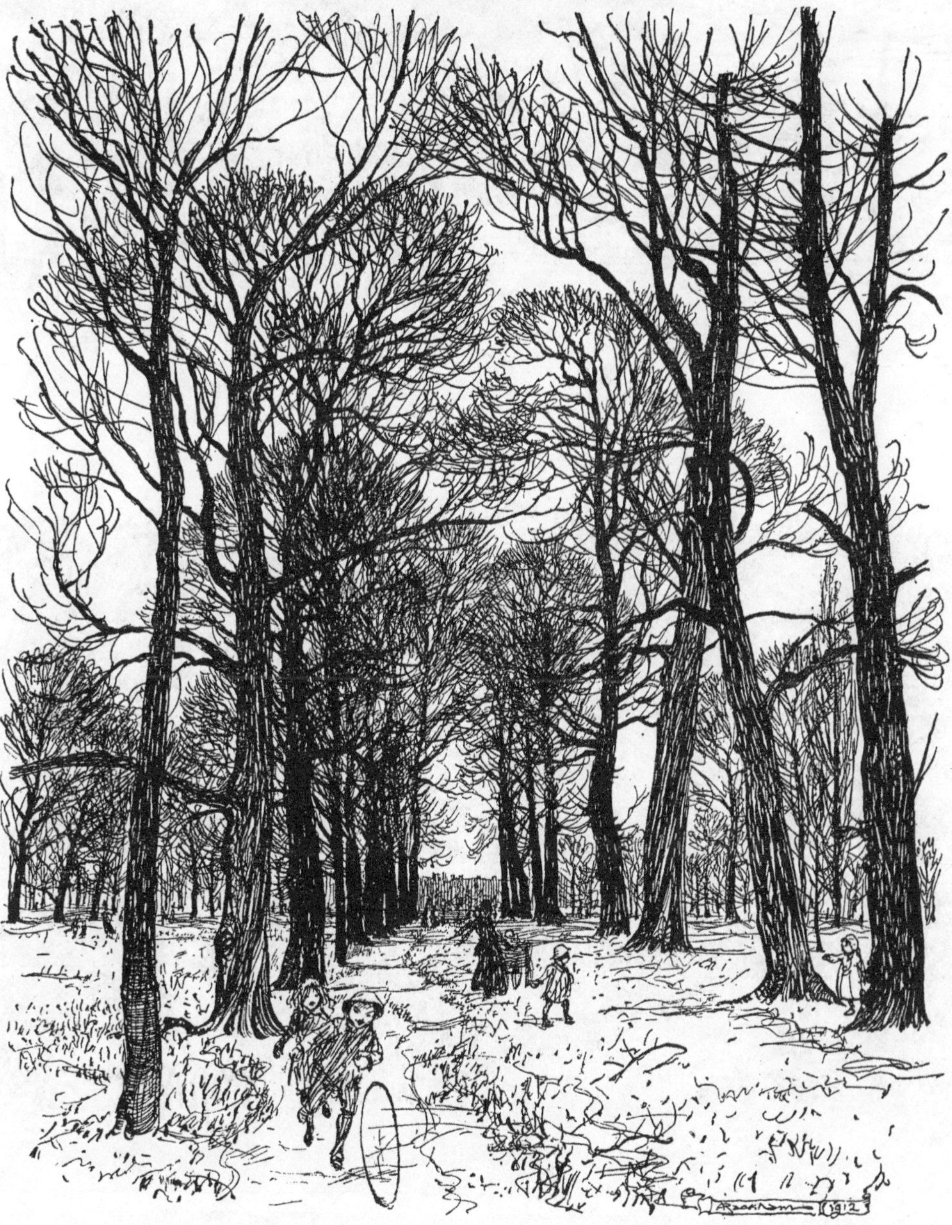

Peter Pan in Kensington Gardens, 1912

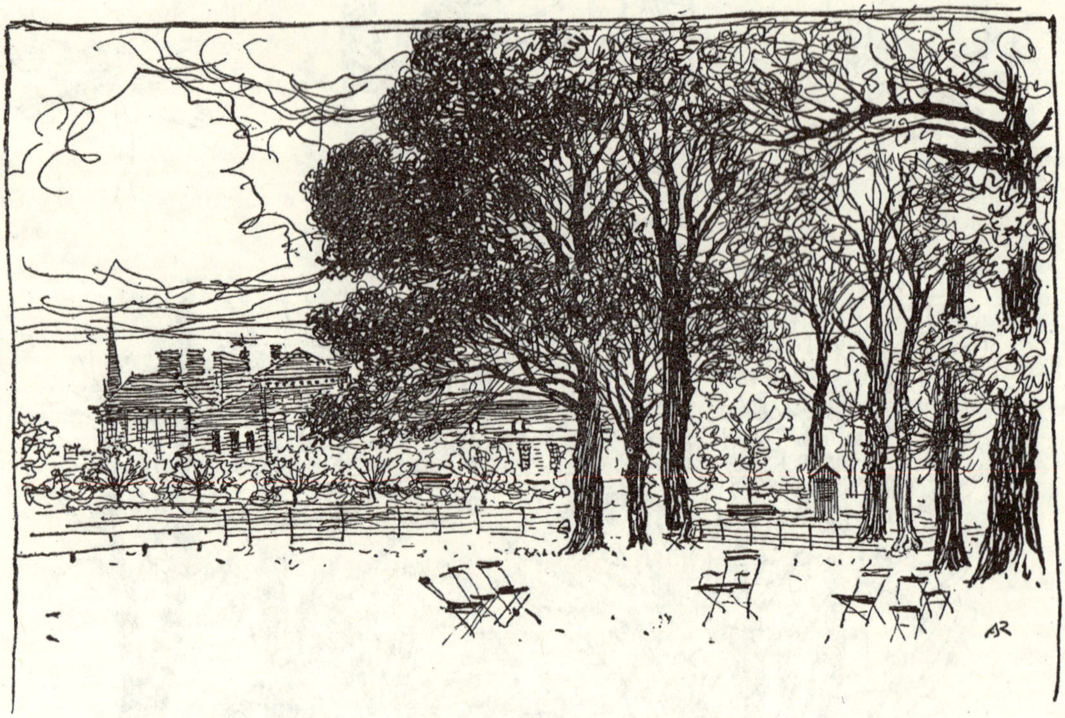

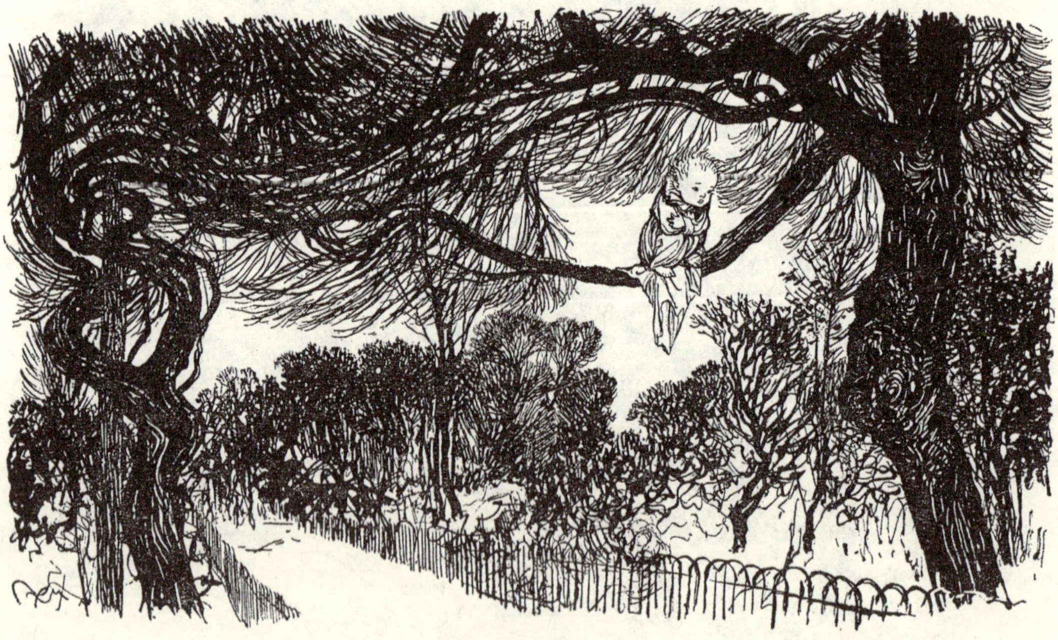

Peter Pan in Kensington Gardens, 1912

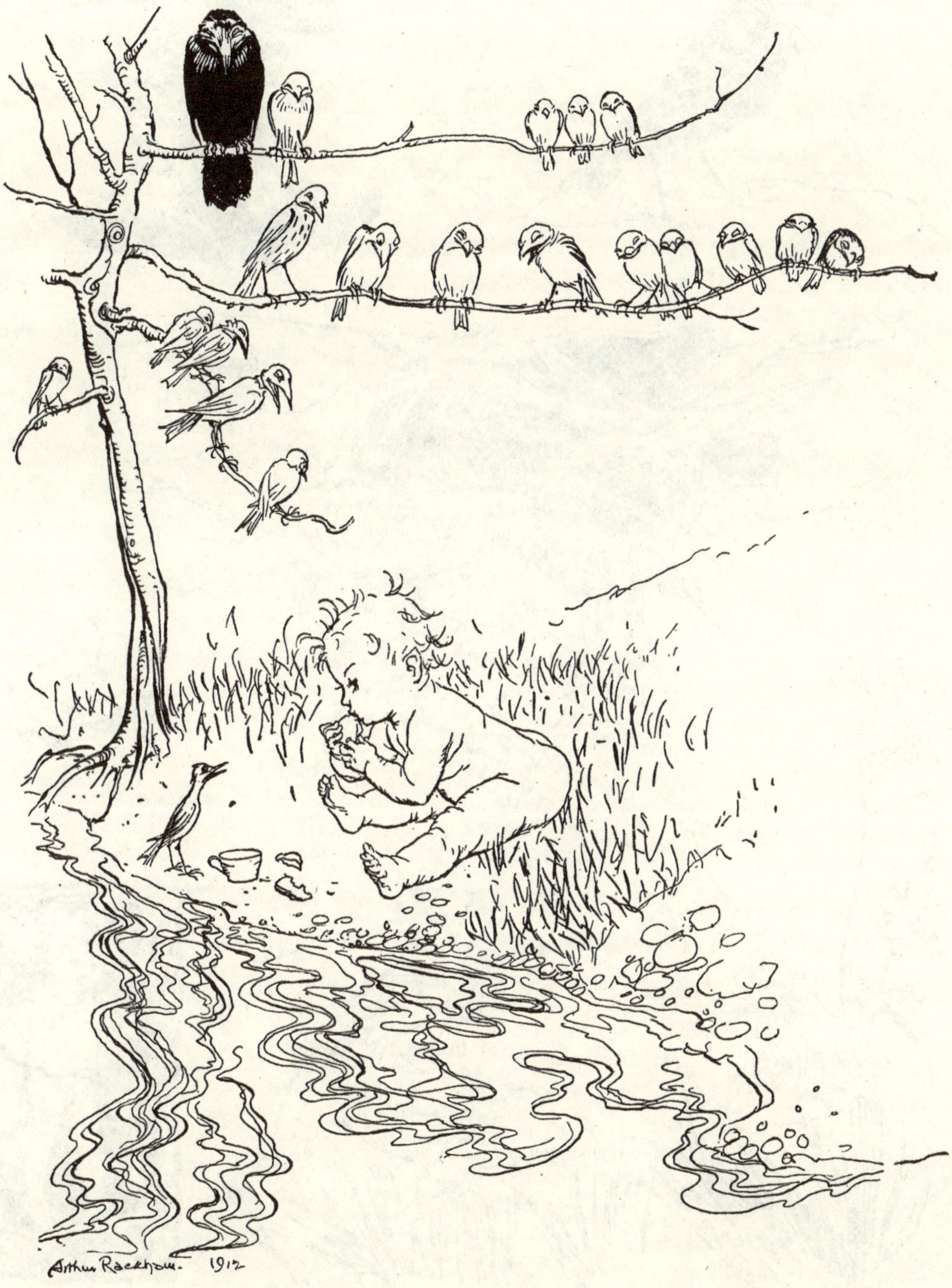

"The birds on the island never got used to him. His oddities tickled them every day."

Peter Pan in Kensington Gardens, 1912

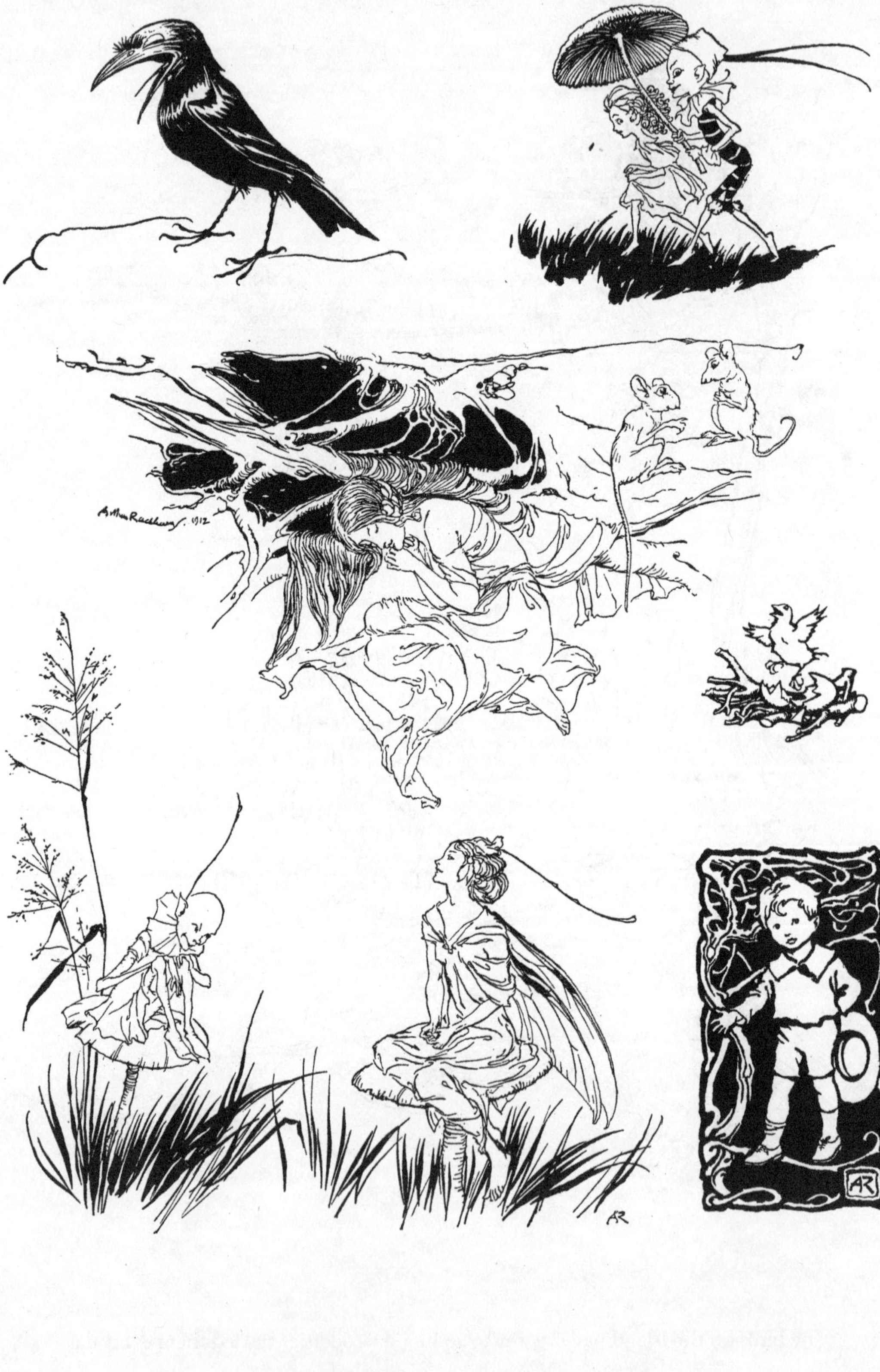

Peter Pan in Kensington Gardens, 1912

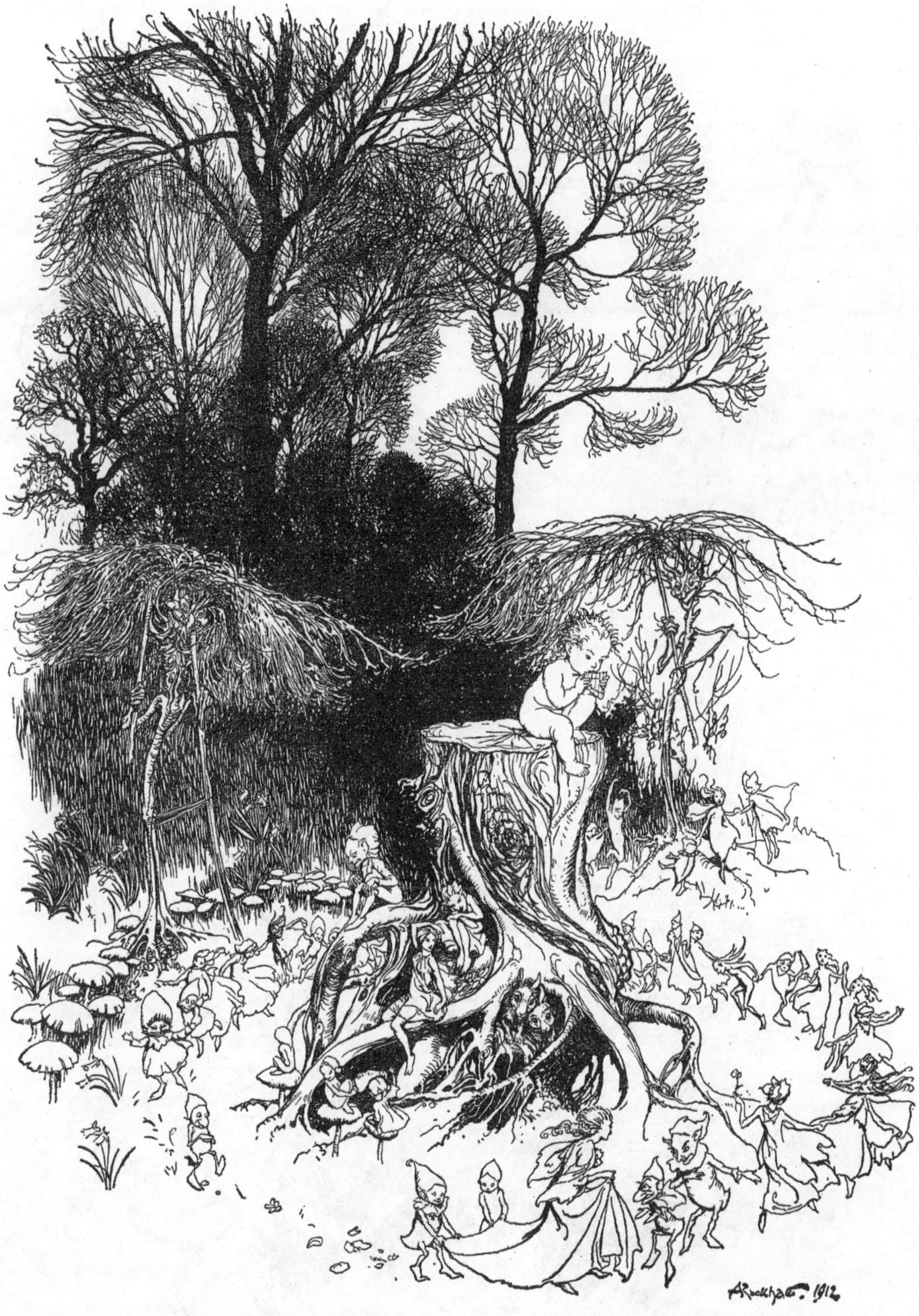

"A Fairy Ring"

Peter Pan in Kensington Gardens, 1912

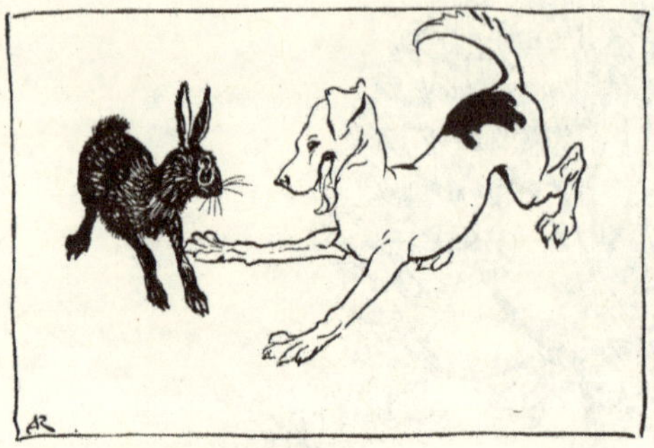

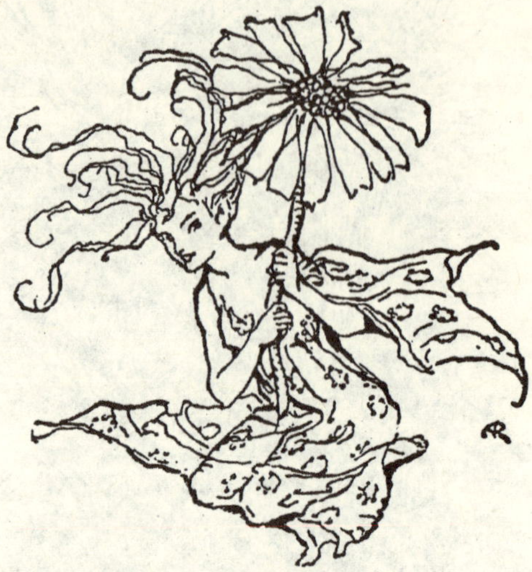

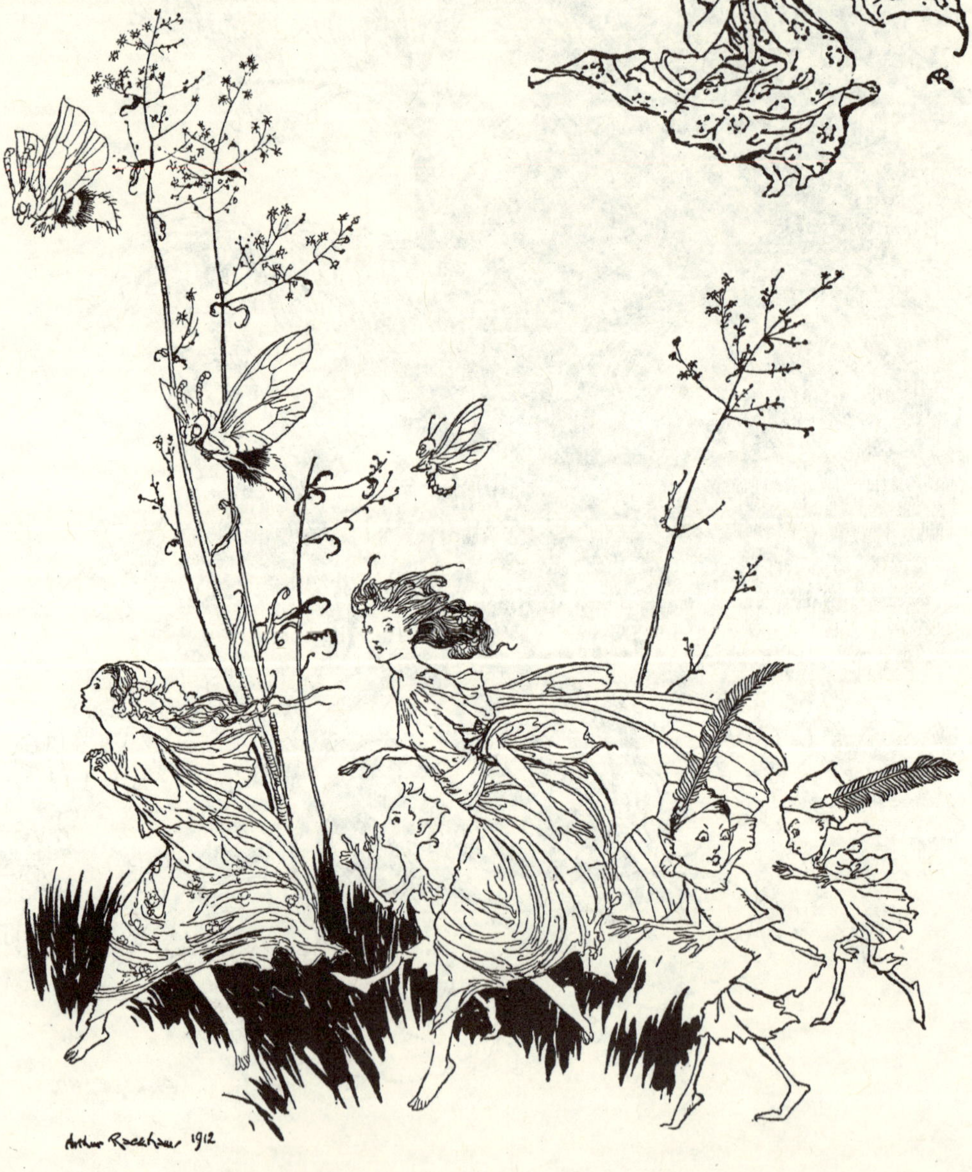

Peter Pan in Kensington Gardens, 1912

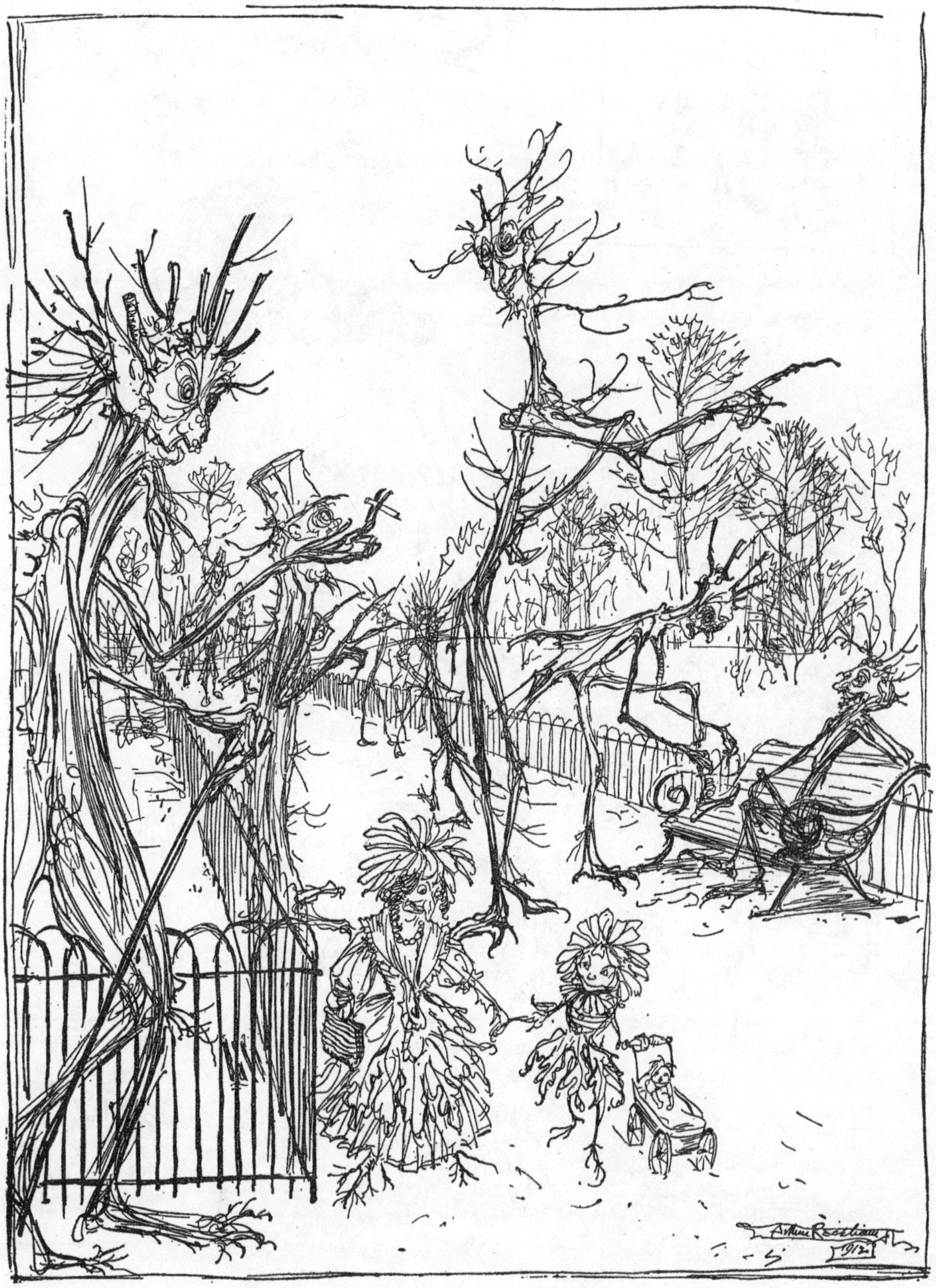

"There was a good deal going on in the baby walk"

PETER PAN IN KENSINGTON GARDENS, 1912

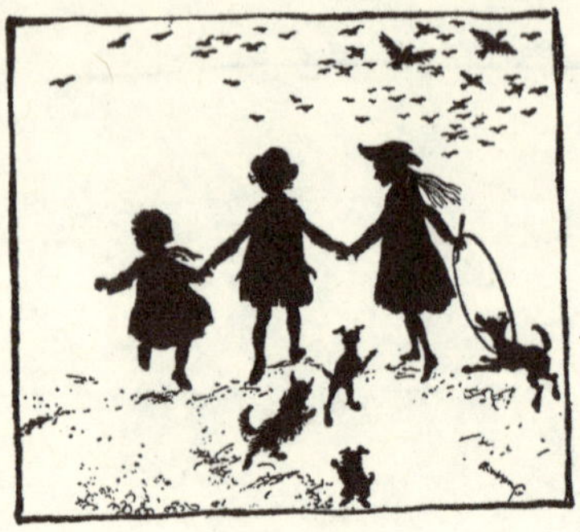

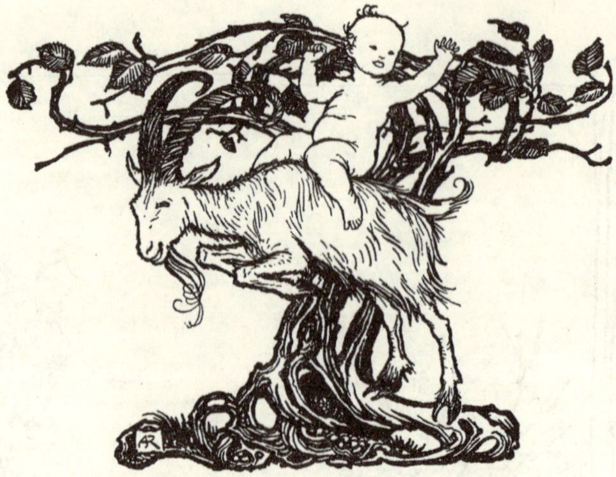

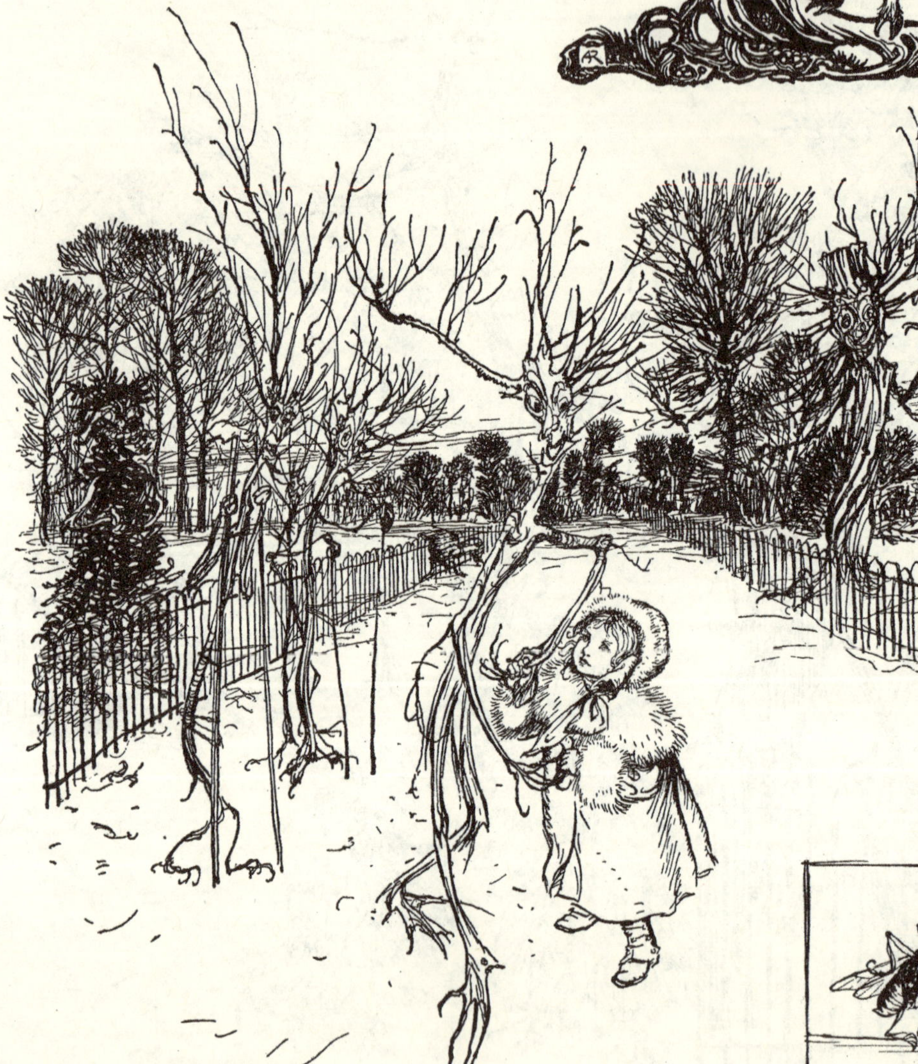

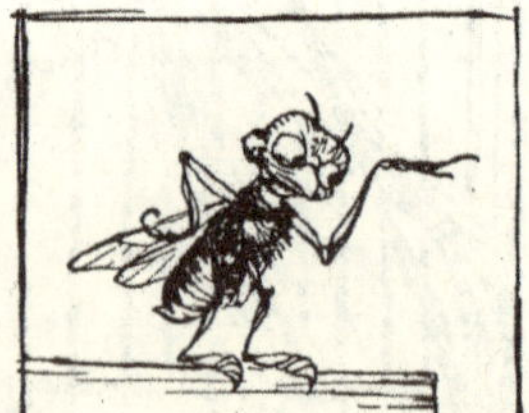

Peter Pan in Kensington Gardens, 1912

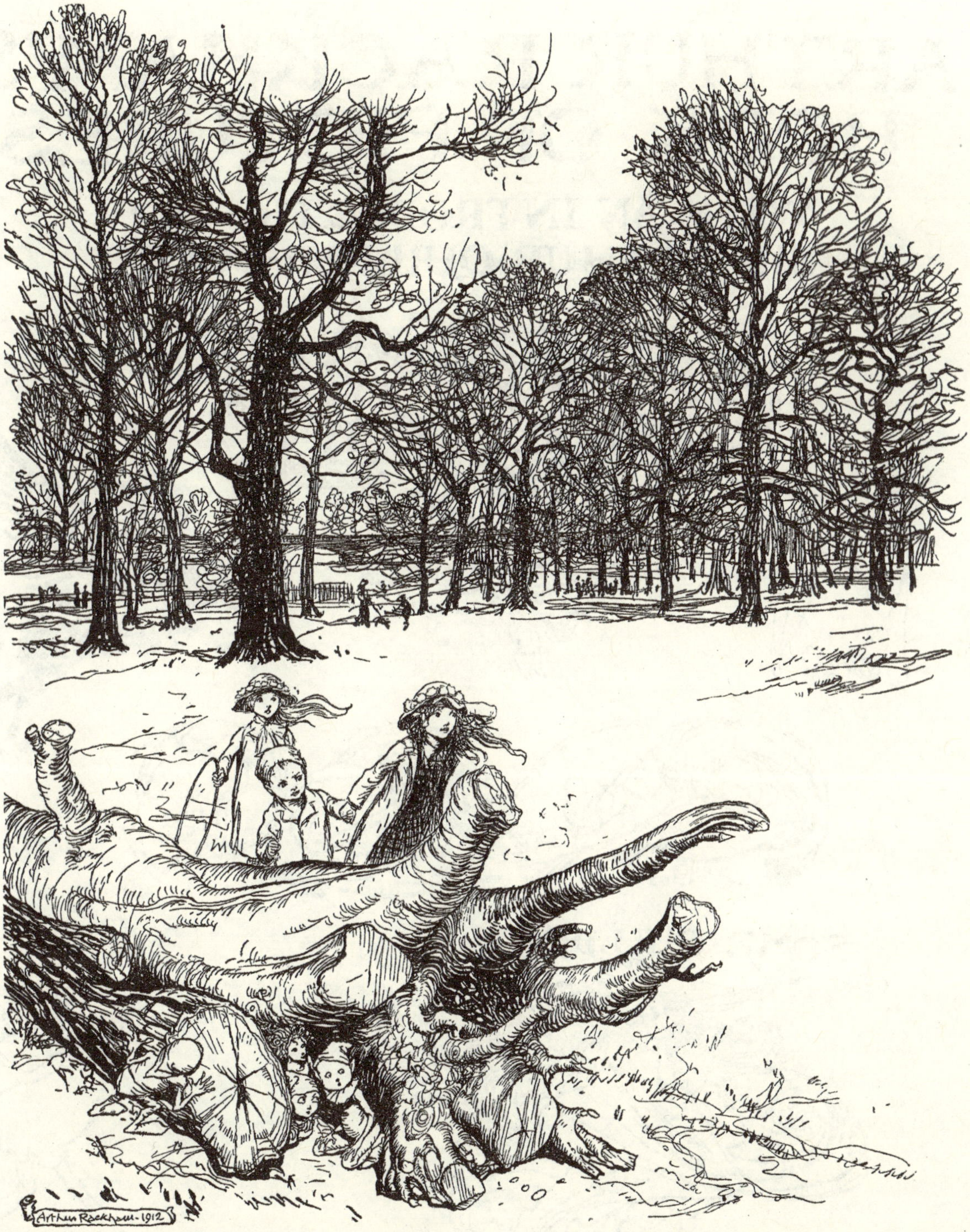

"Kensington Gardens"

Peter Pan in Kensington Gardens, 1912

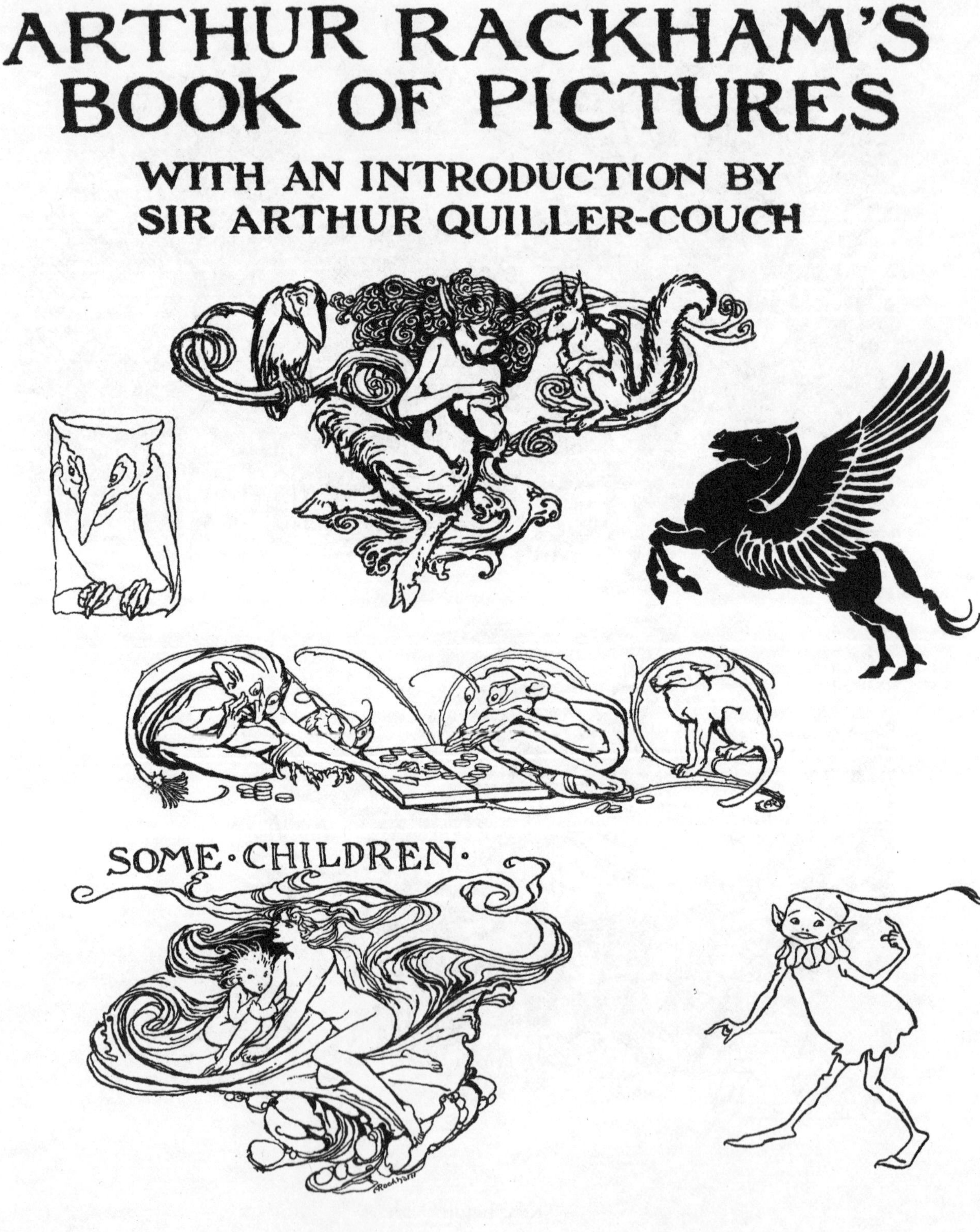
ARTHUR RACKHAM'S
BOOK OF PICTURES
WITH AN INTRODUCTION BY
SIR ARTHUR QUILLER-COUCH

SOME · CHILDREN ·

Arthur Rackham's Book of Pictures, 1913

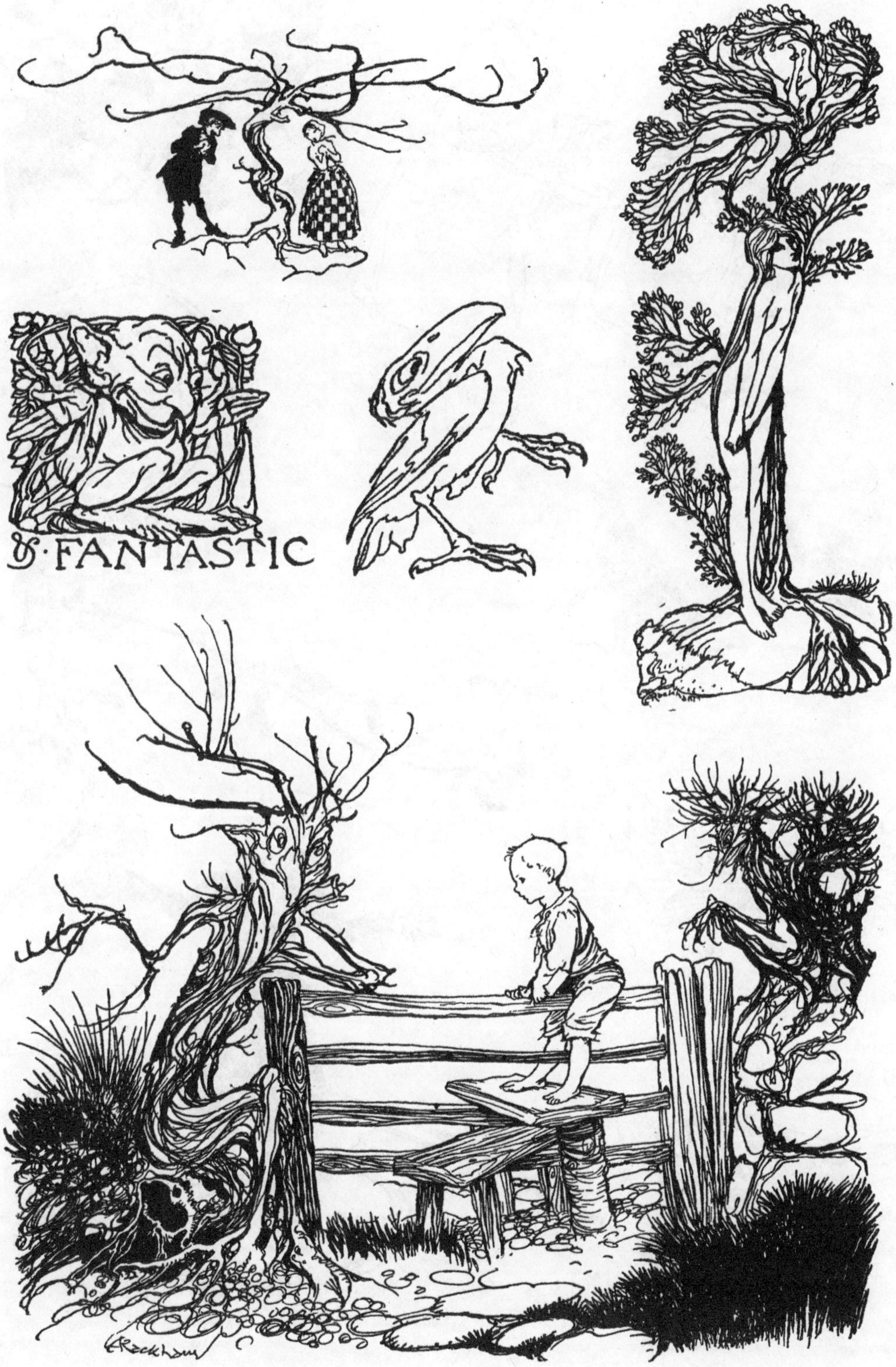

Arthur Rackham's Book of Pictures, 1913

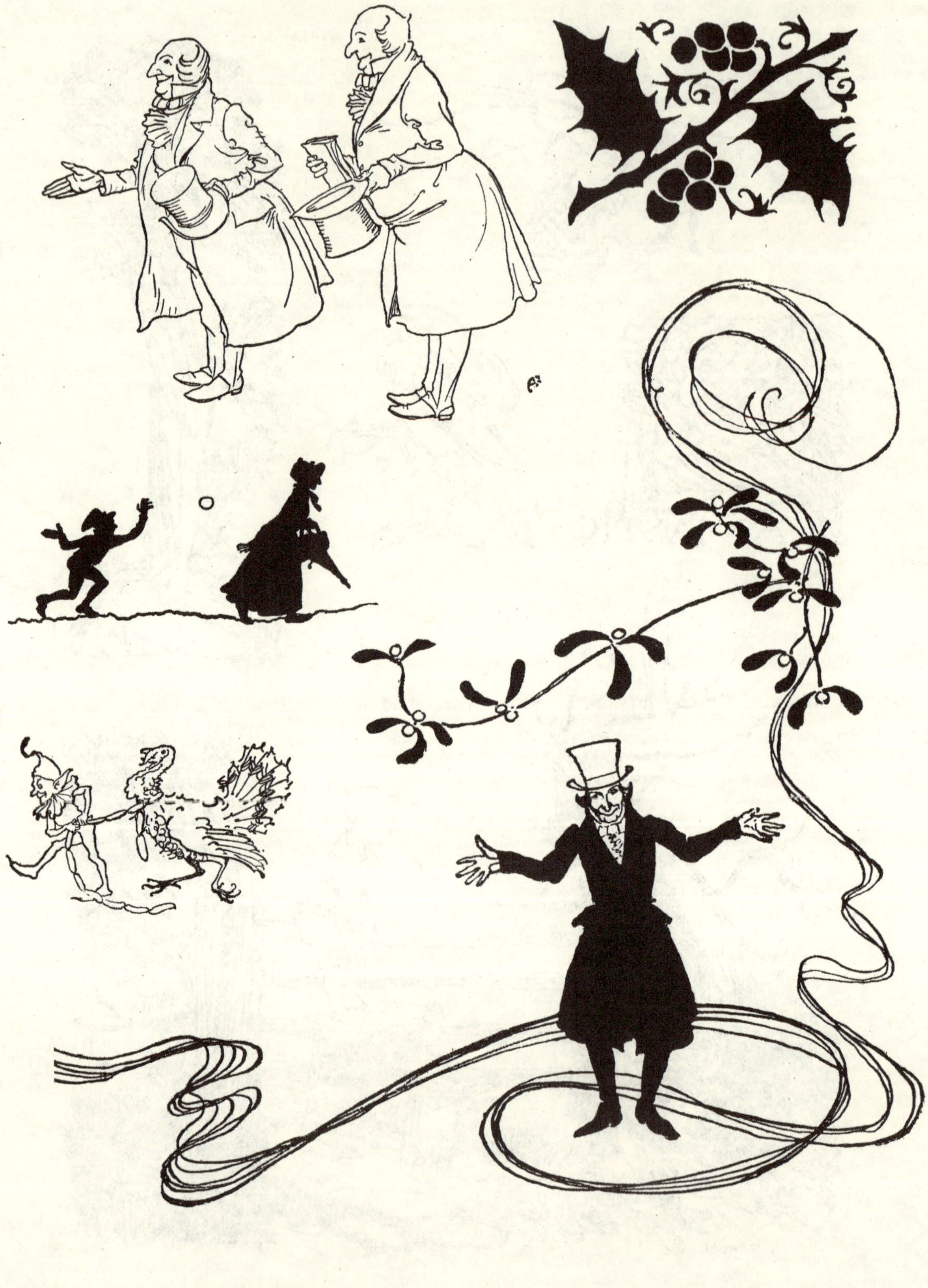

A Christmas Carol, 1915

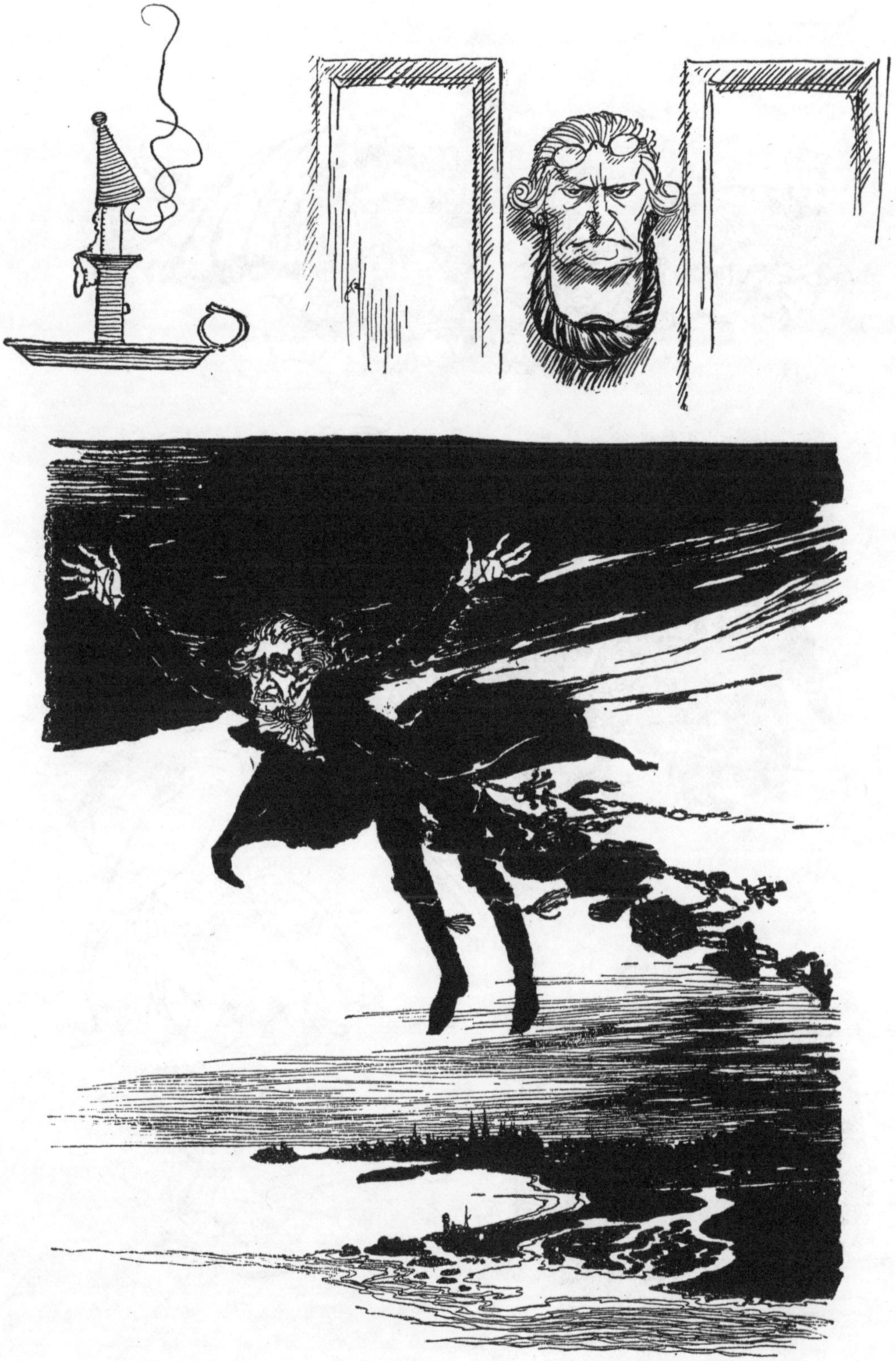

A Christmas Carol, 1915

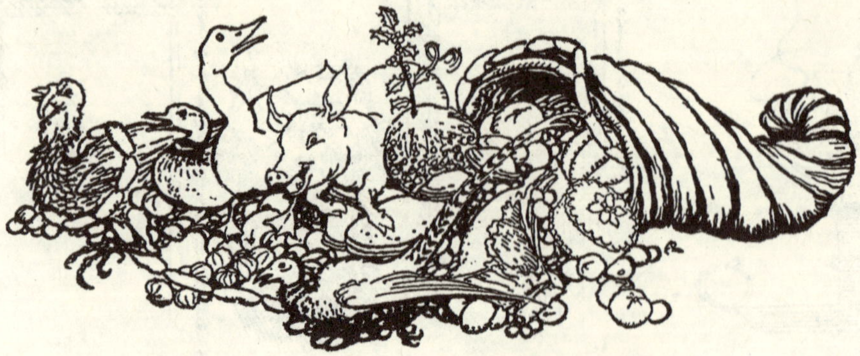

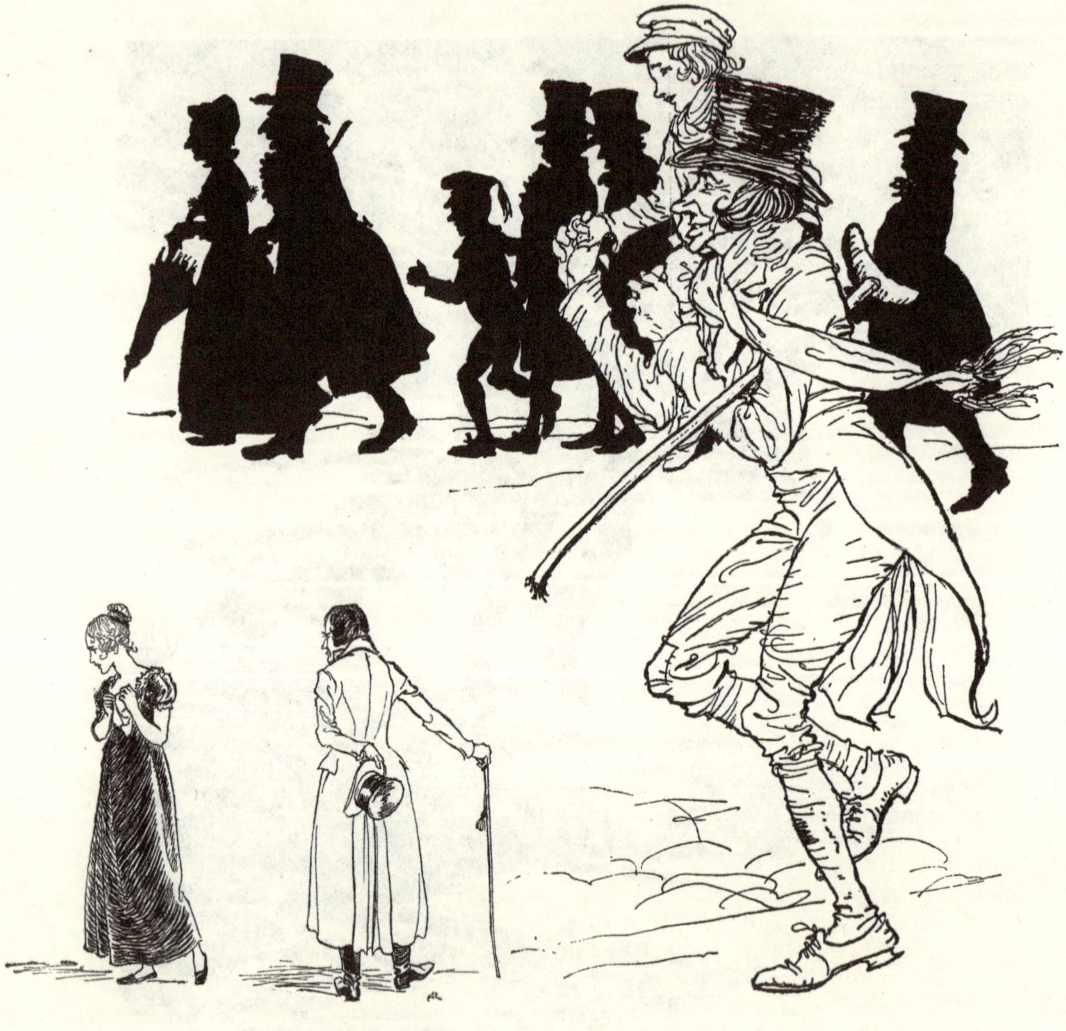

A Christmas Carol, 1915

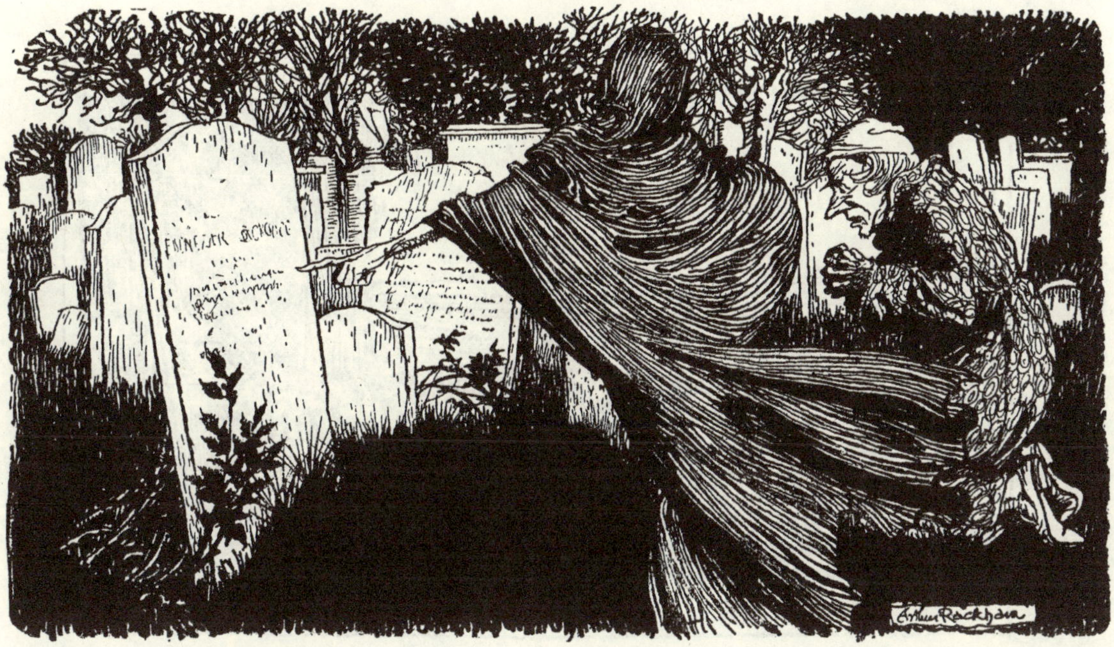

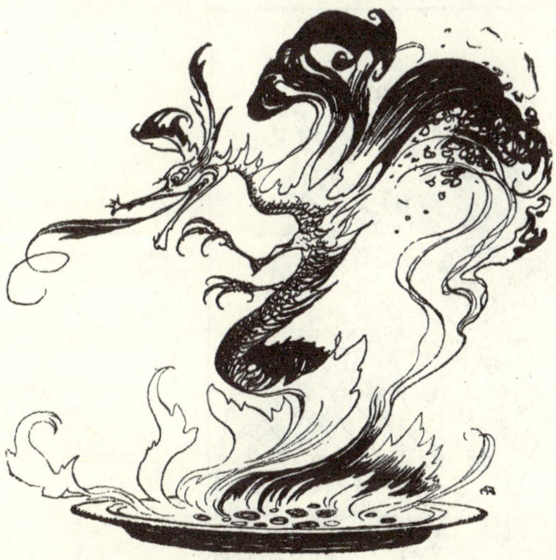

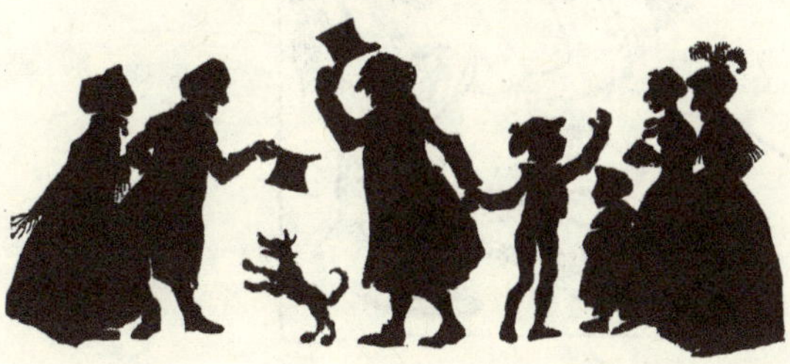

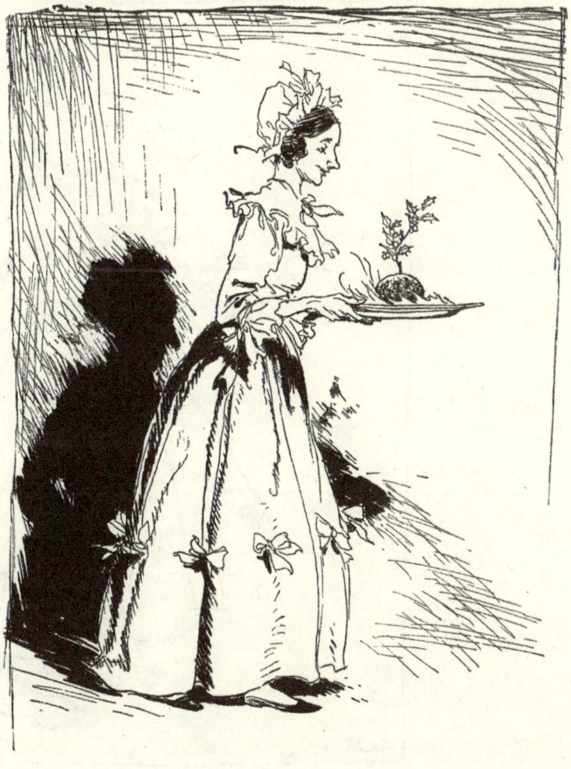

A CHRISTMAS CAROL, 1915

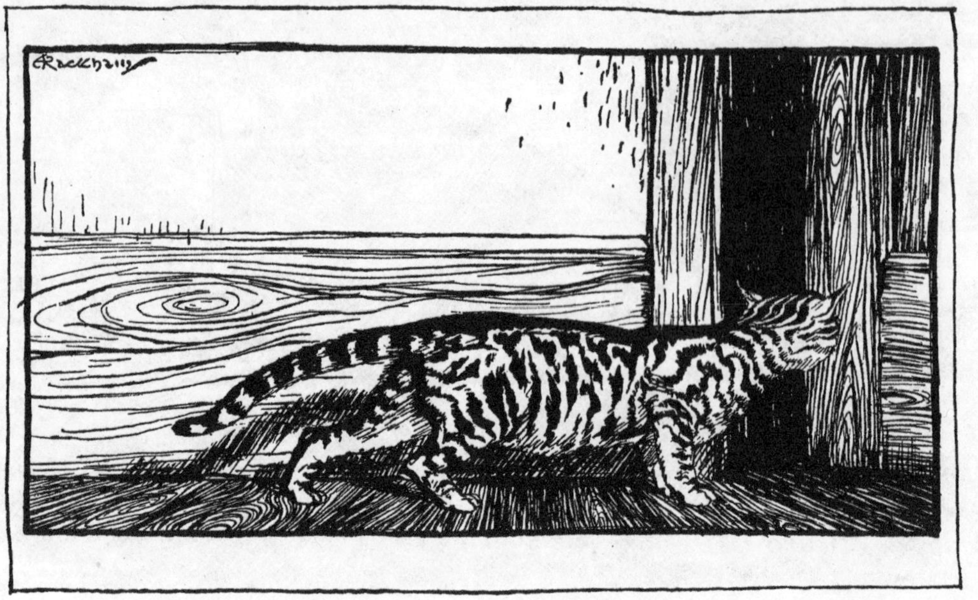

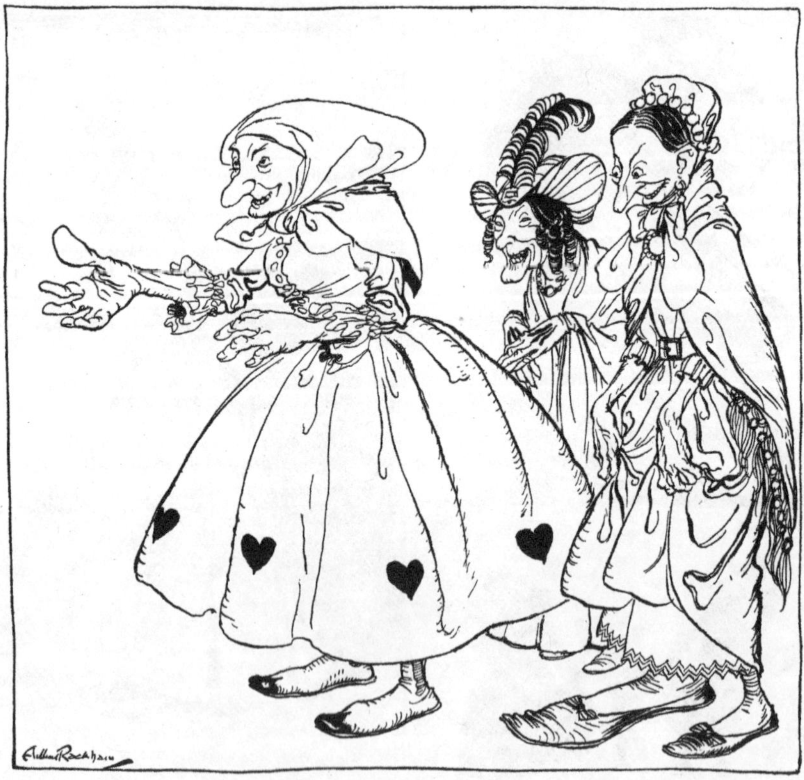

Little Brother and Little Sister, 1917

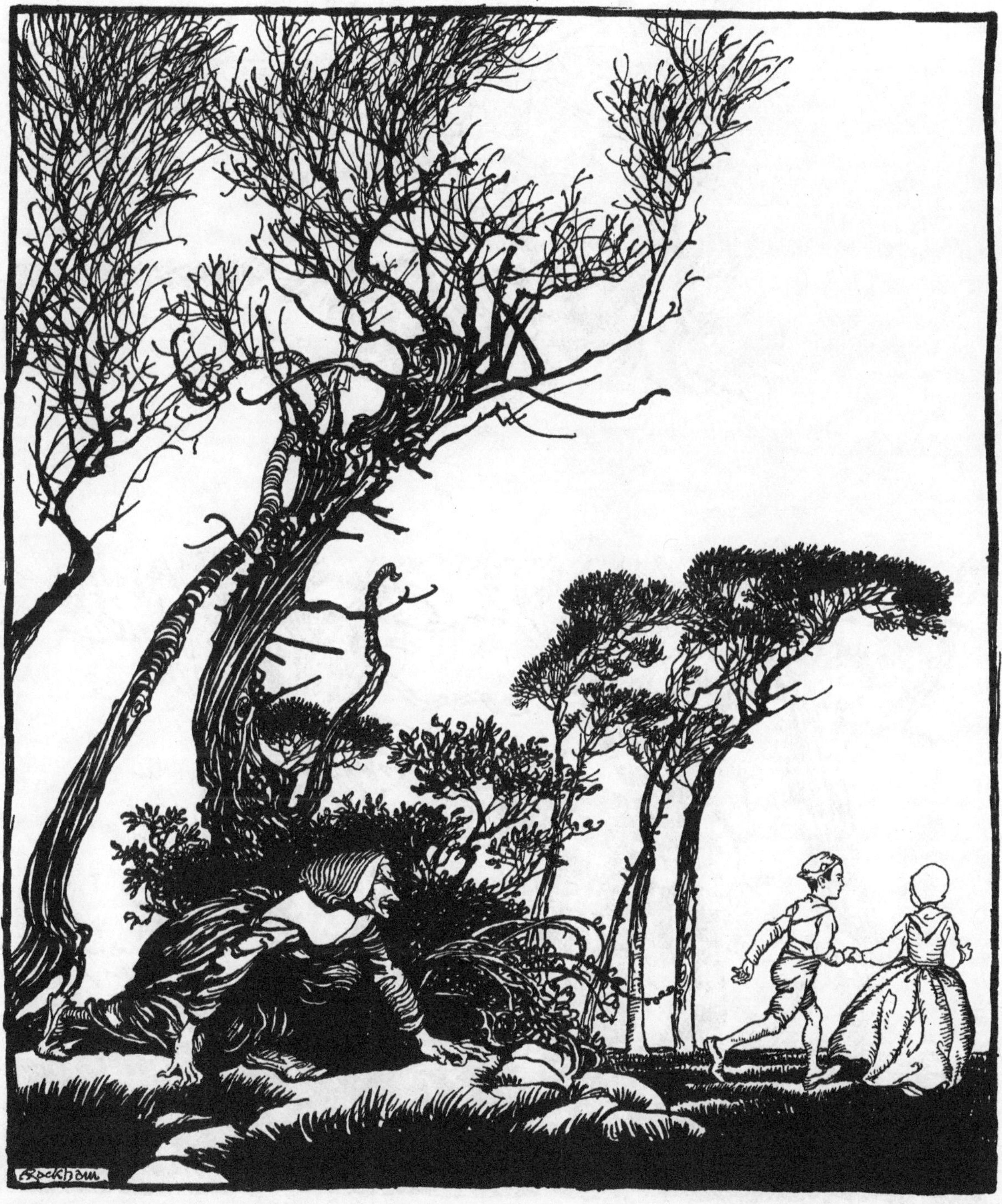

"She crept after them secretly, as witches do creep"

LITTLE BROTHER AND LITTLE SISTER, 1917

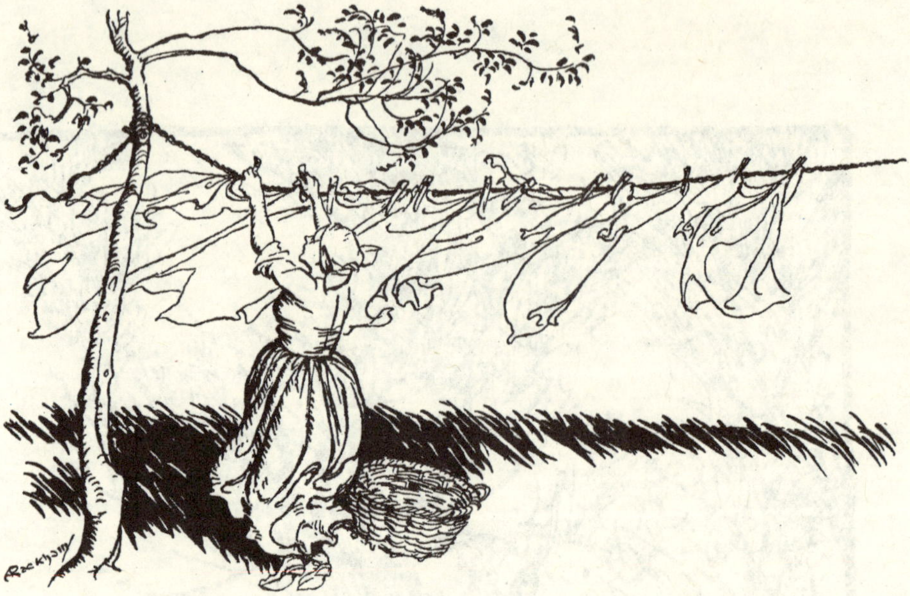

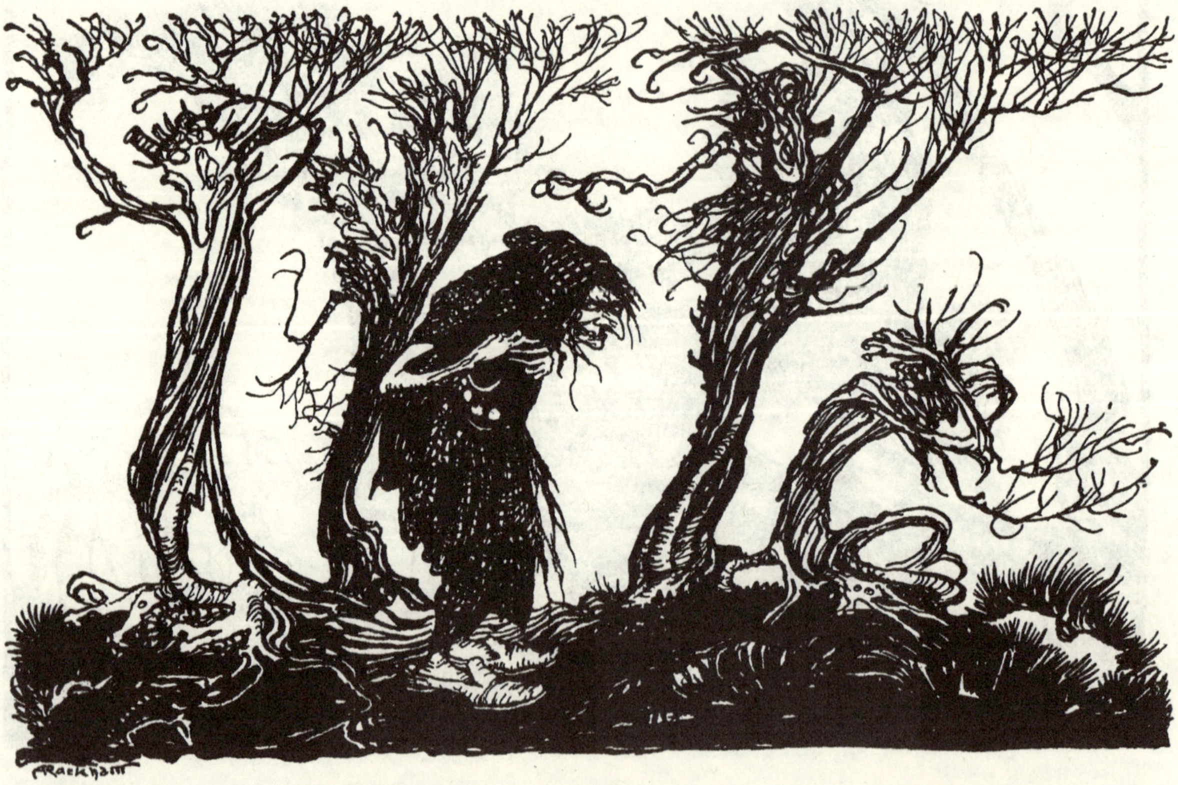

Little Brother and Little Sister, 1917

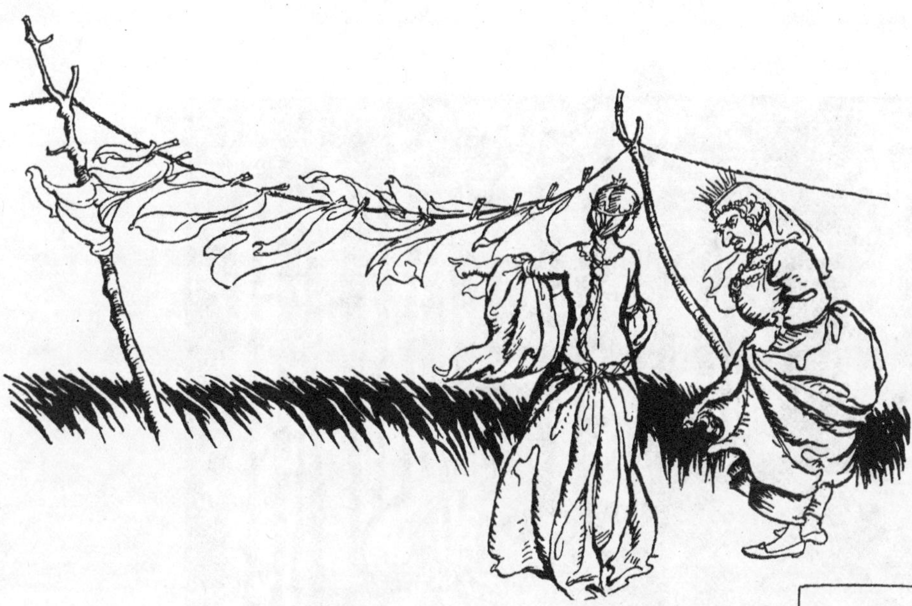

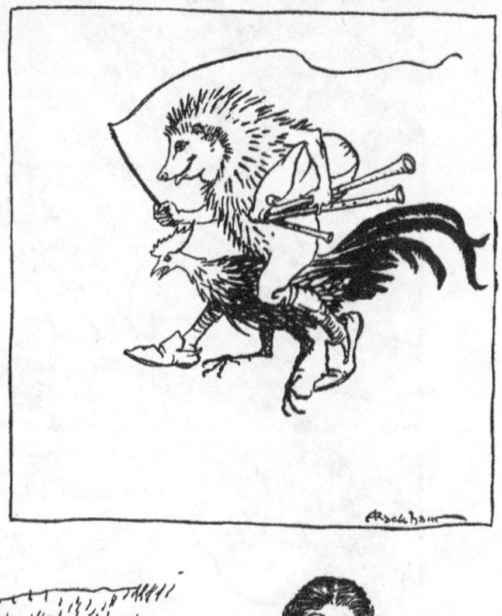

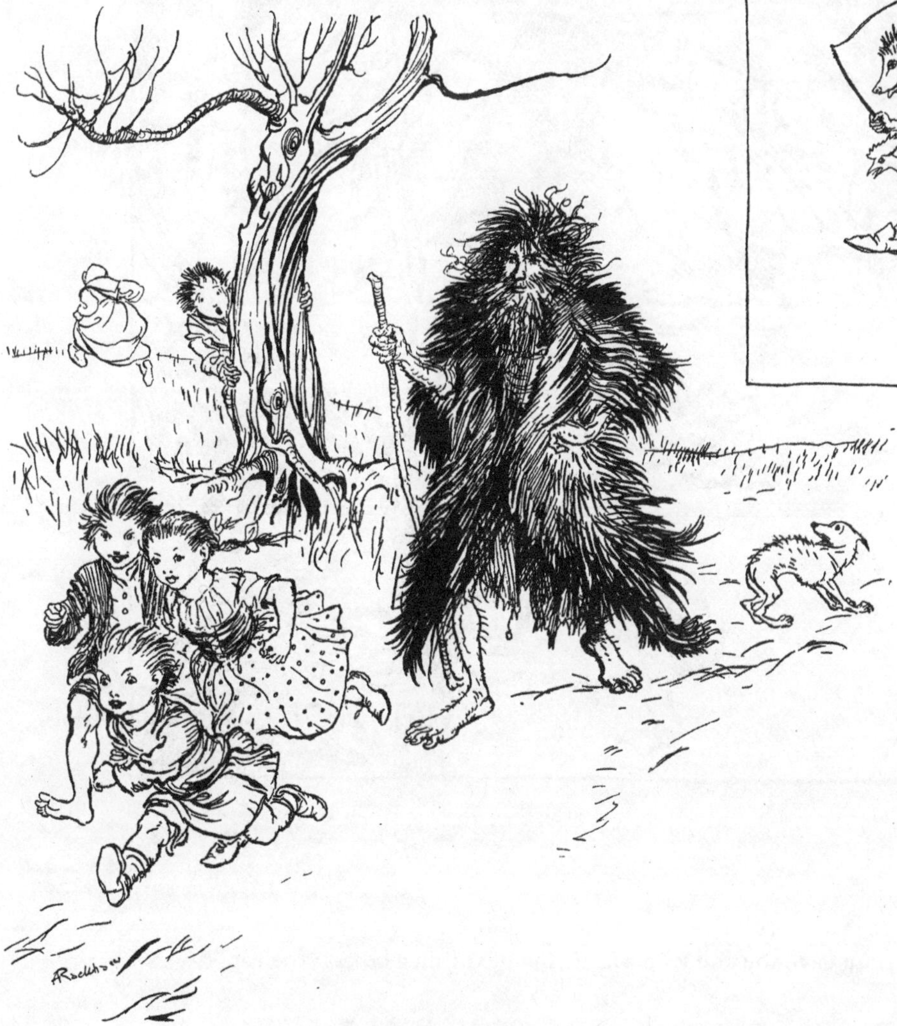

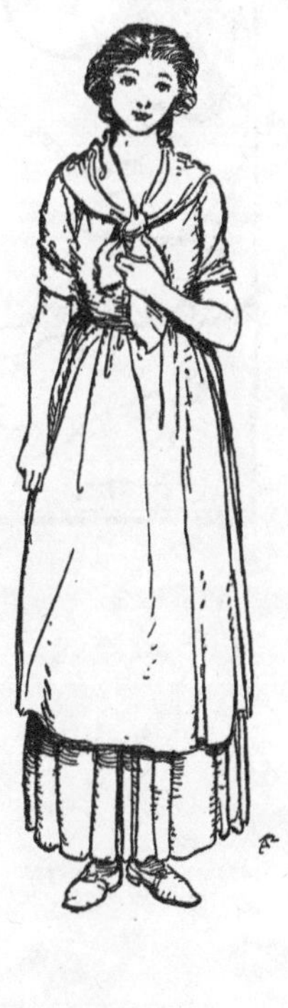

Little Brother and Little Sister, 1917

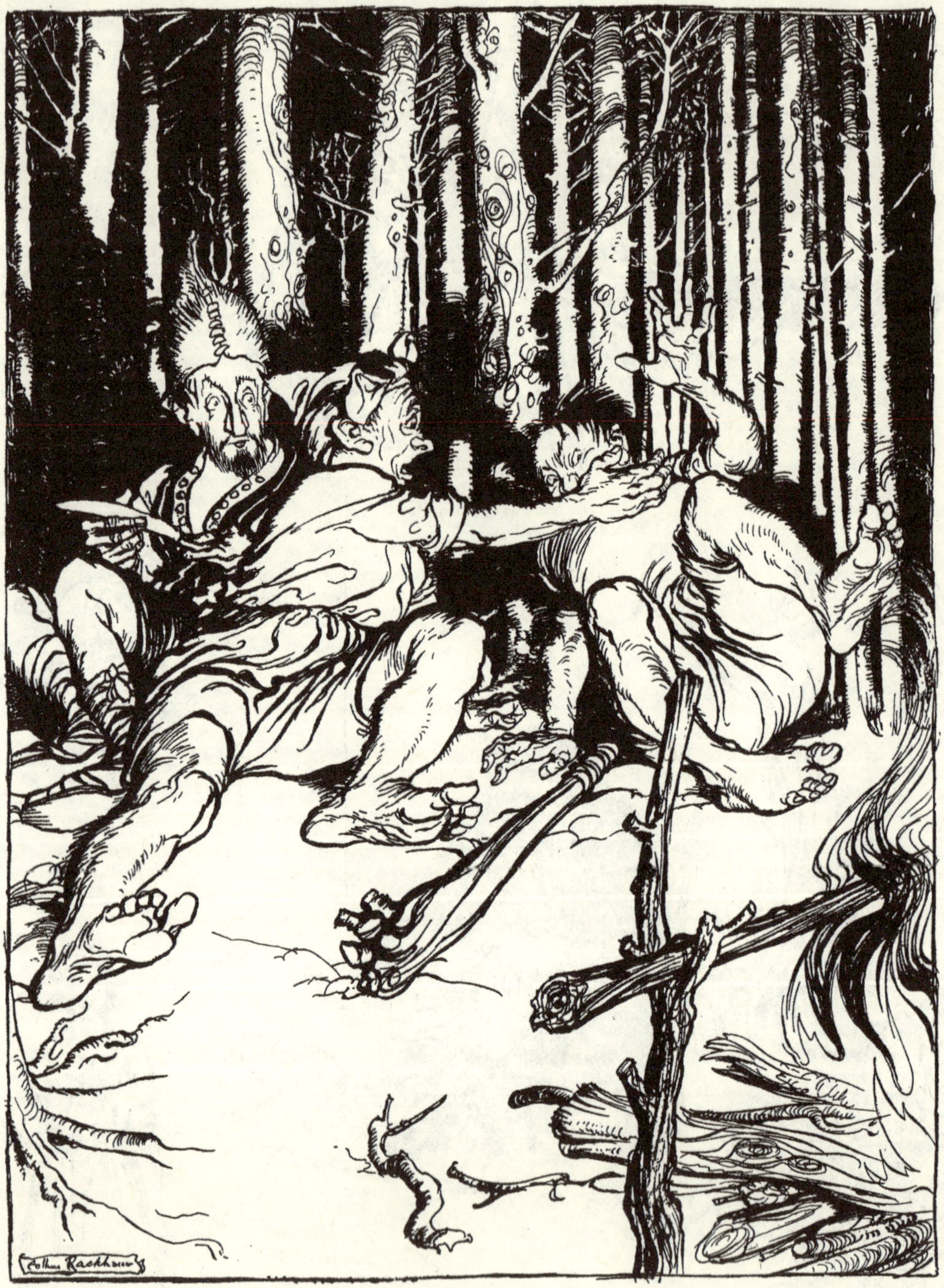

"The giant gave the one who was sitting next him a box on the ear."

LITTLE BROTHER AND LITTLE SISTER, 1917

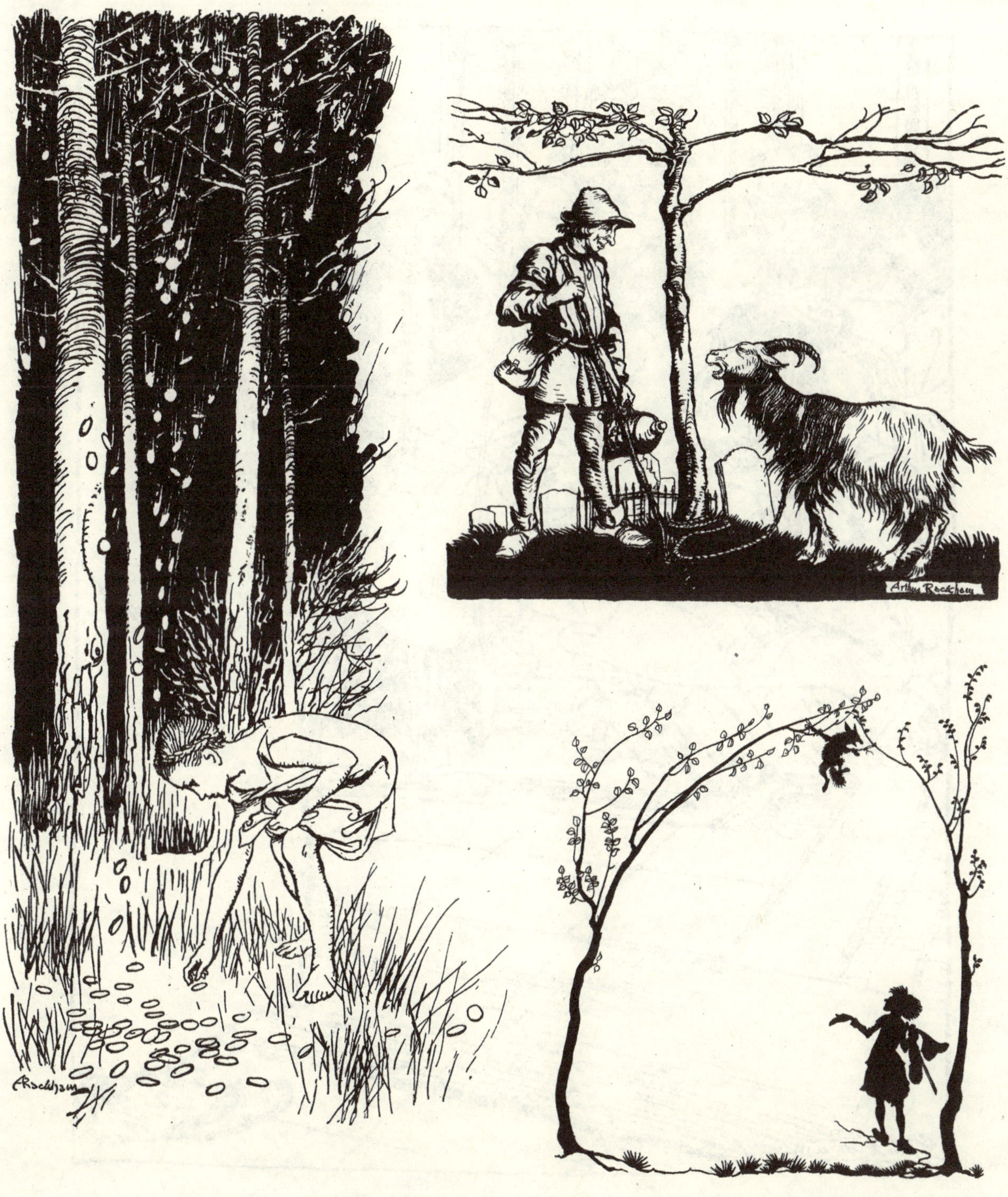

Little Brother and Little Sister, 1917

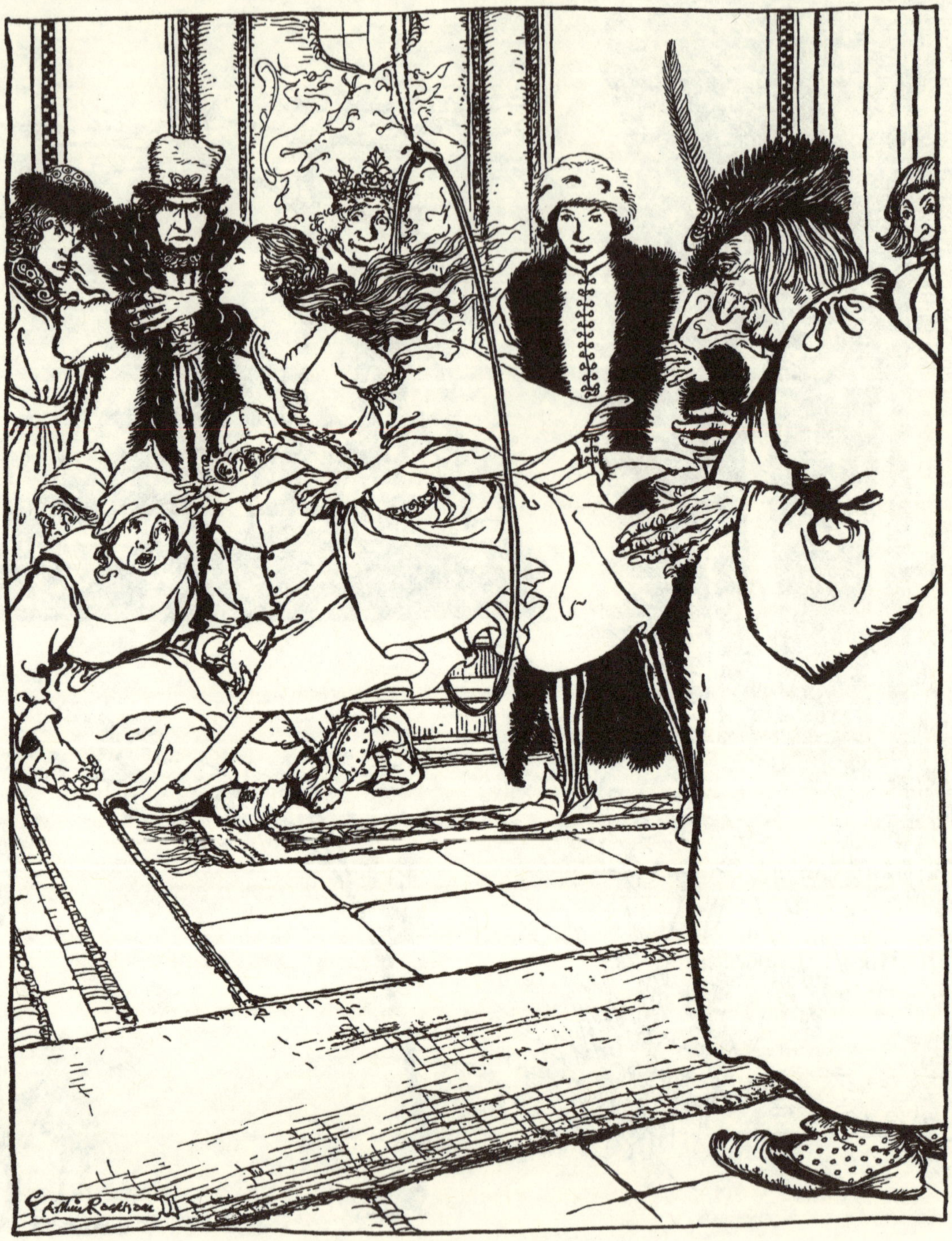

"The pretty maiden skipped through the hoop as lightly as a deer."

LITTLE BROTHER AND LITTLE SISTER, 1917

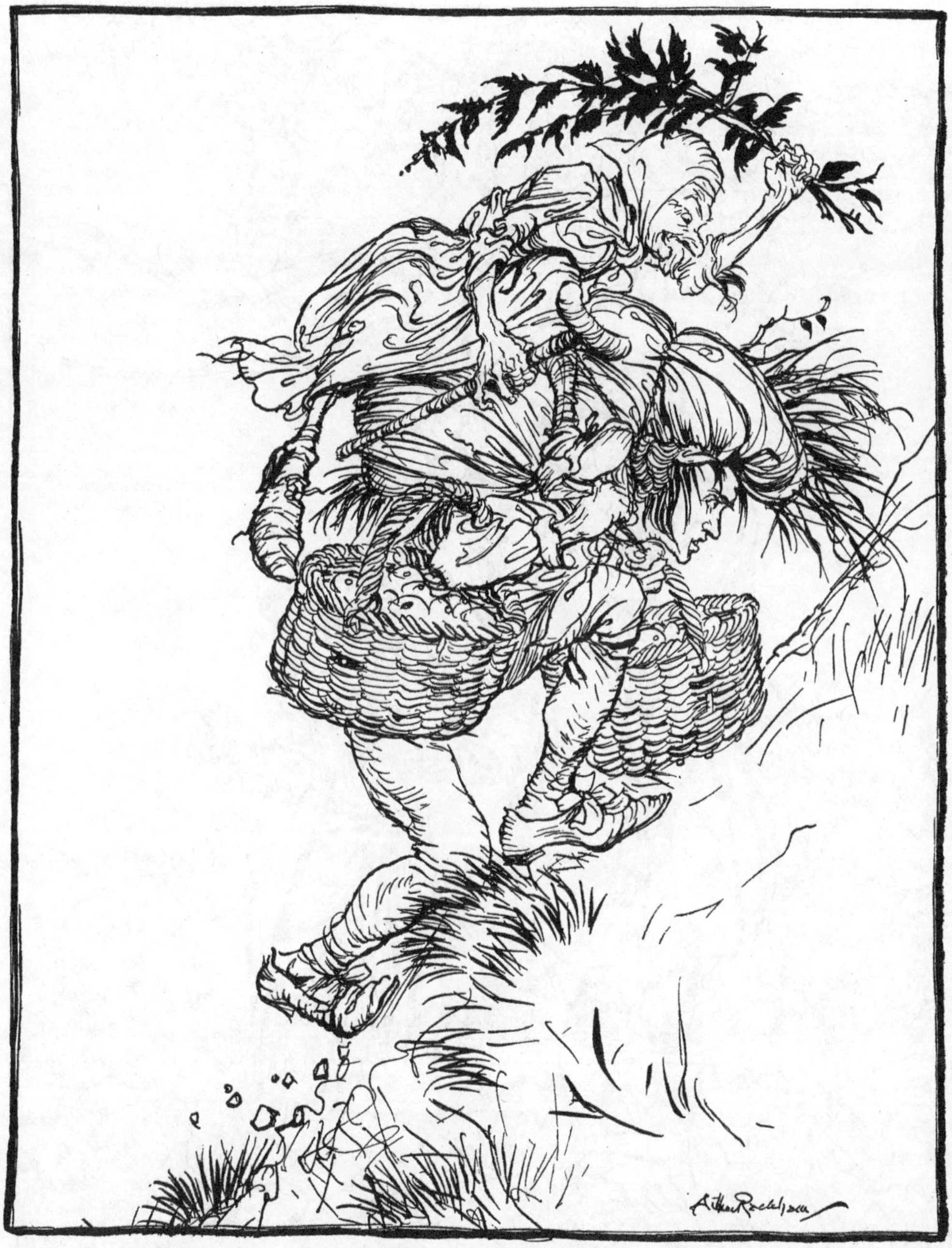

"Groaning continually, he climbed the mountain."

Little Brother and Little Sister, 1917

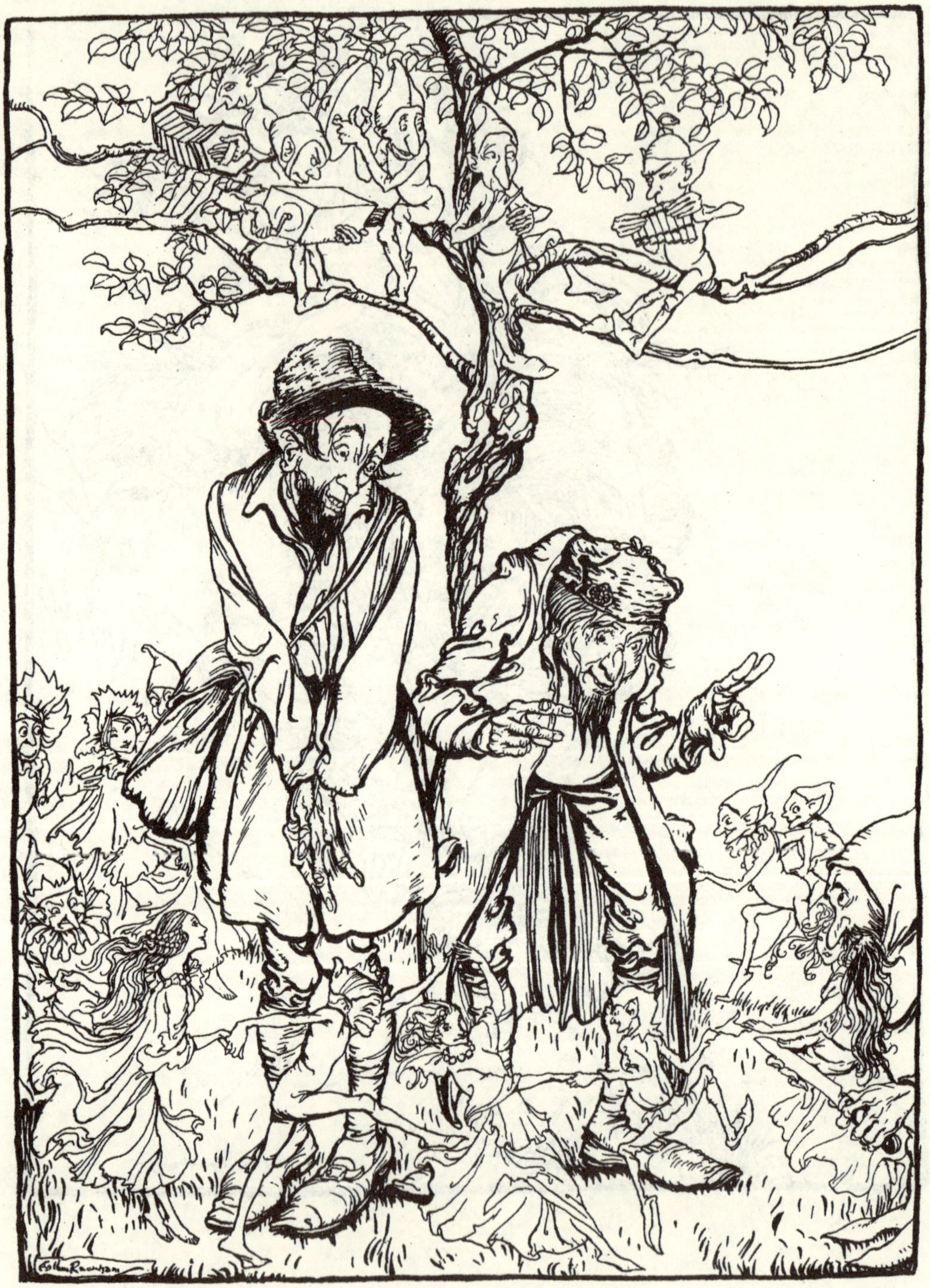

"When it was sharp enough, he looked round at the strangers."

LITTLE BROTHER AND LITTLE SISTER, 1917

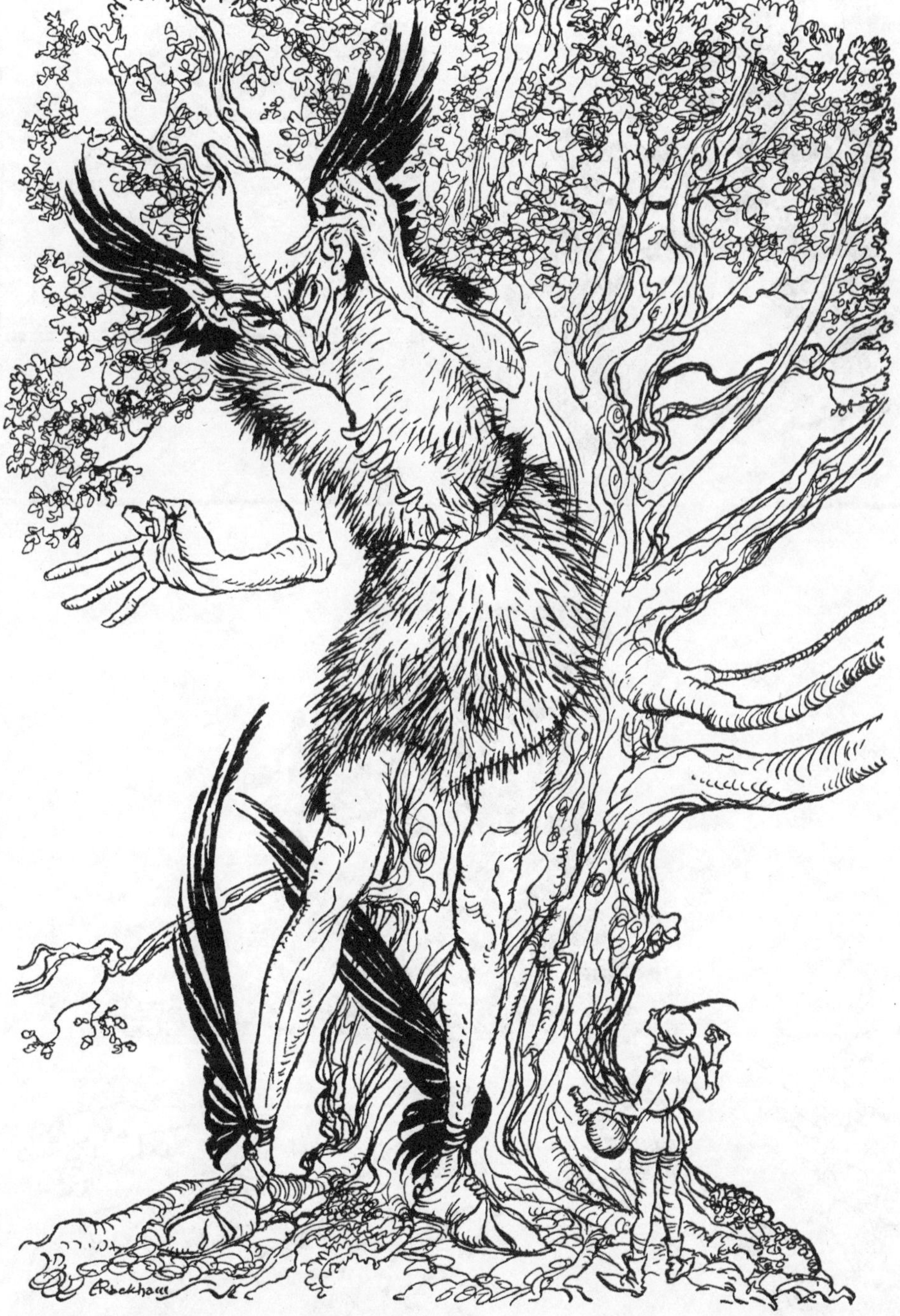

"A terrible fellow was half as big as the tree by which he was standing."

Little Brother and Little Sister, 1917

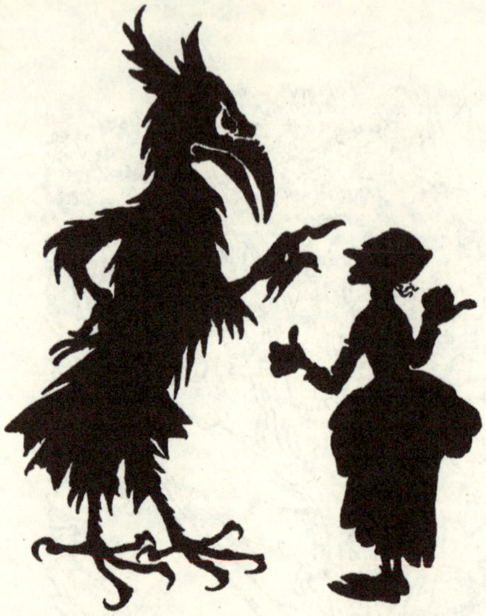

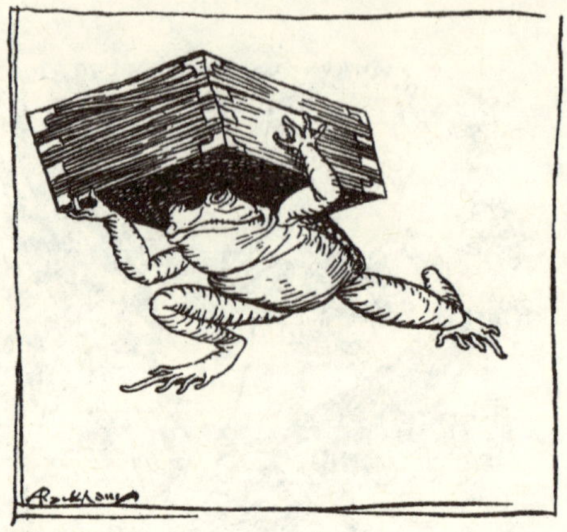

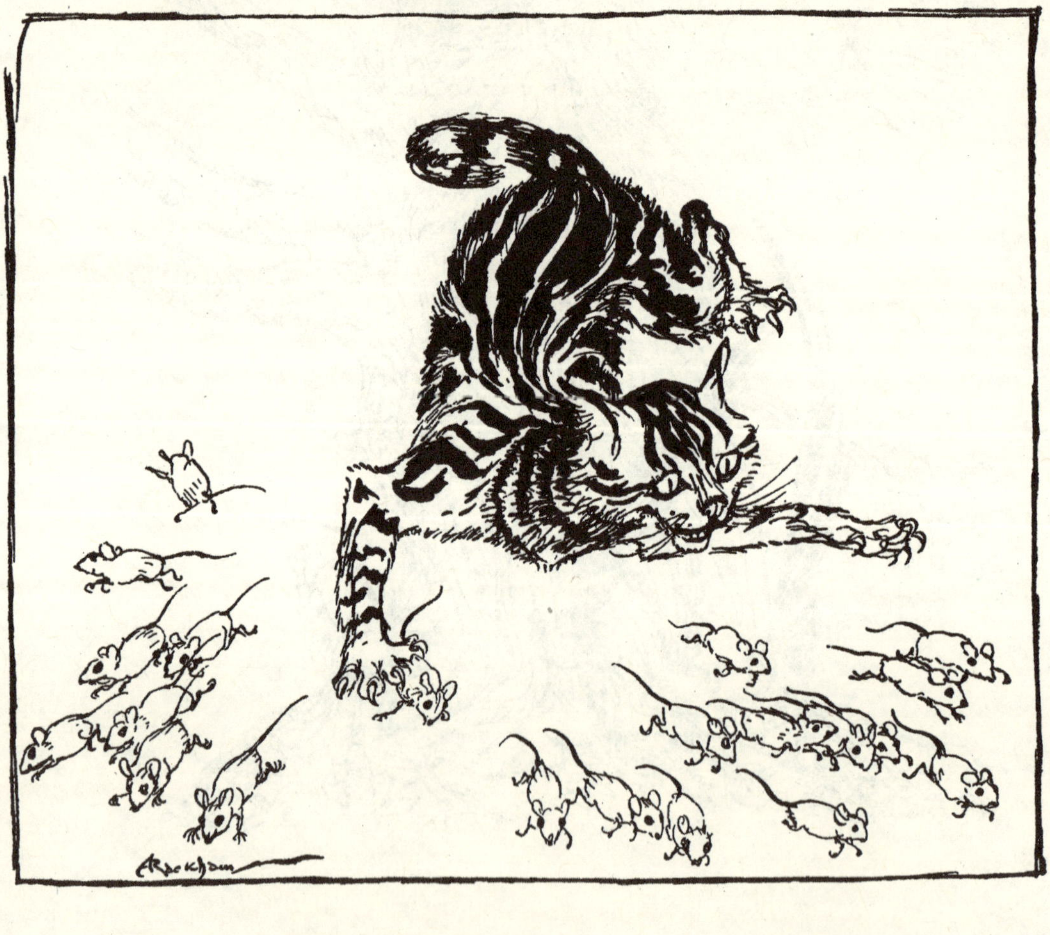

Little Brother and Little Sister, 1917

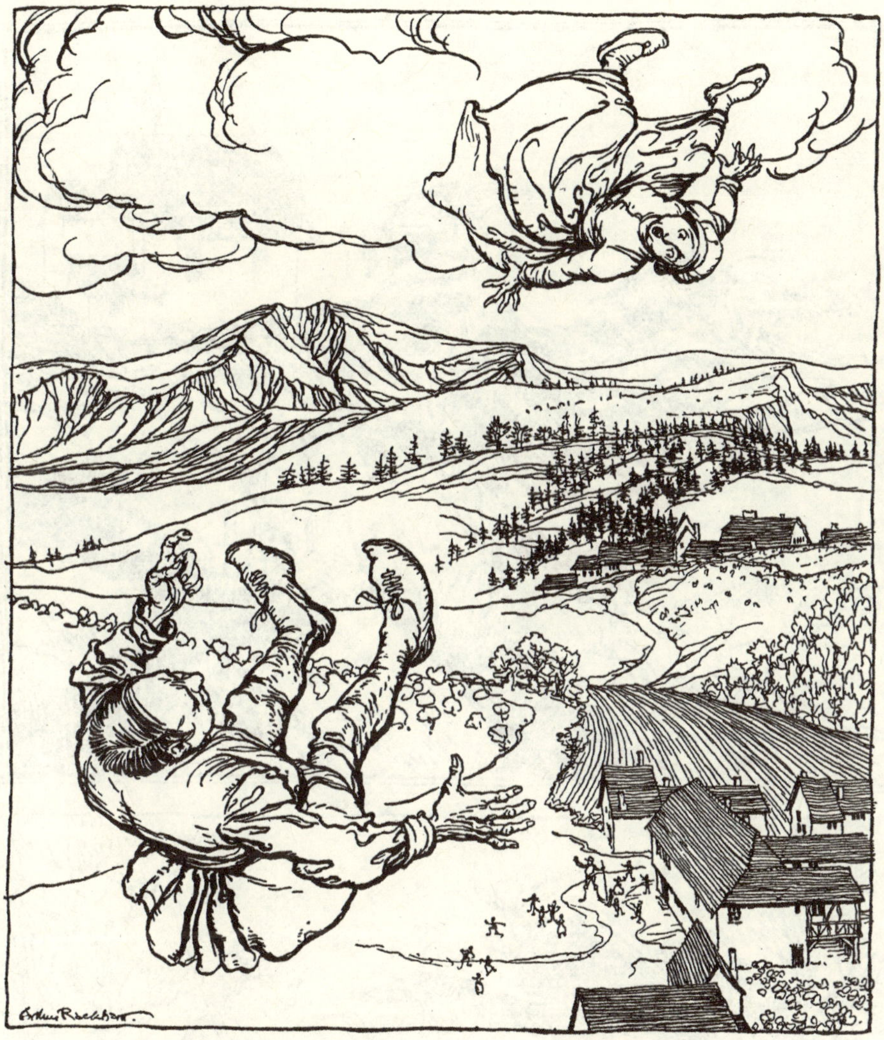

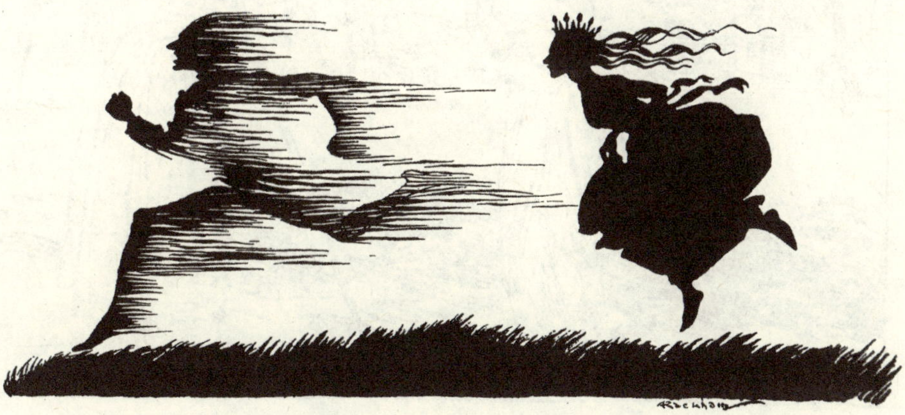

Little Brother and Little Sister, 1917

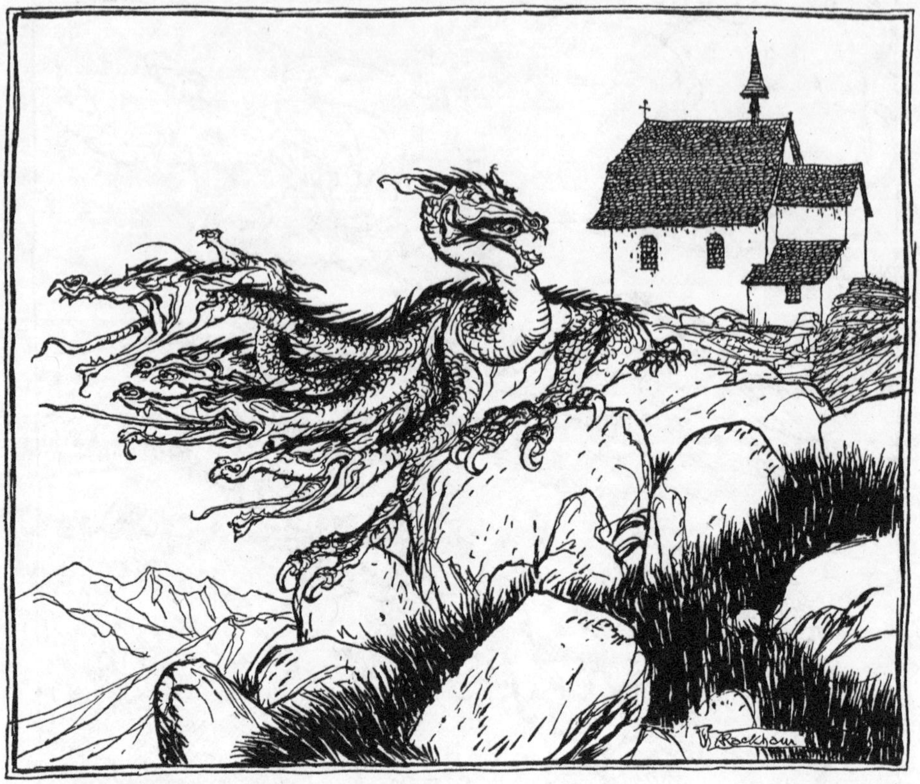

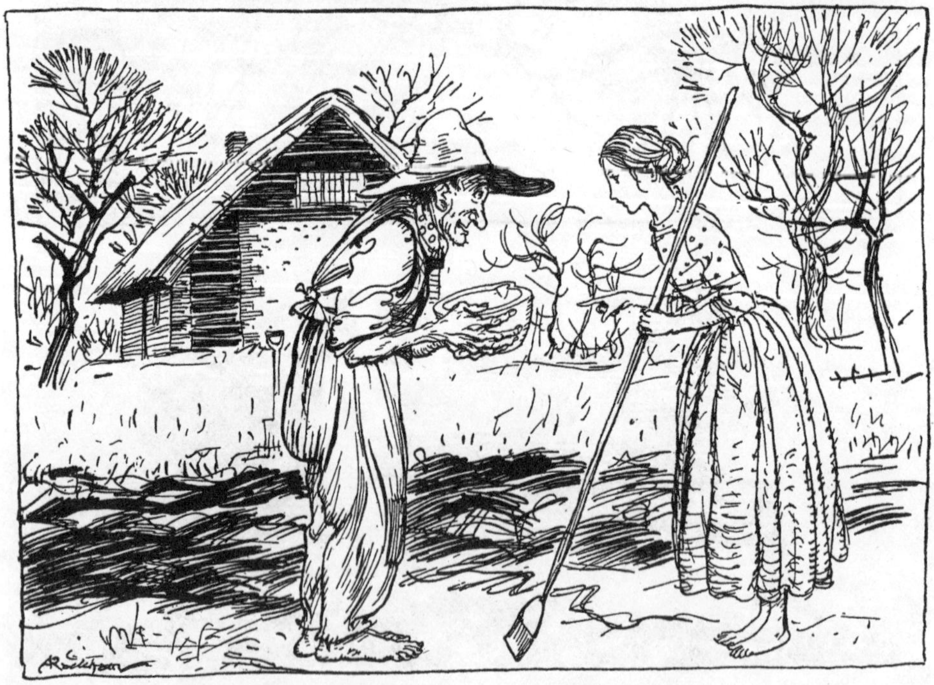

LITTLE BROTHER AND LITTLE SISTER, 1917

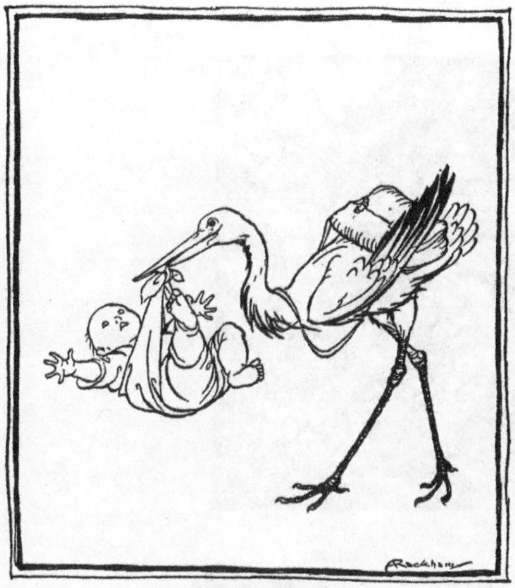

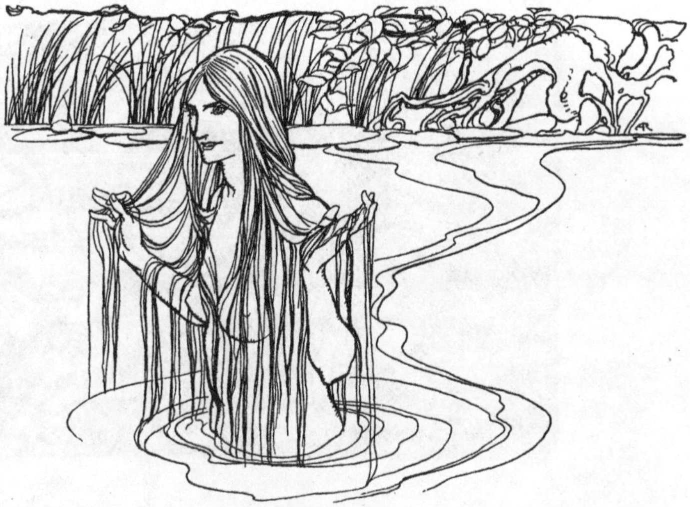

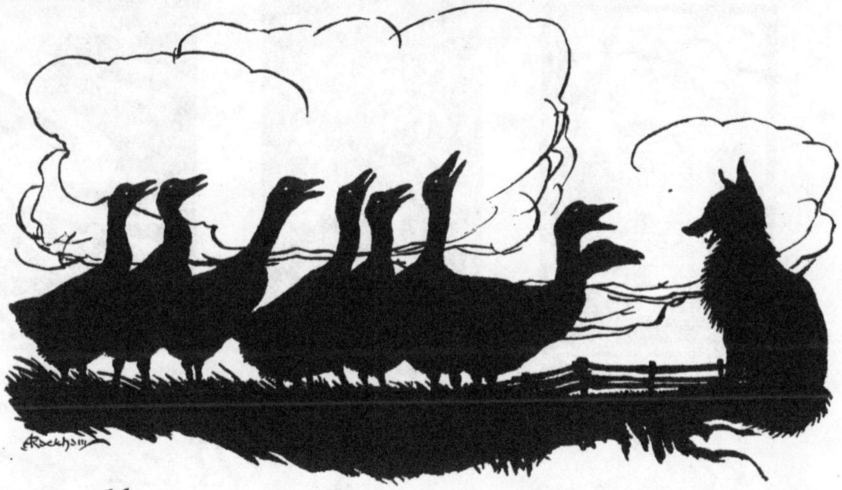

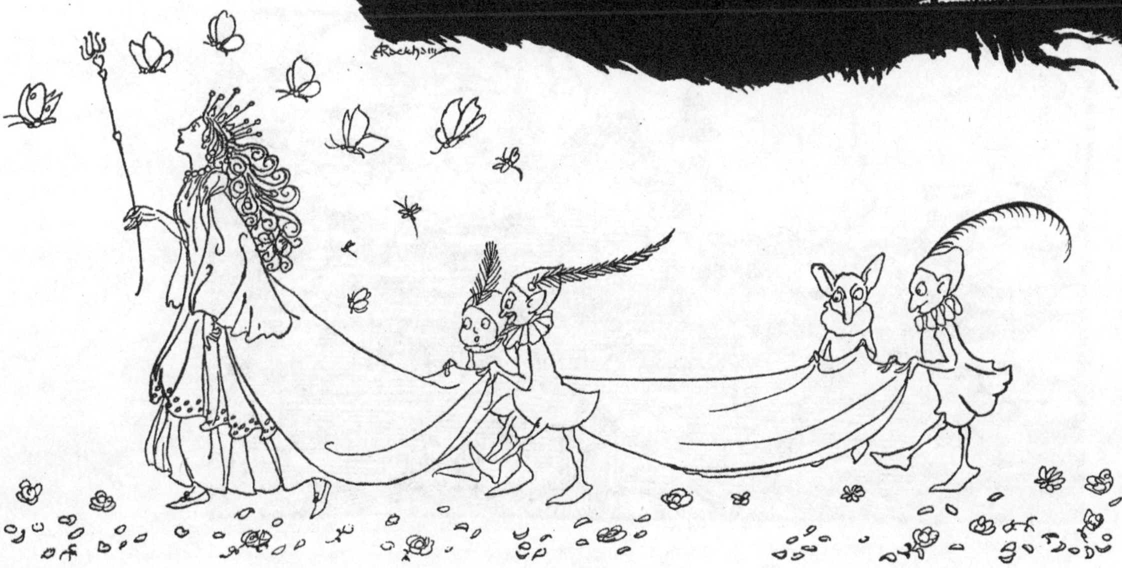

LITTLE BROTHER AND LITTLE SISTER, 1917

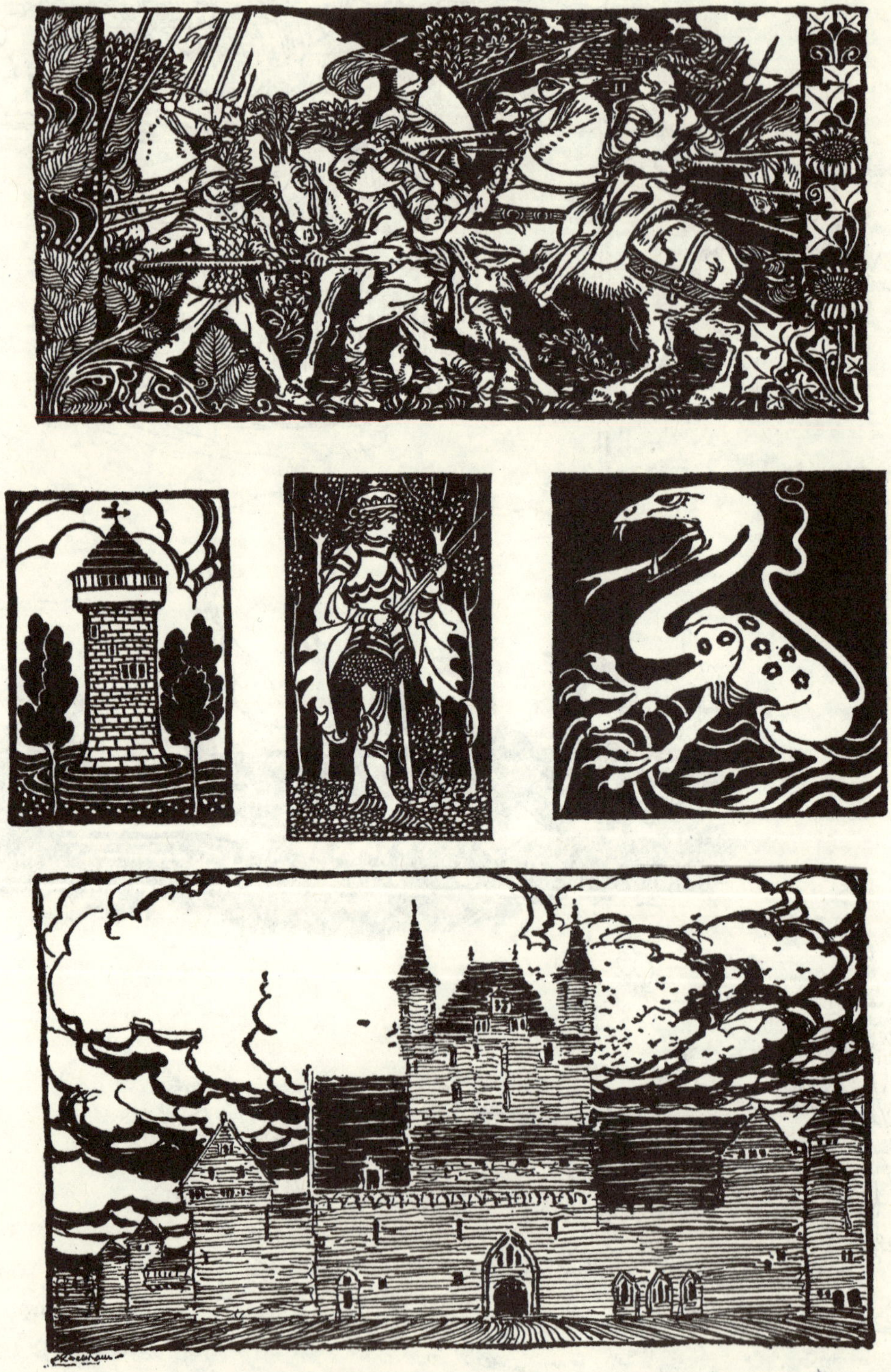

The Romance of King Arthur, 1917

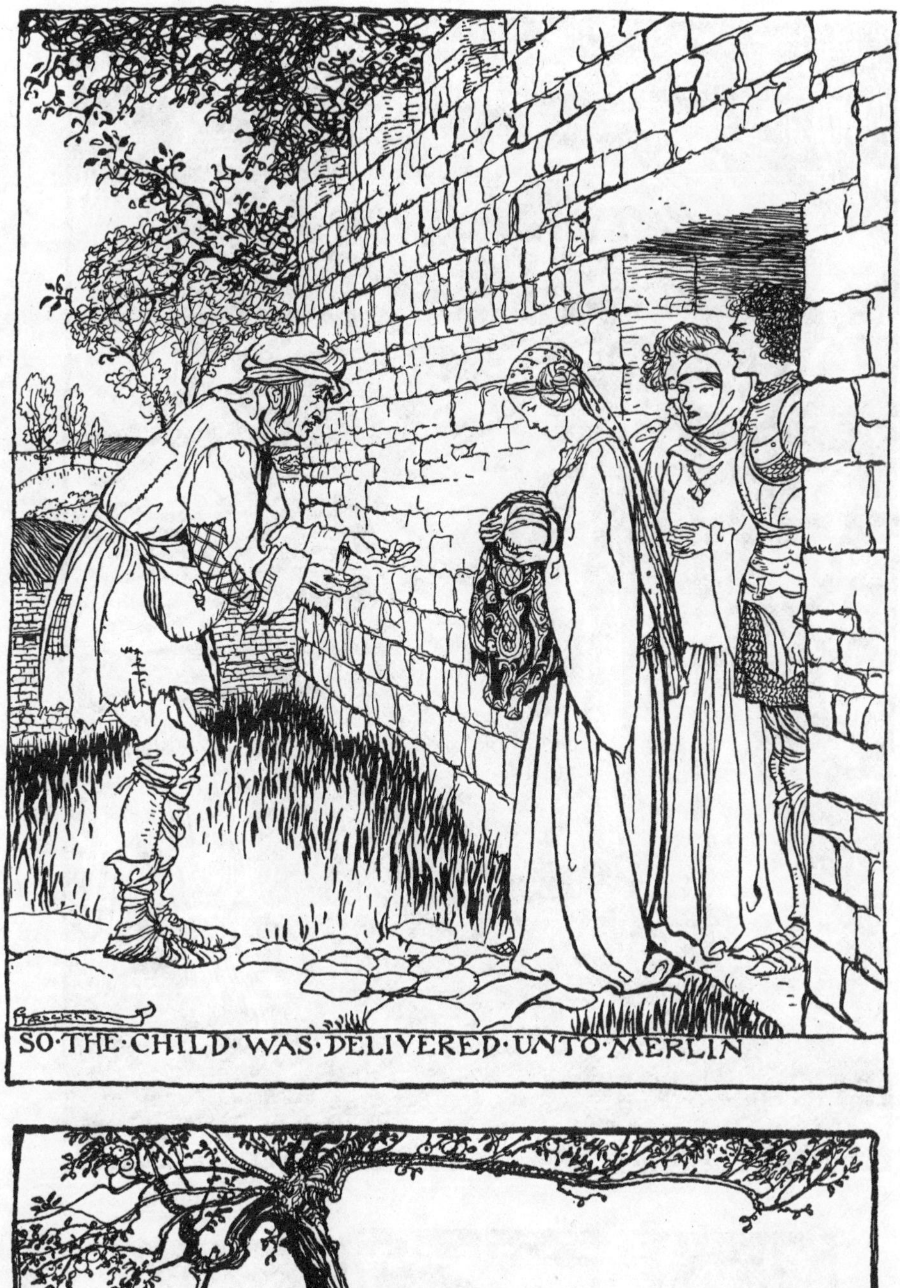

SO·THE·CHILD·WAS·DELIVERED·UNTO·MERLIN

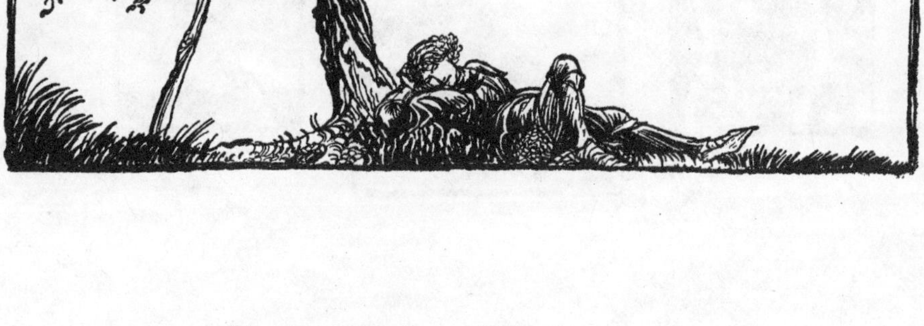

The Romance of King Arthur, 1917

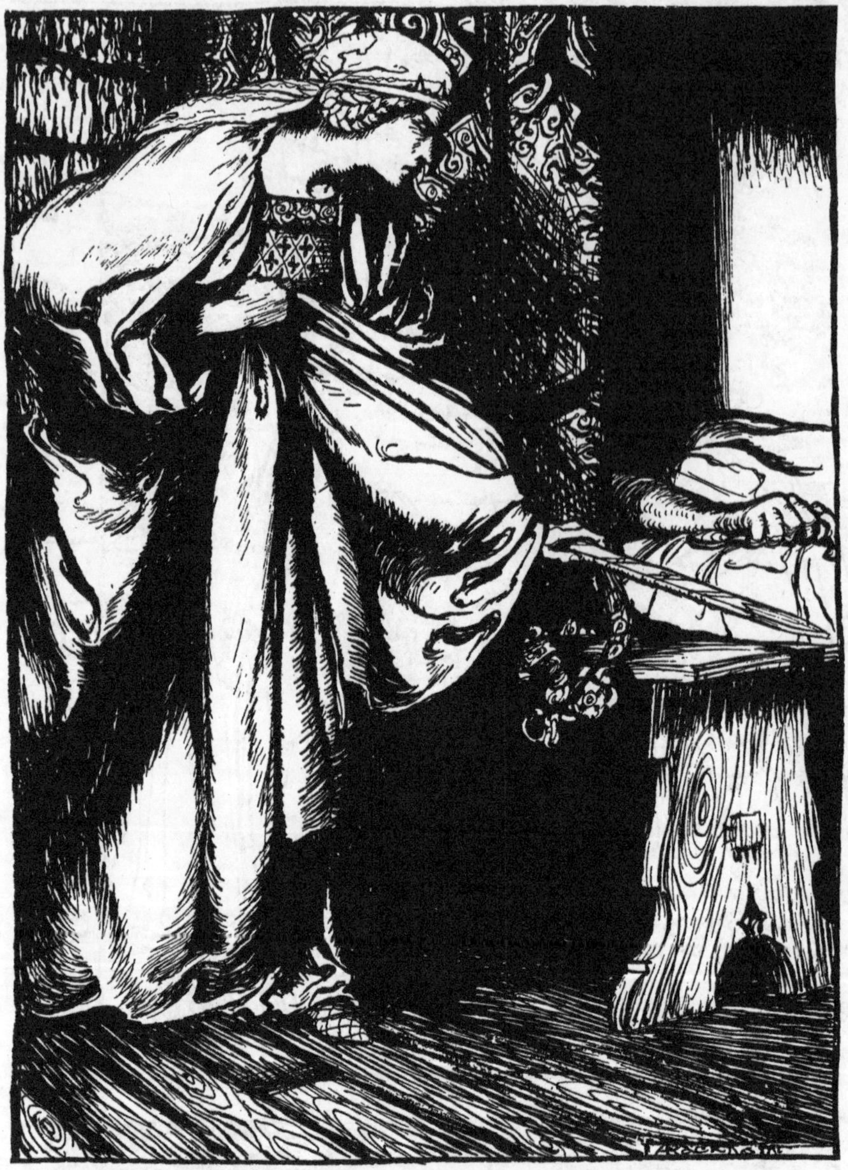

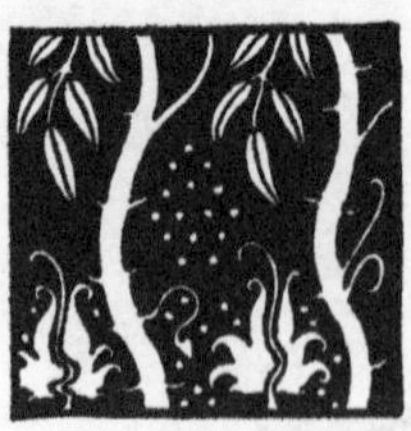

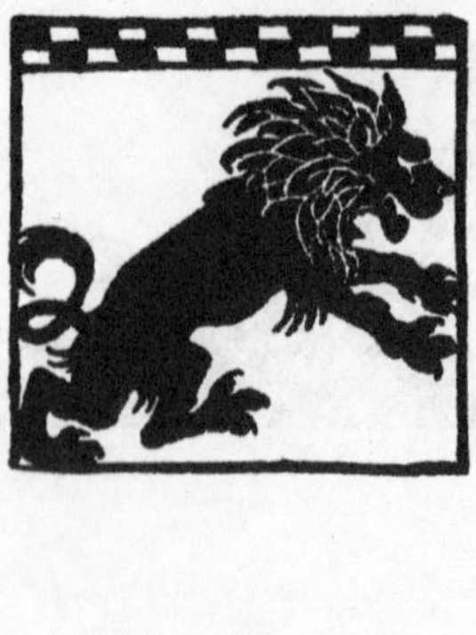

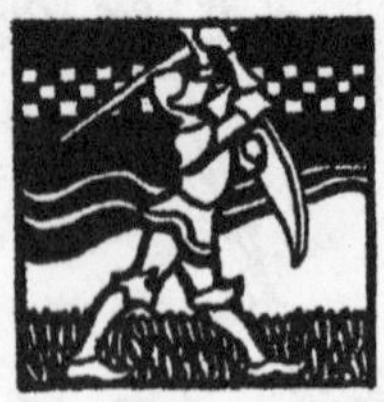

The Romance of King Arthur, 1917

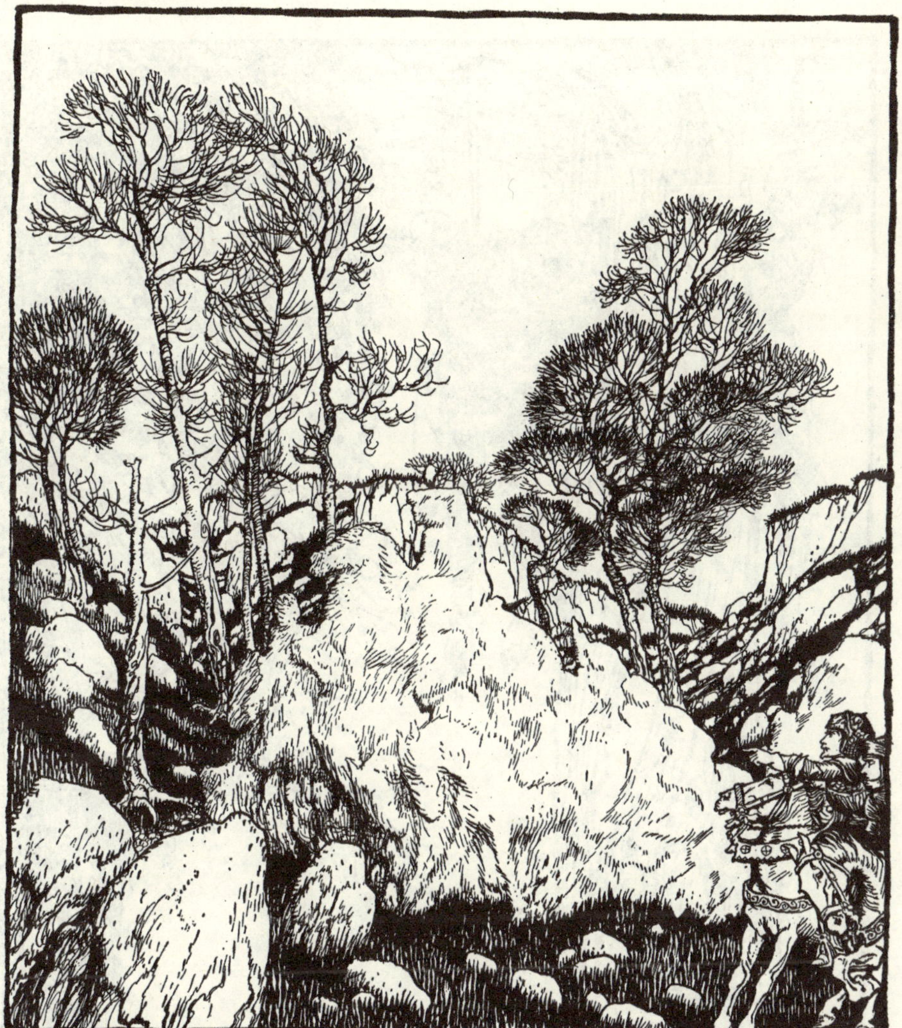

WHEN·SHE·SAW·SHE·MUST·BE·OVERTAKEN·SHE·SHAPED HERSELF·HORSE·AND·MAN·BY·ENCHANTMENT·UNTO·A·GREAT MARBLE·STONE

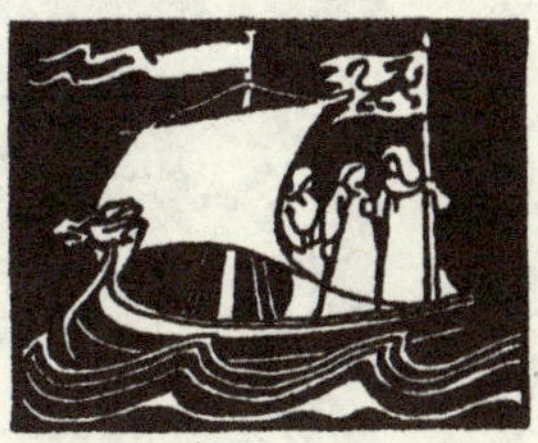

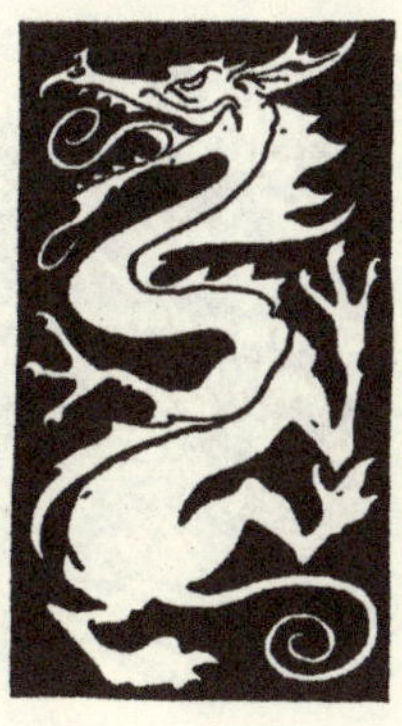

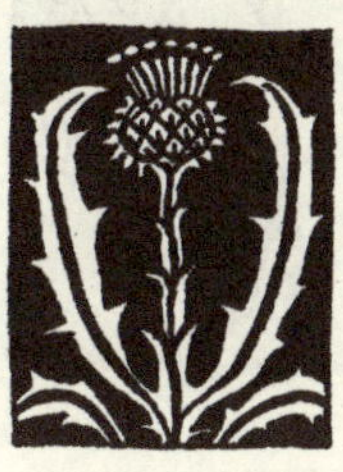

THE ROMANCE OF KING ARTHUR, 1917

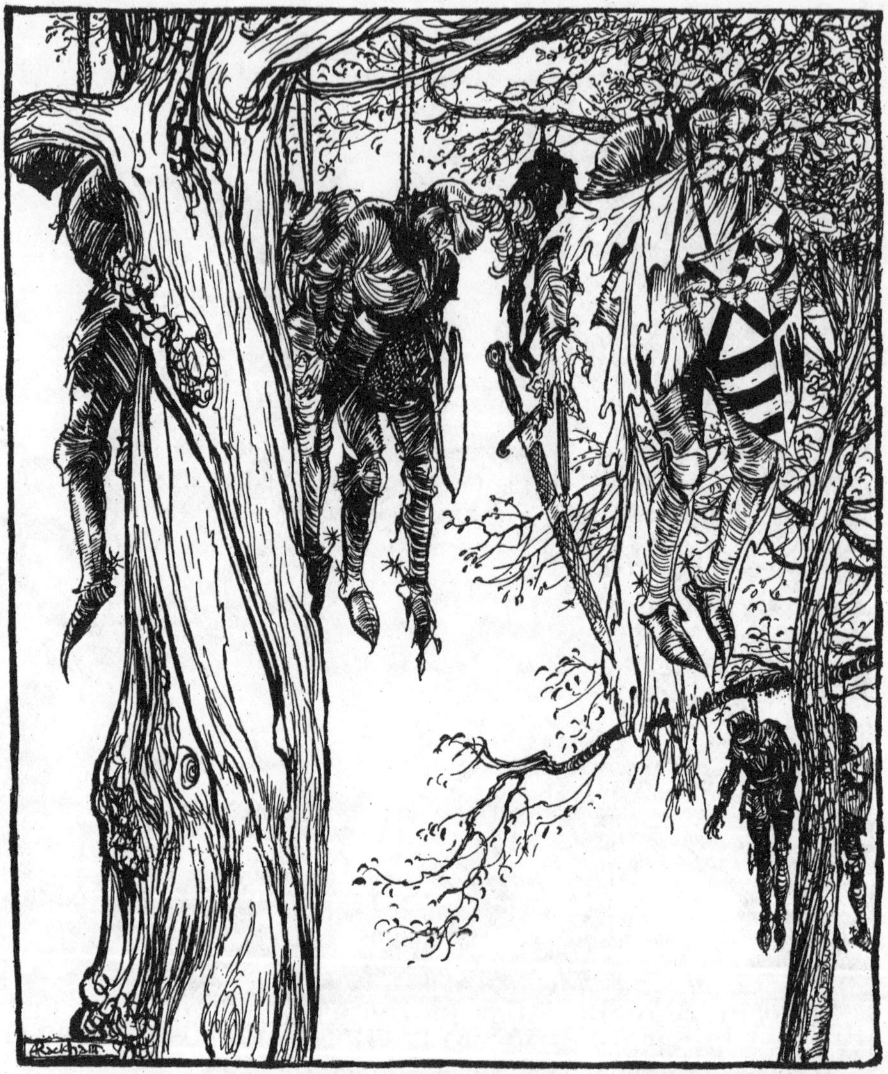

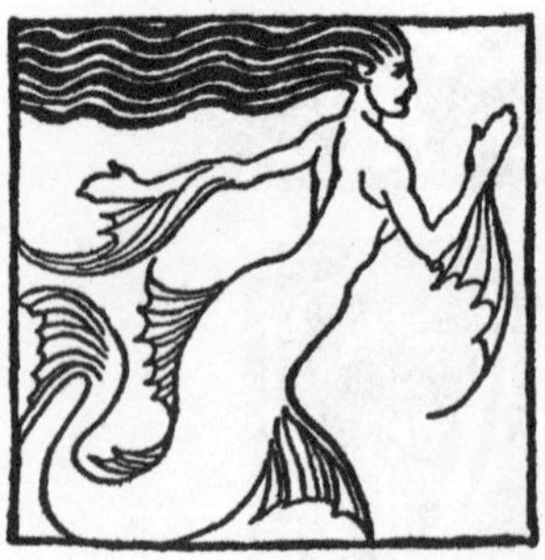

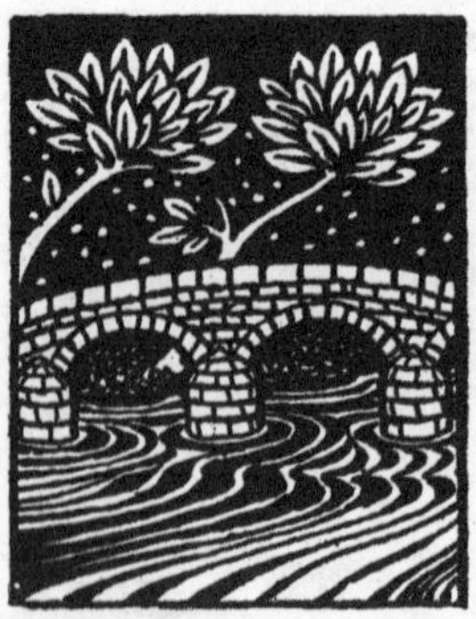

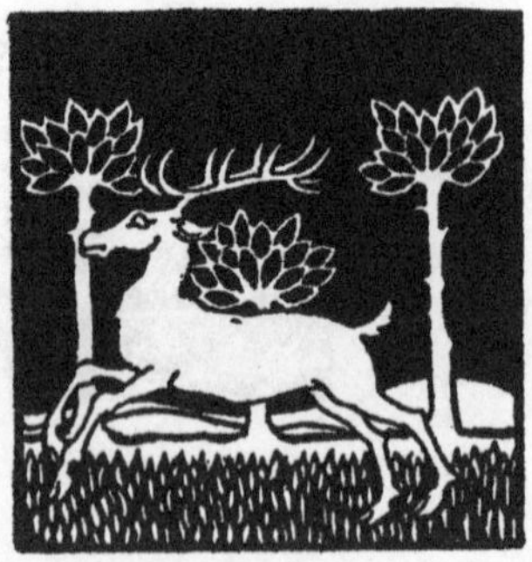

THE ROMANCE OF KING ARTHUR, 1917

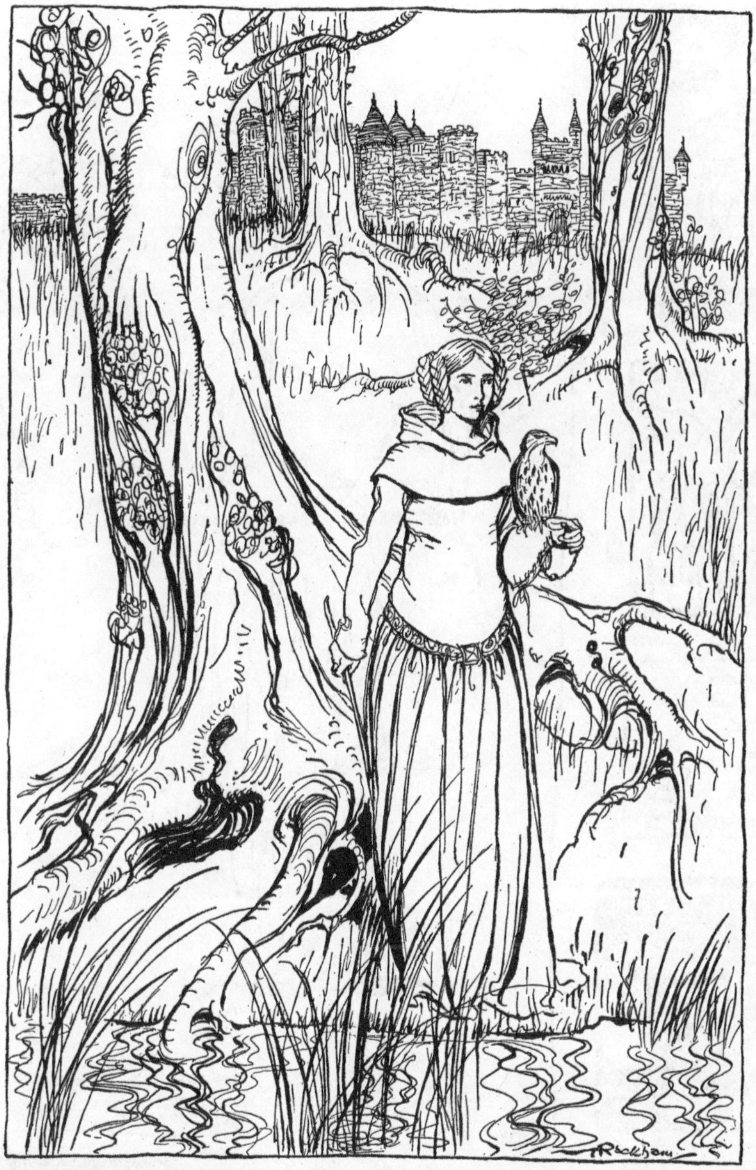

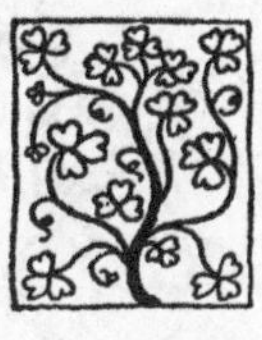

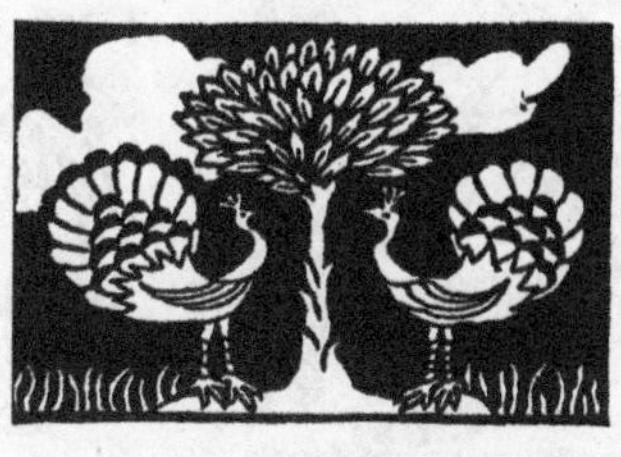

The Romance of King Arthur, 1917

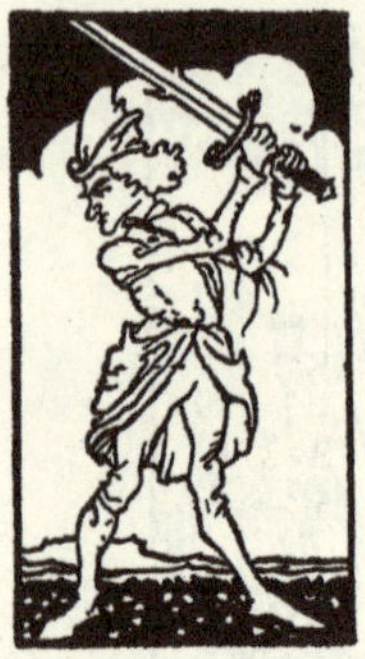
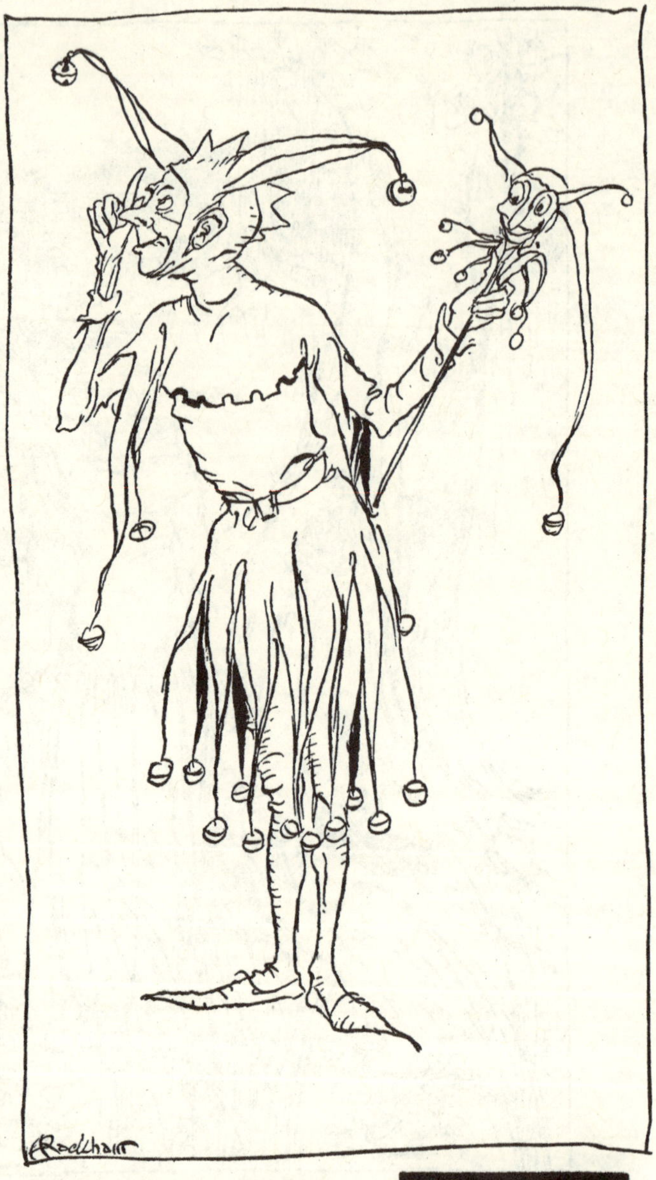
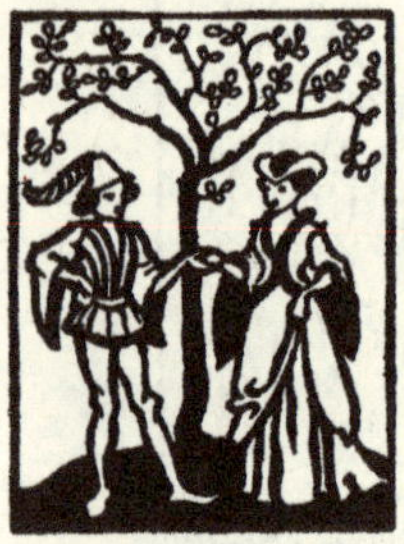
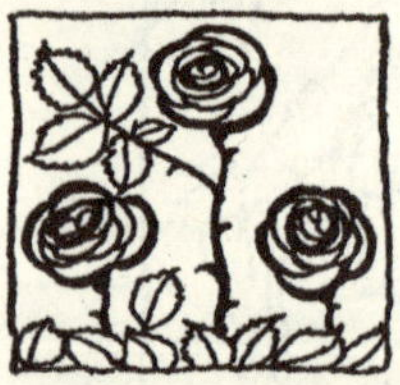
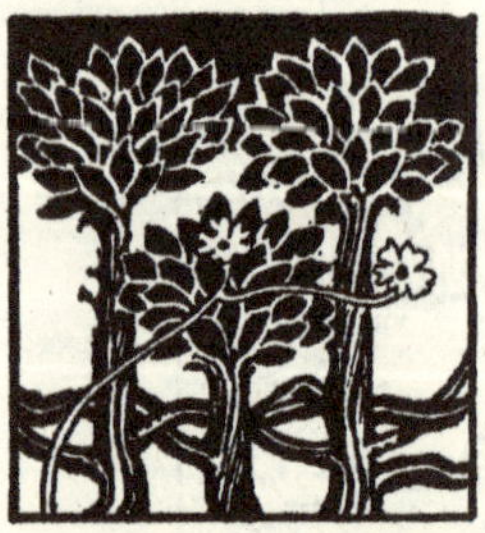
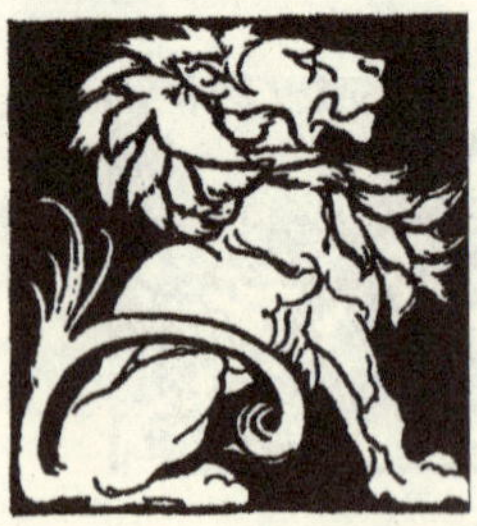
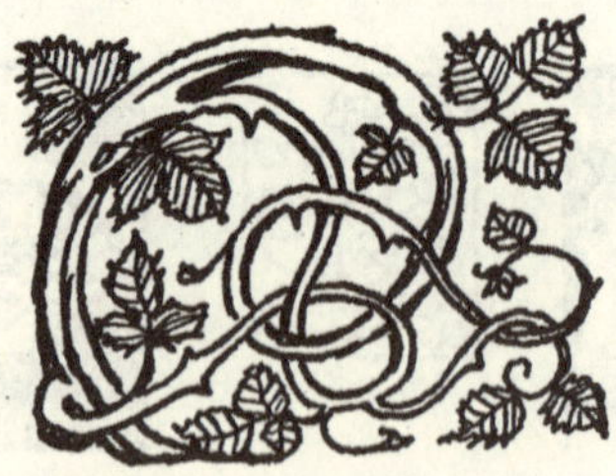
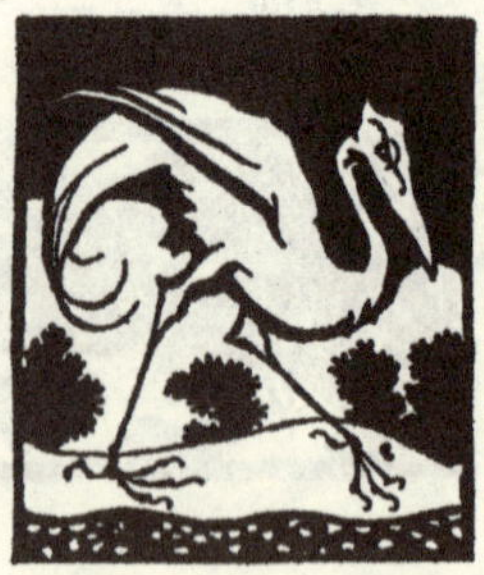

THE ROMANCE OF KING ARTHUR, 1917

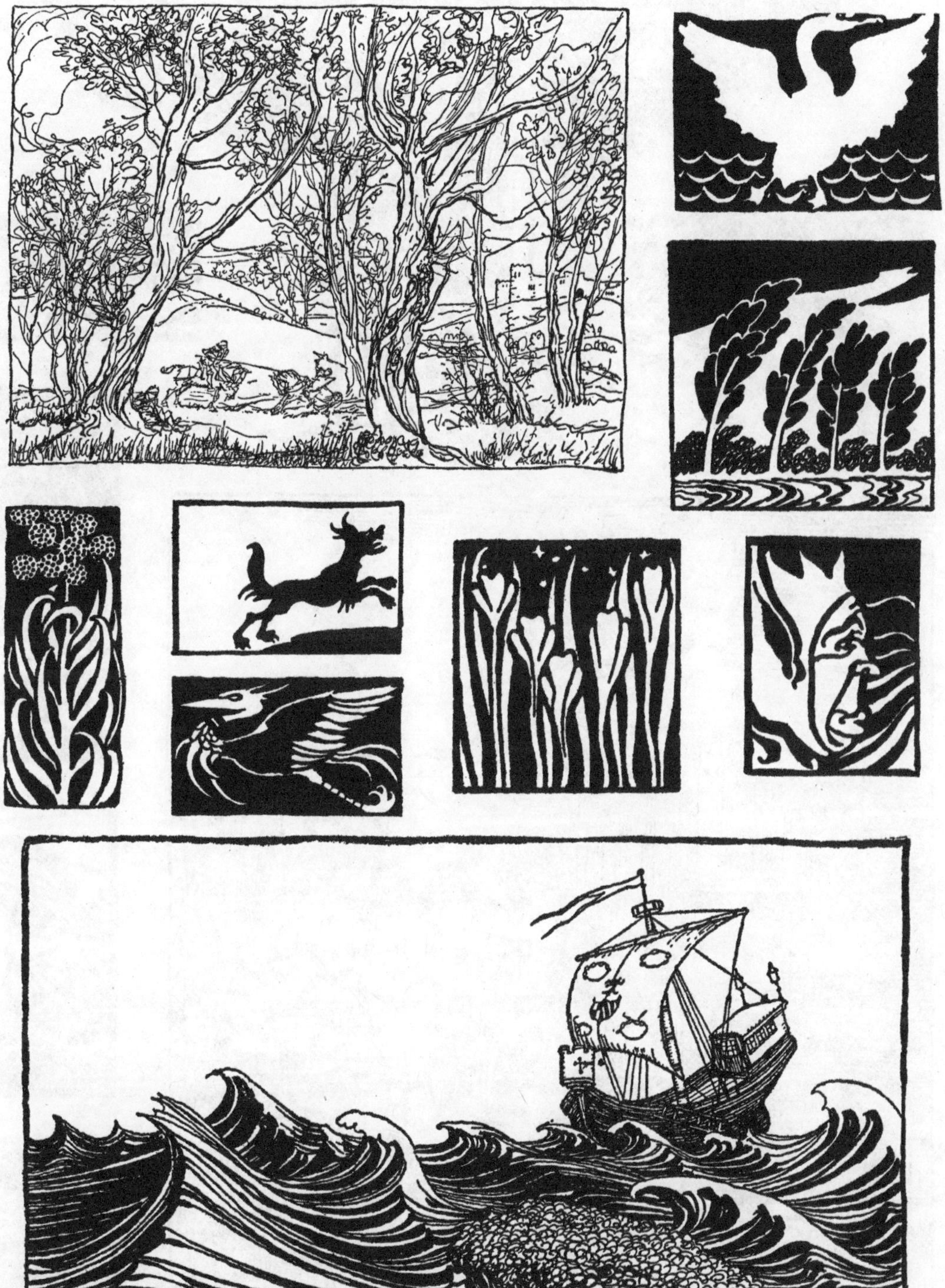

The Romance of King Arthur, 1917

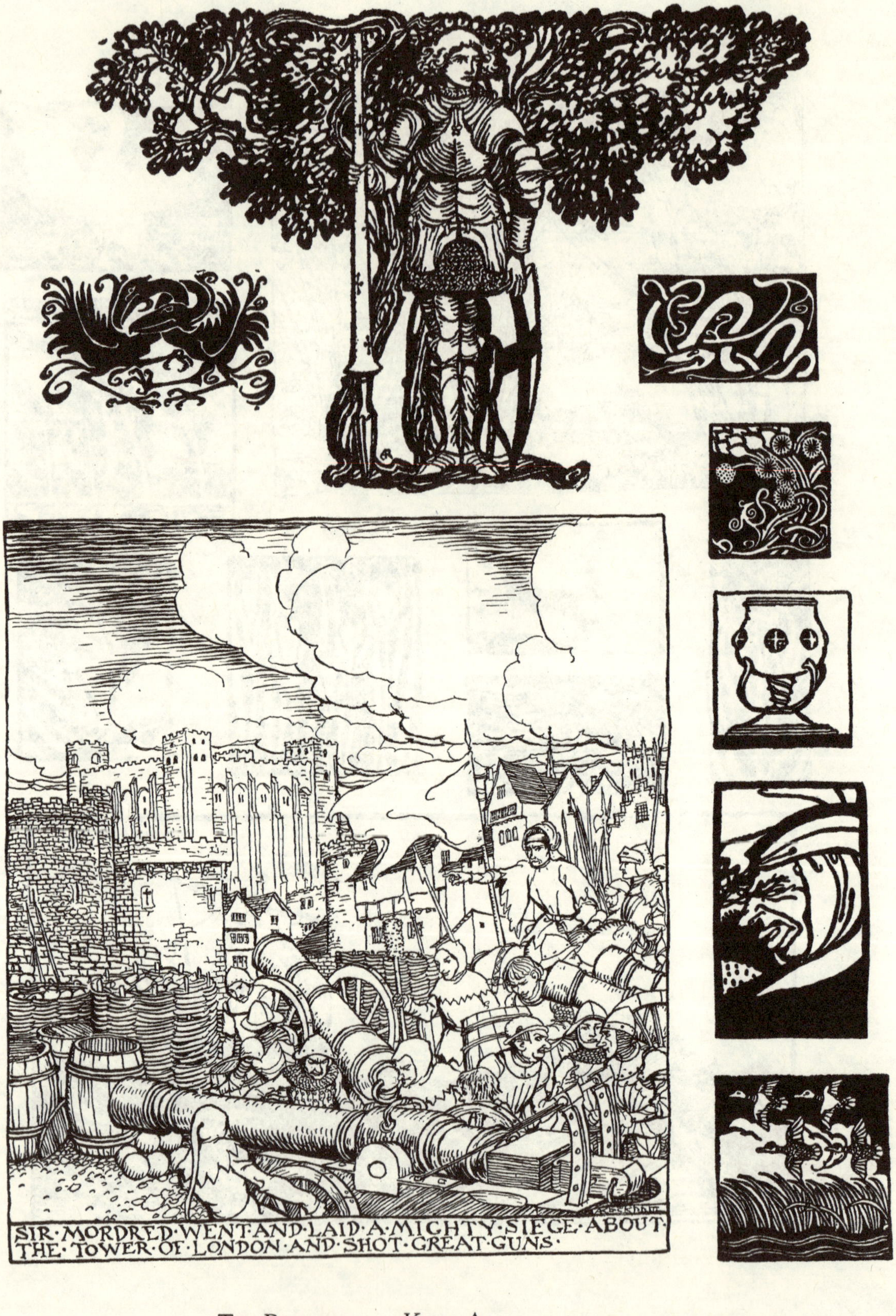

THE ROMANCE OF KING ARTHUR, 1917

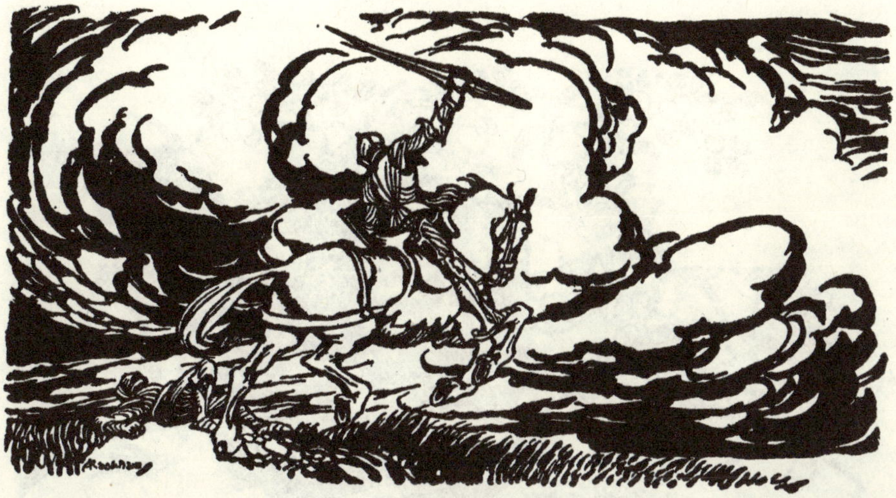

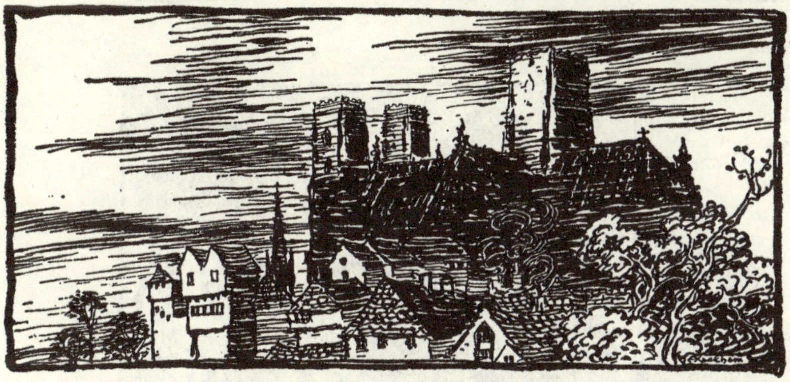

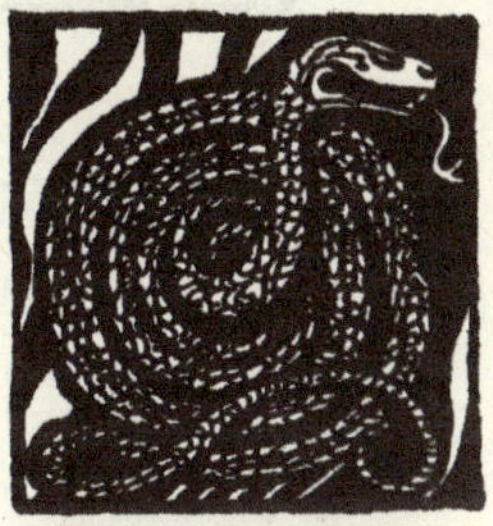

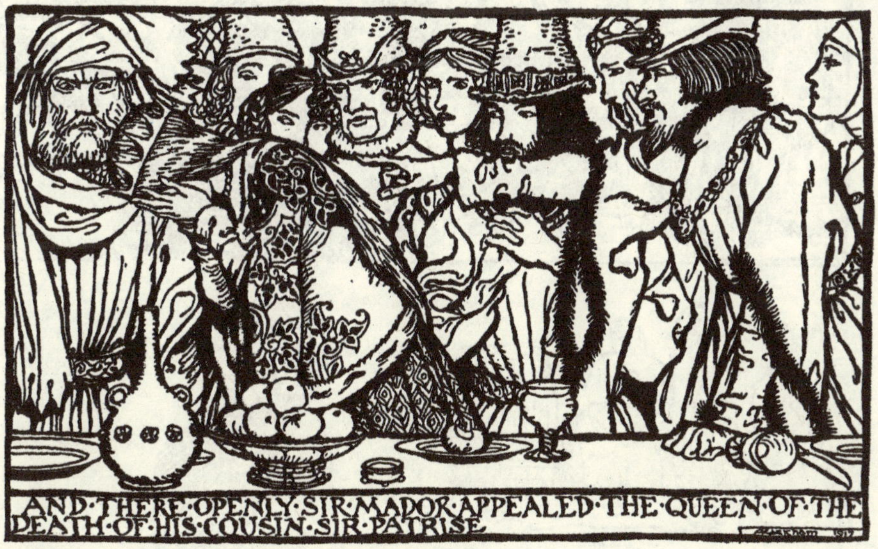

THE ROMANCE OF KING ARTHUR, 1917

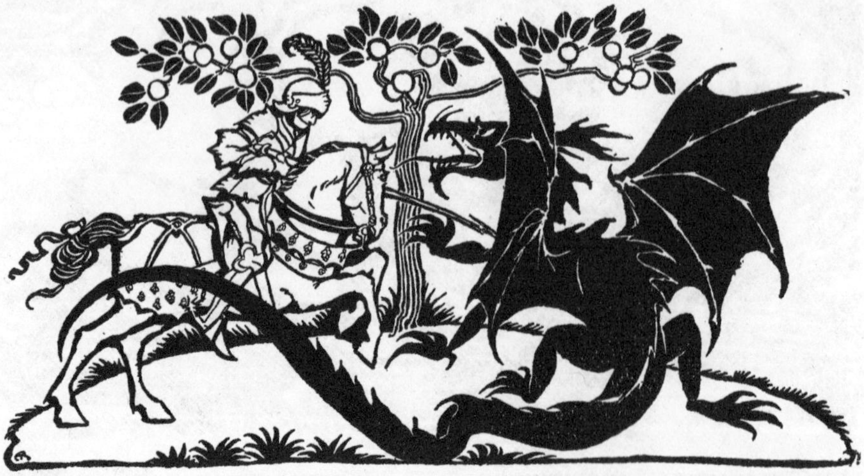

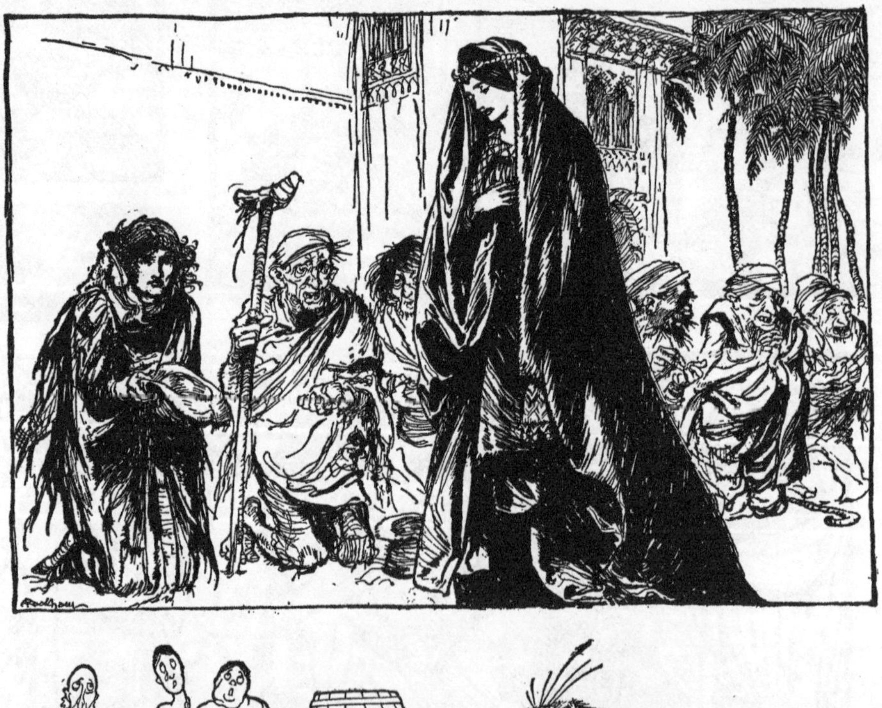

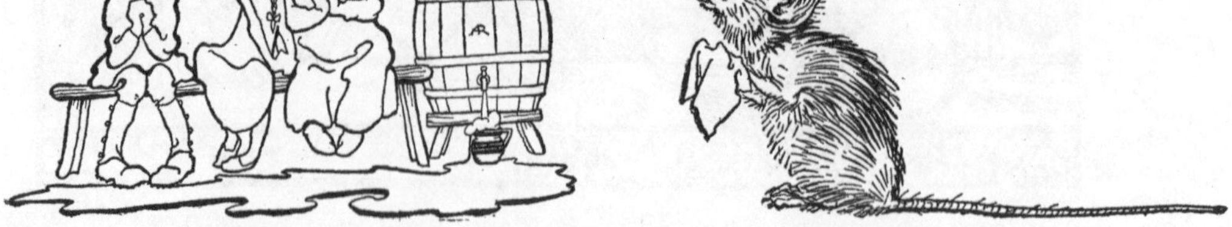

English Fairy Tales, 1918

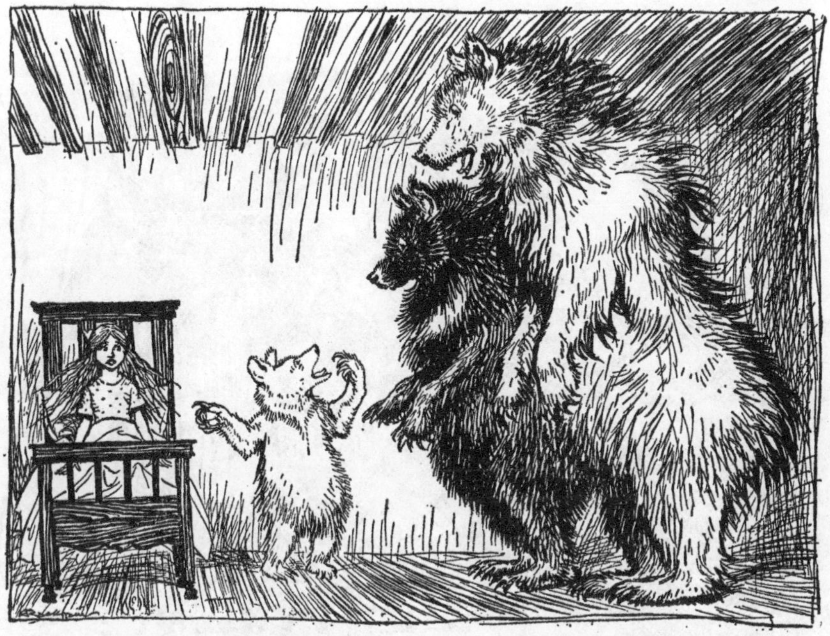

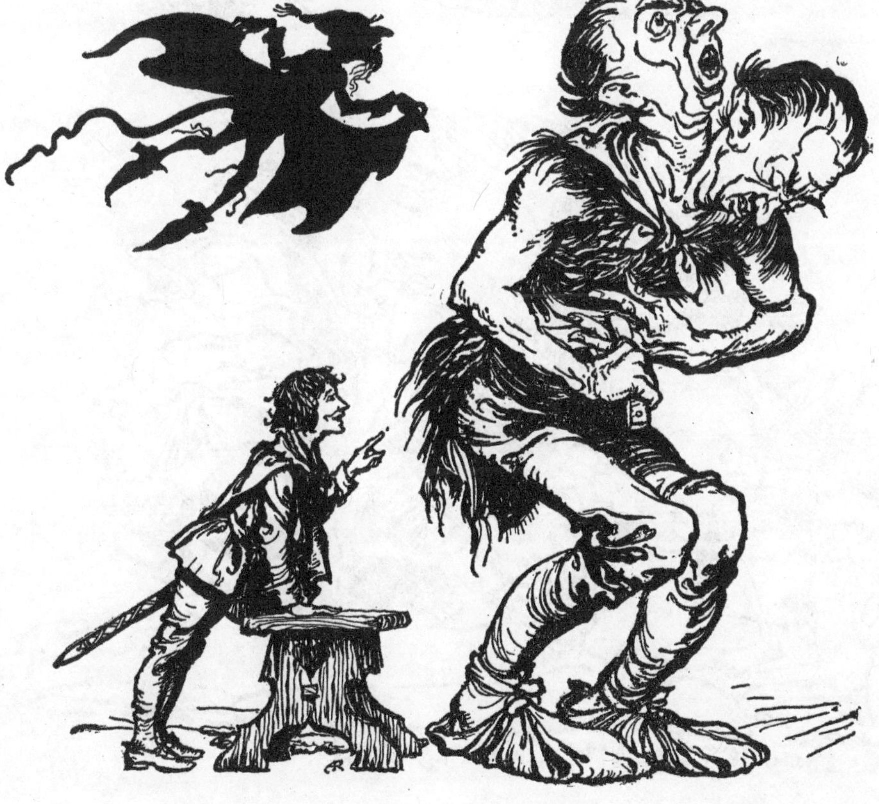

English Fairy Tales, 1918

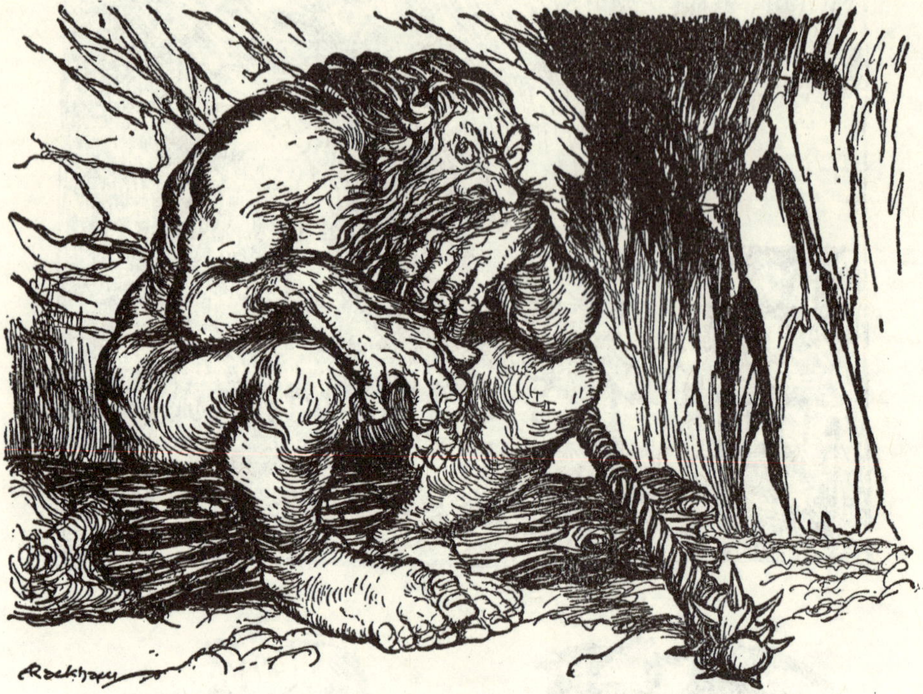

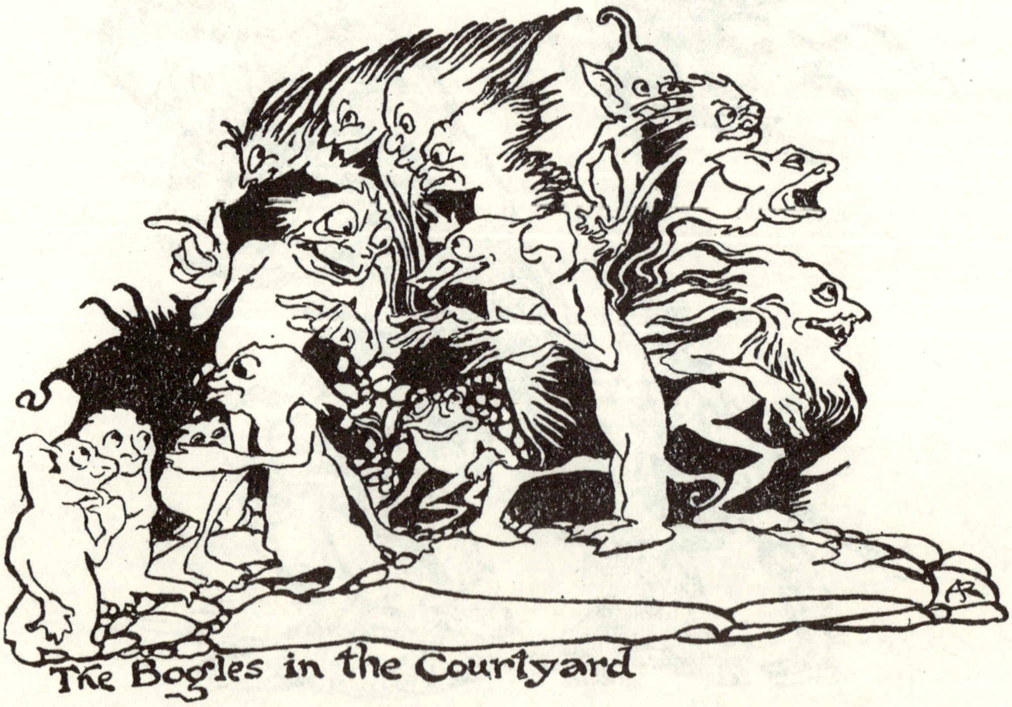

English Fairy Tales, 1918

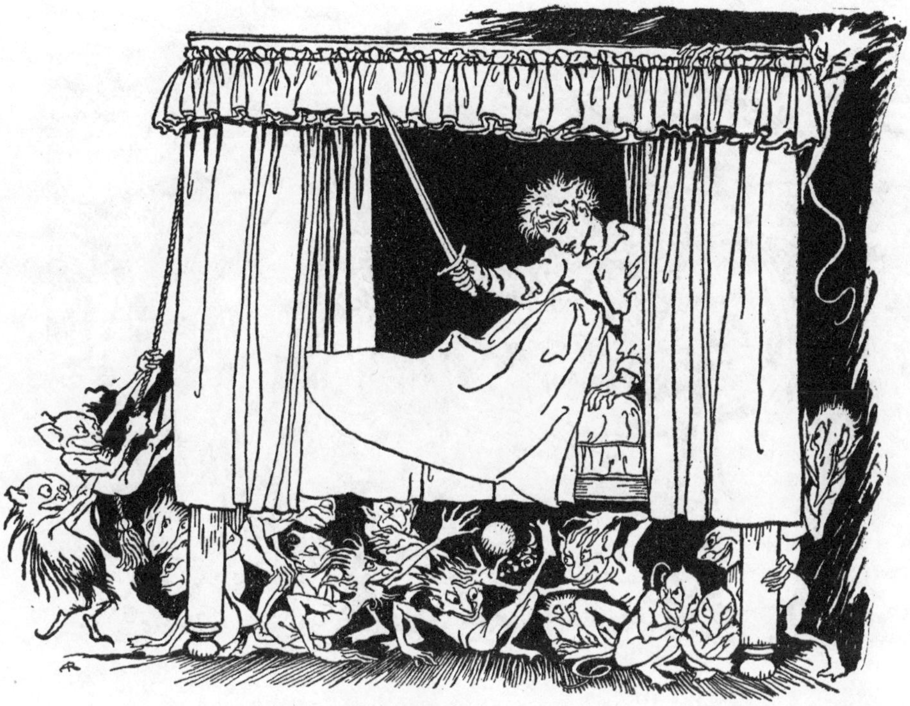

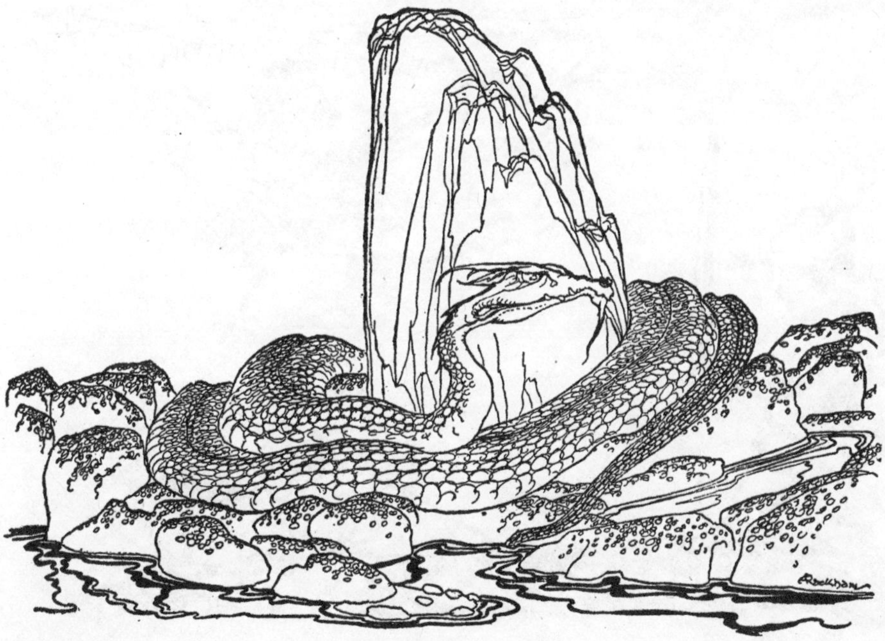

English Fairy Tales, 1918

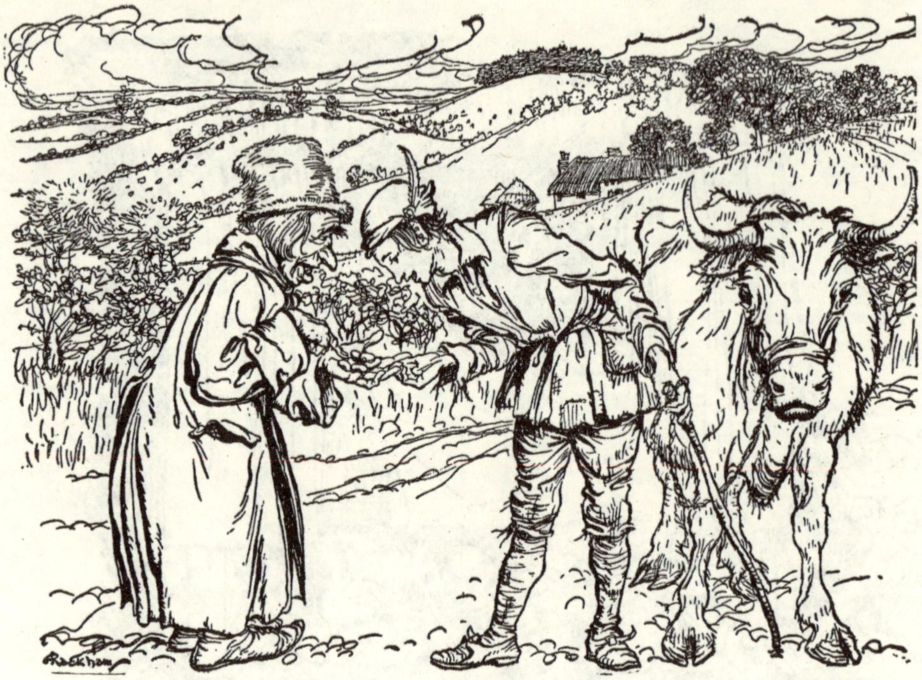

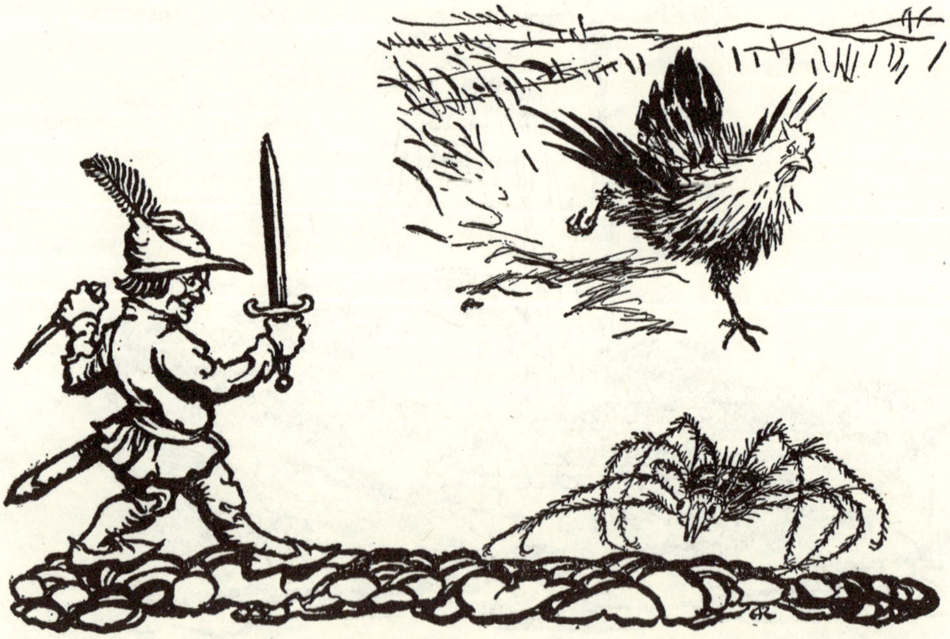

English Fairy Tales, 1918

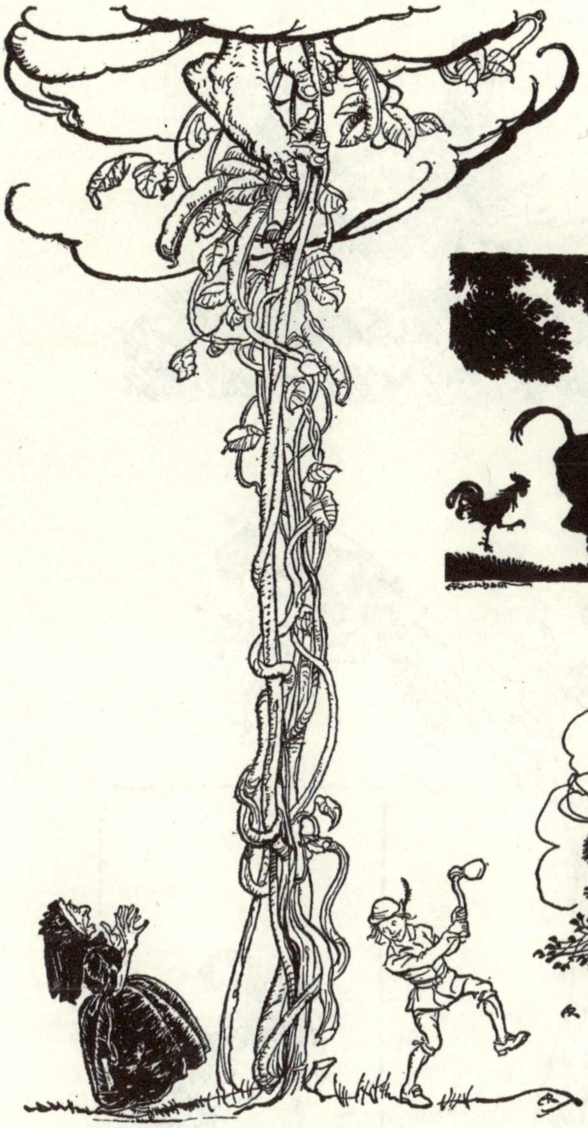

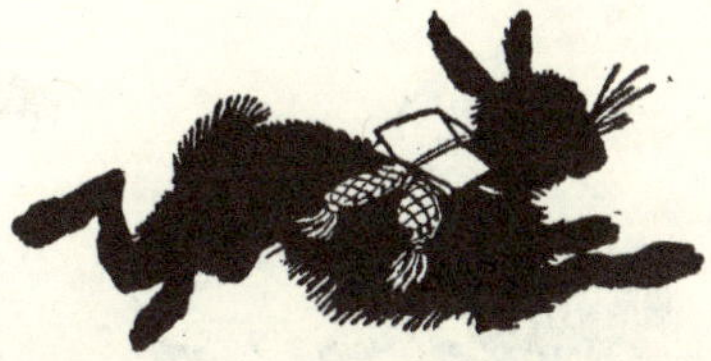

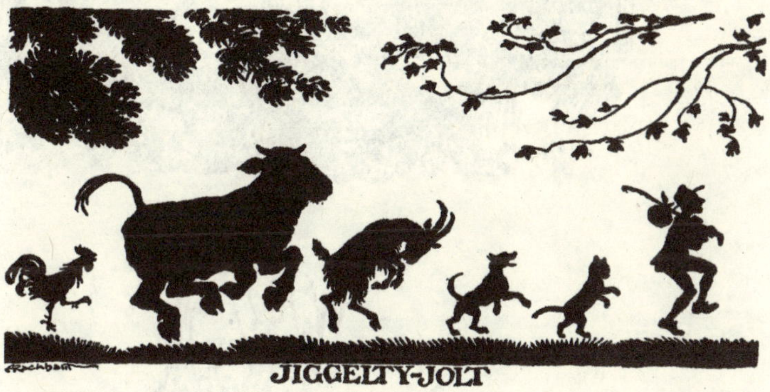

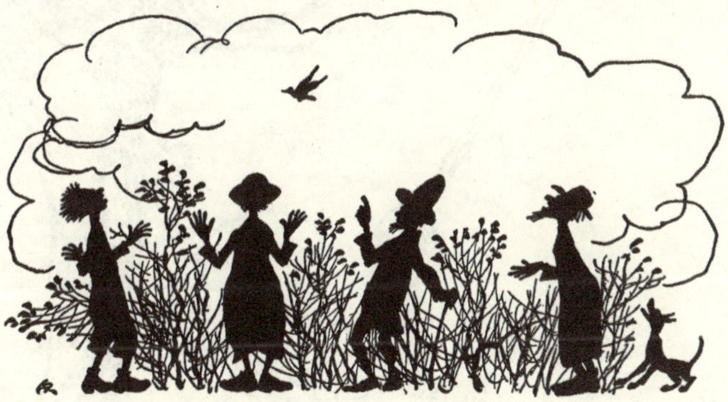

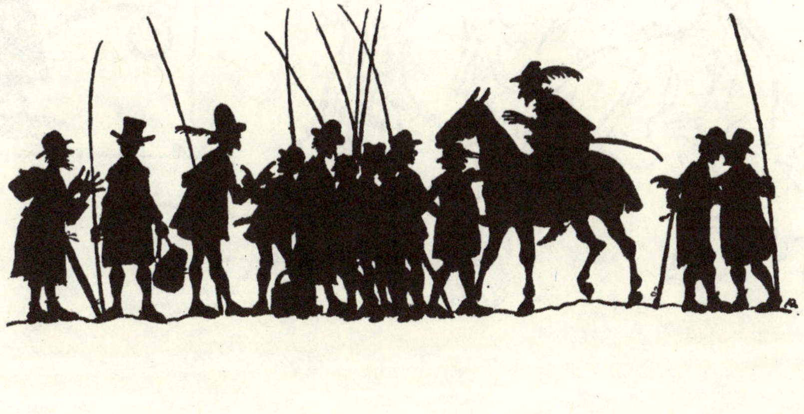

English Fairy Tales, 1918

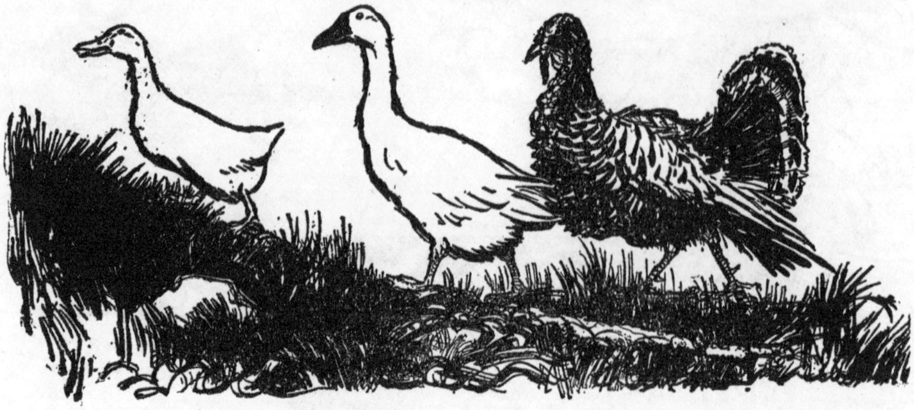

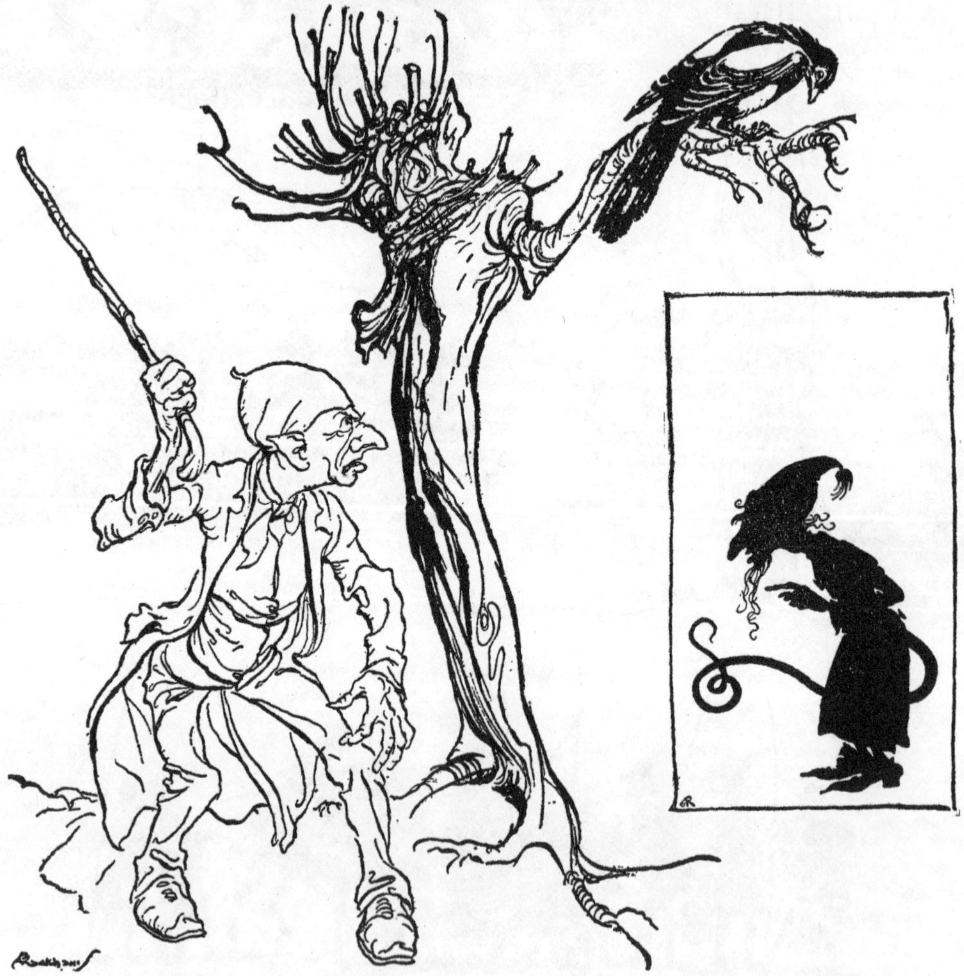

ENGLISH FAIRY TALES, 1918

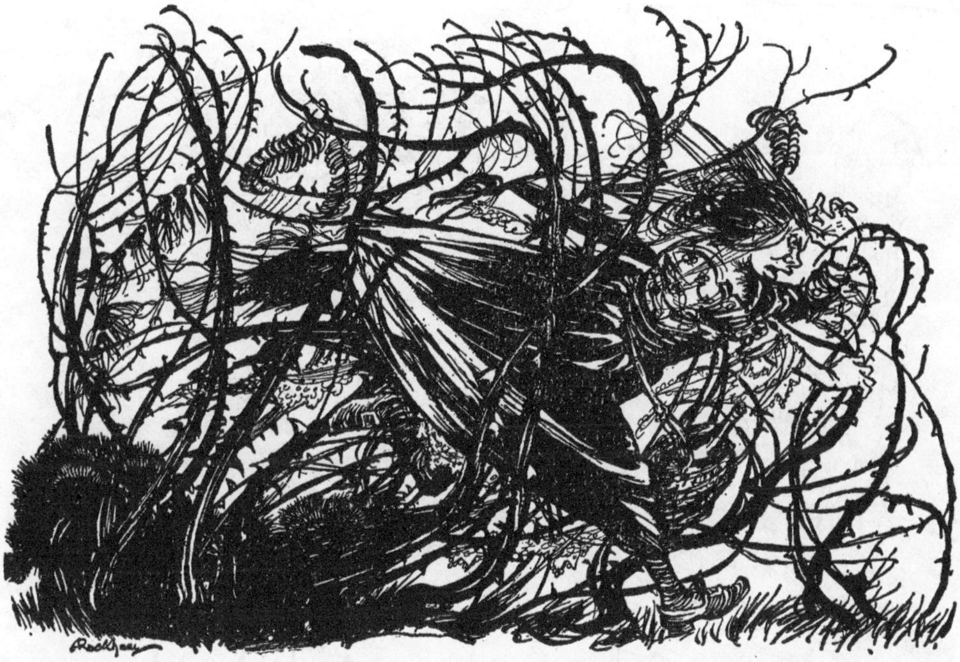

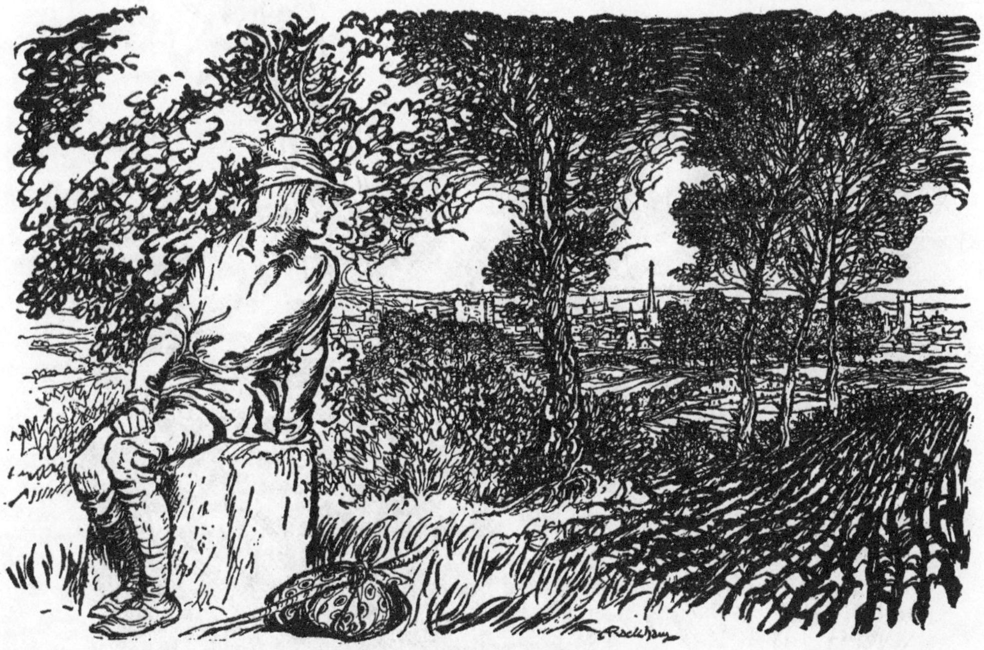

English Fairy Tales, 1918

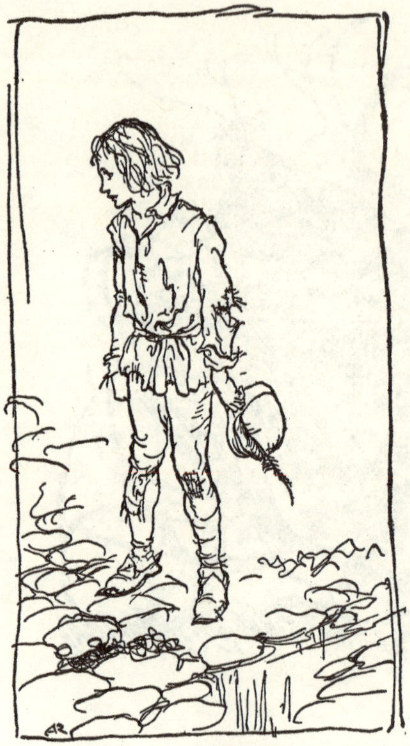

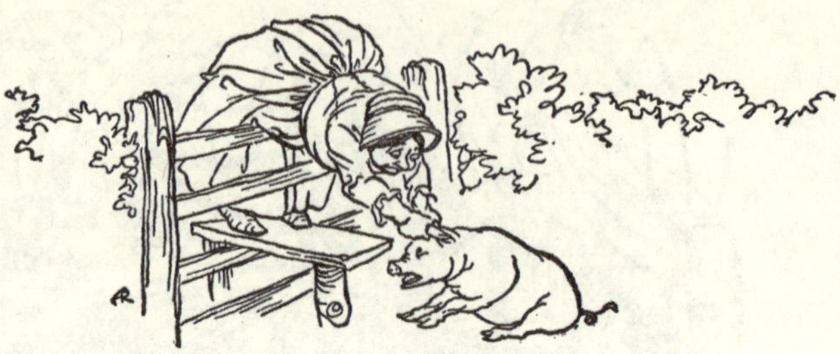

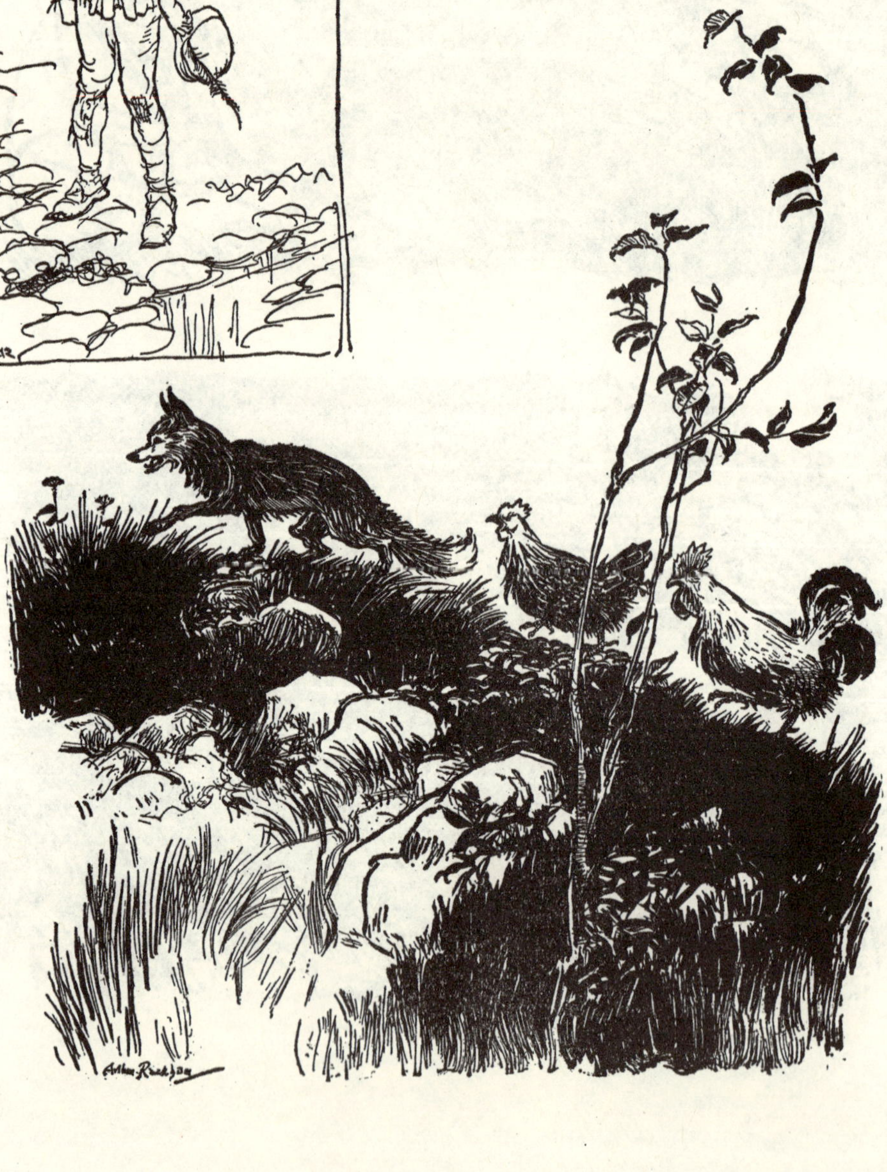

English Fairy Tales, 1918

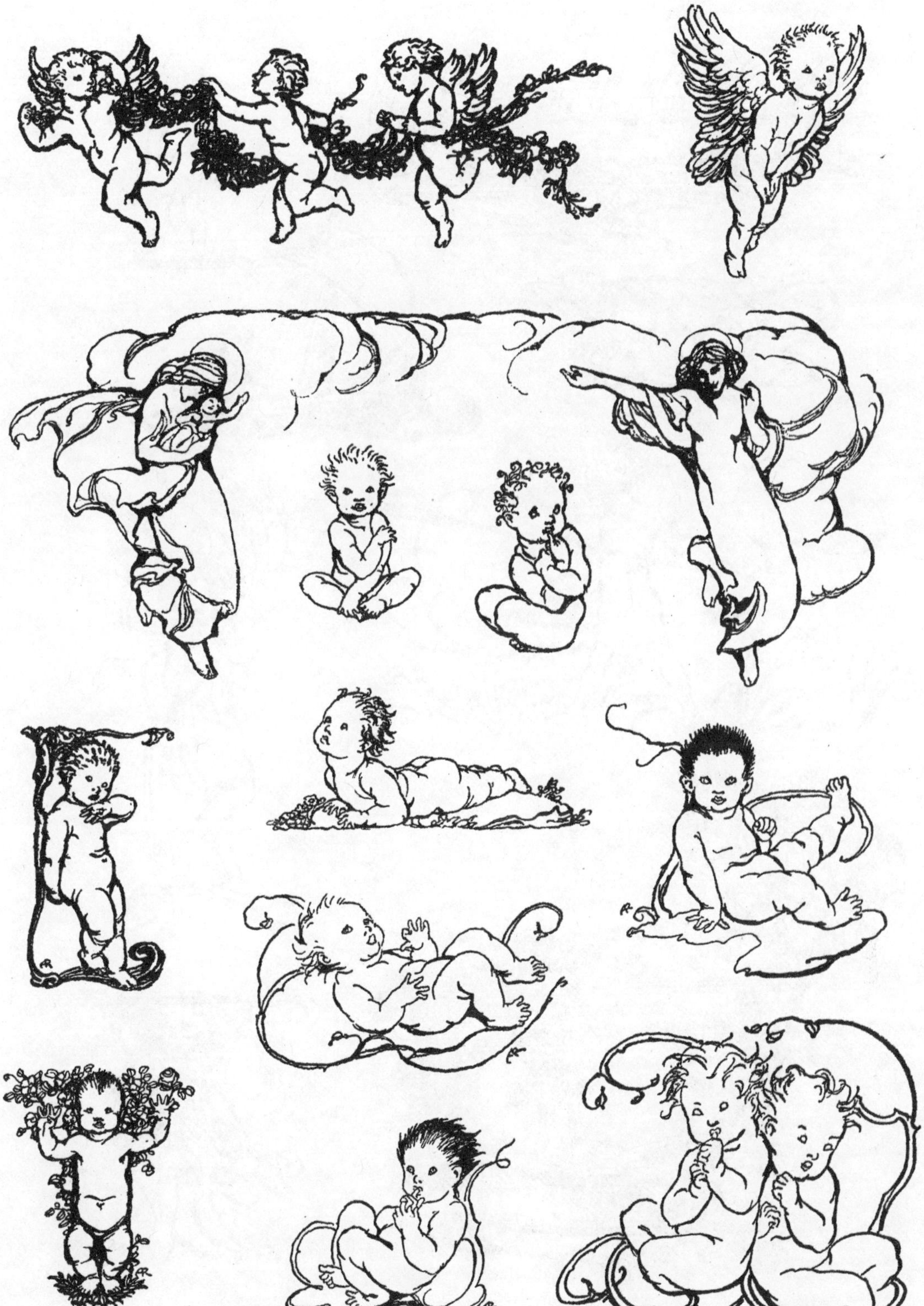

The Springtide of Life: Poems of Childhood, 1918

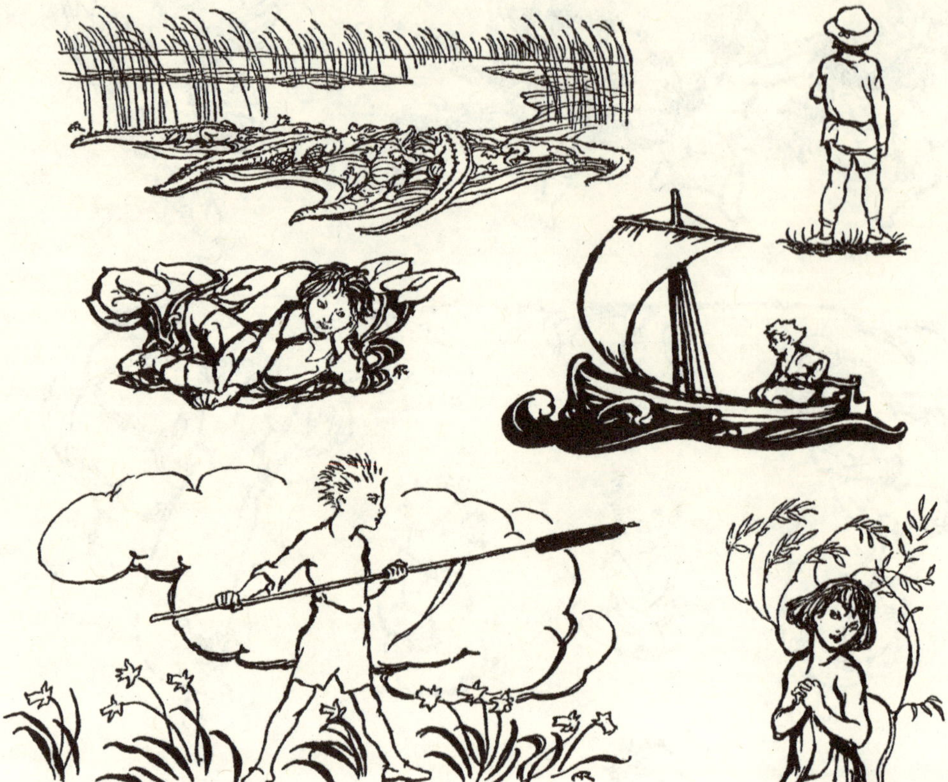

The Springtide of Life: Poems of Childhood, 1918

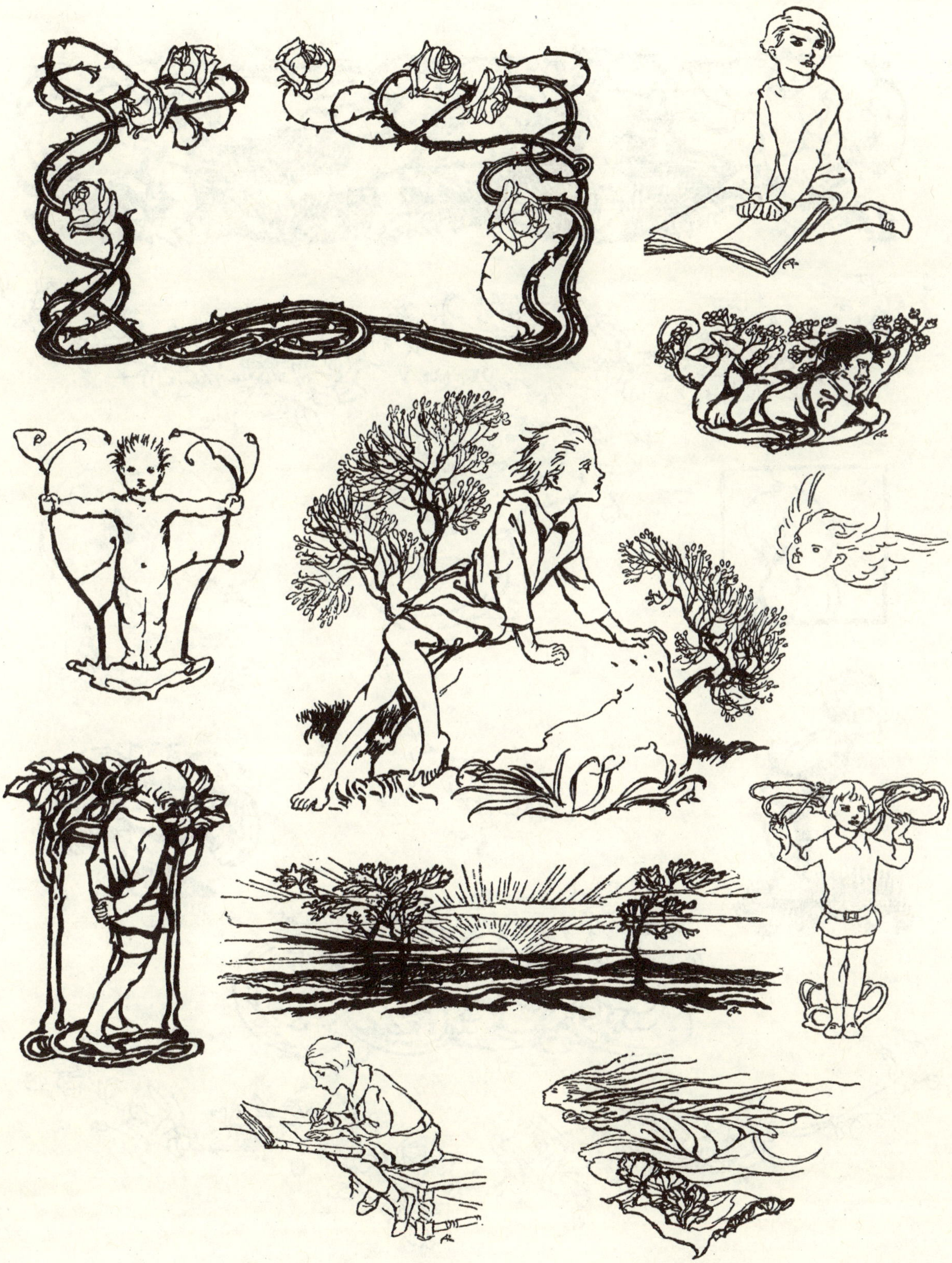

The Springtide of Life: Poems of Childhood, 1918

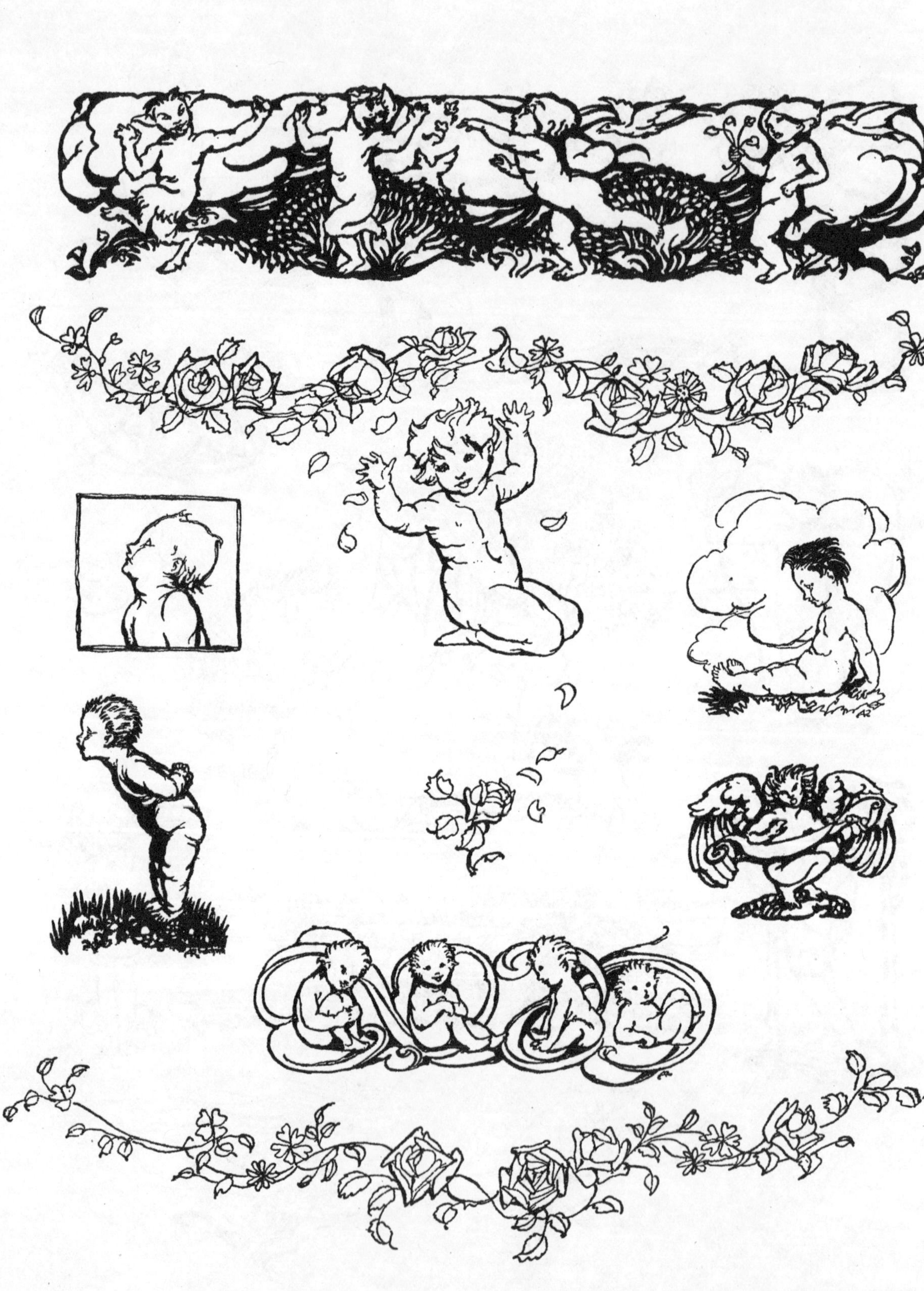

The Springtide of Life: Poems of Childhood, 1918

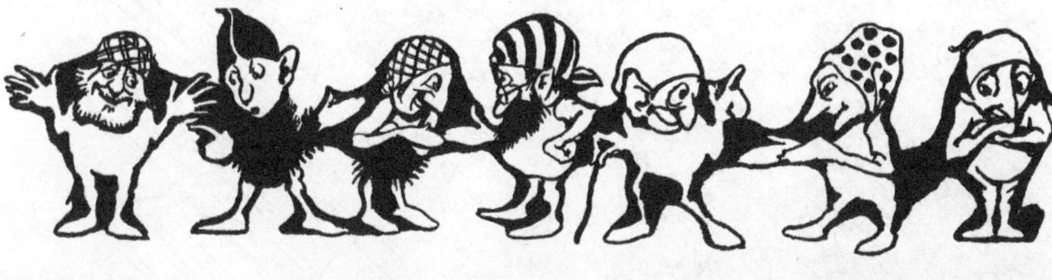

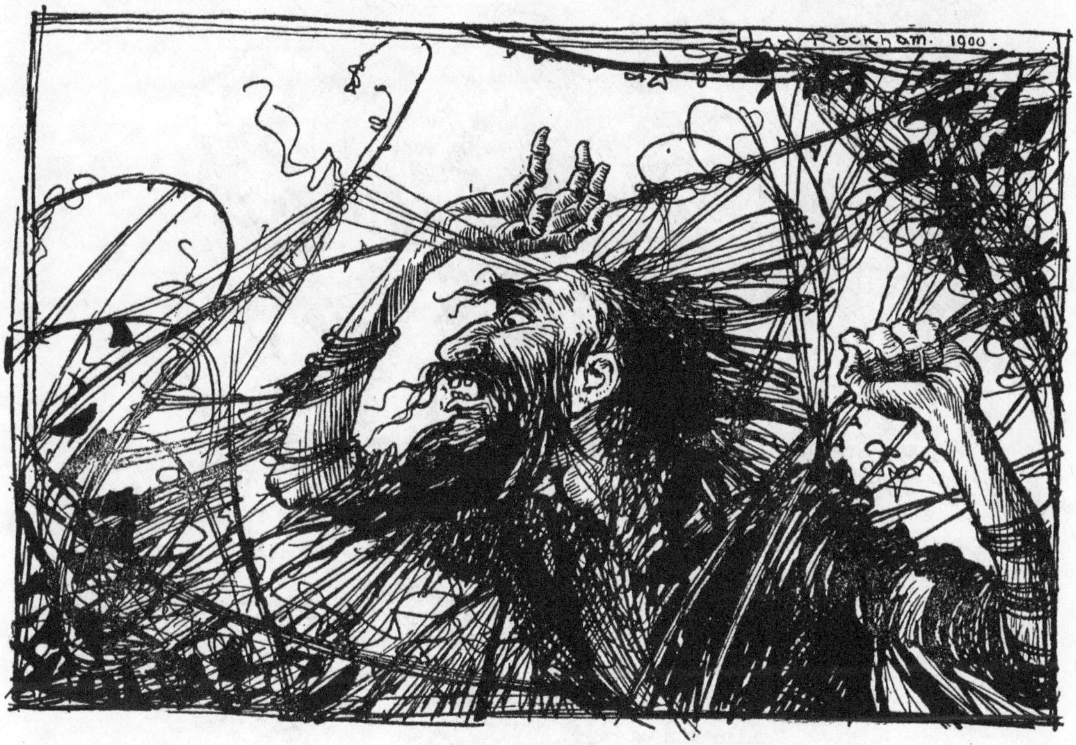

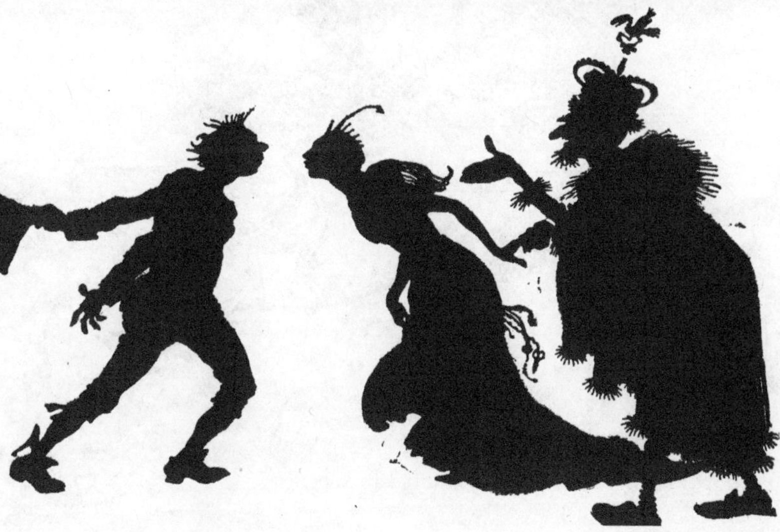

SNOWDROP AND OTHER TALES, 1920

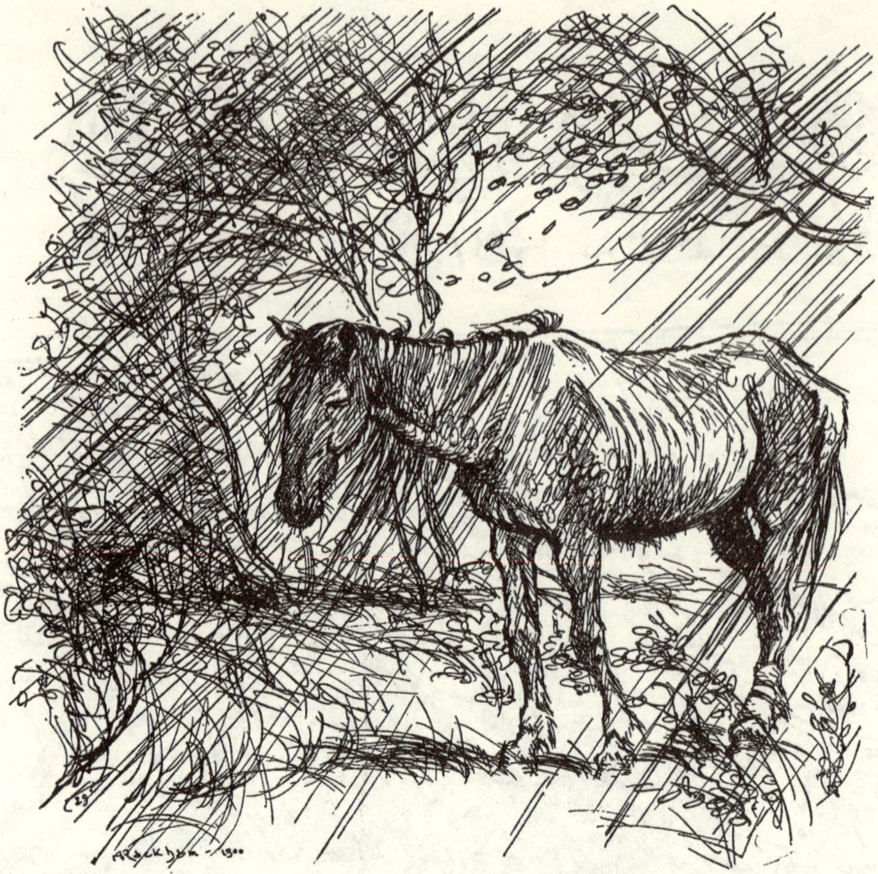

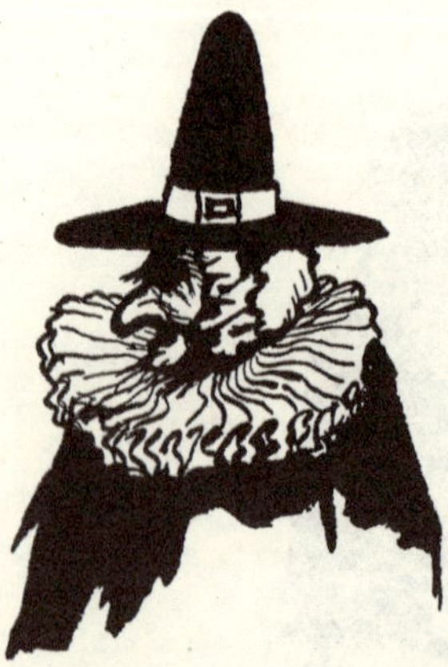

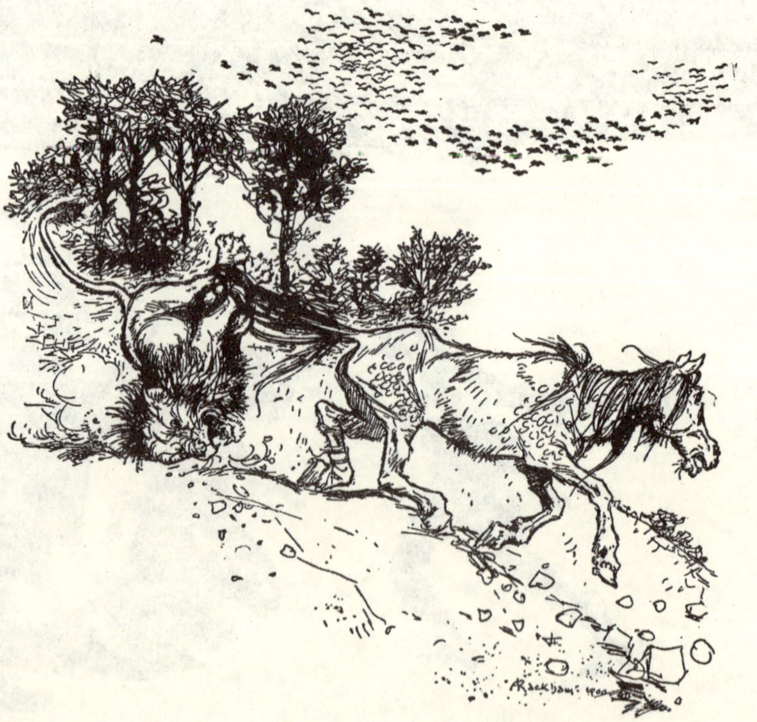

Snowdrop and Other Tales, 1920

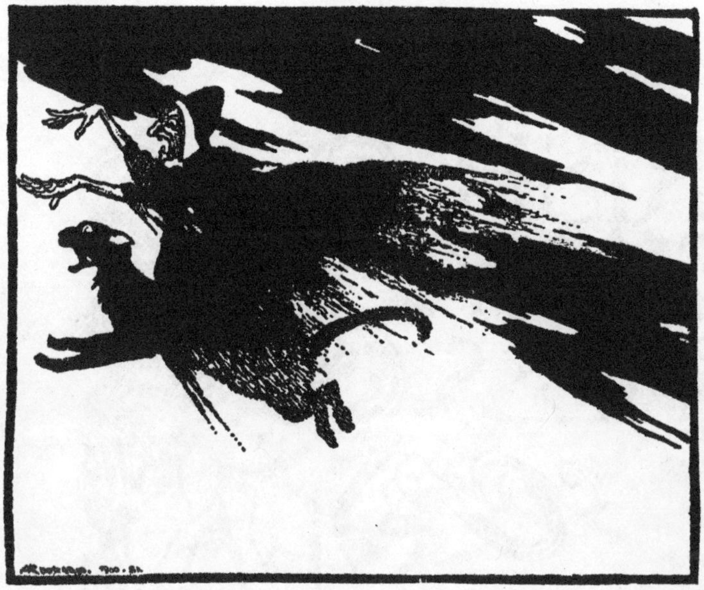
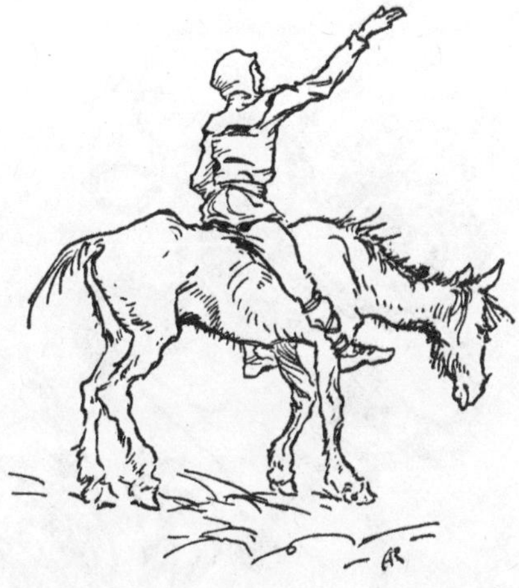
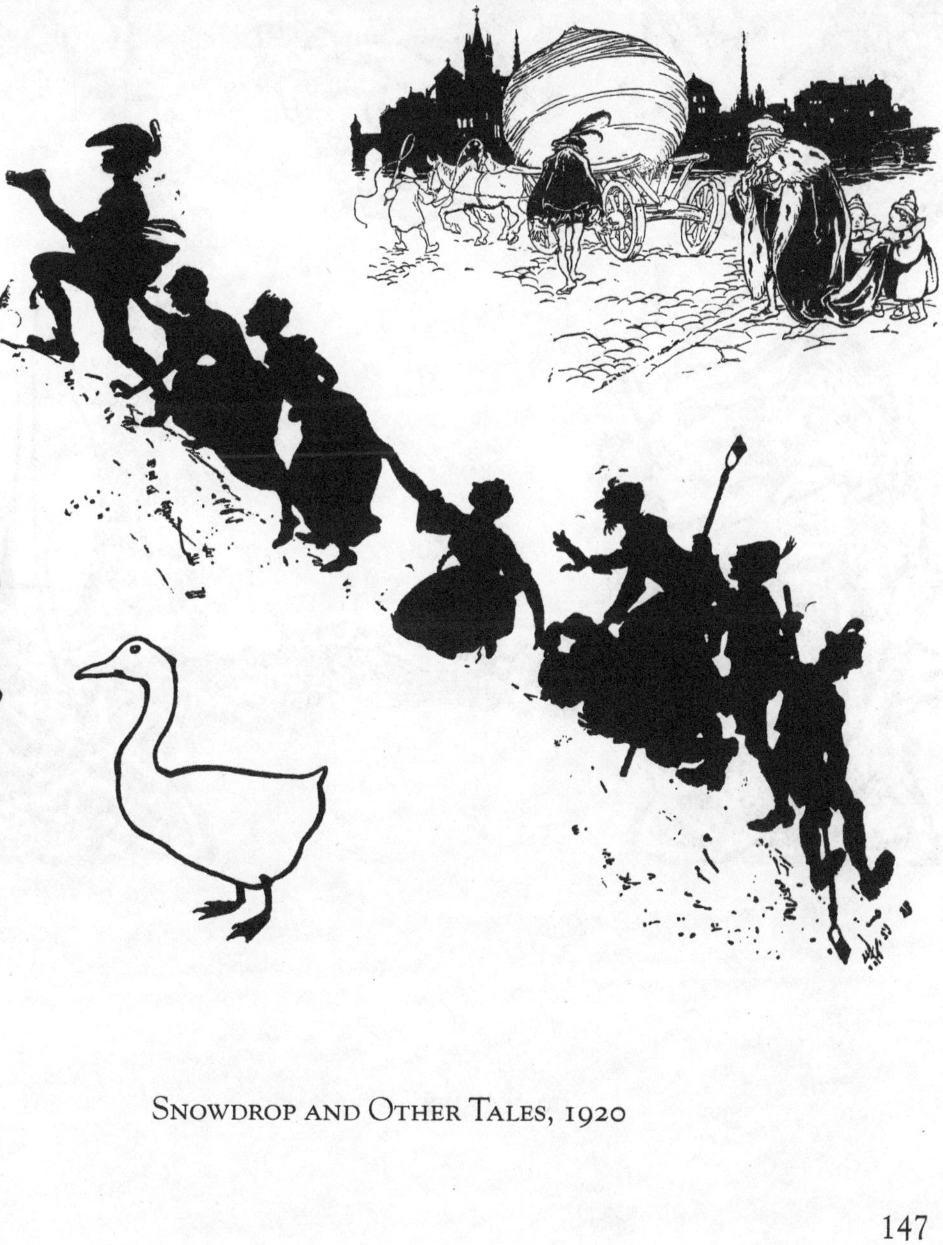
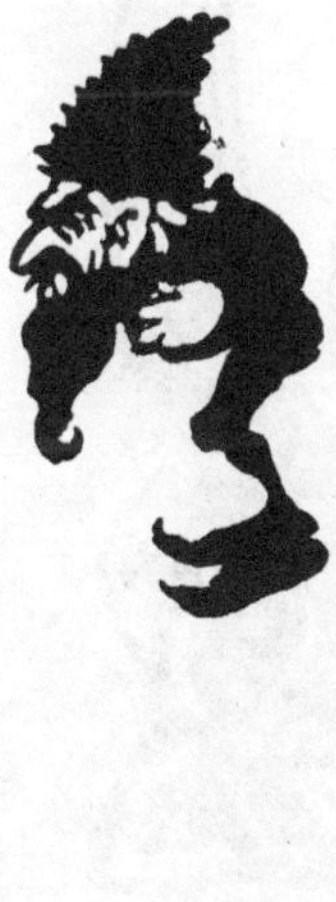

SNOWDROP AND OTHER TALES, 1920

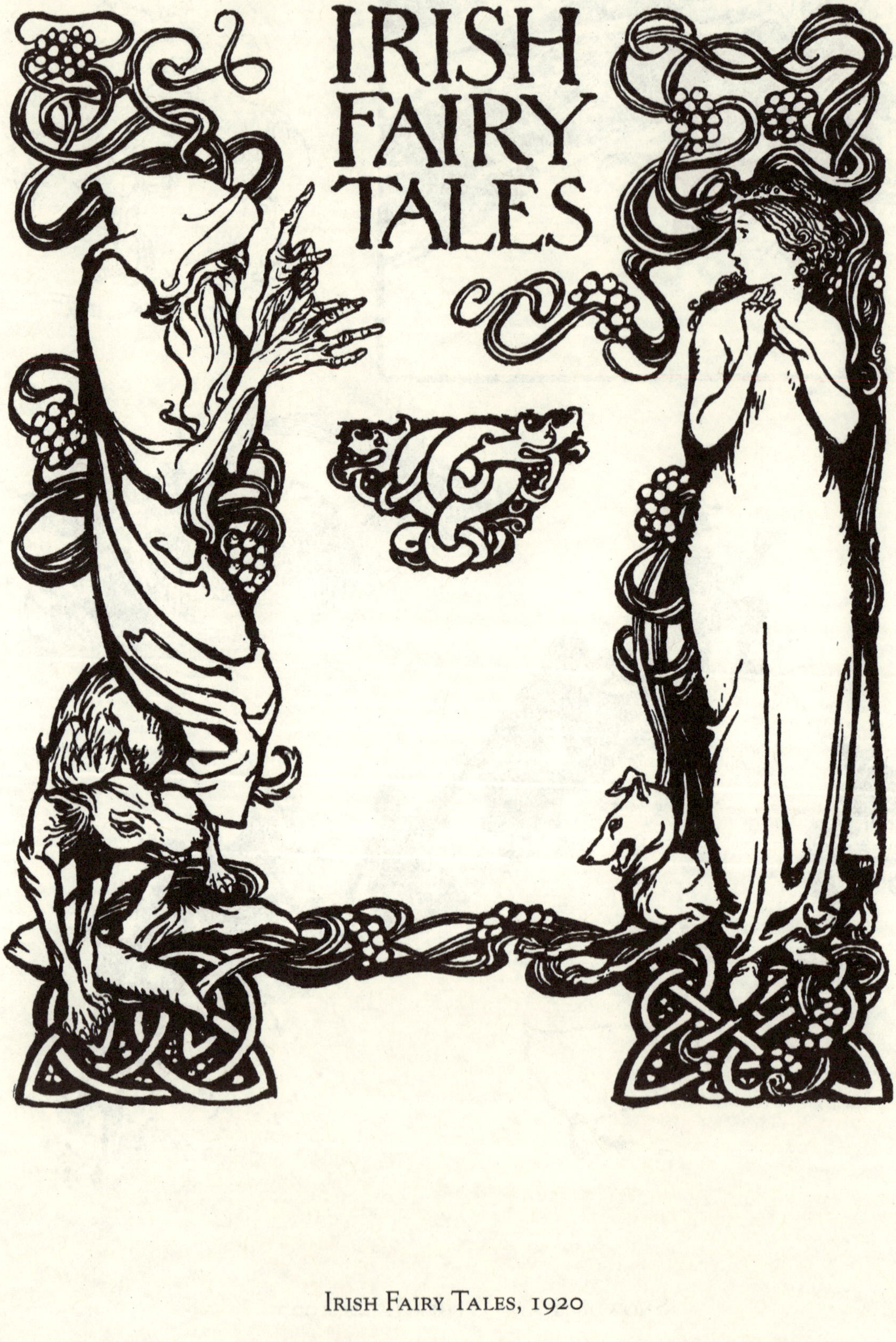

Irish Fairy Tales, 1920

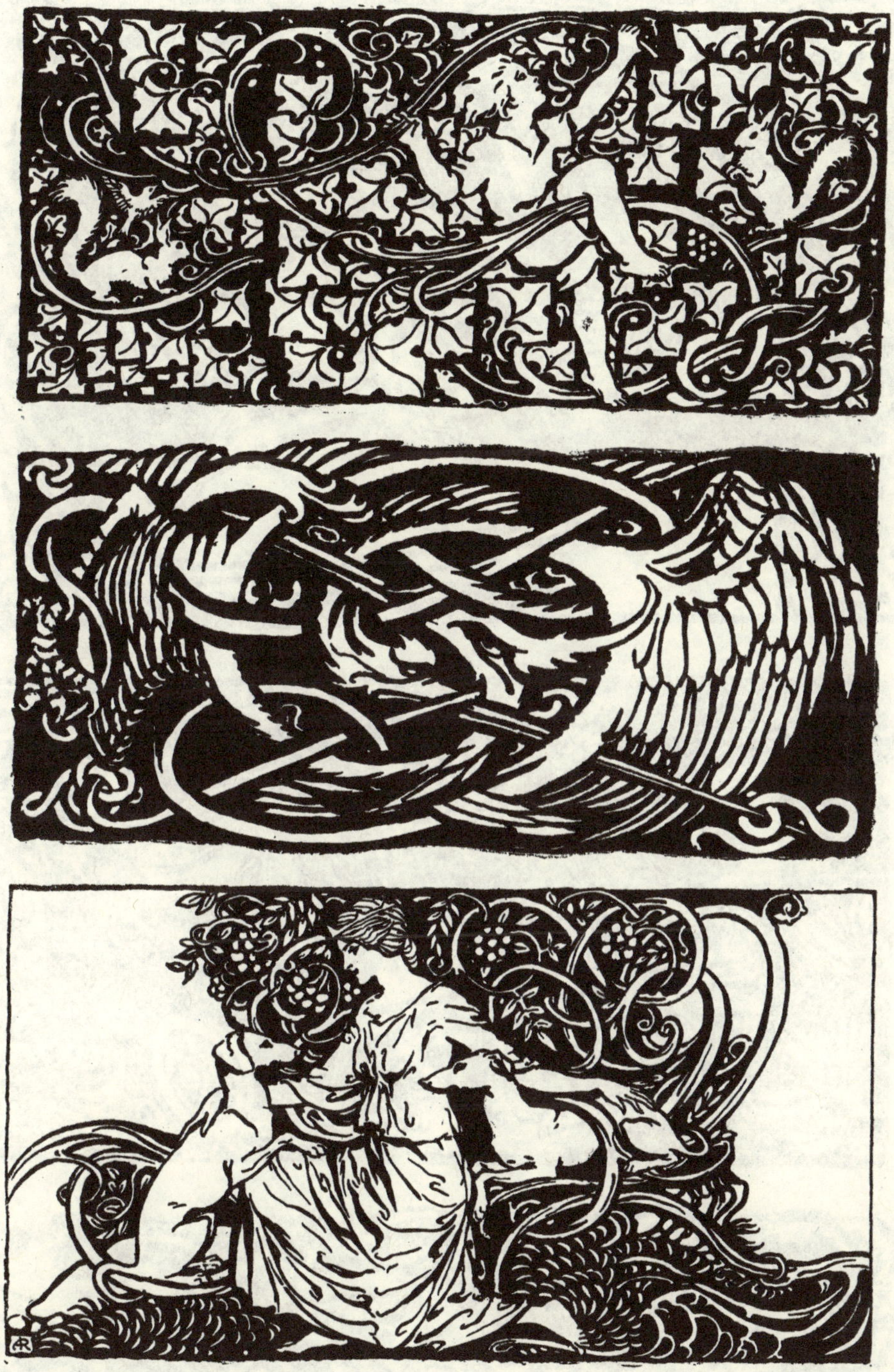

IRISH FAIRY TALES, 1920

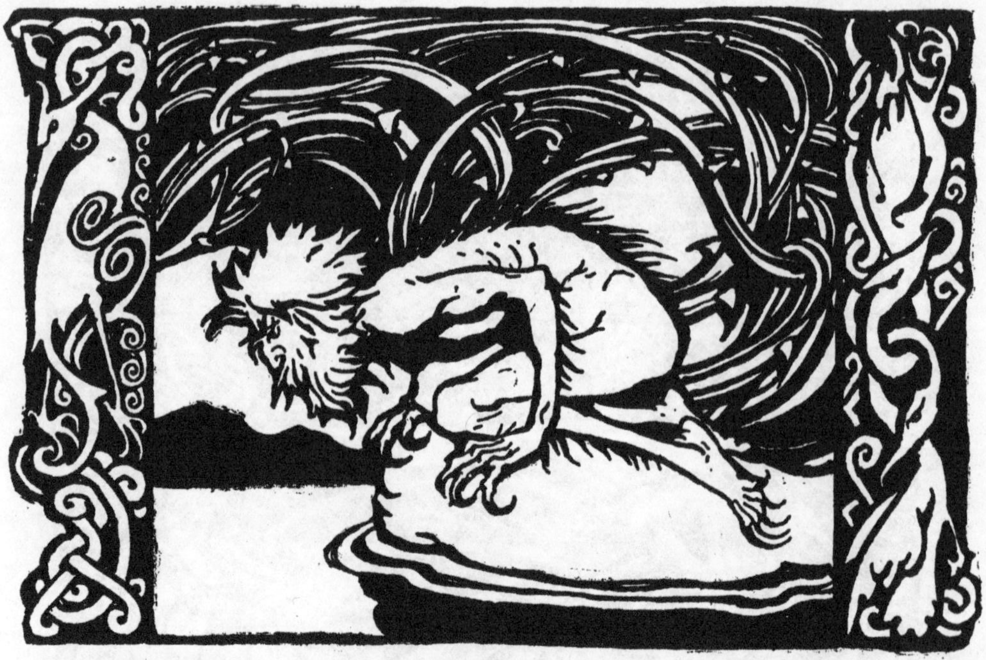

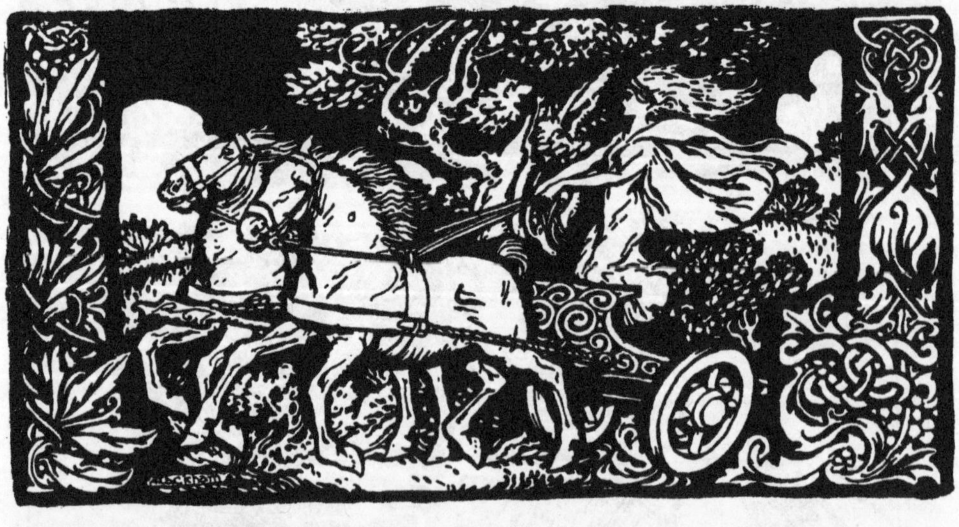

Irish Fairy Tales, 1920

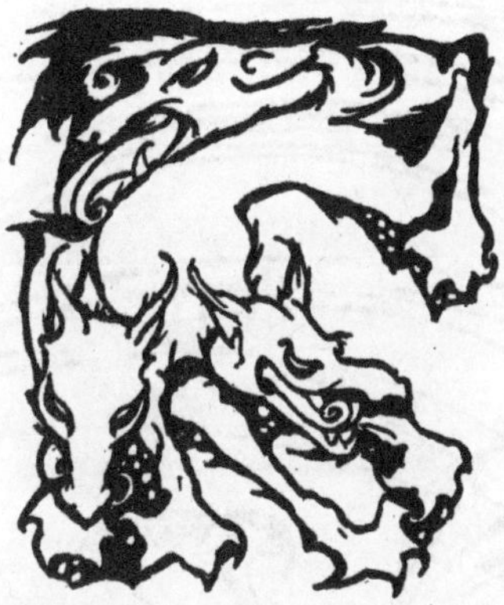

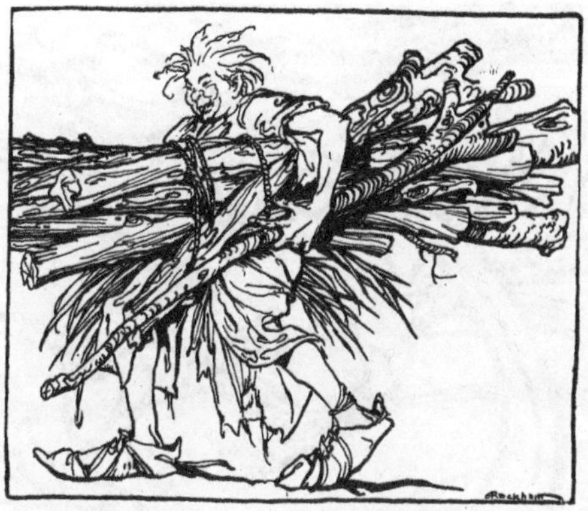

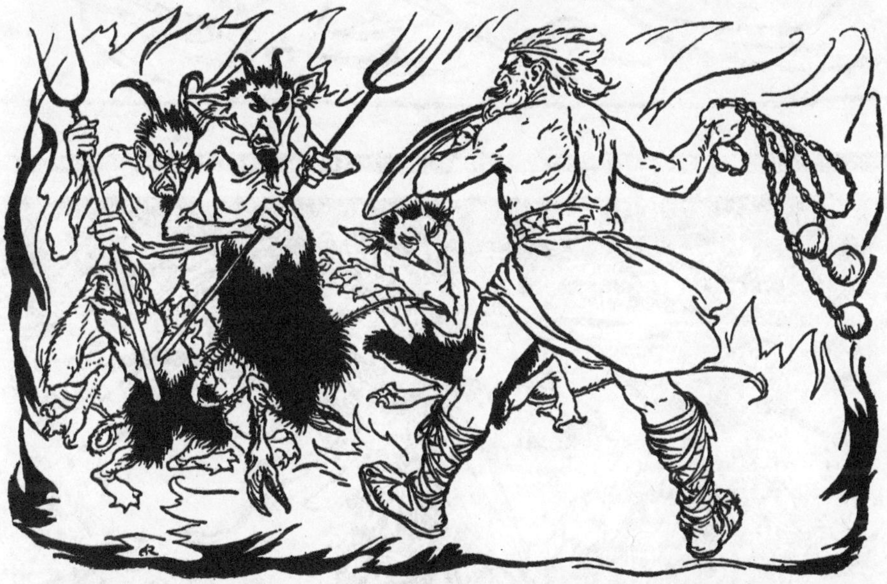

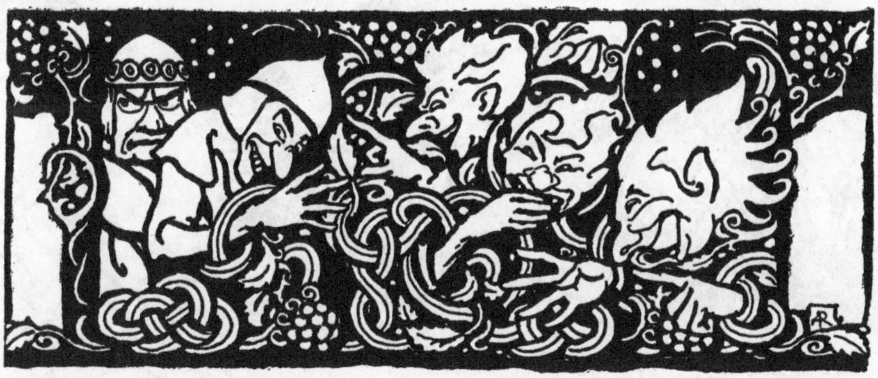

Irish Fairy Tales, 1920

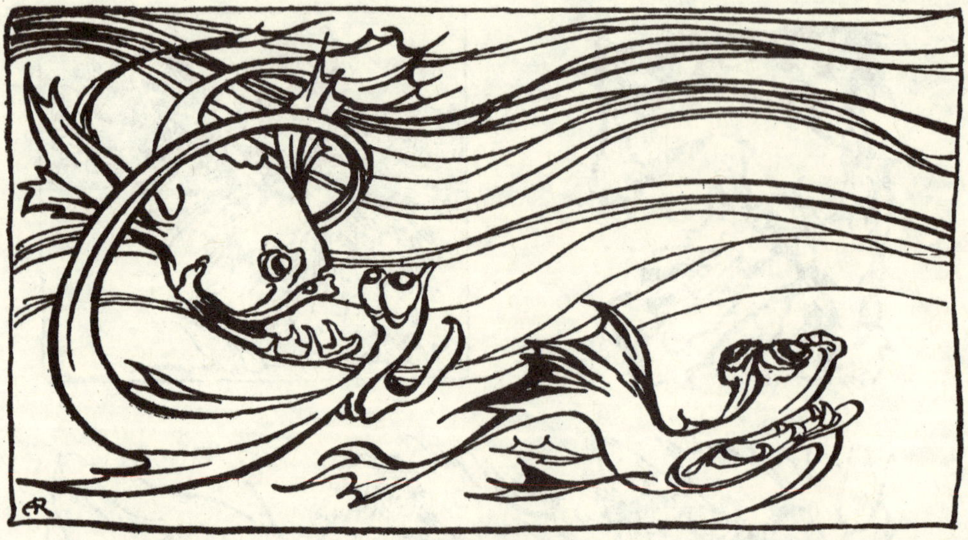

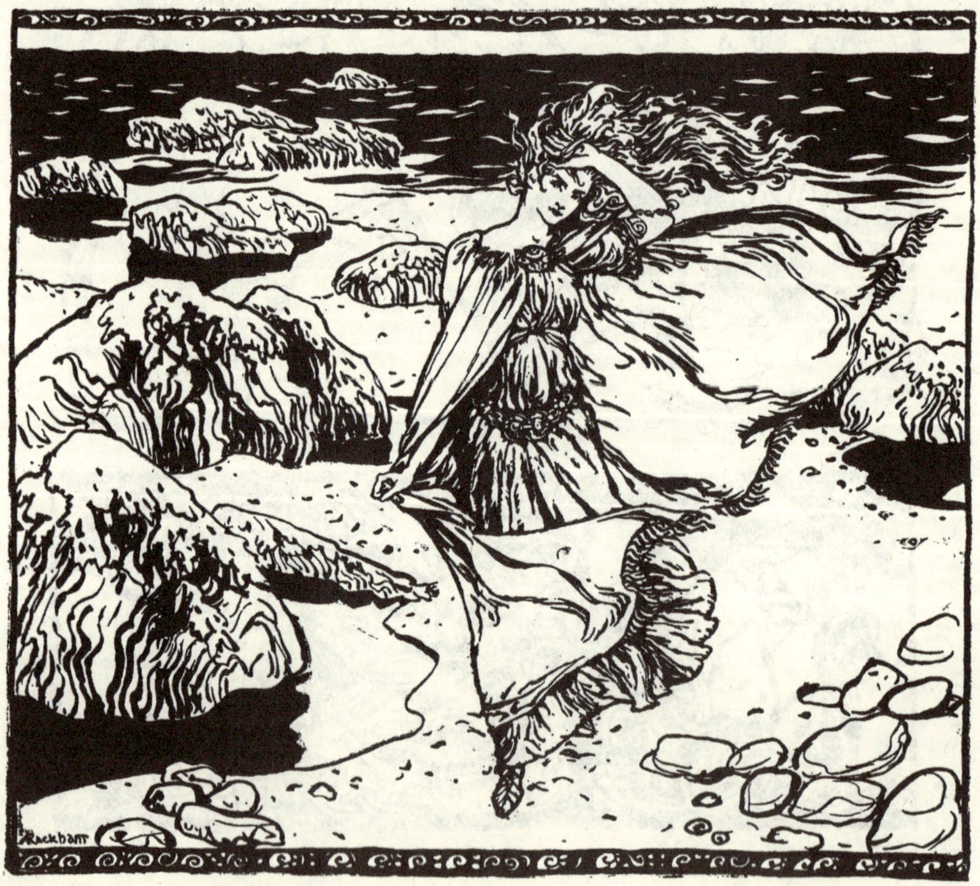

Irish Fairy Tales, 1920

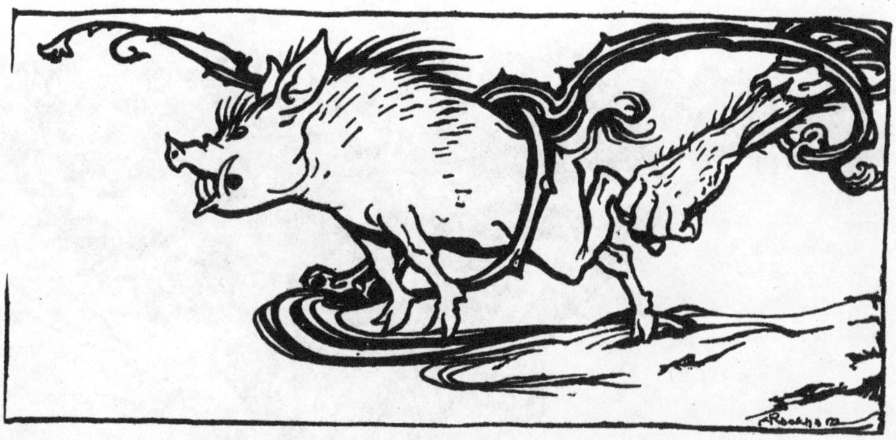

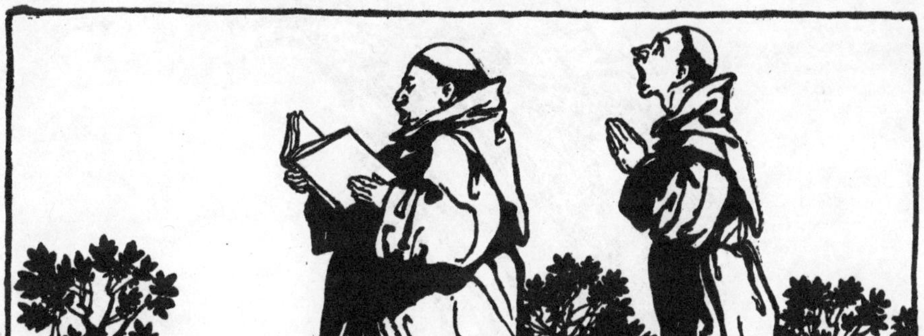

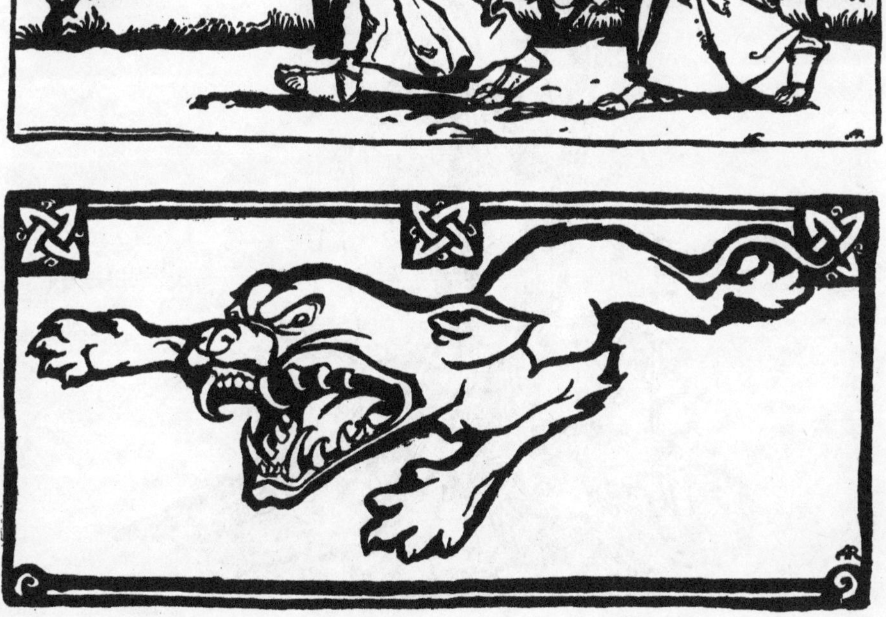

Irish Fairy Tales, 1920

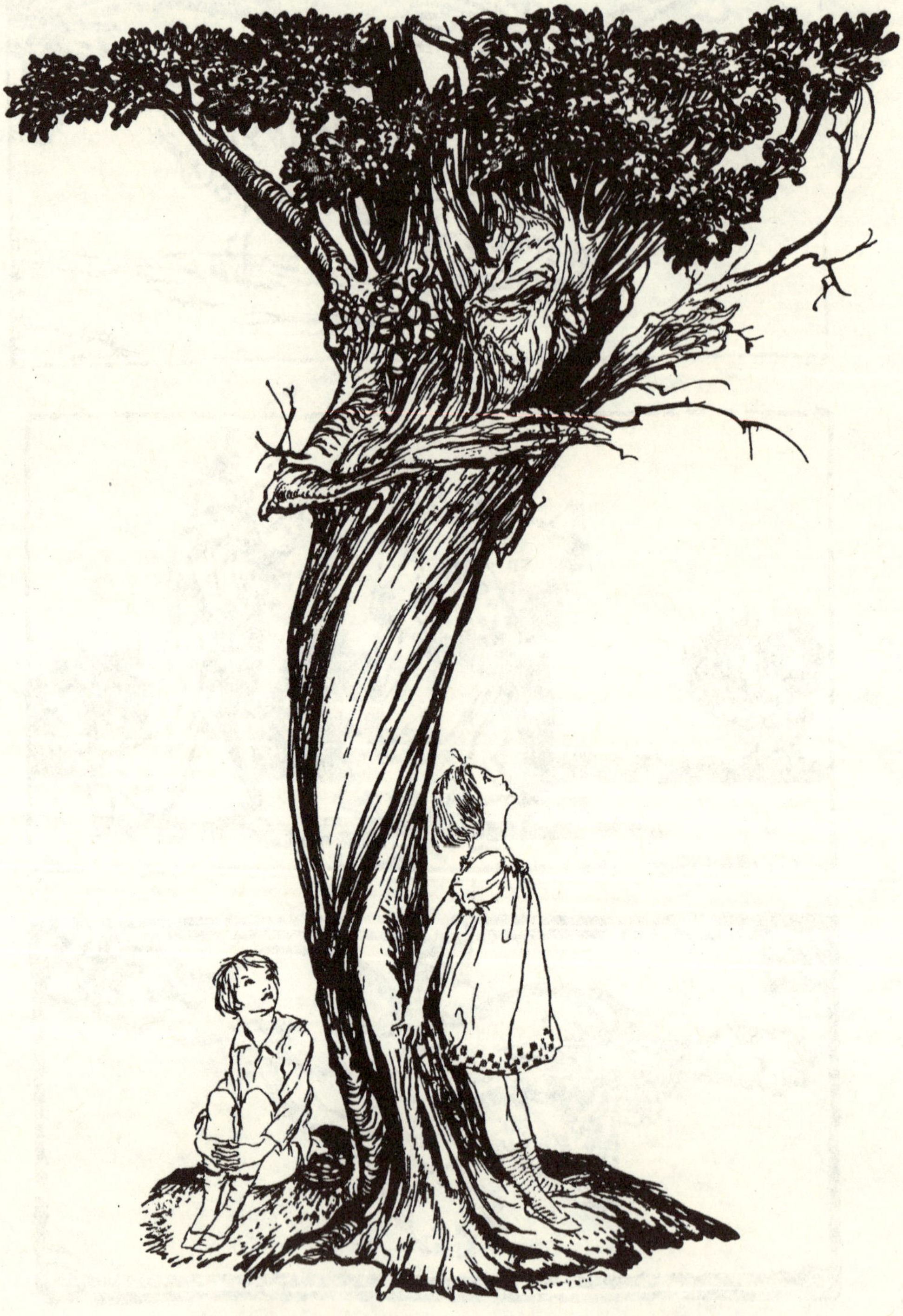

"The Hawthorn Tree"

A Wonder Book, 1922

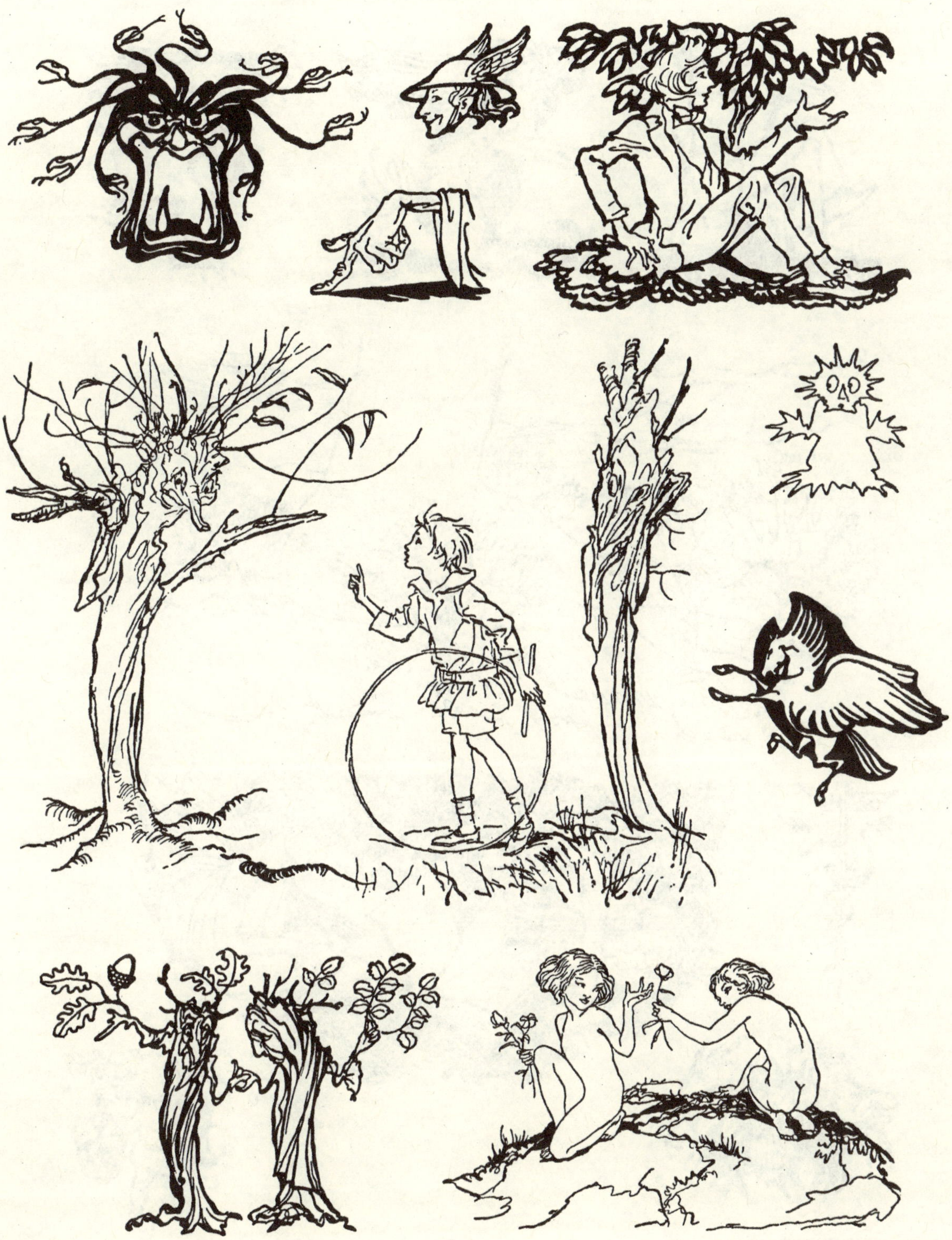

A WONDER BOOK, 1922

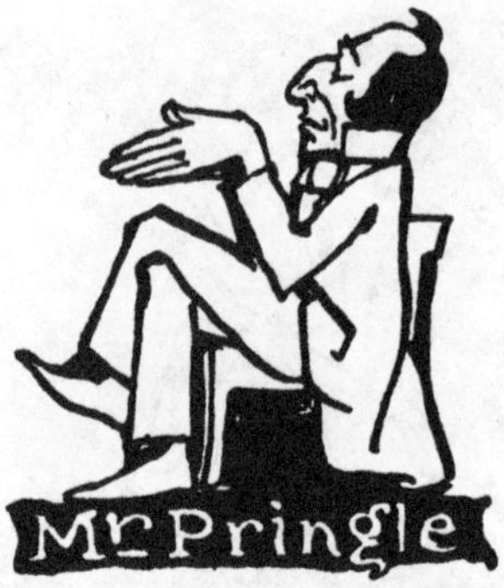

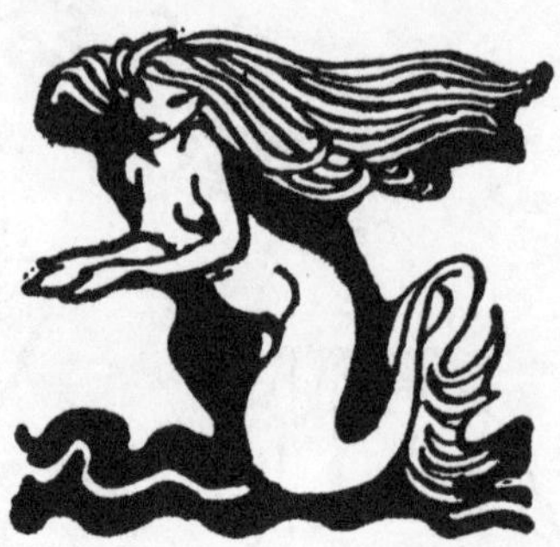

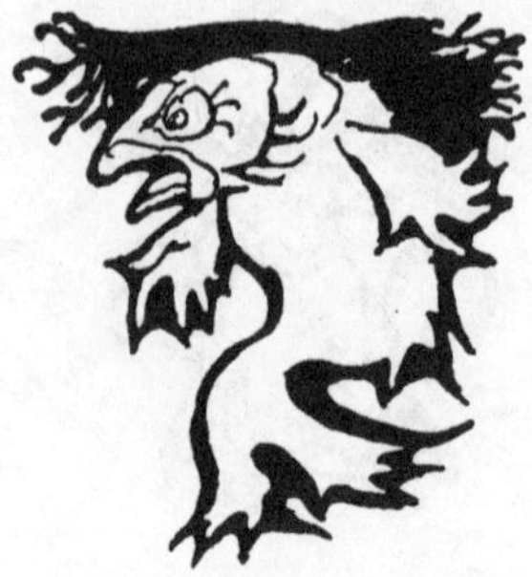

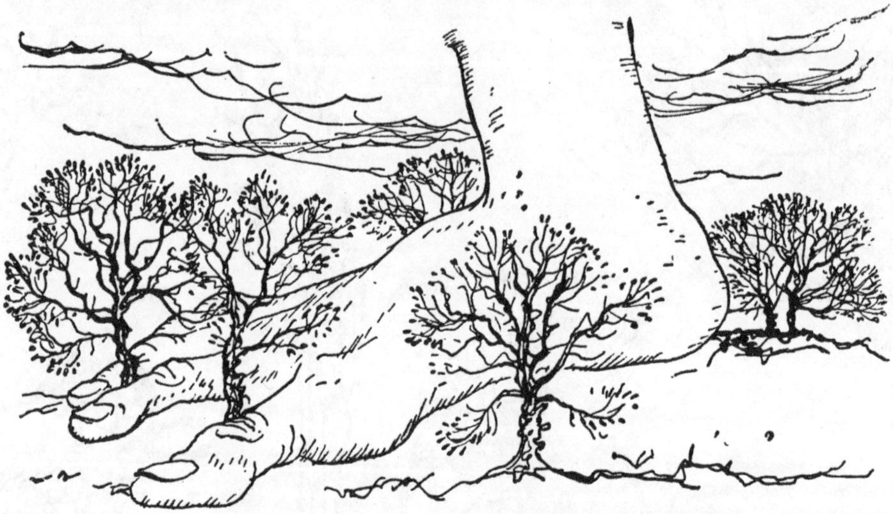

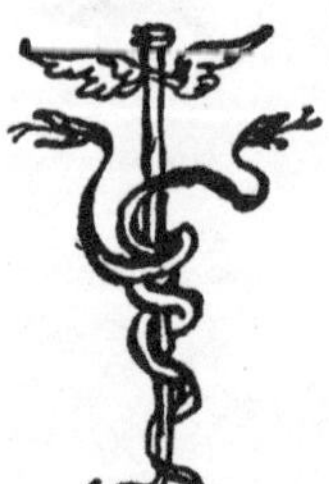

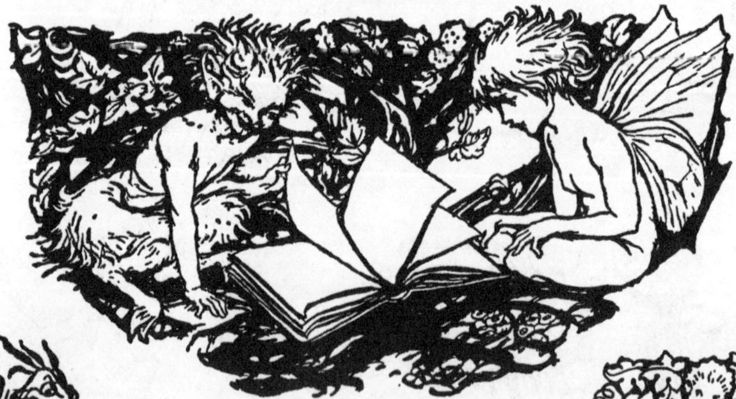

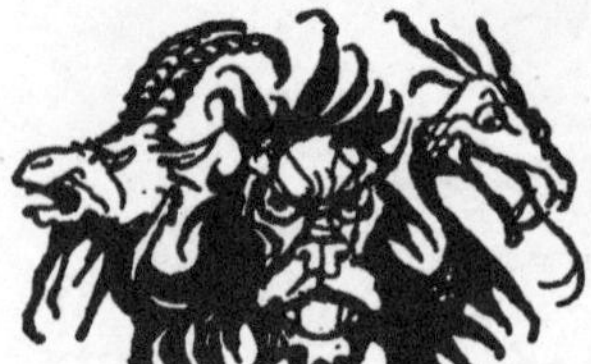

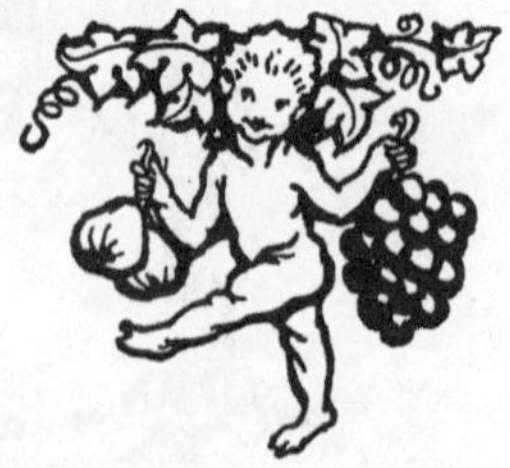

A WONDER BOOK, 1922

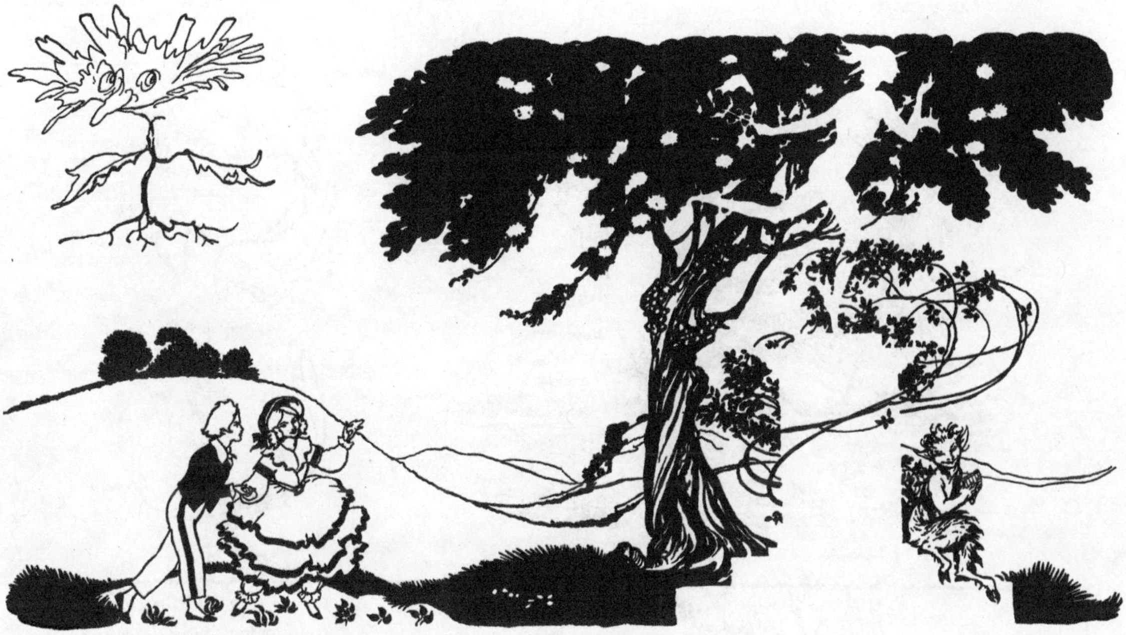

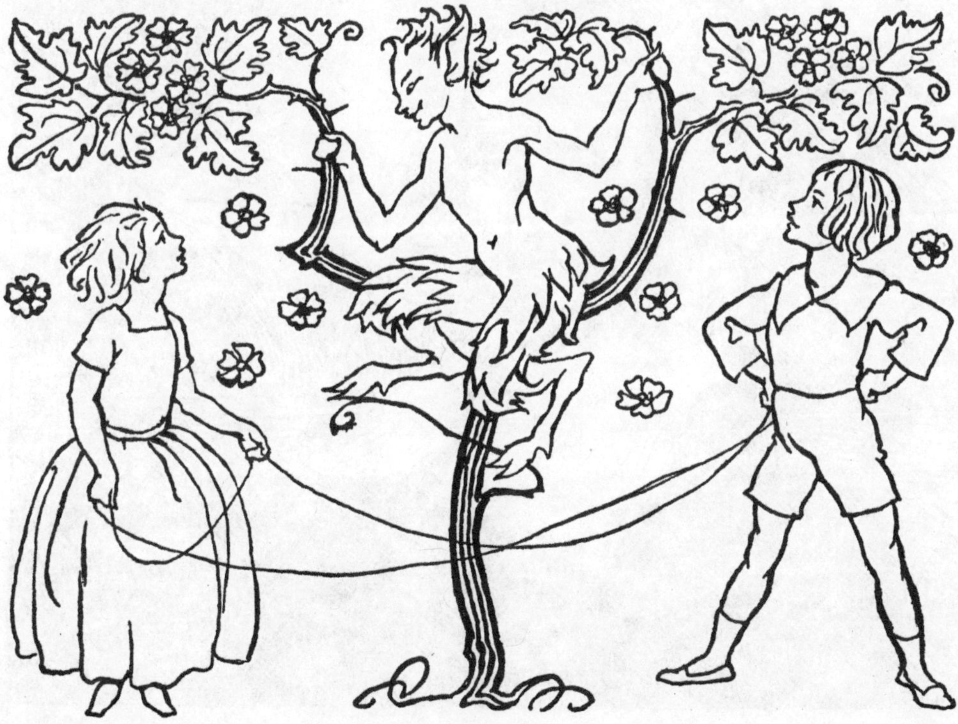

A Wonder Book, 1922

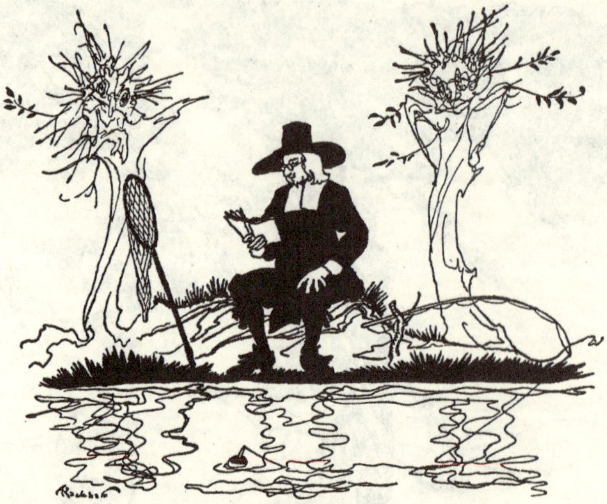

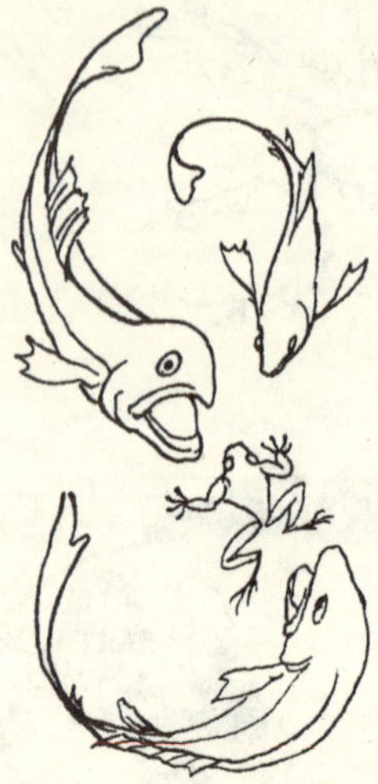

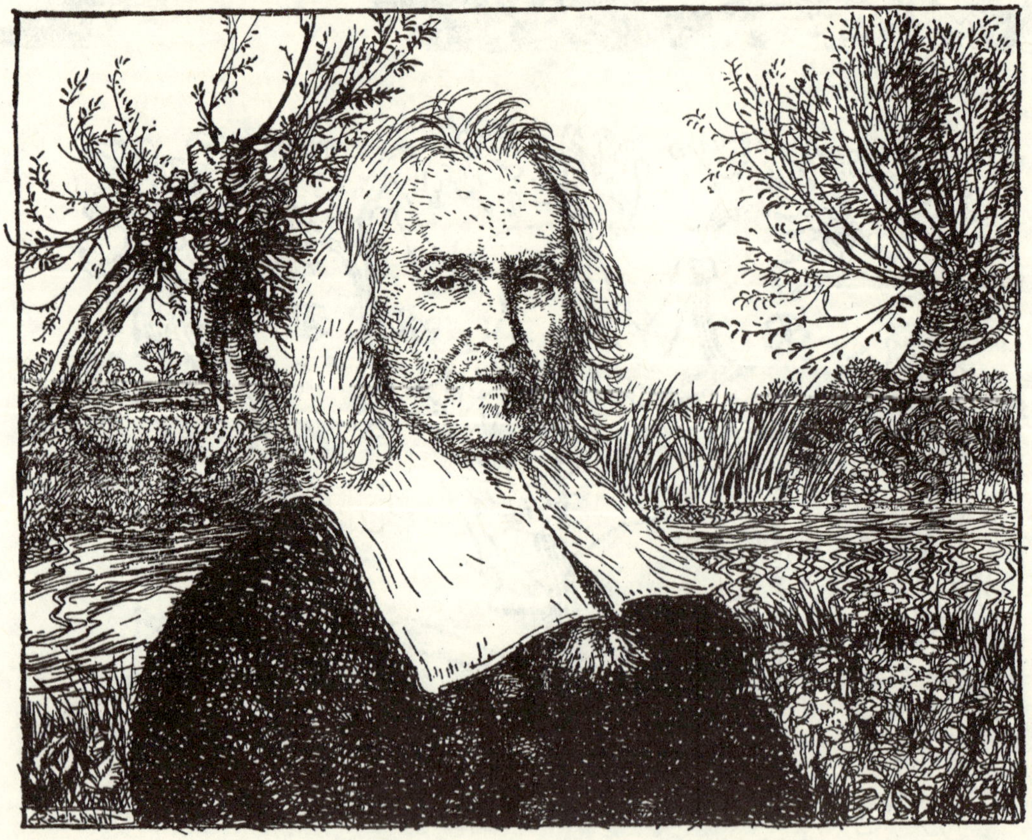

The Compleat Angler, 1931

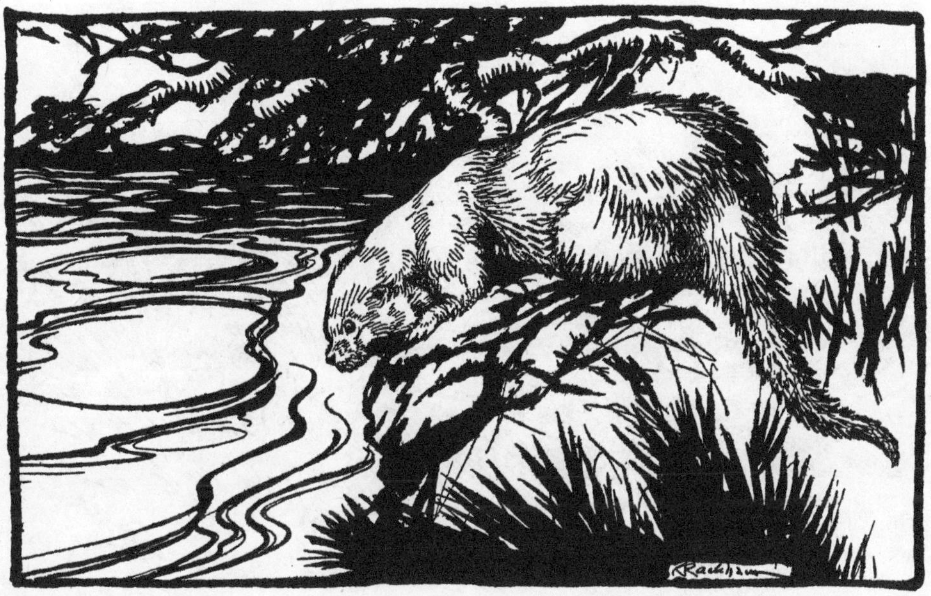

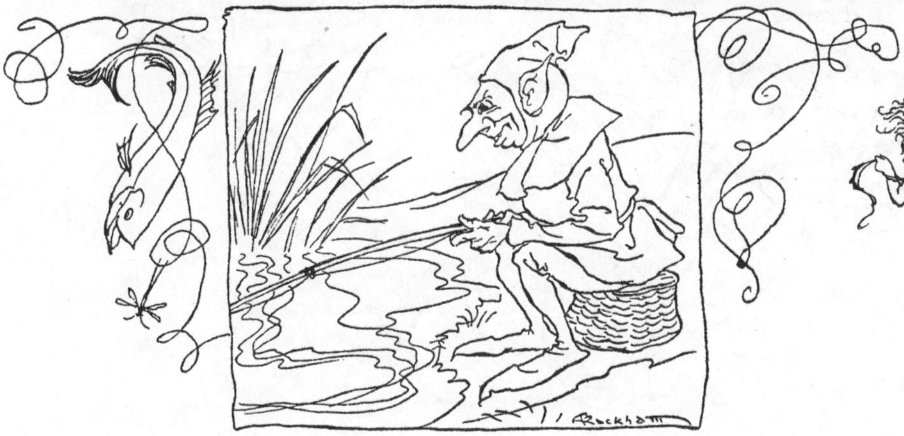

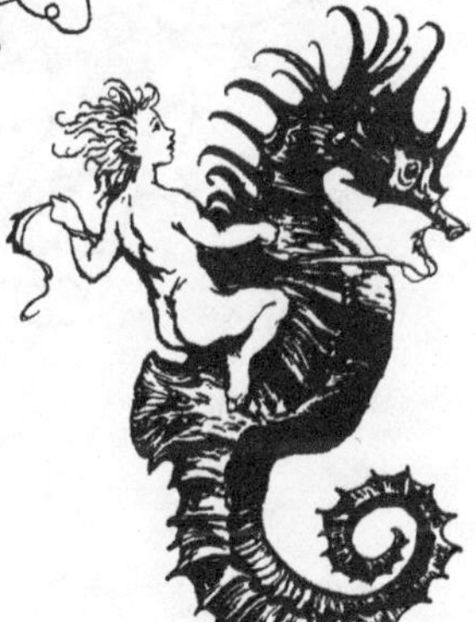

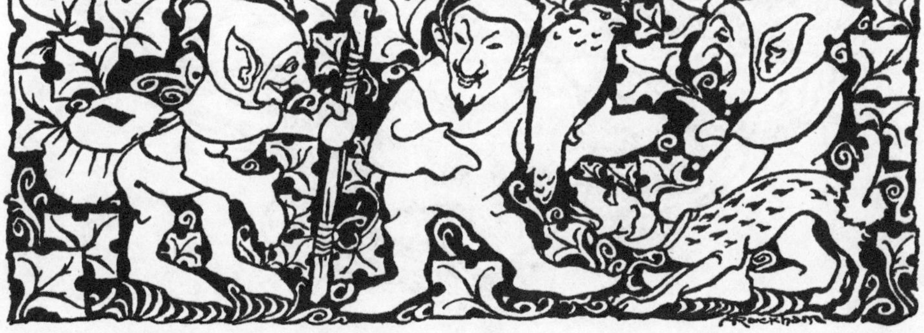

THE COMPLEAT ANGLER, 1931

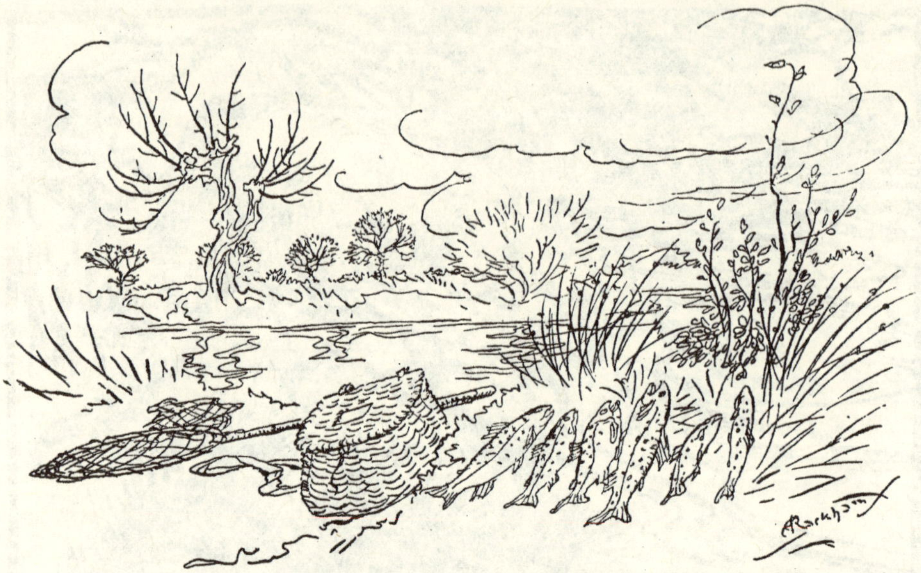

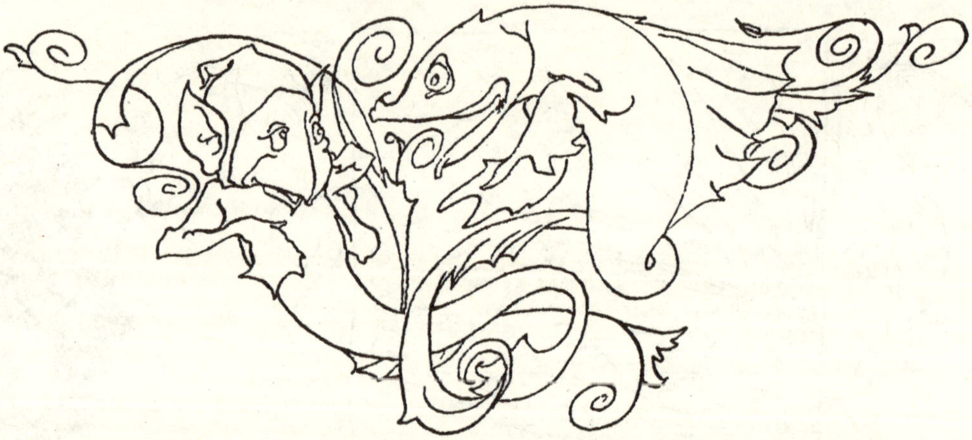

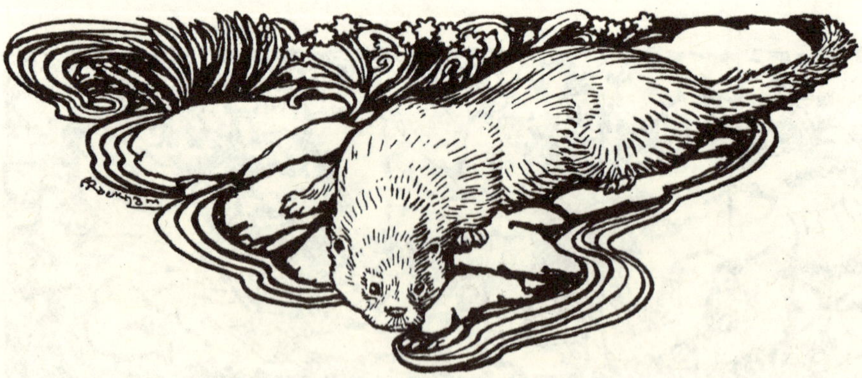

The Compleat Angler, 1931

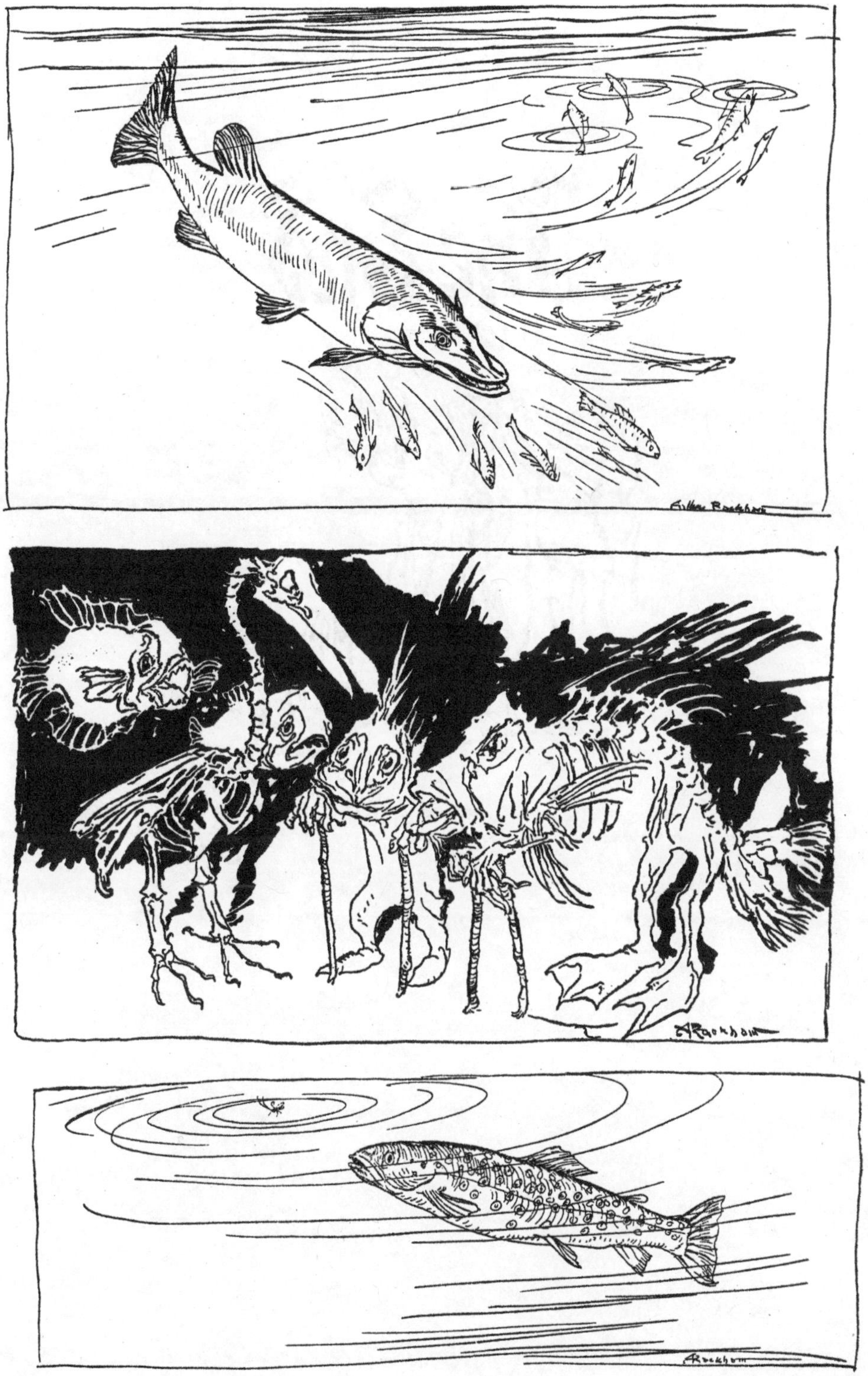

The Compleat Angler, 1931

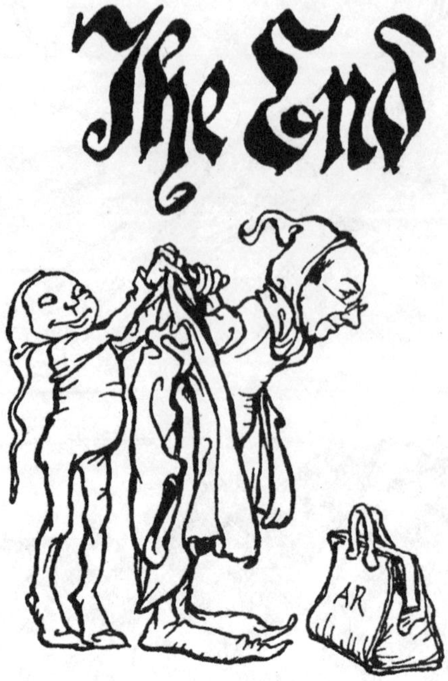

From
Little Brother and Little Sister, 1917